Lecture Notes in Computer Science 15393

Founding Editors

Gerhard Goos
Juris Hartmanis

Editorial Board Members

Elisa Bertino, *Purdue University, West Lafayette, IN, USA*
Wen Gao, *Peking University, Beijing, China*
Bernhard Steffen ⓘ, *TU Dortmund University, Dortmund, Germany*
Moti Yung ⓘ, *Columbia University, New York, NY, USA*

The series Lecture Notes in Computer Science (LNCS), including its subseries Lecture Notes in Artificial Intelligence (LNAI) and Lecture Notes in Bioinformatics (LNBI), has established itself as a medium for the publication of new developments in computer science and information technology research, teaching, and education.

LNCS enjoys close cooperation with the computer science R & D community, the series counts many renowned academics among its volume editors and paper authors, and collaborates with prestigious societies. Its mission is to serve this international community by providing an invaluable service, mainly focused on the publication of conference and workshop proceedings and postproceedings. LNCS commenced publication in 1973.

Shaoying Liu
Editor

Software Fault Prevention, Verification, and Validation

First International Symposium, SFPVV 2024
Hiroshima, Japan, December 2–3, 2024
Proceedings

Editor
Shaoying Liu
Hiroshima University
Hiroshima, Hiroshima, Japan

ISSN 0302-9743　　　　　　ISSN 1611-3349　(electronic)
Lecture Notes in Computer Science
ISBN 978-981-96-1620-6　　　ISBN 978-981-96-1621-3　(eBook)
https://doi.org/10.1007/978-981-96-1621-3

© The Editor(s) (if applicable) and The Author(s), under exclusive license to Springer Nature Singapore Pte Ltd. 2025

This work is subject to copyright. All rights are solely and exclusively licensed by the Publisher, whether the whole or part of the material is concerned, specifically the rights of translation, reprinting, reuse of illustrations, recitation, broadcasting, reproduction on microfilms or in any other physical way, and transmission or information storage and retrieval, electronic adaptation, computer software, or by similar or dissimilar methodology now known or hereafter developed.
The use of general descriptive names, registered names, trademarks, service marks, etc. in this publication does not imply, even in the absence of a specific statement, that such names are exempt from the relevant protective laws and regulations and therefore free for general use.
The publisher, the authors and the editors are safe to assume that the advice and information in this book are believed to be true and accurate at the date of publication. Neither the publisher nor the authors or the editors give a warranty, expressed or implied, with respect to the material contained herein or for any errors or omissions that may have been made. The publisher remains neutral with regard to jurisdictional claims in published maps and institutional affiliations.

This Springer imprint is published by the registered company Springer Nature Singapore Pte Ltd.
The registered company address is: 152 Beach Road, #21-01/04 Gateway East, Singapore 189721, Singapore

If disposing of this product, please recycle the paper.

Preface

Software fault prevention, verification, and validation are crucial approaches to ensuring software productivity, reliability, and quality. Fault prevention aims to reduce or eliminate the introduction of faults in software systems. Verification rigorously checks whether software systems meet specified requirements or properties, while validation confirms whether the behavior and performance align with user expectations. Numerous techniques and supporting tools have been developed to advance fault prevention, verification, and validation. However, significant challenges and unresolved issues remain in achieving comprehensive and efficient solutions in these areas.

The 1st International Symposium on Software Fault Prevention, Verification, and Validation (SFPVV 2024), which took place on December 2–3, 2024, in Hiroshima as a satellite event of the 25th International Conference on Formal Engineering Methods (ICFEM 2024), aimed to bring together researchers and practitioners dedicated to advancing software quality assurance. The symposium encouraged the exchange of ideas and discussion on how formal methods, testing-based techniques, AI-driven approaches, and their combinations can be explored, established, and refined to achieve the goals of software fault prevention, verification, and validation.

There were 39 submissions, each undergoing a two-step review process. Initially, the program committee (PC) chair screened all submissions to verify that they aligned with the symposium's scope and met the formatting and page limit requirements. Submissions failing to meet these criteria were excluded from further review. In the second step, each remaining submission was reviewed by three program committee members or additional reviewers. Ultimately, 18 submissions were accepted for both presentation at the symposium and inclusion in the proceedings.

The SFPVV 2024 program features two keynote talks given by Kazuhiro Ogata of Japan Advanced Institute of Science and Technology (JAIST) and Professor Geguang Pu at East China Normal University, and 18 paper presentations on various techniques and approaches for software fault preventation, verification, and validation in 6 sessions, including Formal Methods, Testing and Analysis, Formal Semantics, Defect Detection, Specification and Implementation, and Language and Blockchain. This year, the symposium welcomed around 45 attendees from over 10 countries worldwide. This volume contains all the papers presented at SFPVV 2024.

The successful organization of SFPVV 2024 was due to the invaluable contributions of numerous individuals and institutions. I extend heartfelt thanks to all authors for submitting and presenting their papers at SFPVV 2024. We are deeply grateful to the program committee members for their dedication and efforts in reviewing and selecting papers. My sincere appreciation also goes to the conference organizing committee for their hard work in handling the many complex tasks required. We also express our gratitude to the Murata Science and Education Foundation, Huawei Technology Co., Ltd., and Kayamori Foundation of Informational Science Advancement for their generous sponsorship of ICFEM 2024 through which SFPVV 2024 has benefited to some extent, and to the Information Processing Society of Japan, Hiroshima University, and IEEE Japan Council for their essential support. Our thanks go to the EasyChair team for their user-friendly platform, which helped us efficiently manage the files needed for this volume, and to Springer-Nature for their support in publishing the SFPVV 2024 proceedings.

November 2024   Shaoying Liu

Organization

Program Committee

Yamine Aït-Ameur	IRIT/INPT-ENSEEIHT, France
Yuting Chen	Shanghai Jiao Tong University, China
Yoonsik Cheon	University of Texas at El Paso, USA
Tadashi Dohi	Hiroshima University, Japan
Dingbang Fang	Fujian Normal University, China
Jiandong Li	Peking University, China
Jingyue Li	Norwegian University of Science and Technology, Norway
Ai Liu	Nanjing University of Aeronautics and Astronautics, China
Shaoying Liu (PC Chair)	Hiroshima University, Japan
Yang Liu	Nanyang Technological University, Singapore
Weikai Miao	East China Normal University, China
Fumiko Nagoya	Nihon University, Japan
Shin Nakajima	National Institute of Informatics, Japan
Hiroyuki Okamura	Hiroshima University, Japan
Yuji Sato	Hosei University, Japan
Xinfeng Shu	Xi'an University of Posts and Telecommunications, China
Pingyan Wang	Guangdong University of Petrochemical Technology, China
Xi Wang	Shanghai University, China
Guangquan Xu	Tianjin University, China
Zhen You	Jiangxi Normal University, China
Naijun Zhan	Institute of Software, Chinese Academy of Sciences, China
Jianjun Zhao	Kyushu University, Japan

Additional Reviewers

An, Jie
Wang, Shuling

Invited Papers

Some Achievements of the International Joint Research Project "Formal Analysis and Verification of Post-quantum Cryptographic Protocols"

Kazuhiro Ogata

JAIST, Nomi, Ishikawa, 923-1292 Japan
ogata@jaist.ac.jp

Abstract

The international joint research project "Formal Analysis and Verification of Post-quantum Cryptographic Protocols" was carried out for April 2021 through March 2024. The main investigators are Santiago Escobar (Spain), Sedat Akleylek (Turkey), Ayoub Otmani (France) and me (Japan). Quantum era will be coming soon, when it is predicted that most of the currently used public-key cryptosystems become insecure because of the Shor's algorithm. Accordingly, cryptographers have been developing new cryptosystems that can replace the currently used public-key cryptosystems and are resistant to the Shor's algorithm running on practical quantum computers that are expected to appear in the near future. Such new cryptosystems are called post-quantum cryptosystems, while the currently used public-key cryptosystems are called classical public-key cryptosystems. Some security protocols, such as TLS and SSH, have been revised such that post-quantum cryptosystems as well as classical public-key cryptosystems are used. The revised versions of TLS and SSH are called hybrid postquantum TLS and hybrid post-quantum SSH because both classical public-key cryptosystems and post-quantum cryptosystems are used. The main outcomes achieved in the international joint research are as follows:

1. Model checking experiments of some post-quantum cryptosystems have been conducted with Maude [5, 2];
2. A tool called Invariant Proof Score Generator (IPSG) that mostly automaticallygenerates proof scores in CafeOBJ has been developed [4];
3. A parallel version of Maude-NPA has been developed [1];
4. Hybrid post-quantum TLS has been formally specified and analyzed with Maude-NPA and its parallel version [3];
5. Hybrid post-quantum SSH has been formally specified and verified (theorem proved) with CafeOBJ and IPSG [6].

This work was supported by JST SICORP Grant Number JPMJSC20C2

References

1. Do, C.M., Riesco, A., Escobar, S., Ogata, K.: Parallel maude-npa for cryptographic protocol analysis. In: WRLA@ETAPS 2022. Lecture Notes in Computer Science vol. 13252, pp. 253–273. Springer (2022). https://doi.org/10.1007/978-3-031-12441-9_13
2. García, V., Escobar, S., Ogata, K., Akleylek, S., Otmani, A.: Modelling and verification of post-quantum key encapsulation mechanisms using maude. PeerJ Comput. Sci. **9**, e1547 (2023). https://doi.org/10.7717/PEERJ-CS.1547
3. Tran, D.D., Do, C.M., Escobar, S., Ogata, K.: Hybrid post-quantum transport layer security formal analysis in maude-npa and its parallel version. PeerJ Comput. Sci. **9**, e1556 (2023). https://doi.org/10.7717/PEERJ-CS.1556.
4. Tran, D.D., Ogata, K.: Formal verification of TLS 1.2 by automatically generating proof scores. Comput. Secur. 123, 102909 (2022). https://doi.org/10.1016/J.COSE.2022.102909
5. Tran, D.D., Ogata, K., Escobar, S., Akleylek, S., Otmani, A.: Kyber, Saber, and SK-MLWR lattice-based key encapsulation mechanisms model checking with Maude. IET Inf. Secur. **2023**, 9399887 (2023). https://doi.org/10.1049/2023/9399887
4. Tran, D.D., Ogata, K., Escobar, S., Akleylek, S., Otmani, A.: Formal analysis of post-quantum hybrid key exchange SSH transport layer protocol. IEEE Access **12**, 1672–1687 (2024). https://doi.org/10.1109/ACCESS.2023.3347914

Developing the Industrial-strength Tools for Modeling, Testing and Verification: A Formal-methods Perspective

Geguang Pu

East China Normal University, China
ggpu@sei.ecnu.edu.cn

Abstract. FM-related techniques are very helpful to ensure the quality of software. For instance, the model checking technique has been successfully applied in hardware/software verification and it becomes the key element for EDA tool chains. In this talk, I will share the experiences of developing the industrial-strength tools for modeling, testing and verification from the formal-methods perspective. We will show how to find the real problems about testing and verification from the industry and show how formal methods can guide us to solve these problems by tool construction. We will illustrate our experiences and insights by three interesting tools under development.

The first one is a formal modeling and verification tool for the formal verification of Interlock system of the train, that is a key part of signal systems in railway. Firstly, we design a formal model to capture the behavior of the Interlock system. And then we illustrate that the verification problem of Interlock system can be transformed into the hardware model checking one, and by the model checker we developed, the formal verification of the Interlock system is both effective and efficient. The second case is the testing tool for embedded systems, where the symbolic execution technique plays an important role. A new symbolic execution engine has been designed to handle complicated memory manipulations like operating pointers/objects in C/C++ programs. The last one is a new model checking solver for hardware verification, and its performance in practice has proved to be efficient by the new observations on the search process in the state space. Surprisingly, the dedicated algorithm based on the new observation is effective in all the state-of-the-art SAT-based model checkers, like Nu-XMV and IC3/PDR.

These tools are successfully applied in our industry partners and their effectiveness is proved by industrial cases. For instance, the testing tool we developed has been used to test millions of lines of code from hundreds of institutes and companies where the testing efficiency has proved to be improved largely by the functionality of automated test cases generation. Finally, we also share the lessons we have learned during the tool development in the last five years.

Contents

A Methodology for Rating Maintainability Metrics of SOFL Formal Specifications 1
   Yu Du and Shaoying Liu

An Executable Operational Semantics of Quantum Programs and Its Application 15
   Canh Minh Do and Kazuhiro Ogata

Automated Software Test Input Generation with Diffusion Models 32
   Yujin Zhu, Xiujing Guo, Hiroyuki Okamura, and Tadashi Dohi

Blockchain Solutions for Cash-on-Delivery: Utilizing Encrypted NFTs, Smart Contracts, and IPFS Technology 49
   Phan Hoang Tuan Trung, Tran Dang Khoa, Thanh Pham Nghiem, Tran Ba Nam, Nguyen Thi Kim Ngan, Doan Minh Hieu, and Van Cao Phu Loc

Revolutionizing Animal Health Privacy: Blockchain and Encrypted NFTs 64
   Phan Hoang Tuan Trung, Tran Dang Khoa, Thanh Pham Nghiem, Tran Ba Nam, Nguyen Thi Kim Ngan, Doan Minh Hieu, and Van Cao Phu Loc

Improving and Evaluating Sparse Decision-Based Black-Box Attacks and Defenses 79
   Jonas Brager Jacobsen, Jingyue Li, and Mathias Lundteigen Mohus

Recovery of Trace Links Between a SOFL Formal Specification and Its Corresponding Incomplete Java Code 97
   Jiandong Li, Shaoying Liu, and Zhi Jin

S3DA: A 3D Point Cloud Based PCB Solder Defect Detection Algorithm 115
   Yilongfei Xu, Zhewei Wang, Jinhao Liang, Yueling Zhang, Jincao Feng, Weikai Miao, Jiangtao Wang, and Geguang Pu

Consistency Naming Between Requirements Analysis and Specifications 131
   Fumiko Nagoya

A Framework for Standardized Partitioning Analysis in Integrated Modular Avionics Systems 141
   Jilu Zhang, Yong Cai, Weikai Miao, and Zhouyang Wang

A Common Declarative Language for UML State Machine Representation,
Model Transformation, and Interoperability of Visualization Tools 158
   Ali Jannatpour and Constantinos Constantinides

The Three-Point Optimization Algorithm: A Novel Physics-Based
Metaheuristic Approach 177
   Xiong Deng, Shaoying Liu, and Yanli Liu

Generating Simulink Models from Hybridised Event-B Models 189
   *Neeraj Kumar Singh, Guillaume Dupont, Yamine Aït Ameur,
   and Marc Pantel*

Formal Specification and Model Checking of a Synchronous Leader
Election Protocol in Maude 208
   Tomoyoshi Ogura, Canh Minh Do, and Kazuhiro Ogata

Relational Denotational and Algebraic Semantics Based on UTP 226
   Zhiru Hou and Huibiao Zhu

ASTD Patterns for Integrated Continuous Anomaly Detection in Data Logs 245
   Chaymae El Jabri, Marc Frappier, and Pierre-Martin Tardif

Towards a Novel Approach to Railway Safety Using STPA and Promise
Theory 263
   Felix Schaber, Atif Mashkoor, and Michael Leuschel

Functional Modelling of the Matroid and Application to the Knapsack
Problem 280
   *Zikang Wan, Zhen You, Chen Zhang, Zhengkang Zuo, Changjing Wang,
   and Qimin Hu*

Author Index 293

A Methodology for Rating Maintainability Metrics of SOFL Formal Specifications

Yu Du and Shaoying Liu[✉]

Graduate School of Advanced Science and Engineering, Hiroshima University, Hiroshima 7398511, Japan
{d243489,sliu}@hiroshima-u.ac.jp

Abstract. In this work, we present a novel methodology to evaluate the maintainability of Structured Object-oriented Formal Language (SOFL) specifications, addressing an existing gap in maintainability assessment for formal specifications compared to source code. We then introduce a structured rating methodology based on a weighted Z-score approach to define and quantify essential maintainability factors, including analysability, complexity, modifiability, and testability. Additionally, we implement a supporting tool that automates this evaluation process, making the SOFL maintainability assessment method practical for real-world applications. Our results demonstrate that the proposed methodology and tool provide a comprehensive assessment, effectively identifying weaker modules within the specification and establishing a basis for pinpointing potential issues.

Keywords: SOFL · Software maintainability · Formal specification

1 Introduction

Maintainability refers to the degree of effectiveness and efficiency with which the intended maintainers can modify a product or system. As a critical attribute of system and software quality, maintainability plays a pivotal role in software development, with maintenance activities constituting a significant portion of the software life cycle costs [1–3]. Since the inception of software systems, the necessity for high maintainability has been widely recognized [4,5]. Software products are developed to fulfill specific user or industry requirements, but these requirements inevitably evolve due to changing needs or environmental factors. Consequently, ensuring that software systems maintain high levels of maintainability is essential. Despite this widespread understanding, achieving and accurately measuring maintainability remains a significant challenge.

Formal methods, grounded in mathematical theory, employ formal specifications and verification to ensure the reliability of software development [6]. Formal methods are extracting and refining the specification, using set theory and logic to describe the software specification, this allows the system functionality to be progressively clarified, resulting in a more precise and unambiguous requirements analysis of the software functionality. Formal methods are particularly valued in developing safety-critical systems, as they provide a rigorous framework for clarifying requirements and enhancing software reliability while potentially reducing development costs [7,8]. Structured Object-Oriented Formal Language (SOFL), developed at the University of Manchester in 1989, exemplifies such formal methods. Over the past three decades, SOFL has gained prominence in software system development due to its integration of traditional graphical symbols with formalized notations and its structured approach to specification development [9].

Despite the advantages of SOFL, maintaining formal specifications poses significant challenges, particularly due to the complexity of formal notations and the specialized concepts involved. This highlights the critical need for tool support in the maintenance process. Effective tools can streamline the assessment of complex logic conditions and provide actionable recommendations for maintaining specifications.

This paper makes several key contributions, particularly focusing on developing and applying a novel methodology for assessing the maintainability of SOFL formal specifications. First, we introduce an innovative method specifically tailored to evaluate SOFL formal specifications. This approach builds on existing principles but is adapted to address the unique characteristics of formal specifications. By incorporating specific metrics and criteria relevant to SOFL, the methodology enhances the accuracy and relevance of the maintainability assessment. Second, we establish a comprehensive set of hierarchical rating rules that support the application of the new method. These rules are designed to systematize the evaluation process, providing a structured framework for assessing various maintainability aspects. This approach ensures that the ratings are consistent and meaningful, facilitating a more nuanced understanding of the maintainability of formal specifications. Third, we validate the effectiveness of the methodology and its associated rules through empirical testing. By applying the method to real-world formal specification cases, we demonstrate its practical utility and ability to provide actionable insights. This validation underscores the methodology's effectiveness in identifying and addressing potential issues within SOFL specifications.

The remainder of this paper is structured as follows. Section 2 reviews existing evaluation methods for software maintainability, outlining their strengths and limitations. It then positions our approach by demonstrating how it improves upon or differs from these established methods. Section 3 provides a detailed explanation of the maintainability measurement methodology for SOFL specifications, including the maintainability assessment framework, the specific metrics used, and the implementation of the method for calculating ratings for maintainability metrics. Section 4 presents a case study that illustrates how our proposed rating approach and developed tool operate in practice. This section focuses on the practical application of our tool, showcasing its effectiveness in evaluating maintainability. Finally, Sect. 5 summarizes the key findings, discusses the broader implications of our work, and suggests areas for future research and improvements to the tool and its evaluation.

2 Background and Related Work

Current methodologies for evaluating software maintainability predominantly focus on implementing source code or project documentation. One such approach is the widely utilized Maintainability Index (MI), originally developed by Oman and Hagemeister [10]. The MI offers an objective measure of software maintainability by consolidating multiple metrics-such as Halstead Volume, Cyclomatic Complexity, and Lines of Code -into a single polynomial expression that reflects overall system maintainability. This index has been extensively validated across various procedural programming languages, making it a widely accepted method in the field [11].

The MI has two primary variants, aiming to provide a comprehensive maintainability assessment. The first variant is represented by the following formula [12]:

$$MI3 = 171 - 5.2 \times \ln(aveV) - 0.23 \times aveV(g') - 16.2 \times \ln(aveLOC). \quad (1)$$

In this formula, $aveV$ represents the average Halstead Volume per module, $aveV(g')$ refers to the average extended Cyclomatic Complexity per module, and $aveLOC$ indicates the average number of lines of code per module. These metrics are assessed at the module level, where a module typically represents the smallest functional unit, such as a function or method. Halstead Volume (HV) measures the complexity of a module by examining the density of operators and operands, offering insight into the complexity of variable usage. Cyclomatic Complexity (CC) counts the number of possible execution paths in a system, indicating its logical complexity. Meanwhile, the Lines of Code (LOC) metric captures the program size.

A refined variant of the MI introduces an additional factor that considers the percentage of comments in the codebase, reflecting the degree of internal documentation. By incorporating this variable, the second variant provides a more comprehensive evaluation of maintainability, acknowledging that well-documented code tends to be easier to maintain and understand. Both MI variants serve as valuable tools for quantitatively assessing maintainability. The second variant, including comments as a factor, reflects an evolving understanding of the elements contributing to software maintainability, particularly in large-scale systems.

In addition to MI, researchers have explored other techniques for evaluating maintainability. Zhuo et al. compared expert assessments with maintainability indices derived from multiple models [13], while Coleman et al. examined the practical application of these models in industrial settings [14]. Bosch et al. proposed methods for analyzing software architecture maintainability [15], and

Anan et al. introduced entropy-based metrics for assessing structural dependencies [16]. Despite these advancements, many of these methods struggle to fully capture the complexity and quality characteristics of software systems, particularly when applied to formal specifications.

While traditional metrics and static analysis tools have made significant strides, they fall short of addressing the specific needs of formal specifications. The distinct features of SOFL, such as its formal notation and specialized concepts, necessitate an alternative approach to maintainability assessment. Due to differences in representation and complexity, existing code-based metrics are insufficient for evaluating formal specifications. To overcome these limitations, this research proposes a novel methodology that adapts established principles to the context of SOFL, which will be discussed in detail in Sect. 3.1. By developing a set of tailored metrics and an automated tool to apply them, we offer a more precise and practical solution for maintainability assessment in formal specifications, providing early feedback during the specification phase and improving the overall efficiency of the software development lifecycle (see Fig. 1).

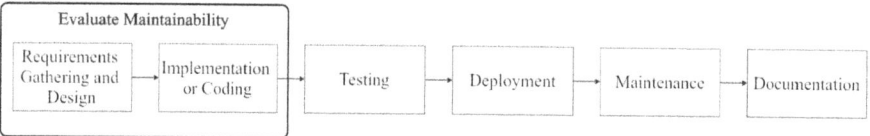

Fig. 1. Software development lifecycle

3 Maintainability Assessment Methodology

This section briefly describes the software maintainability assessment methodological framework and related metrics, followed by a discussion of the SOFL specification and its features, and a description of the metrics' rating methodology.

3.1 Maintainability Assessment Framework

Our maintainability assessment framework is grounded in the ISO/IEC 25010:2023 standard, which provides a comprehensive model of software quality with eight characteristics [17], for assessing maintainability, the standard highlights five key sub-characteristics: testability, modifiability, reusability, modularity, and analysability. These elements are essential in evaluating how easily software can be maintained.

Modularity refers to the degree to which a system's components are separated, which minimizes the impact of changes in one component on others. Reusability assesses the potential to use software components in various contexts.

Analysability measures how effectively and efficiently changes can be assessed, defects diagnosed, and modification requirements identified. Modifiability evaluates how easily a system can be altered without introducing defects. Testability concerns the ease of establishing and performing tests to ensure that criteria are met.

In the context of SOFL specifications, our focus narrows to four sub-factors: analysability, complexity, modifiability, and testability. Although reusability is an important aspect of software design, it is less relevant to our current study and has been excluded. This is because reusability primarily concerns how a specification or its components can be applied to another project, rather than focusing on the maintainability of the system being developed. Key features impacting our selected factors include the total size of the specification, which influences complexity and modifiability; the number of units, reflecting cohesion and coupling; process coupling, affecting complexity and analysability; the logical structure of conditions, which impacts both complexity and testability; and data usage, which is important for analysability and modifiability. Furthermore, the style of the specification-such as typography, naming conventions, and comments-also contributes to its overall comprehensibility and maintainability.

In our previous research, we have developed a SOFL maintainability metric model that contains eight quantifiable metrics to evaluate these characteristics [18]. The SOFL formal specification maintainability metric hierarchy is shown in Fig. 2 (see Fig. 2). These metrics include Lines of Expressions (LOE) for measuring the total size, Number of Processes (NOP) reflecting cohesion, Number of Control Data Flows (NOCDF) for process coupling complexity, Cyclomatic Complexity (CC) for logical complexity, Module Halstead Volume (MHV) for lexical complexity, Number of Data Stores Used (NODSU) to capture data usage complexity, Extensiveness of Comments (EOC) to evaluate comment coverage, Extensiveness of Blank Lines (EOBL) to assess typographic features. These metrics are designed to help developers identify complex and error-prone modules, thereby improving maintainability.

3.2 Rating Criteria for Maintainability Metrics

We employ a Weighted Z-score methodology to rank the maintainability metrics of SOFL formal specifications, which provides a standardized way to compare metrics across specifications with different characteristics. The Z-score is commonly used in statistical analysis to measure how far a specific data point deviates from the mean of the dataset, expressed in terms of standard deviations. This allows for comparing metrics with different units or scales, making it especially useful for assessing various maintainability attributes.

The Z-score is computed using the following formula:

$$Z = \frac{X - \mu}{\sigma}, \qquad (2)$$

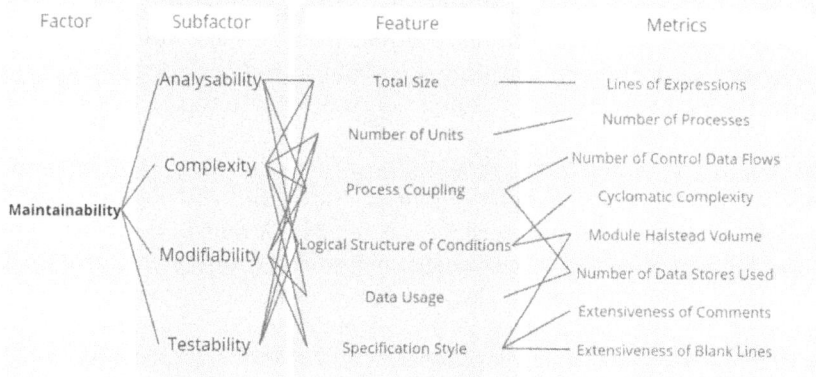

Fig. 2. SOFL formal specifications maintainability metrics hierarchy

where X represents the value of the maintainability metric for a given module, μ is the mean value of the metric across all modules being assessed, and σ is the standard deviation of the metric values, reflecting the variability of the data.

While the basic Z-score offers a useful means for standardizing different metrics, it has limitations when applied to smaller specifications. In such cases, smaller specifications might exhibit lower complexity or other metric values, which can lead to distorted conclusions if not adjusted properly. To address this issue, we introduce a Weighted Z-score (Zw), which accounts for the size of the specification by incorporating the Lines of Expressions into the calculation. This adjustment ensures that smaller specifications are not inaccurately represented and maintainability ratings are more consistent across different-sized modules.

The Weighted Z-score is calculated as follows:

$$Zw = \frac{X - \left(\frac{LOE_i}{\text{avg}(LOE)}\right) \times \mu}{\sigma}, \tag{3}$$

Here, LOE_i represents the Lines of Expressions for the module, which refers to the number of expressions in the formal specification, and $avg(LOE)$ is the average LOE value.

This adjustment normalizes the metric value according to the relative size of the module, ensuring that the maintainability ratings reflect not only the raw metric values but also the scale of the module being evaluated. This is crucial for fairness in maintainability assessments, particularly in projects with both large and small modules.

Once the Weighted Z-score is calculated, it is classified into various categories to indicate the magnitude of deviation from the average maintainability level. This classification helps developers prioritize their maintenance efforts based on the severity of the maintainability concerns. The classification thresholds are defined as follows:

- A difference of less than 1 is considered small, indicating that the module is close to the average maintainability level.
- A difference between 1 and 2 is classified as moderate, suggesting a noticeable deviation that may require attention.
- A difference between 2 and 3 is considered large, highlighting significant maintainability concerns that should be prioritized.
- A difference of 3 or greater is classified as very large, indicating critical maintainability issues that need immediate intervention.

This classification allows for a more structured approach to maintainability assessment, as shown in Table 1. By categorizing the results, developers can focus on modules that deviate significantly from the mean and take corrective actions accordingly. The classification system ensures a standardized and fair assessment, enabling the identification of problematic modules and helping teams allocate resources effectively during the maintenance phase.

By using weighted Z-scores and their categorization, the methodology provides objective comparisons of modules and contextualizes these comparisons in a way that makes sense for both small and large specifications. This ensures that maintainability ratings reflect real-world concerns and helps developers identify, prioritize, and efficiently resolve maintainability issues.

Table 1. The classification of differences using weighted Z-score

Value	Degree	Grade
$|Zw| < 1$	Small difference	A
$1 \leq |Zw| < 2$	Moderate difference	B
$2 \leq |Zw| < 3$	Large difference	C
$|Zw| \geq 3$	Very large difference	D

3.3 Implementation of the Rating Methodology

The methodology for calculating ratings for maintainability metrics is designed to help developers identify and prioritize modules that significantly deviate from standard maintainability norms. This process is implemented in C# and involves several key steps.

First, the methodology begins with the CalculateOverallStatistics function, which is responsible for computing the weighted Z-scores for each maintainability metric. This step involves normalizing the metrics by calculating the Z-score for each value, which measures how far a given metric deviates from the mean of all metrics. By standardizing the metrics in this way, it becomes possible to compare them consistently, despite variations in their units or scales. This calculation is essential for understanding the overall dispersion of the metrics, highlighting the relative maintainability of different modules within the specification.

Second, once the Z-scores are calculated, the GetGrade function is invoked to assign grades based on the magnitude of these weighted Z-scores. This step introduces a qualitative aspect to the quantitative Z-score data by categorizing the deviations into predefined ranges. For example, small deviations from the mean may receive a high grade, indicating good maintainability, while larger deviations may receive lower grades, signaling potential areas of concern. This grading system is critical for offering a clear and intuitive interpretation of the maintainability metrics, allowing developers to quickly differentiate between modules that are performing well and those that require attention.

Next, the CalculateOverallGrade function quantifies the average score for each metric across all modules in the specification. This step is crucial because it provides an overall rating for each metric by averaging the scores from multiple modules, which offers a more comprehensive view of how well each metric performs within the whole specification. By summarizing the performance across modules, this function provides a more holistic view of how each metric contributes to the maintainability of the entire specification, rather than focusing on individual modules in isolation.

Finally, the GetOverallGrade function assigns a final rating based on the calculated average scores. By providing a clear visual indication of each metric average level of maintainability, developers can quickly identify which metrics may require attention. This function aggregates the results, allowing developers to easily see which areas of the formal specification most urgently need improvement. The overall grade serves as a practical guide for targeting maintenance efforts, helping to allocate resources effectively, and ensuring that critical issues are addressed promptly.

By implementing this methodology, developers can evaluate the maintainability of SOFL formal specifications in a systematic, data-driven way. This structured approach allows for targeted improvements and better maintenance planning, ensuring the specification's long-term maintainability is effectively managed.

4 Case Study

We applied our methodology to a real-world case study involving an Automated Teller Machine (ATM) system to validate the effectiveness of our maintainability metrics and the support tool. This case study serves as a practical demonstration of how our tool can be utilized to assess software maintainability. By evaluating the SOFL formal specification of the ATM system, we aim to illustrate how our methodology can be implemented in a structured development process to identify potential maintenance challenges and offer targeted improvements.

4.1 System Overview and Case Study Setup

The ATM system was selected due to its critical business functionality and complexity, making it an ideal candidate for maintainability assessment. The system provides essential services, such as authentication, account operations, money transfers, and password changes, which are crucial to a wide range of users. These functionalities are represented in the SOFL formal specification, which includes a top-level SYSTEM_ATM module, further divided into six interconnected sub-modules. The use of SOFL formal specifications is important in this study because it allows for precise system modeling, which supports the rigorous evaluation of maintainability.

The goal of the case study is to evaluate the maintainability of this system using our tool, focusing on key metrics such as complexity, modifiability, analysability, and testability, as introduced in Sect. 3. The maintainability of each module was assessed, and the results are aggregated to provide a holistic view of the entire system's maintainability. By applying this methodology, we aim to demonstrate the utility of our tool in a real-world development environment.

4.2 Maintainability Assessment and Results

The application of our methodology begins with the user importing the ATM system's specification file into the tool using the "File" menu. A comprehensive user guide is available to facilitate the process, providing clear instructions on operating the tool and explaining its various features. Once the ATM specification is uploaded, the tool automatically calculates maintainability metrics based on the formulas and weighted Z-score approach described earlier in Sect. 3. The tool's interface, as shown in Fig. 3, is designed to be intuitive, allowing users to seamlessly switch between different sections of the maintainability assessment. The initial results are displayed on two primary pages within the tool: the Summary Page and the Metrics Page. The Summary Page provides an aggregated view of maintainability scores across all modules, along with a composite score for the entire system. This high-level overview enables users to quickly identify modules that significantly deviate from maintainability norms, highlighting areas that may require further investigation.

For more granular analysis, the Metrics Page presents detailed information for each module. It showcases specific metrics such as Cyclomatic Complexity, Halstead Volume, and Extensiveness of Comments, alongside statistical values like their means and standard deviations. This detailed comparison helps users evaluate the maintainability of individual modules, particularly in identifying potential issues such as high complexity that could negatively impact maintainability.

To enhance the analytical experience, the tool includes interactive visualizations in the Analysis Report section (Fig. 4). These visualizations are powered by LiveCharts, which allows users to explore the data more thoroughly. By interacting with the charts, users can observe the distribution of maintainability metrics across the different modules, zoom in on specific areas, and analyze how each module's performance contributes to the overall system's maintainability. This feature helps users gain deeper insights into how specific metrics affect

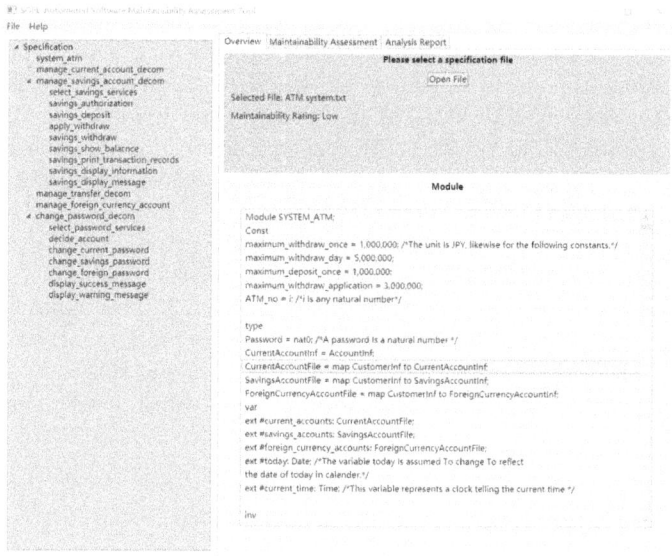

Fig. 3. A snapshot of the Overview page

the maintainability of the entire system and pinpoints areas that might need improvement.

Moreover, the tool offers the capability to save the results of the analysis for future reference. The "Save" feature ensures that users can document their findings and later compare them against subsequent versions of the specification. This is especially useful for tracking progress over time and ensuring that maintainability improvements are sustained throughout the system's evolution.

Table 2 summarizes the maintainability ratings of the ATM system, highlighting significant findings. Modules that handle critical operations such as authentication and account management are shown to have higher complexity, leading to lower maintainability ratings. On the other hand, the password change module demonstrates lower complexity and higher modifiability, which suggests it would require less effort to maintain. These results emphasize the tool's capability to pinpoint areas within the system that may need targeted attention, ensuring that developers can focus their efforts on improving the overall maintainability of the system.

4.3 Discussion

The results of the case study confirm the effectiveness of our tool and methodology in assessing the maintainability of formal specifications. By applying the weighted Z-score methodology, we standardize the evaluation process, allowing for consistent comparisons across modules with varying levels of complexity. This methodology is particularly useful in systems like the ATM, where

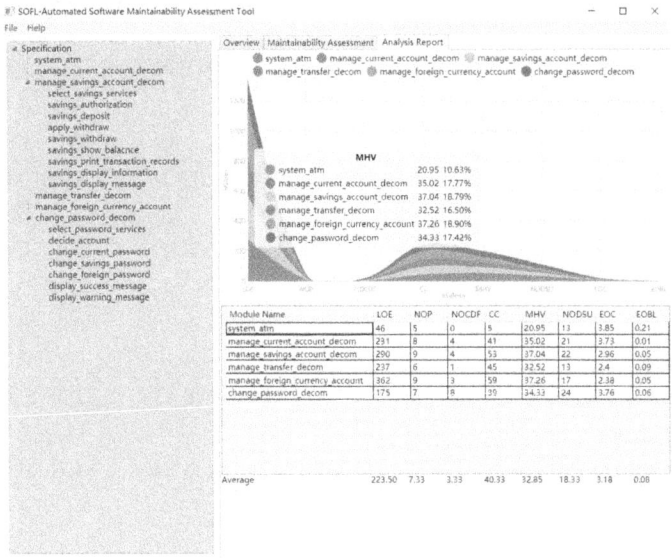

Fig. 4. A snapshot of the Analysis Report page

different modules serve critical but distinct functions, and their maintainability needs can vary.

One of the key findings is that Cyclomatic Complexity and Halstead Volume play significant roles in determining the maintainability of certain modules. For example, modules with higher Cyclomatic Complexity and Halstead Volume scores tend to require more frequent modifications and testing, which aligns with known software maintenance patterns. However, we also observed that metrics such as the Extensiveness of Comments and the Extensiveness of Blank Lines have relatively small values, making it challenging to assess their impact on maintainability through direct analysis. Nevertheless, by applying our weighted Z-score methodology, we were able to resolve this issue, as the approach allows for a more balanced rating of these metrics, preventing smaller values from being overlooked in the overall maintainability evaluation.

Our tool and methodology, though currently tailored to SOFL formal specifications, can be adapted to other formal languages by integrating domain-specific maintainability metrics. This adaptability enables the approach to be applied to a broader range of formal specifications, enhancing its versatility across different domains.

Table 2. Maintainability Assessment Summary of the ATM system

No.	Module	LOE	NOP	NOCDF	CC	MHV	NODSU	EOC	EOBL
1	SYSTEM_ATM	46 / B	5 / C	0 / A	5 / A	20.95 / C	13 / C	3.85 / D	0.21 / D
2	Manage_Current_Account_Decom	231 / A	8 / A	4 / A	41 / A	35.02 / A	21 / A	3.73 / A	0.01 / B
3	Manage_Savings_Account_Decom	290 / A	9 / A	4 / A	53 / A	37.04 / B	22 / A	2.96 / B	0.05 / A
4	Manage_Transfer_Decom	237 / A	6 / B	1 / A	45 / A	35.52 / A	13 / B	2.4 / B	0.09 / A
5	Manage_Foreign_Currency_Account	362 / A	9 / B	3 / A	59 / A	37.26 / C	17 / C	2.38 / D	0.05 / B
6	Change_Password_Decom	175 / A	7 / A	8 / C	39 / A	34.33 / B	24 / C	3.76 / C	0.06 / A

5 Conclusion

This paper describes a comprehensive methodology for enhancing software maintainability assessment in the SOFL formal specification. We developed a novel framework for evaluating maintainability, supported by an automated assessment tool that integrates targeted metrics for a structured evaluation of analyzability, complexity, modifiability, and testability. This methodology addresses the growing need for consistent and reliable maintainability metrics in formal development processes.

The case study involving an Automated Teller Machine (ATM) system validated the effectiveness of both the tool and methodology. By applying a weighted Z-score approach, the tool provided a detailed and nuanced maintainability rating, helping developers identify potential challenges and prioritize areas for improvement. This structured assessment process allows for consistent comparisons across modules with varying complexity, improving decision-making in system maintenance.

In future work, we aim to refine the Z-score standardization process to address the limitations observed in smaller modules and to incorporate additional metrics that better capture the complexities of formal specification maintainability. Expanding the applicability of both the tool and methodology beyond SOFL to other formal languages will further enhance their relevance across diverse software development contexts. Our long-term goal is to provide actionable recommendations for improving maintainability and facilitate rapid, comprehensive assessments in various domains of formal specification.

References

1. Alsolai, H., Roper, M.: Application of ensemble techniques in predicting object-oriented software maintainability. In: Proceedings of the 23rd International Conference on Evaluation and Assessment in Software Engineering, pp. 370–373 (2019). https://doi.org/10.1145/3319008.3319716
2. Boehm, B.W., Brown, J.R., Lipow, M.: Quantitative evaluation of software quality. In: Proceedings of the 2nd International Conference on Software Engineering, pp. 592–605. IEEE Computer Society Press (1976). https://doi.org/10.5555/800253.807736
3. Malhotra, R., Chug, A.: Software maintainability: systematic literature review and current trends. Int. J. Software Eng. Knowl. Eng. **26**(08), 1221–1253 (2016). https://doi.org/10.1142/s0218194016500431
4. Koskinen, J., Laplante, P.: Software maintenance fundamentals. In: Laplante, P. (ed.) Encyclopedia of Software Engineering. Taylor & Francis Group (2009)
5. Maxim, B.R., Kessentini, M.: An introduction to modern software quality assurance. In: Software Quality Assurance, pp. 19–46. Morgan Kaufmann (2016). https://doi.org/10.1016/b978-0-12-802301-3.00002-8
6. Hall, A.: Realising the benefits of formal methods. In: Formal Methods and Software Engineering, vol. 3785, pp. 1–4 (2005). https://doi.org/10.1007/11576280_1
7. Kurita, T., Chiba, M., Nakatsugawa, Y.: Application of a formal specification language in the development of the 'Mobile FeliCa' IC chip firmware for embedding in mobile phone. In: Cuellar, J., Maibaum, T., Sere, K. (eds.) FM 2008: Formal Methods. FM 2008. LNCS, vol. 5014, pp. 425–429. (2008). https://doi.org/10.1007/978-3-540-68237-0_31
8. Woodcock, J., Larsen, P. G., Bicarregui, J., Fitzgerald, J.: Formal methods. In: ACM Computing Surveys, vol. 41, no. 4, pp. 1–36 (2009). https://doi.org/10.1145/1592434.1592436
9. Liu, S.: Formal engineering for industrial software development - an introduction to the SOFL specification language and method. In: Proceedings of the International Conference on Formal Engineering Methods, vol. 3308, pp. 7–8 (2004)
10. Oman, P., Hagemeister, J.: Construction and testing of polynomials predicting software maintainability. J. Syst. Softw. **24**(3), 251–266 (1994). https://doi.org/10.1016/0164-1212(94)90067-1
11. Oppedijk, F.R.: Comparison of the SIG Maintainability Model and the Maintainability Index (2008)
12. VanDoren, E., Sciences, K., Springs, C.: Maintainability index technique for measuring program maintainability. In: Software Tech Review SEI. http://www.sei.cmu.edu/str/descriptions/mitmpm_body.html
13. Zhuo, F., Lowther, B., Oman, P., Hagemeister, J.: Constructing and testing software maintainability assessment models. In: Proceedings First International Software Metrics Symposium, pp. 61–70 (1993). https://doi.org/10.1109/metric.1993.263800
14. Coleman, D., Lowther, B., Oman, P.: The application of software maintainability models in industrial software systems. J. Syst. Softw. **29**(1), 3–16 (1995). https://doi.org/10.1016/0164-1212(94)00125-7
15. Bosch, J., Bengtsson, P.: Assessing optimal software architecture maintainability. In: Proceedings Fifth European Conference on Software Maintenance and Reengineering, Lisbon, pp. 168–175 (2001). https://doi.org/10.1109/CSMR.2001.914981

16. Anan, M., Saiedian, H., Ryoo, J.: An architecture-centric software maintainability assessment using information theory. J. Softw. Mainten. Evol.: Res. Pract. **21**(1), 1–18 (2009). https://doi.org/10.1002/smr.396
17. International Organization for Standardization, ISO/IEC 25010:2023. https://www.iso.org/standard/78176.html. Accessed 15 May 2024
18. Du, Y., Liu, S.: Maintainability assessment for SOFL formal specifications. In: 2023 10th International Conference on Dependable Systems and Their Applications (DSA), Tokyo, pp. 680–687 (2023). https://doi.org/10.1109/DSA59317.2023.00099

An Executable Operational Semantics of Quantum Programs and Its Application

Canh Minh Do(✉) and Kazuhiro Ogata

Japan Advanced Institute of Science and Technology (JAIST), Nomi, Japan
{canhdo,ogata}@jaist.ac.jp

Abstract. This paper presents the syntax and operational semantics of quantum **while**-programs, an extension of classical while programs, using pure states for representing quantum states. Although the syntax presented here is the same as in [19], the operational semantics is different due to the use of pure states instead of density matrices for quantum state representation. The transition relation between configurations of the operational semantics is naturally mapped into a rewriting relation between terms that represent configurations in rewriting logic. This mapping allows us to implement an executable operational semantics of quantum **while**-programs in Maude, a high-level specification/programming language based on rewriting logic. The executable operational semantics is used as a part of a reachability analysis tool, called QRAT, for quantum programs by utilizing the search command, a built-in reachability analyzer in Maude. Specifically, given a system module for the executable semantics, a source term for an initial configuration, and a target term for a target configuration, the search command is used to automatically check whether the target configuration is reachable from the initial configuration. As a case study, we use QRAT to verify the correctness of Quantum Teleportation to demonstrate the usefulness of our approach.

Keywords: Executable Operational Semantics · Quantum Programs · Reachability Analysis · Maude

1 Introduction

With recent exponential investments from big companies and governments, there is a widespread belief that building a large-scale quantum computer capable of efficiently running advanced quantum algorithms, such as Shor's fast algorithms for discrete logarithms and factoring [14], is only a matter of time and effort. As with classical computers, quantum programming languages and software development techniques will be essential to harness the unique power of quantum computing once quantum computers become available. In recent years, several

---

The research was supported by JAIST Research Grant for Fundamental Research and by JSPS KAKENHI Grant Numbers JP23K28060, JP23K19959, JP24K20757, JP24KK0185.

quantum programming languages and platforms have been introduced by leading companies, including Qiskit [12] from IBM, Q# [15] from Microsoft, and Cirq [3] from Google, reflecting the rapid advancements in quantum hardware development. Quantum computing is fundamentally different and counter-intuitive compared to classical computing, making it difficult to develop efficient quantum algorithms for problems considered very hard in current computing. This difference also increases the likelihood of errors in quantum programs compared to classical ones. Therefore, it is crucial to provide formal semantics of quantum programming languages and formal methods to ensure the correctness of quantum programs.

This paper presents the syntax and operational semantics of quantum **while**-programs, an extension of classical while programs, using pure states for representing quantum states. Although the syntax presented here is the same as in [19], the operational semantics is different due to the use of pure states instead of density matrices for quantum state representation. The operational semantics is described as a transition relation between configurations by transition rules. It is natural to map the transition relation between configurations of the operational semantics into a rewriting relation between terms that represent configurations in rewriting logic [9]. This mapping allows us to implement an executable operational semantics of quantum **while**-programs in Maude [2], a high-level specification/programming language based on rewriting logic [10]. In order to develop the executable operational semantics, we need to express complex numbers, quantum states, quantum gates, and measurement operators, and reason about quantum computation. Therefore, we reuse symbolic reasoning about quantum computation with Dirac notation in Maude from our previous work [5–8,16]. The executable operational semantics is used as a part of a reachability analysis tool, called QRAT, for quantum programs by utilizing the `search` command, a built-in reachability analyzer in Maude. Specifically, given a system module for the executable operational semantics, a source term for an initial configuration, and a target term for a target configuration, the `search` command is used to automatically check whether the target configuration is reachable from the initial configuration. As a case study, we use QRAT to verify the correctness of Quantum Teleportation through reachability analysis so as to demonstrate the usefulness of our approach. QRAT and the case study are publicly available at https://github.com/canhminhdo/trs-qrat.

The rest of the paper is organized as follows. Section 2 provides basic notation from quantum computation. Section 3 describes quantum programs, where the syntax and operational semantics of quantum **while**-programs are introduced using pure states for representing quantum states. Section 4 presents an executable operational semantics of quantum **while**-programs implemented in Maude. Section 5 shows the application of the executable operational semantics for reachability analysis of quantum programs with a case study, namely Quantum Teleportation. Section 6 presents some existing work. Section 7 finally concludes the paper with some pieces of future work.

2 Basic Notations from Quantum Computation

This section briefly describes some basic notations from quantum computation based on linear algebra (refer to [11] for more details).

Quantum Bits (or Qubits). In classical computing, the fundamental unit of information is a bit whose value is either 0 or 1. In quantum computing, the counterpart is a *quantum bit* or *qubit*, which has two basis states, conventionally written in Dirac notation [4] as $|0\rangle$ and $|1\rangle$. These denote two column vectors $(1,0)^T$ and $(0,1)^T$, respectively, where T is the transpose operator. In quantum computation, a general state of a quantum system is a superposition or linear combination of basis states. A quantum state is a unit vector in a Hilbert space $\mathcal{H}$, which is a complex vector space equipped with an inner product such that each Cauchy sequence has a limit. A single-qubit state is $|\psi\rangle = \alpha|0\rangle + \beta|1\rangle$, where α and β are complex numbers and $|\psi\rangle$ is normalized such that $|\alpha|^2 + |\beta|^2 = 1$. The coefficients α and β are called the amplitudes of this quantum state. The set $\{|0\rangle, |1\rangle\}$ forms an orthonormal basis of the two-dimensional Hilbert space. States $|\psi\rangle$ can be also represented by column complex vectors as $(\alpha, \beta)^T$. The basis $\{|0\rangle, |1\rangle\}$ is called the *computational* basis besides other orthonormal bases of interest, such as *diagonal* (or *dual*, or *Hadamard*) basis consisting of two vectors $|+\rangle = \frac{1}{\sqrt{2}}(|0\rangle + |1\rangle)$ and $|-\rangle = \frac{1}{\sqrt{2}}(|0\rangle - |1\rangle)$.

Tensor Product. For multiple qubits, we use the tensor product of Hilbert spaces. Let $\mathcal{H}_1$ and $\mathcal{H}_2$ be two Hilbert spaces. Their tensor product $\mathcal{H}_1 \otimes \mathcal{H}_2$ is defined as a vector space consisting of linear combinations of the vectors $|\psi_1\psi_2\rangle = |\psi_1\rangle|\psi_2\rangle = |\psi_1\rangle \otimes |\psi_2\rangle$, where $|\psi_1\rangle \in \mathcal{H}_1$ and $|\psi_2\rangle \in \mathcal{H}_2$. Systems of two or more qubits may be in *entangled* states, meaning that states of qubits are correlated and inseparable. For instance, entanglement shows that an entangled state of two qubits cannot be expressed as a tensor product of single-qubit states.

Unitary Transformation. The evolution of a closed quantum system can be performed by a unitary transformation. If the state of a qubit is represented by a column vector, then a unitary transformation U can be represented by a complex-value matrix such that $UU^\dagger = U^\dagger U = I$ or $U^\dagger = U^{-1}$, where $U^\dagger$ is the conjugate transpose of U. U acts on the Hilbert space $\mathcal{H}$ transforming a state $|\psi\rangle$ to a state $|\psi'\rangle$ by a matrix multiplication such that $|\psi'\rangle = U|\psi\rangle$. There are some frequently used quantum gates in applications: the Hadamard gate H, the identity gate I, the Pauli gates X, Y, and Z, and the controlled-NOT gate CX. Note that the CX gate performs on two qubits, while the remaining gates perform on a single qubit. Their matrix representations are as follows:

$$I_2 = \begin{pmatrix} 1 & 0 \\ 0 & 1 \end{pmatrix}, \quad X = \begin{pmatrix} 0 & 1 \\ 1 & 0 \end{pmatrix}, \quad Y = \begin{pmatrix} 0 & -i \\ i & 0 \end{pmatrix},$$

$$Z = \begin{pmatrix} 1 & 0 \\ 0 & -1 \end{pmatrix}, \quad H = \frac{1}{\sqrt{2}}\begin{pmatrix} 1 & 1 \\ 1 & -1 \end{pmatrix}, \quad CX = \begin{pmatrix} 1 & 0 & 0 & 0 \\ 0 & 1 & 0 & 0 \\ 0 & 0 & 0 & 1 \\ 0 & 0 & 1 & 0 \end{pmatrix}.$$

where i is the imaginary unit. For example, the Hadamard gate on a single qubit performs the mapping $|0\rangle \mapsto \frac{1}{\sqrt{2}}(|0\rangle + |1\rangle)$ and $|1\rangle \mapsto \frac{1}{\sqrt{2}}(|0\rangle - |1\rangle)$. The controlled-NOT gate on a pair of qubits performs the mapping $|00\rangle \mapsto |00\rangle, |01\rangle \mapsto |01\rangle, |10\rangle \mapsto |11\rangle, |11\rangle \mapsto |10\rangle$, which can be understood as inverting the second qubit (referred to as the *target*) if and only if the first qubit (referred to as the *control*) is one.

Measurement. A quantum measurement is described as a collection $\{M_m\}$ of measurement operators, where the indices m refer to the measurement outcomes. It is required that the measurement operators satisfy the completeness relation, which is $\sum_m M_m^\dagger M_m = I$. If the state of a quantum system is $|\psi\rangle$ before the measurement, then the probability for the result m is $p(m) = \langle\psi|M_m^\dagger M_m|\psi\rangle$, and the state of the quantum system after the measurement is $\frac{M_m|\psi\rangle}{\sqrt{p(m)}}$. Note that $M_m|\psi\rangle$ is divided by its norm $\|M_m|\psi\rangle\| = \sqrt{p(m)}$ for normalizing to a unit vector. For instance, we consider a measurement $\{M_0 = |0\rangle\langle 0|, M_1 = |1\rangle\langle 1|\}$. It is obvious that the completeness relation is satisfied as $M_0 + M_1 = |0\rangle\langle 0| + |1\rangle\langle 1| = I$. Let us suppose the single-qubit state being measured is $|\psi\rangle = \alpha|0\rangle + \beta|1\rangle$, where the amplitudes have been normalized such that $|\alpha|^2 + |\beta|^2 = 1$. The result 0 will occur with probability $|\alpha|^2$ and the result 1 with probability $|\beta|^2$. Moreover, the measurement causes the quantum state to collapse to either $|0\rangle$ or $|1\rangle$ depending on the measurement result.

The measurement involving multiple qubits is more complex. Let us consider a two-qubit system in a state $|\psi\rangle = \alpha|00\rangle + \beta|01\rangle + \gamma|10\rangle + \delta|11\rangle$, where the amplitudes are normalized. We again use the measurement $\{M_0 = |0\rangle\langle 0|, M_1 = |1\rangle\langle 1|\}$, but note that we do not normalize quantum states after each measurement. When we measure the first qubit, one of the following will occur:

- the result 0 with probability of $p_0 = |\alpha|^2 + |\beta|^2$, collapsing the quantum state to $\alpha|00\rangle + \beta|01\rangle$, and
- the result 1 with probability of $p_1 = |\gamma|^2 + |\delta|^2$, collapsing the quantum state to $\gamma|10\rangle + \delta|11\rangle$.

Next, we measure the second qubit. The possible outcomes are illustrated in the following diagram.

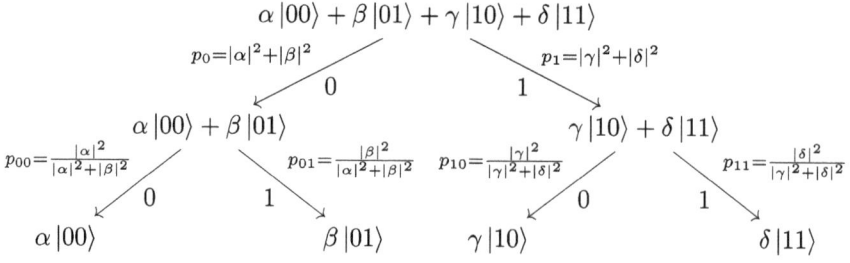

In this diagram, nodes represent quantum states, and transitions are labeled with the probabilities and measurement results. The total probabilities of obtaining 00, 01, 10, and 11 as the result of the two measurements are $p_0 p_{00} = |\alpha|^2$, $p_0 p_{01} = |\beta|^2$, $p_1 p_{10} = |\gamma|^2$, and $p_1 p_{11} = |\delta|^2$. It is common to normalize quantum states to unit vectors after each measurement, ensuring that the sum of the squares of the amplitudes is 1. However, the diagram shows that a different normalization is more convenient. Therefore, we adopt the normalization convention from [13] in this present paper as follows.

Convention 2.1 (Normalization Convention). *Each state is normalized so that the sum of the squares of the amplitudes equals the total probability of reaching that state.*

With this convention, normalizing the state after measurement is unnecessary, significantly simplifying our representation and computation. However, we need to define the equivalence relation on quantum states with this normalization convention as follows:

$$|\psi\rangle \sim |\phi\rangle \text{ if and only if } \frac{|\psi\rangle}{|||\psi\rangle||} \approx_{e^{i\theta}} \frac{|\phi\rangle}{|||\phi\rangle||}$$

where $|\varphi\rangle, |\phi\rangle$ may not be unit vectors, $\theta \in [0, \pi)$, and $e^{i\theta}$ is called the global phase. The fact is that quantum states normalized to unit vectors that differ only by a global phase are physically indistinguishable and equivalent under observation [11]. In order to check whether $|\psi\rangle \sim |\phi\rangle$, we can verify whether $|\phi\rangle$ belongs to the one-dimensional subspace spanned by $|\psi\rangle$, that is checking if

$$|\phi\rangle = \frac{|\psi\rangle\langle\psi| \, |\phi\rangle}{|||\psi\rangle||^2}.$$

3 Quantum Programs

This section presents the syntax and operational semantics of quantum **while**-programs, a quantum extension of classical while-programs. In the sequel, we may call quantum programs rather than quantum **while**-programs for brevity.

3.1 Syntax of Quantum Programs

A quantum variable q refers to a single-qubit state, while a quantum register $\overline{q}$ is a finite sequence of distinct quantum variables. Let *Var* be a set of quantum variables in quantum programs. We use BNF (Backus-Naur form) to describe the syntax of quantum **while**-programs. Although the syntax presented here is the same as in [19], the operational semantics of quantum **while**-programs is different. Specifically, we represent quantum states in pure states, while their approach deals with both pure and mixed states using density operators. As also noted in [19], pure states are more intuitive and convenient in applications than density operators for representing quantum states. Therefore, pure states deserve more attention. Since we use pure states for the representation, we do not provide the assignment statement $q := |0\rangle$ because assigning q to a basis state $|0\rangle$ may generally affect other quantum variables.

Definition 3.1 (Syntax [19]). *The quantum **while**-programs are defined by the grammar:*

$$S ::= \text{skip} \mid \bar{q} := U[\bar{q}] \mid S_1 \ ; \ S_2$$
$$\mid \text{if } \Box m \cdot M[\bar{q}] = m \rightarrow S_m \text{ fi}$$
$$\mid \text{while } M[\bar{q}] = 1 \text{ do } S \text{ od }.$$

The meaning of the quantum **while**-programs are described as follows. The statement **skip** is a constant program that does nothing and terminates. The statement $\bar{q} := U[\bar{q}]$ is an atomic program that shows the unitary transformation U being applied to a quantum register $\bar{q}$. The sequential composition $S_1 \ ; \ S_2$ first executes S_1 and when S_1 terminates, S_2 is executed. The selection statement **if** $\Box m \cdot M[\bar{q}] = m \rightarrow S_m$ **fi** is called a quantum case statement, which is the abbreviation of the following program

$$\begin{aligned}
&\text{if } M[\bar{q}] = m_1 \rightarrow S_{m_1} \\
&\Box \qquad\qquad m_2 \rightarrow S_{m_2} \\
&\qquad\qquad\qquad \ldots \\
&\Box \qquad\qquad m_n \rightarrow S_{m_n} \\
&\text{fi.}
\end{aligned}$$

The quantum case statement involves performing a quantum measurement $M = \{M_m\} = \{M_{m_1}, \ldots, M_{m_n}\}$ on a quantum register $\bar{q}$ and S_m is the subprogram that will be executed next based on the measurement outcome $m \in \{m_1, \ldots, m_n\}$. In the while-loop statement **while** $M[\bar{q}] = 1$ **do** S **od**, a yes-no measurement $M = \{M_0, M_1\}$ is used in the while-loop condition with two possible outcomes 0 (indicating "no") and 1 (indicating "yes"). If the outcome is 1, the subprogram S in the loop body is executed, and the loop continues. Otherwise, the loop terminates. Note that only measurement-based conditions are used in the program constructs **while** ... **od** and **if** ... **fi**.

3.2 Operational Semantics of Quantum Programs

We use operational semantics to give the meaning or semantics of quantum programs presented in Sect. 3.1. Operational means a transition relation $\rightarrow$ between so-called configurations. Let $\mathcal{H}_S$ be the Hilbert space of quantum variables for a quantum program S. A configuration is a pair $\langle S, |\psi\rangle\rangle$, where S is a quantum program and $|\psi\rangle \in \mathcal{H}_S$ is a pure quantum state. Intuitively, a transition relation $\langle S, |\psi\rangle\rangle \rightarrow \langle S', |\psi'\rangle\rangle$ means that executing S for one step in a state $|\psi\rangle$ results in state $|\psi'\rangle$ with S' being the remaining program of S to be executed next. To indicate termination, we use an empty quantum program denoted by $\downarrow$ in

(SK) $\langle \mathbf{skip}, |\psi\rangle\rangle \to \langle \downarrow, |\psi\rangle\rangle$

(UT) $\langle \bar{q} := U[\bar{q}], |\psi\rangle\rangle \to \langle \downarrow, U|\psi\rangle\rangle$

where U on the left-hand side is a syntactical symbol to represent the cylindrical extension of the actual unitary matrix U applied to $\bar{q}$ on the right-hand side.

(SC) $\dfrac{\langle S_1, |\psi\rangle\rangle \to \langle S_1', |\psi'\rangle\rangle}{\langle S_1\ ;\ S_2, |\psi\rangle\rangle \to \langle S_1'\ ;\ S_2, |\psi'\rangle\rangle}$

where we use the convention that $\downarrow\ ;\ S_2 = S_2$ and $S_2\ ;\ \downarrow\ = S_2$.

(IF) $\langle \mathbf{if}\ \Box m \cdot M[\bar{q}] = m \to S_m\ \mathbf{fi}, |\psi\rangle\rangle \to \langle S_m, M_m|\psi\rangle\rangle$

for each outcome $m \in \{m_1, \ldots, m_n\}$ of measurement $M = \{M_m\} = \{M_{m_1}, \ldots, M_{m_n}\}$.

(L0) $\langle \mathbf{while}\ M[\bar{q}] = 1\ \mathbf{do}\ S\ \mathbf{od}, |\psi\rangle\rangle \to \langle \downarrow, M_0|\psi\rangle\rangle$

for outcome 0 of measurement $M = \{M_0, M_1\}$.

(L1) $\langle \mathbf{while}\ M[\bar{q}] = 1\ \mathbf{do}\ S\ \mathbf{od}, |\psi\rangle\rangle \to \langle S\ ;\mathbf{while}\ M[\bar{q}] = 1\ \mathbf{do}\ S\ \mathbf{od}, M_1|\psi\rangle\rangle$

for outcome 1 of measurement $M = \{M_0, M_1\}$.

Fig. 1. Transition rules for quantum **while**-programs in pure states

configurations such that $S' \equiv\ \downarrow$, to mean that S terminates in state $|\psi'\rangle$. We conveniently use $\downarrow\ ;\ S$ and $S\ ;\ \downarrow$ as the abbreviations of S in this context. It is important to note that $|\psi\rangle$ denotes the whole quantum state of a quantum program S, a quantum variable q refers to a specific single qubit in $|\psi\rangle$, and a quantum register $\bar{q}$ refers to multiple qubits in $|\psi\rangle$.

Definition 3.2 (Operational Semantics). *The operational semantics of quantum **while**-programs is defined inductively based on the structure of programs as a transition relation $\to$ specified by transition rules in Fig. 1.*

Let us briefly explain the transition rules in Fig. 1. The rule (SK) makes the program terminate with no change in state $|\psi\rangle$. The rule (SC) presents a one-step execution of the program. The rules (UT), (IF), (L0), (L1) are based on the fundamental principles of quantum mechanics, using the normalization convention from [13] as detailed in Convention 2.1. Although measurements typically result in a probability distribution of post-measurement states, this normalization convention allows the transition rules to be used as an ordinary transition rather than a probabilistic one, which is different from the probabilistic transition rules in pure states presented in [19]. The transition rules (IF), (L0), (L1) introduce nondeterministic transitions between configurations due to varying choices of measurement operators. Therefore, the semantics $\to$ can be viewed as a nondeterministic transition relation, which can be naturally expressed by a rewriting relation specified by rewrite rules in rewriting logic as discussed in Sect. 4.

The transition relation $\to$ specified by transition rules in Fig. 1 induces a formal proof system called a transition system. A transition $\langle S, |\psi\rangle\rangle \to \langle S', |\psi'\rangle\rangle$ is possible if and only if it can be deduced within the transition system. The computation of quantum programs can be defined as follows.

Definition 3.3. *Let S be a quantum program and $|\psi\rangle \in \mathcal{H}_S$ be a quantum state.*

- A transition sequence of S starting in $|\psi\rangle$ is a finite or infinite sequence of configurations $\langle S_i, |\psi_i\rangle\rangle$ for $i \geq 0$ such that

$$\langle S, |\psi\rangle\rangle = \langle S_0, |\psi_0\rangle\rangle \to \langle S_1, |\psi_1\rangle\rangle \to \ldots \to \langle S_i, |\psi_i\rangle\rangle \to \ldots$$

- A computation of S starting in $|\psi\rangle$ is a transition sequence of S that starts in $|\psi\rangle$ and cannot be extended further. That is, the number of distinct quantum states with respect to the equivalence relation for quantum states along the computation is finite.
- A computation of S terminates in $|\psi'\rangle$ if it is finite and its last configuration is $\langle \downarrow, |\psi'\rangle\rangle$.
- A computation of S diverges if it is infinite. Furthermore, S can diverge from $|\psi\rangle$ if there exists an infinite computation of S starting in $|\psi\rangle$.
- To describe the reachability between two configurations, we use the transitive, reflexive closure $\to^*$ of $\to$:

$$\langle S, |\psi\rangle\rangle \to^* \langle S', |\psi'\rangle\rangle$$

holds if and only if there exits configurations $\langle S_1, |\psi_1\rangle\rangle, \ldots, \langle S_n, |\psi_n\rangle\rangle$ for $n \geq 0$ such that

$$\langle S, |\psi\rangle\rangle = \langle S_1, |\psi_1\rangle\rangle \to \ldots \to \langle S_n, |\psi_n\rangle\rangle = \langle S', |\psi'\rangle\rangle$$

holds. In the case $n = 0$, $\langle S, |\psi\rangle\rangle = \langle S', |\psi'\rangle\rangle$ holds. Then, we say that $\langle S', |\psi'\rangle\rangle$ is reachable from $\langle S, |\psi\rangle\rangle$.
- Transitions where the quantum state of the target configuration is a zero vector may be discarded due to its zero probability.

Let us use a simple quantum program to illustrate the above definition.

Example 3.1. *Consider the quantum program with a single qubit*

$$S \equiv q :- H[q] \ ; \ S'$$

where H is the Hadamard transformation, $M = \{M_0 = |0\rangle\langle 0|, M_1 = |1\rangle\langle 1|\}$, and $S' \equiv$ while $M[\bar{q}] = 1$ do $q :- H[q]$ od.

Then the computations of S starting in $|1\rangle_q$ (written $|1\rangle$ for short) are:

$$\langle S, |1\rangle\rangle \to \langle S', \frac{|0\rangle - |1\rangle}{\sqrt{2}}\rangle$$

$$\to \begin{cases} \langle q :- H[q] \ ; \ S', -\frac{|1\rangle}{\sqrt{2}}\rangle \to \langle S', \frac{|1\rangle - |0\rangle}{2}\rangle \to \ldots \\ \langle \downarrow, \frac{|0\rangle}{\sqrt{2}}\rangle. \end{cases}$$

Notice that $\frac{|0\rangle - |1\rangle}{\sqrt{2}}$ is equivalent to $\frac{|1\rangle - |0\rangle}{2}$. Therefore, $\langle S', \frac{|1\rangle - |0\rangle}{2}\rangle$ can produce an infinite sequence of configurations. As a result, S diverges from $|1\rangle$. Moreover, the distinct quantum states reachable from $|1\rangle$ are only $\frac{|0\rangle - |1\rangle}{\sqrt{2}}$, $|0\rangle$, and $|1\rangle$ due to the equivalence relation on quantum states.

4 An Executable Operational Semantics of Quantum Programs

This section presents an executable operational semantics of quantum programs implemented in Maude [2], a high-level specification/programming language based on rewriting logic [10]. We then use this executable semantics as a part of a reachability analysis tool, called QRAT, for quantum programs by utilizing the search command in Maude to perform a reachability analysis for verifying the correctness of Quantum Teleportation. Note that we use Maude syntax in some code blocks in this section (see [2] for more details about Maude).

4.1 Transition Rules as Rewrite Rules

Rewriting logic has been utilized as a logical and semantic framework by showing various ways for mapping inference systems into rewriting logic [9]. For instance, a general inference rule of the form

$$\frac{S_1 \ldots S_n}{S_0}$$

can be mapped to a rewrite rule of the form $S_1 \ldots S_n \longrightarrow S_0$, which rewrites multisets of judgements S_i for $i \in [0, n]$. In operational semantics, the judgment S_i typically takes the form $P_i \to Q_i$ between configurations. Thus, it is natural to map this transition relation between configurations to a rewriting relation between terms that represent the configurations. With this mapping, an inference rule of the form

$$\frac{P_1 \to Q_1 \ldots P_n \to Q_n}{P_0 \to Q_0}$$

becomes a conditional rewrite rule of the form

$$P_0 \longrightarrow Q_0 \text{ if } P_1 \longrightarrow Q_1 \wedge \cdots \wedge P_n \longrightarrow Q_n,$$

where the condition includes rewrites. In cases where the inference rule has empty premises, we simply have a non-conditional rewrite rule $P_0 \longrightarrow Q_0$. Thereby, the semantic transition rules (with $\to$) are mapped into (conditional) rewrite rules (with $\longrightarrow$), where the transition in the conclusion becomes the main rewrite of the rule, and the transitions in the premises become rewrite conditions.

4.2 Syntax Definition

For the sake of simplicity, we only use a fixed yes-no measurement $M = \{M_0 = |0\rangle\langle 0|, M_1 = |1\rangle\langle 1|\}$ for measuring a single qubit at a time in the syntax of quantum **while**-programs. Consequently, the quantum case statement is reduced to a quantum conditional statement of the form **if** $M[q] = 1$ **then** S_1 **else** S_2 **fi**. With this restriction, we define the syntax of quantum **while**-programs in the functional module SYNTAX. Note that the signature structure in this module closely follows the syntax structure shown in Definition 3.1 as follows:

```
fmod SYNTAX is
   protecting QID .
   protecting NAT .
   sorts Var Reg Com Prog Gate Meas .
   subsort Var < Reg .
   subsort Com < Prog .
   --- for quantum variables
   op v : Qid -> Var [ctor] .
   --- for quantum registers
   op nil : -> Reg [ctor] .
   op _,_ : Reg Reg -> Reg [ctor assoc] .
   --- for measurements
   op M[_] : Var -> Meas .
   --- for quantum gates
   ops I X Y Z H S T CX CY CZ SWAP CCX CCZ CSWAP : -> Gate .
   --- for program constructs
   op skip : -> Com [ctor] .
   op _:=_[_] : Reg Gate Reg -> Com [ctor] .
   op _;_ : Com Com -> Com [ctor prec 42 gather (e E)] .
   op if_=_then_else_fi : Meas Nat Prog Prog -> Com [ctor] .
   op while_=_do_od : Meas Nat Prog -> Com [ctor] .
endfm
```

The sort Var is used for quantum variables, the sort Reg is used for registers, the sort Com is used for commands, the sort Prog is used for programs that are built up from commands, the sort Gate is used for quantum gates, and the sort Meas is used for measurements.

To facilitate the identification of quantum variables for applying unitary transformations and measurements, we define a functional module ENV for environments that associate quantum variables with indices of qubits in quantum states as follows:

```
fmod ENV is
   protecting SYNTAX .
   sort Entry Env .
   subsort Entry < Env .
   --- for Entry
   op _->_ : Var Nat -> Entry .
   --- for Environment
   op empEnv : -> Env [ctor] .
   op __ : Env Env -> Env [ctor comm assoc id: empEnv] .
   op _[_] : Env Var -> Nat .
   --- variable declaration in Maude syntax
   var V : Var . var N : Nat . var E : Env .
   eq ((V -> N) E)[V] = N .
   eq (V -> N) (V -> N) = (V -> N) .
endfm
```

The sort Entry is used for entries that are pairs of quantum variables and indices, where indices are nonzero natural numbers starting from zero (with zero indicating the first qubit counted from the left in quantum states and so forth). The sort Env is used for environments, where an environment is a set of entries. The last two equations (starting with **eq**) are used to obtain the index of the qubit referred by a quantum variable and to remove duplicate entries in an environment.

4.3 Executable Semantics

To specify the executable semantics of quantum **while**-programs, we need to express complex numbers, quantum states, quantum gates, and measurement operators, and reason about quantum computation. In our previous work [5–8,16], we have developed symbolic reasoning about quantum computation with Dirac notation in Maude that can be easily reused by importing a functional module QC. Therefore, we conveniently reuse this module to implement our executable semantics. The module QC has some essential sorts, such as the sort Cpx for complex numbers, the sort Vect for quantum states, and the sort Mat for quantum gates and measurement operators. To map syntactical symbols of quantum gates and measurement operators to actual quantum gates and measurements of the sort Mat, we define a functional module QC-EXT that imports both two functional modules SYNTAX and QC. For brevity, we do not present the module QC-EXT in detail here. However, the reader of interest can find the full implementation publicly available at https://github.com/canhminhdo/trs-qrat. The functional module QC-EXT provides two essential functions: buildGate and buildMeasOp, which map syntactical symbols to quantum gates and measurement operators, respectively. The executable semantics of quantum **while**-programs is specified in the system module SEMANTICS, which imports the module QC-EXT and closely follows the semantics shown in Fig. 1, as follows:

```
mod SEMANTICS is
    protecting QC-EXT .
    sort Config .
    --- for configuration
    op <_,_,_> : Prog Vect Env -> Config .
    vars S S1 S1' S2 : Prog .       vars V V' : Vect .
    vars Q : Var . vars R : Reg . vars U : Gate . vars E : Env .
    --- convention for the empty program
    op emp : -> Com [ctor] .
    eq emp ; S = S .
    eq S ; emp = S .
    --- rewrite rules for transition rules
    rl  [SK]  : < skip, V, E > => < emp, V, E > .
    rl  [UT]  : < R := U[R], V, E > =>
                < emp, buildGate(U, R, E) x V, E > .
    crl [SC]  : < S1 ; S2, V, E > => < S1' ; S2, V', E >
            if < S1, V, E > => < S1', V', E > /\ S1 =/= S1' .
```

```
crl [IF0] : < if M[Q] = 1 then S1 else S2 fi, V, E > =>
            < S2, V', E >
          if V' := buildMeasOp(0, Q, E) x V /\ V' =/= 0 .
crl [IF1] : < if M[Q] = 1 then S1 else S2 fi, V, E > =>
            < S1, V', E >
          if V' := buildMeasOp(1, Q, E) x V /\ V' =/= 0 .
crl [L0]  : < while M[Q] = 1 do S od, V, E > =>
            < emp, V', E >
          if V' := buildMeasOp(0, Q, E) x V /\ V' =/= 0 .
crl [L1]  : < while M[Q] = 1 do S od, V, E > =>
            < S ; (while M[Q] = 1 do S od), V', E >
          if V' := buildMeasOp(1, Q, E) x V /\ V' =/= 0 .
endm
```

The sort Config is used for configurations, where a configuration is represented as a triple of a program, a quantum state, and an environment, rather than just a pair of a program and a quantum state. As mentioned above, including an environment in the configuration simplifies referencing quantum variables in quantum states. Note that emp is used to denote the empty program. The rewrite rules SK, UT, SC, IF0, IF1, L0, and L1 (starting with **rl** and **crl** for non-conditional and conditional rewrite rules) closely follow the transition rules shown in Fig. 1, adapted to our restriction of using the fixed yes-no measurement. Note that we use conditional rewrite rules for IF0, IF1, L0, and L1 with the assertion condition V' =/= 0 (indicating a non-zero vector for the post-measurement quantum state) to discard transitions with zero probability caused by measurement.

As an application of the executable operational semantics of quantum while-programs specified above, let us revisit the simple quantum program from Example 3.1. We want to find the last configuration in a finite computation of S starting from $|1\rangle$ by using the search command in Maude as follows:

```
search [1] in SEMANTICS :
< v('q) := H[v('q)]; while M[v('q)] = 1 do v('q) := H[v('q)] od,
  |1>, (v('q) -> 0) > =>! < emp, V:Vect, E:Env > .
Solution 1:
V --> (1 ./ sqrt(2)) . |0>
E --> v('q) -> 0
```

where [1] is used to limit the number of solutions to one. Without this restriction, there would be infinite solutions due to the divergence of S starting from $|1\rangle$, as shown in Example 3.1. As expected, the command returns a solution where the quantum state in the last configuration is (1./sqrt(2)).|0>, which corresponds to $\frac{|0\rangle}{\sqrt{2}}$. A further discussion of the search command will be provided in the next section.

5 Rechability Analysis of Quantum Programs

This section presents the application of the executable operational semantics of quantum programs specified in Sect. 4 for reachability analysis of quantum

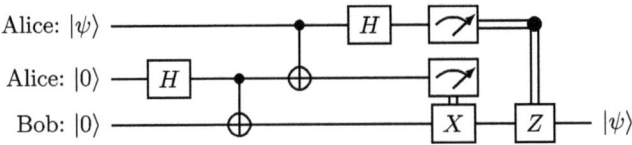

Fig. 2. Quantum Teleportation

programs. Maude supports the search command as a reachability analyzer, allowing us to automatically check whether a target term is reachable from a source term under a system module. As a case study, we use this approach to verify the correctness of Quantum Teleportation through a reachability analysis.

5.1 Quantum Teleportation

Quantum Teleportation [1], illustrated in Fig. 2, utilizes entanglement in quantum mechanics to transmit an unknown quantum state $|\psi\rangle$ from Alice to Bob using only three qubits and two classical bits. Given the no-cloning theorem [17], which prevents copying an arbitrary unknown quantum state, the protocol is crucial for transmitting an arbitrary unknown quantum state from one party to another. Initially, Alice owns the first and second qubits, which are set to an arbitrary quantum state $|\psi\rangle$ and a quantum state $|0\rangle$, respectively. Meanwhile, Bob owns the third qubit that is initialized to $|0\rangle$. The process of Quantum Teleportation is described as follows:

- *Entanglement preparation*: Alice and Bob first establish an entangled state. Alice applies the Hadamard gate on the second qubit and the CX gate on the second and third qubits.
- *State manipulation*: Alice then applies the CX gate on the first and second qubits, followed by the Hadamard gate on the first qubit.
- *Measurement and communication*: Alice measures the first and second qubits and sends the measurement results to Bob.
- *Conditional operations*: Based on Alice's measurement results, Bob applies the X and Z gates conditionally on the third qubit.

At the end of this process, Bob will have the quantum state $|\psi\rangle$ while Alice no longer retains it. Through reachability analysis with our executable operational semantics, we want to verify whether Alice correctly transmits an arbitrary unknown quantum state to Bob at the end.

5.2 Rechability Analysis of Quantum Teleportation

To conduct a reachability analysis for Quantum Teleportation, we define the system module TELEPORT as follows:

```
mod TELEPORT is
    protecting SEMANTICS .
```

```
    var C : Cpx .
    ops a b : -> Cpx .
    eq a .* (a)^* .+ b .* (b)^* = 1 .
    eq C .* a .* (a)^* .+ C .* b .* (b)^* = C .
    --- define an initial configuration
    op prog : -> Prog . op qs : -> Vect . op env : -> Env .
    eq qs = (a . |0> + b . |1>) (x) |0> (x) |0> .
    eq env = (v('q1) -> 0) (v('q2) -> 1) (v('q3) -> 2) .
    eq prog =
        v('q2) := H[v('q2)] ;
        v('q2), v('q3) := CX[v('q2), v('q3)] ;
        v('q1), v('q2) := CX[v('q1), v('q2)] ;
        v('q1) := H[v('q1)] ;
        if M[v('q2)] = 1 then v('q3) := X[v('q3)] else skip fi ;
        if M[v('q1)] = 1 then v('q3) := Z[v('q3)] else skip fi .
endm
```

The system module SEMANTICS is imported in TELEPORT. Within this module, a and b are constants of sort Cpx representing two arbitrary complex numbers such that the sum of the absolute square of two complex numbers is one. prog, qs, and env are defined to describe the quantum program of Quantum Teleportation, the initial quantum state, and the associated environment, respectively. It is important to note that qs corresponds to the quantum state $|\psi\rangle \otimes |0\rangle \otimes |0\rangle$, where the first qubit is in an arbitrary quantum state $|\psi\rangle = a|0\rangle + b|1\rangle$.

Given the module TELEPORT, the initial configuration <prog,qs,env>, and the target configuration <emp,V:Vect,E:Env>, we can use the search command to find all computations that start from the initial configuration and end in the target configuration. The desired search command is as follows:

search in TELEPORT : < prog, qs, env > =>! < emp,V:Vect,E:Env >.

where V:Vect and E:Env denote arbitrary values for the quantum state and the configuration in the target configuration, respectively; the symbol =>! in the command instructs Maude to find only final configurations that cannot be further rewritten as solutions. The command completes in just 1 millisecond and returns the four solutions in total with substitutions for V:Vect as follows:

```
Solution 1:
(a .* 1/2) . |0>(x)|0>(x)|0> + (b .* 1/2) . |0>(x)|0>(x)|1>
Solution 2:
(a .* 1/2) . |1>(x)|0>(x)|0> + (b .* 1/2) . |1>(x)|0>(x)|1>
Solution 3:
(a .* 1/2) . |0>(x)|1>(x)|0> + (b .* 1/2) . |0>(x)|1>(x)|1>
Solution 4:
(a .* 1/2) . |1>(x)|1>(x)|0> + (b .* 1/2) . |1>(x)|1>(x)|1>
```

The four quantum states above actually correspond to $\frac{1}{2}|00\rangle|\psi\rangle$, $\frac{1}{2}|10\rangle|\psi\rangle$, $\frac{1}{2}|01\rangle|\psi\rangle$, and $\frac{1}{2}|11\rangle|\psi\rangle$, respectively. These states indicate that the third qubit is in the state ψ at the final configuration for all computations, and the probability to reach each final quantum state is equal to its norm square that is $\frac{1}{4}$.

Additionally, the first qubit in the quantum state of each final configuration is not in the state $|\psi\rangle$ anymore. This reachability analysis confirms the correctness of Quantum Teleportation using our executable operational semantics with the search command in Maude, referred to as the reachability analysis tool QRAT.

6 Related Work

Recently, M. Ying introduced Quantum Hoare Logic (QHL) [18] for verifying quantum programs, addressing both partial correctness and total correctness with (relative) completeness. His work provided operational semantics, denotational semantics, and axiomatic semantics of quantum programs using density operators for representing quantum states and Hermitian operators (or observables) for assertions. While this approach makes the theory concise, it poses challenges for practical use in applications. To address this issue, his research group [20] then proposed an applied version of QHL, restricting assertions to projections, a specific class of Hermitian operators. However, as M. Ying [19] also noted, using pure states instead of density operators for representing quantum states is more convenient for practical use in applications. Therefore, our operational semantics use pure states rather than density operators to represent quantum states. Our work can be regarded as a complement to their work. We also demonstrated the practical application of our executable operational semantics for the reachability analysis of quantum programs by using QRAT to verify the correctness of Quantum Teleportation in Sect. 5.

7 Conclusion

We have described the syntax and operational semantics of quantum **while**-programs using pure states for representing quantum states. By mapping transition rules into rewrite rules in rewriting logic, we have implemented an executable operational semantics of quantum **while**-programs in Maude and have used it as a part of a reachability analysis tool, called QRAT, for quantum programs by utilizing the search command to automatically conduct reachability analysis in Maude. As a case study, we have used QRAT to verify the correctness of Quantum Teleportation, demonstrating the usefulness of our approach. Notably, QRAT facilitates symbolic and automated reasoning about arbitrary quantum states within Maude thanks to [5–8,16]. For future work, we aim to conduct more case studies, especially in cases where the while-loop construct is used in quantum programs, to demonstrate further the usefulness of QRAT and the executable operational semantics of quantum programs. Additionally, we plan to develop the denotational and axiomatic semantics of quantum programs in pure states, moving toward a proof system for quantum programs.

References

1. Bennett, C., Brassard, G., Crépeau, C., Jozsa, R., Peres, A., Wootters, W.: Teleporting an unknown quantum state via dual classical and Einstein-Podolsky-Rosen channels. Phys. Rev. Lett. **70**, 1895–1899 (1993). https://doi.org/10.1103/PhysRevLett.70.1895
2. Clavel, M., Durán, F., Eker, S., Lincoln, P., Martí-Oliet, N., Meseguer, J., Talcott, C.: All About Maude – A High-Performance Logical Framework: How to Specify, Program and Verify Systems in Rewriting Logic. LNCS, vol. 4350. Springer, Heidelberg (2007). https://doi.org/10.1007/978-3-540-71999-1
3. Developers, C.: Cirq (2024). https://doi.org/10.5281/zenodo.11398048
4. Dirac, P.A.M.: A new notation for quantum mechanics. Math. Proc. Cambridge Philos. Soc. **35**(3), 416–418 (1939). https://doi.org/10.1017/S0305004100021162
5. Do, C.M., Ogata, K.: Symbolic model checking quantum circuits in Maude. In: The 35th International Conference on Software Engineering and Knowledge Engineering. SEKE 2023, pp. 103–108 (2023). https://doi.org/10.18293/SEKE2023-014
6. Do, C.M., Ogata, K.: Equivalence checking of quantum circuits based on dirac notation in Maude. In: Ogata, K., Martí-Oliet, N. (eds.) WRLA 2024. LNCS, vol. 14953, pp. 84–103. Springer, Cham (2024). https://doi.org/10.1007/978-3-031-65941-6_5
7. Do, C.M., Ogata, K.: Symbolic model checking quantum circuits in Maude. PeerJ Comput. Sci. **10**, e2098 (2024). https://doi.org/10.7717/PEERJ-CS.2098
8. Do, C.M., Tsubasa, T., Ogata, K.: Automated quantum program verification in probabilistic dynamic quantum logic. In: The 2nd International Workshop on Formal Analysis and Verification of Post-Quantum Cryptographic Protocols. FAVPQC 2023, pp. 36–51 (2023). https://favpqc2023.gitlab.io/files/papers/3-Canh.pdf
9. Martí-Oliet, N., Meseguer, J.: Rewriting logic as a logical and semantic framework. Electron. Notes Theor. Comput. Sci. **4**, 190–225 (1996). https://doi.org/10.1016/S1571-0661(04)00040-4, RWLW96, First International Workshop on Rewriting Logic and its Applications
10. Meseguer, J.: Twenty years of rewriting logic. J. Logic Algebr. Program. **81**(7), 721–781 (2012). https://doi.org/10.1016/j.jlap.2012.06.003, Rewriting Logic and its Applications
11. Nielsen, M.A., Chuang, I.L.: Quantum Computation and Quantum Information: 10th Anniversary Edition. Cambridge University Press, Cambridge (2010). https://doi.org/10.1017/CBO9780511976667
12. Qiskit Community: Qiskit: an open-source framework for quantum computing (2017). https://doi.org/10.5281/zenodo.2562110
13. Selinger, P.: Towards a quantum programming language. Math. Struct. Comput. Sci. **14**(4), 527–586 (2004). https://doi.org/10.1017/S0960129504004256
14. Shor, P.: Algorithms for quantum computation: discrete logarithms and factoring. In: Proceedings 35th Annual Symposium on Foundations of Computer Science, pp. 124–134 (1994). https://doi.org/10.1109/SFCS.1994.365700
15. Svore, K., et al.: Q#: enabling scalable quantum computing and development with a high-level DSL. In: Proceedings of the Real World Domain Specific Languages Workshop 2018. RWDSL2018. Association for Computing Machinery, New York, NY, USA (2018). https://doi.org/10.1145/3183895.3183901
16. Takagi, T., Do, C.M., Ogata, K.: Automated quantum program verification in dynamic quantum logic. In: Gierasimczuk, N., Velázquez-Quesada, F.R. (eds.) DaLí 2023. LNCS, vol. 14401, pp. 68–84. Springer, Cham (2024). https://doi.org/10.1007/978-3-031-51777-8_5

17. Wootters, W.K., Zurek, W.H.: A single quantum cannot be cloned. Nature **299**(5886), 802–803 (1982). https://doi.org/10.1038/299802a0
18. Ying, M.: Floyd–Hoare logic for quantum programs. ACM Trans. Program. Lang. Syst. **33**(6) (2012). https://doi.org/10.1145/2049706.2049708
19. Ying, M.: Foundations of Quantum Programming, , 2nd edn. Morgan Kaufmann Publishers Inc., San Francisco (2024). https://doi.org/10.1016/C2022-0-02250-9
20. Zhou, L., Yu, N., Ying, M.: An applied quantum Hoare logic. In: Proceedings of the 40th ACM SIGPLAN Conference on Programming Language Design and Implementation. PLDI 2019, pp. 1149–1162. Association for Computing Machinery, New York, NY, USA (2019). https://doi.org/10.1145/3314221.3314584

Automated Software Test Input Generation with Diffusion Models

Yujin Zhu[✉], Xiujing Guo, Hiroyuki Okamura, and Tadashi Dohi

Hiroshima University, Hiroshima, Japan
zhuyujin0502@outlook.com, {okamu,dohi}@hiroshima-u.ac.jp

Abstract. With the rapid growth of software size and complexity, traditional software testing methods are becoming increasingly costly. To improve test efficiency, we propose a novel approach for automated test input generation based on diffusion models, which are advanced techniques for generating high-quality data. Our approach leverages diffusion models to generate test inputs aimed at achieving higher code coverage. In our framework, diffusion models are used to generate test inputs that evaluate program behavior on programs using LLVM as an intermediate language. By training the diffusion model with execution path information, we can generate diverse test inputs that increase code coverage without requiring detailed analysis of branch expressions. We conducted experiments to compare the performance of diffusion models with GAN-based methods in terms of test input generation. The results show that the diffusion model-based framework significantly outperforms GAN-based methods in terms of test coverage. Our tests on two modules in the GNU Scientific Library showed that diffusion models can effectively generate test inputs that improve branch coverage. These results suggest that diffusion models hold great promise in the area of automated test input generation, providing an efficient and effective approach to increasing test coverage and software reliability.

Keywords: Software testing · test case generation · test input · execution path · Diffusion Mode

1 Introduction

Software testing is a crucial process for ensuring the reliability and stability of software systems. Its primary objective is to identify and correct errors and defects in a program to enhance software quality. In modern software development, testing not only impacts product reliability and performance but also affects the development timeline and costs. Thus, software testing is a key component of software engineering and is worth thorough research.

Our research focuses on test input generation. Test input generation is central to ensuring software quality because it directly impacts test coverage and effectiveness. By generating test inputs with a wide coverage range, testers can more easily discover potential defects and errors. On the other hand, in terms of software reliability, an increase in the number of test cases may correspond to improved software reliability. However, the proliferation of test cases inevitably incurs substantial testing costs. Thus, the challenge lies in striking a balance between reducing the number of test cases and maintaining a desirable level of software reliability.

In recent years, with the rise of artificial intelligence, researchers have started exploring the application of AI in test input generation. AI technology can generate varied test inputs, improving test coverage and effectiveness.

The GAN (Generative Adversarial Network) model has made remarkable achievements in the field of image generation. Lyu et al. [1] employed a GAN model to learn the characteristics of valuable inputs, subsequently generating seed files for fuzz testing. This approach contributed to test input diversity and increased fuzz testing effectiveness. Joffe and Clark [2] proposed a search-based software testing (SBST) framework built on a deconvolutional generative neural network, comparing its performance with the AFL fuzzing tool. Moreover, Li et al. [3] utilized Wasserstein GANs (WGANGP) to generate fuzzing data for industrial control systems. For industrial control systems, Hu et al. [4] proposed an automatical and intelligent fuzzing framework(GANFuzz) for testing implementations of industrial network protocols, in which the protocol grammar is learned by deep learning. More recently, Lv et al. [5] designed an automated and intelligent fuzzing framework BLSTM-DCNNFuzz for industry control protocols. Guo et al. [6] proposed a framework for automatic test input generation based on the generative adversarial network (GAN), aiming to generate test inputs that can improve test coverage.

Deep learning techniques, such as deep neural networks (DNNs), provide a versatile platform for automated test input generation, allowing models to learn from large datasets and generate diverse test inputs. Zong et al. [7] adopted deep learning techniques to predict input reachability, aiding grey-box fuzzing in filtering out unreachable inputs. This enhancement improves fuzz testing performance by focusing on reachable code paths. Guo et al. [8] train an Multilayer Perceptron-based discriminator to identify software boundaries and use Markov Chain Monte Carlo (MCMC) to automatically generate test inputs with Boundary Value Analysis. Demir et al. [9] proposed a novel CGF solution for structural testing of DNNs. The proposed fuzzer employs Monte Carlo Tree Search to drive the coverage-guided search in the pursuit of achieving high coverage. Moreover, Jiang et al. [10] propose AugTest, a DNN testing method based on stochastic optimization with momentum, searching for optimal compositions of data augmentation parameters to efficiently generate diverse and valid test inputs.

Reinforcement Learning (RL) for test input generation offers a dynamic and adaptive approach, where models utilize feedback to optimize their behavior in generating test inputs. Reddy et al. [11] propose and study a black-box approach for generating valid test inputs and then propose a solution based on reinforcement learning, using a tabular, on-policy RL approach to guide the generator. Kim et al. [12] present GunPowder, a novel framework for SBST which extends SUT to the environment. They train a Double Deep Q-Networks (DDQN) agent with deep neural network and evaluate the effectiveness of their approach by conducting a small empirical study.

Evolutionary algorithms are a subset of evolutionary computation in AI. In software testing, Evolutionary algorithms can be used to automate test input generation by evolving a population of test inputs toward optimal coverage. Ferrer et al. [13] have studied the multi-objective TDGP with the aim of analyzing the performance of a direct multi-objective approach versus the application of mono-objective algorithms followed by a test case selection. Suresh et al. [14] explores the automatic generation of test data for object-oriented programs based on the concept of the extended control flow graph by utilizing the binary particle swarm optimization and artificial bee colony optimization algorithms.

The field of software testing has seen significant advancements with the application of various AI models. This paper focuses on input generation based on generative model. Guo et al. [6] proposed a framework for automatic test input generation based on the generative adversarial network (GAN). GANs are widely known for their ability to generate complex data by employing a generator-discriminator framework, which helps improve the quality of generated data through competition. However, despite their success in various domains, GANs have certain limitations when it comes to test data generation for software testing. GANs can be difficult to train due to issues such as mode collapse, where the generator fails to capture the full diversity of the data distribution. Additionally, GANs are prone to instability during training, which can lead to inconsistent results. These limitations are particularly challenging when generating test inputs and execution paths, as software testing often requires a high level of diversity and consistency to ensure thorough coverage.

Given these challenges, we propose a new approach for generating test inputs and execution paths using Diffusion models. Diffusion models are a recent development in AI, known for their stability and ability to generate high-quality data with a diverse distribution. Diffusion models work through a process of iterative denoising, gradually transforming noise into meaningful data. This approach provides greater stability and can produce a broader range of test input, making it highly suitable for software testing applications. In our framework, diffusion models are used to generate test inputs that evaluate program behavior on programs using LLVM (Low Level Virtual Machine) as an intermediate language. LLVM is a versatile compiler framework used in many software development projects, and by generating test data compatible with LLVM, our approach aims to contribute to a more robust and effective software testing process. By training the diffusion model with execution path information, we can generate diverse test inputs that increase code coverage without requiring detailed analysis of branch expressions.

The remaining parts of the paper are organized as follows. Section 2 is dedicated to the review of diffusion models. Section 3 describes the details of the proposed framework. In Section 4, we exhibit experiments using the diffusion model to generate test inputs. Section 5 concludes the paper with some remarks and presents the future direction.

2 Denoising Diffusion Probabilistic Model (DDPM)

2.1 Overview of DDPM

Denoising Diffusion Probabilistic Model (DDPM) represent a class of generative models that have gained significant attention due to their ability to generate high-quality data with diverse distributions [15]. The core concept of DDPM is based on a diffusion process that gradually adds noise to data and a reverse process that progressively removes noise to recover the original data. This forward and reverse diffusion process is a key characteristic that distinguishes DDPM from other generative models.

2.2 DDPM: Basic Concept

In the forward diffusion process, start with a sample x_0 from the real-world data distribution $q(x_0)$. The diffusion process is then defined through a series of steps where noise is incrementally added. Specifically, for each time step t in the set $\{1, 2, \ldots, T\}$, the conditional distribution for the next state in the diffusion process, x_t, is given by

$$q(x_t \mid x_{t-1}) = \mathcal{N}\left(x_t; \sqrt{1-\beta_t} \cdot x_{t-1}, \beta_t \cdot I\right), \tag{1}$$

where x_t is the data at step t, β_t is the noise scale, and I is the identity matrix. The process starts with original data (x_0), then adds noise through T steps to create a distribution of noise (x_T). As t increases, the process gradually diffuses the original data sample into a simpler distribution, ultimately converging to a standard Gaussian distribution. This progression toward a Gaussian distribution is a key feature of diffusion models and forms the basis for the subsequent reverse process

In the reverse process, we start from the final state (x_T) which is obtained from a standard Gaussian distribution, and gradually reconstruct the data by iteratively moving back through the reverse diffusion steps. For each time step t (from T down to 1), the conditional distribution for generating the previous state x_{t-1} from x_t, is defined as:

$$p(x_{t-1}|x_t) = \mathcal{N}(x_{t-1}; \mu_t(x_t, t), \Sigma_t(x_t, t)), \tag{2}$$

where $\mu_t(x_t, t)$ is the mean predicted by the model, and $\Sigma_t(x_t, t)$ is the variance indicating the uncertainty in the prediction.

Training DDPM involves learning a model that can accurately predict the denoising step, essentially learning the distribution of the original data. This is achieved by minimizing the difference between the predicted denoising and the original data at each time step. The objective function typically used in DDPMs involves a variational lower bound (VLB), where the model is trained to maximize the likelihood of recovering the original data from the noisy data.

The loss function for each time step t is defined as:

$$\mathbb{E}_{t,\epsilon}[\|\epsilon - \epsilon_\theta(x_t, t)\|^2], \tag{3}$$

where ϵ is the noise in the forward process, and $\epsilon_\theta(x_t, t)$ is the predicted denoising result. The expected value is calculated by sampling across various time steps t and corresponding noise.

2.3 Application in Software Testing

Applying artificial intelligence technologies to unstructured data, such as computer programs and software testing, poses the significant challenge of identifying suitable inputs for AI systems. Our approach involves leveraging not just the test inputs but also their associated execution paths as inputs for DDPMs. This combination provides valuable information about the program's behavior. Furthermore, gathering execution paths during dynamic testing is relatively straightforward, adding to the feasibility of our approach.

In our study, we focus on branch coverage as the metric for evaluating test inputs. And define the execution path as the combination of the execution state of each branch in the program under a specific input. To extract execution paths, we use the LLVM-cov tool [16], a source code coverage analysis and profiling tool that works with the LLVM compiler framework. LLVM-cov can provide detailed information on how many times each statement in a program is executed and can generate coverage reports with precise branch execution counts. LLVM-cov is a part of the LLVM project and is designed to work with LLVM-based compilers. LLVM is a compiler framework that supports multiple programming languages by converting source code into an intermediate language (IR), which is then transformed into machine-readable code [17]. The intermediate language in LLVM represents a level of abstraction where various programming constructs are translated into a common format, allowing for more consistent test case generation and analysis. This flexibility allows LLVM to be used with a wide range of languages, making it a valuable target for software testing. By focusing on achieving high coverage in LLVM, we can ensure that our approach is applicable across multiple languages and software projects. Given LLVM's widespread use, enhancing test coverage in LLVM means that our approach can be widely applicable, covering a broader range of software projects and languages.

When executing a program, we use LLVM-cov to write branch frequencies to the output file, and then extract the branch information in the file as a path. For example, Fig. 1 is a C program designed to determine whether and what kind of triangle a three-sided triangle forms. When the input score is $3, 4, 5$, we compile the program with LLVM and use LLVM-cov to collect branch coverage information to get the "triangle.c.gcov" file, as shown in Fig. 2. The resulting output file contains detailed branch execution data, indicating which branches were taken and which were not. This data can be converted into a simplified representation where: A branch marked as "taken" is represented by "1", indicating that the branch was executed at least once. A branch marked as "not taken" is represented by "0", indicating that the branch was not executed. A branch marked as "never

```
int Triangle_Classifier(float A , float B ,float C){
    bool isTriangle = (A + B > C) && (B + C > A) && (C + A > B);
    if (isTriangle) {
        printf("These sides form a triangle.\n");
        if (A == B && B == C) {
            printf("Triangle type: Equilateral\n");
        } else if (A == B || B == C || C == A) {
            printf("Triangle type: Isosceles\n");
        } else {
            printf("Triangle type: Scalene\n");
        }
    } else {
        printf("These sides do not form a triangle.\n");
    }

    return 0;
}
```

Fig. 1. A code of `triangle.c`

executed" is represented by "-1", indicating that it was entirely bypassed during program execution. Thus, "$-1, 0, 1$" is treated as the three execution states of the branch, and the execution path for the program under the input of $3, 4, 5$ is defined as a combination of branch states: $1, 0, 0, 1, 1, 0, 0, 1, 1, 0, 1, 0, 0, 1$. This approach provides a straightforward and systematic way to determine branch coverage in LLVM-based programs, allowing us to define and analyze execution paths effectively. By using LLVM-cov, we can obtain detailed branch-level data that helps us evaluate test case effectiveness and identify areas for improvement in our test input generation process. This information plays a crucial role in assessing branch coverage and ensuring a comprehensive testing strategy.

In our approach, we use DDPMs to generate test inputs and their associated execution paths for software testing. The ability of DDPMs to traverse from a noisy state back to a structured state allows for a flexible exploration of the testing space, helping to uncover test inputs that may provide higher test coverage. Fig. 3 illustrates the input and output of DDPMs in our framework. The input of DDPM is a set of inputs of the program with their corresponding executed paths extracted by LLVM-cov. The output of DDPMs is a set of new inputs of the program with their corresponding expected paths. There are two phases from input to output: training and sampling.

During the training phase, we start by adding noise to the original data. This noise is introduced through various schemes, which dictate the pattern of noise addition. In this phase, we create a noise schedule based on the chosen scheme and then use it to transform the original data. The process of adding noise mimics the diffusion process in DDPMs. The goal is to train the model to understand the relationship between the noisy data and the underlying original data, and to achieve the conversion between the input-path distribution and the noise distribution (e.g. Gaussian noise).

During the sampling stage, a noise vector sampled from the noise distribution (e.g. Gaussian noise) is provided as input to the model. After sampling T time points, we obtain a new denoising result, which represents a new input and corresponding predicted path that conforms to the input-path distribution.

```
-:    0:Source:triangle.c
-:    0:Graph:triangle.gcno
-:    0:Data:triangle.gcda
-:    0:Runs:1
-:    0:Programs:1
-:    1://Automatic Test Data Generation for Unit Testing
-:    2:
-:    3:#include <math.h>
-:    4:#include<stdio.h>
-:    5:#include<stdlib.h>
-:    6:#include <string.h>
-:    7:#include <stdbool.h>
-:    8:
-:    9:
function Triangle_Classifier called 1 returned 100% blocks executed 75%
1:   10:int Triangle_Classifier(float A , float B ,float C){
-:   11:
1:   12:   bool isTriangle = (A + B > C) && (B + C > A) && (C + A > B);
branch  0 taken 1
branch  1 taken 0
branch  2 taken 0
branch  3 taken 1
1:   13:   if (isTriangle) {
branch  0 taken 1
branch  1 taken 0
1:   14:     printf("These sides form a triangle.\n");
1:   15:     if (A == B && B == C) {
branch  0 taken 0
branch  1 taken 1
branch  2 never executed
branch  3 never executed
#####:   16:     printf("Triangle type: Equilateral\n");
1:   17:   } else if (A == B || B == C || C == A) {
branch  0 taken 1
branch  1 taken 0
branch  2 taken 1
branch  3 taken 0
branch  4 taken 0
branch  5 taken 1
#####:   18:     printf("Triangle type: Isosceles\n");
#####:   19:   } else {
1:   20:     printf("Triangle type: Scalene\n");
-:   21:   }
1:   22:   } else {
#####:   23:     printf("These sides do not form a triangle.\n");
-:   24:   }
-:   25:
1:   26:   return 0;
-:   27:}
-:   28:
```

Fig. 2. `triangle.c.gcov` file

3 Framework for Test Generation Based on Diffusion Models

We propose a framework for automated test input generation. The proposed framework using Diffusion models is designed to generate diverse test inputs with high coverage. Figure 4 illustrates the structure of the framework. It contains the following five steps:

– Step 1: Select m test inputs and their corresponding paths as initial training data, and set a maximum training data limit k.
– Step 2: Train DDPMs with m training data.
– Step 3: Generate m data by DDPMs.
– Step 4: According to the path information of the generated data, select $p(p < m)$ data from m data sets that may cover not-executed branches in the training data.

Training phase

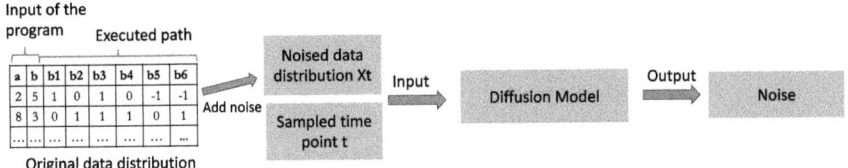

Sampling phase

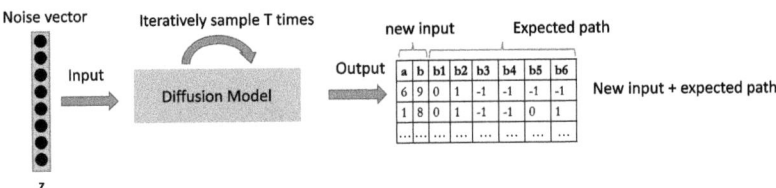

Fig. 3. The input and output of DDPM in our framework

- Step 5: Add the selected p input data and their corresponding executed paths to the training data (At this time, the number of training data is $m = m+p$). After adding, if the total number of training data is less than k, return to Step 2; otherwise, terminate the process.

Figure 5 shows a practical example of our proposed framework. The program under test has two inputs, "a" and "b", and four branches, labeled b1 through b4. The process starts with step 1, where we choose 10 test inputs and their corresponding execution paths to use as training data. Notably, in this initial dataset, branches 2 and 3 are not covered.

Then, we train a DDPMs on this training data to generate m new test inputs and their associated expected paths. The goal is to increase branch coverage, particularly focusing on those that were previously not taken, such as branches 2 and 3.

In step 4, we select the test inputs with path information indicating coverage of branches 2 and 3. For example, the selected inputs might include patterns like a = 0, b = 3; ...; a = 2, b = 1; a = 7, b = 10; where the generated path information shows that these inputs are likely to traverse branch 2 or 3.

In step 5, we execute the program with these selected test inputs to gather the actual execution paths. We then add these paths to the training dataset for further refinement. After running the selected test inputs, the new data shows that branch 2 and 3 has been covered.

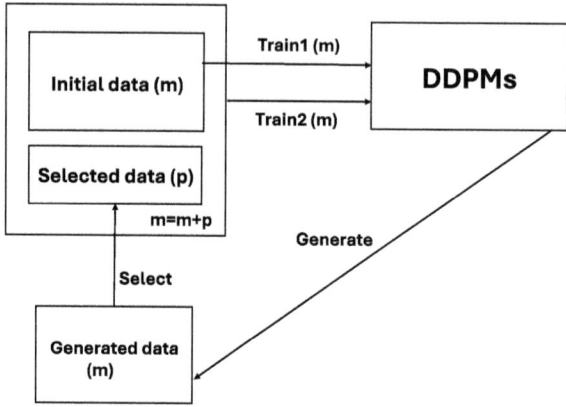

Fig. 4. A framework for the test input generation indenting to increase test coverage

Through this process, a high-precision DDPMs model can enhance test coverage by generating test inputs that target previously uncovered branches. This capability allows our framework to continually improve its effectiveness in finding test inputs that achieve broader branch coverage.

4 Experiment

In this section, we conduct a series of experiments to evaluate the effectiveness of our proposed framework, which uses diffusion models. To establish a baseline for comparison, we selected the WGANGP structure because, as noted by Guo et al.[6], it outperformed other GAN variants in generating automated software test inputs. This makes it a solid reference point for evaluating the effectiveness of GAN models in comparison to Diffusion models within our framework. Our experiments aim to determine how diffusion models perform in our framework compared to GAN models.

4.1 Programs Under Test

In the experiment, we have considered two modules in the GNU Scientific Library [18] (a numerical library for C and C++ programmers): the gamma_inc.c module and the hyperg_1F1.c module. The gamma_inc.c module is used to calculate the incomplete gamma function. It contains 13 functions and the total number of branches included is 138. The hyperg 1F1.c module is used to calculate the confluent hypergeometric function. It contains 21 functions with branches, and the total number of branches is 590. In this experiment, we focused on unit testing and conducted experiments for 3 functions in the gamma_inc.c module and 5 functions in the hyperg_1F1.c module. The name of the selected functions and the number of branches it contains are shown in Table 1.

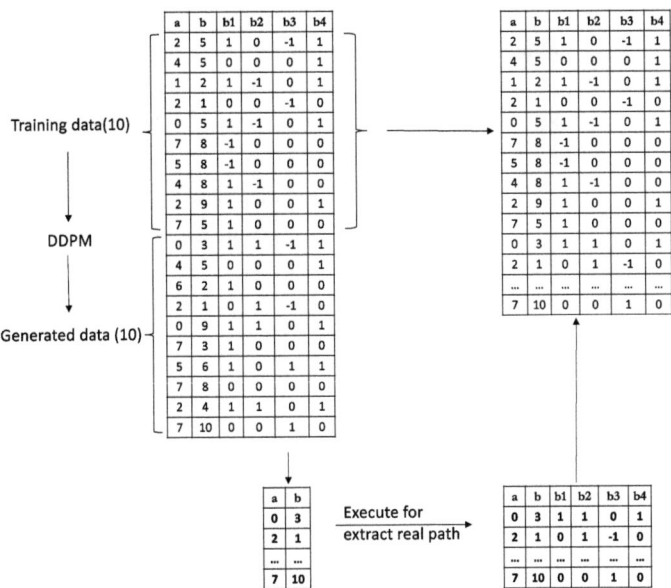

Fig. 5. An example of proposed framework

4.2 Experimental Setup

The structure of the noise generator in the diffusion model is a fully connected neural network, and the training hyperparameters are shown in the Table 3. In the experiment, the diffusion steps were set to 100, and different sampling steps were investigated: $T_s = 100$ and $T_s = 90$. When the sampling steps were set to 100, complete denoising was performed. When set to 90, some noise was retained. Then we compare the coverage of the generated test inputs under these two settings.

Besides, we conducted experiments using three different noise addition methods and three different sampling strategies for diffusion models.

The three noise addition schemes we use are Linear, Cosine, and Sqrt, each defining a unique method to incrementally corrupt the data with noise over a series of time points.

- Linear Schedule: This method gradually increases noise in a linear fashion throughout the diffusion process. It's simple and widely used due to its stability.
- Cosine Schedule: This method employs a cosine-based progression for noise addition, offering a smoother transition of noise levels.
- Sqrt Schedule: This schedule uses a square root function, providing a rapid noise increase at the beginning and slowing down toward the end of the diffusion process.

Table 1. The functions names

Modules	Functions	Function name	Number of branches
gamma_inc.c	F1	gsl_sf_gamma_inc_Q_e	24
	F2	gsl_sf_gamma_inc_P_e	20
	F3	gsl_sf_gamma_inc_e	16
hyperg_1F1.c	F1	hyperg_1F1_small_a_bgt0	38
	F2	hyperg_1F1_ab_posint	68
	F3	hyperg_1F1_ab_pos	94
	F4	hyperg_1F1_ab_neg	58
	F5	gsl_sf_hyperg_1F1_int_e	42

For the sampling strategies, we explored:

- Uniform Sampling: This strategy provides equal probability to all time steps during sampling, offering a straightforward and unbiased approach.
- Fix Sampling: This method assigns predefined weights to certain time steps, allowing for more focused sampling in specific regions.
- LossAware Sampling: This strategy adjusts sampling weights based on the loss at each time step, emphasizing the steps that are most significant in terms of model learning.

Combining the three noise addition methods and the three sampling strategies, 9 methods can be obtained and marked as in Table 2.

Table 2. Combining the three noise addition methods and the three sampling strategies in 9 methods

Sampling Methods \ Noise	Linear	Cosine	Sqrt
Uniform	UL	UC	US
LossAware	LL	LC	LS
Fix	FL	FC	FS

Table 3. Training hyperparameters of DDPM

DDPM	Hidden Layers	Hidden Units	Activations Functions	Learning Rate	Layer norm	optimizer
Noise Generater	7	64	ReLU	0.001	FALSE	Adam

By running experiments with these different configurations, we aimed to understand how variations in noise addition and sampling impact the performance of diffusion models in generating test inputs for software testing.

For the GAN model, we use WGANGP as the baseline for GAN comparison. The network structure of the generator and discriminator is a simple fully connected neural network (dense layer), and training hyperparameters are shown in the Table 4

In both two experiments, we generated 100 initial training data, and then selected 10 data from the sampled data as test inputs in each iteration. This process was iterated 10 times to generate 100 test inputs.

Through these experiments we were able to determine which diffusion model settings are most effective for software testing tasks and how they stack up against GAN-based approaches. The comparison with GAN provides insights into the strengths and limitations of both Diffusion and GAN models in the context of automated test input generation.

4.3 Results and Discussion

Table 5 shows the coverage of test inputs generated by WGANGP based method and DDPMs based method. The initial coverage represents the percent of branches executed by 100 initial training data. The trained coverage represents the percent of branches executed by 200 input data, where 200 input data contains 100 initial training data and 100 generated data. From the coverage results, it can be seen that DDPMs outperforms GAN methods in all three functions of the `gamma_inc.c` module. At the same time, in the five functions of the `hyperg_1F1.c` module, DDPMs's coverage rate exceeds that of GAN in three functions. Overall, when $T_s = 100$, among the 9 combinations of sampling methods and noise addition methods, DDPMs combined with the uniform sampling method and the linear schedule noise addition method produced better coverage than the other combinations. In addition, compared with sampling at $T_s = 90$, the coverage of the four functions of the data sampled at $T_s = 100$ exceeds that of the data sampled at $T_s = 90$.

We chose three commonly used metrics in classification models: "accuracy", "precision", and "recall", as evaluation metrics. In our work, we use generative model to learn the distribution of inputs and path information of programs. In path definition, the path is composed of the execution states of several branches, where each branch has three states. Generating the status of each branch in the path information is similar to a three-classification problem. Therefore, we selected these three metrics to assess the model's understanding of program

Table 4. Training hyperparameters of WGANGP

WGAN-GP	Hidden Layers	Hidden Units	Activations Functions	Learning Rate	Layer norm	optimizer	GP_WEIGHT
Generater	3	64	LeakyReLU	0.001	TRUE	RMSprop	10
Discriminator	3	64	LeakyReLU	0.001	TRUE	RMSprop	

Table 5. Comparison of the coverage achievement of GAN and DDPMs

Modules	Func	Initial coverage	Trained coverage																	
			WGAN-GP	DDPM ($T_s = 100$)								DDPM ($T_s = 90$)								
				UL	UC	US	LL	LC	LS	FL	FC	FS	UL	UC	US	LL	LC	LS	FL	FC	FS
gamma_inc.c	F1	0.54	0.58	**0.70**	0.66	**0.70**	0.66	0.66	0.66	0.66	0.66	0.66	0.62	0.62	**0.70**	0.62	0.62	0.62	0.66	0.62	0.66
	F2	0.75	0.8	0.80	**0.85**	**0.85**	0.75	**0.85**	0.75	0.75	**0.85**	**0.85**	0.80	0.75	0.75	0.75	0.75	**0.80**	0.80	0.75	0.80
	F3	0.68	0.68	**0.81**	0.68	0.68	0.75	0.68	0.75	0.75	0.68	0.68	**0.81**	0.68	0.75	0.81	0.68	0.68	0.75	0.68	0.75
hyperg_1F1.c	F1	0.36	**0.57**	0.55	0.55	**0.57**	0.55	0.55	0.55	0.55	0.52	0.55	0.55	0.55	0.55	**0.57**	0.55	0.55	**0.57**	0.55	0.55
	F2	0.42	0.73	**0.76**	0.69	0.42	0.64	0.54	0.66	0.64	0.60	0.70	0.75	0.75	0.66	0.73	0.75	0.75	0.64	0.75	0.75
	F3	0.73	0.76	**0.77**	0.75	**0.77**	0.75	0.75	0.75	**0.77**	0.75	0.76	0.75	0.75	**0.77**	0.76	0.75	0.75	0.74	0.75	**0.77**
	F4	0.56	**0.79**	0.63	0.56	0.60	0.60	0.58	0.62	0.59	0.56	0.58	0.56	0.56	0.58	0.60	0.58	0.56	0.60	0.58	0.56
	F5	0.59	0.78	**0.80**	0.78	0.78	0.76	0.78	0.78	**0.8**	0.78	0.76	0.78	0.78	0.76	0.76	0.78	0.78	0.78	0.78	0.76

Table 6. Average path accuracy

Modules	Func	Average path accuracy																		
		WGAN-GP	DDPM ($T_s = 100$)									DDPM ($T_s = 90$)								
			UL	UC	US	LL	LC	LS	FL	FC	FS	UL	UC	US	LL	LC	LS	FL	FC	FS
gamma_inc.c	F1	0.43	0.42	0.53	0.51	0.39	0.49	0.38	0.44	0.53	0.46	0.41	0.38	0.42	0.42	0.43	0.40	0.42	0.39	0.41
	F2	0.39	0.50	0.49	0.42	0.43	0.40	0.31	0.38	0.36	0.43	0.53	0.36	0.38	0.53	0.38	0.40	0.52	0.39	0.38
	F3	0.31	0.53	0.20	0.21	0.45	0.21	0.45	0.46	0.25	0.17	0.46	0.28	0.35	0.46	0.23	0.36	0.41	0.24	0.35
hyperg_1F1.c	F1	0.21	0.38	0.40	0.41	0.41	0.43	0.41	0.37	0.43	0.42	0.43	0.41	0.40	0.36	0.41	0.41	0.38	0.41	0.42
	F2	0.27	0.45	0.44	0.43	0.44	0.43	0.43	0.44	0.43	0.44	0.45	0.44	0.43	0.43	0.42	0.43	0.42	0.43	0.42
	F3	0.15	0.44	0.45	0.44	0.44	0.46	0.43	0.45	0.46	0.44	0.43	0.47	0.45	0.44	0.47	0.45	0.44	0.47	0.44
	F4	0.36	0.42	0.42	0.42	0.43	0.42	0.41	0.43	0.42	0.44	0.39	0.42	0.42	0.43	0.43	0.42	0.42	0.42	0.41
	F5	0.35	0.53	0.33	0.34	0.38	0.36	0.35	0.33	0.35	0.34	0.49	0.33	0.35	0.41	0.33	0.36	0.32	0.36	0.34

Table 7. Average path precision

Modules	Func	Average path precision																		
		WGAN-GP	DDPM ($T_s = 100$)									DDPM ($T_s = 90$)								
			UL	UC	US	LL	LC	LS	FL	FC	FS	UL	UC	US	LL	LC	LS	FL	FC	FS
gamma_inc.c	F1	0.8	0.48	0.21	0.28	0.17	0.17	0.17	0.20	0.27	0.20	0.32	0.11	0.10	0.37	0.10	0.11	0.25	0.09	0.10
	F2	0.65	0.72	0.38	0.17	0.41	0.27	0.41	0.19	0.20	0.25	0.54	0.13	0.13	0.50	0.12	0.13	0.47	0.13	0.14
	F3	0.76	0.70	0.05	0.11	0.47	0.05	0.47	0.44	0.06	0.10	0.65	0.15	0.19	0.65	0.13	0.24	0.42	0.14	0.17
hyperg_1F1.c	F1	0.56	0.18	0.05	0.12	0.20	0.04	0.11	0.09	0.06	0.11	0.38	0.05	0.08	0.16	0.05	0.09	0.11	0.05	0.11
	F2	0.84	0.12	0.11	0.10	0.12	0.09	0.12	0.11	0.10	0.11	0.11	0.08	0.12	0.12	0.13	0.12	0.13	0.09	0.12
	F3	0.38	0.11	0.09	0.12	0.12	0.08	0.50	0.12	0.08	0.11	0.13	0.09	0.11	0.14	0.09	0.12	0.11	0.07	0.12
	F4	0.68	0.12	0.12	0.14	0.12	0.13	0.15	0.14	0.12	0.12	0.14	0.12	0.12	0.13	0.12	0.13	0.15	0.11	0.14
	F5	0.44	0.69	0.23	0.23	0.26	0.24	0.25	0.25	0.25	0.22	0.58	0.22	0.23	0.30	0.24	0.24	0.27	0.25	0.24

path information. For each branch in the path information, compare the predicted state with the actual state to evaluate the generated program path. If the predicted state matches the actual state, count it as a correct prediction. "accuracy" can be calculated as

$$accuracy = \frac{Number\ of\ correct\ predictions}{Total\ number\ of\ branches} \qquad (4)$$

so as to understand the overall prediction accuracy of the model.

Since, in our proposed framework, we selected data based on the branch information with state 1 (branches being covered) in the generated path information, we used "precision" to measure the proportion of correctly predicted branches as 1 (True positives) to all branches predicted as 1 (True positives + False positives) by the model. This helps us understand how accurately the

Table 8. Average path recall

Modules	Func	Average path recall																
		WGAN-GP	DDPM ($T_s = 100$)								DDPM ($T_s = 90$)							
			UL	UC	US	LL	LC	LS	FL	FC	FS	UL	UC	US	LL	LC	LS	FL	FC	FS
gamma_inc.c	F1	0.36	0.34	0.51	0.52	0.31	0.46	0.31	0.34	0.53	0.40	0.44	0.43	0.45	0.53	0.45	0.43	0.43	0.33	0.44
	F2	0.27	0.66	0.72	0.48	0.31	0.57	0.43	0.31	0.66	0.53	0.60	0.52	0.43	0.54	0.46	0.48	0.50	0.60	0.47
	F3	0.36	0.42	0.30	0.44	0.38	0.32	0.38	0.43	0.38	0.48	0.32	0.49	0.49	0.32	0.49	0.50	0.29	0.55	0.42
hyperg_1F1.c	F1	0.35	0.42	0.42	0.49	0.53	0.41	0.46	0.39	0.44	0.49	0.44	0.48	0.45	0.32	0.0	0.44	0.48	0.42	0.51
	F2	0.39	0.52	0.50	0.49	0.52	0.51	0.49	0.45	0.48	0.49	0.48	0.46	0.43	0.48	0.50	0.50	0.50	0.44	0.47
	F3	0.22	0.51	0.52	0.49	0.48	0.49	0.13	0.48	0.49	0.51	0.46	0.54	0.45	0.52	0.47	0.51	0.48	0.00	0.47
	F4	0.34	0.44	0.45	0.49	0.51	0.44	0.49	0.49	0.49	0.51	0.47	0.49	0.49	0.0	0.48	0.47	0.50	0.42	0.48
	F5	0.79	0.44	0.47	0.47	0.49	0.48	0.49	0.46	0.48	0.46	0.46	0.44	0.49	0.53	0.47	0.50	0.42	0.46	0.34

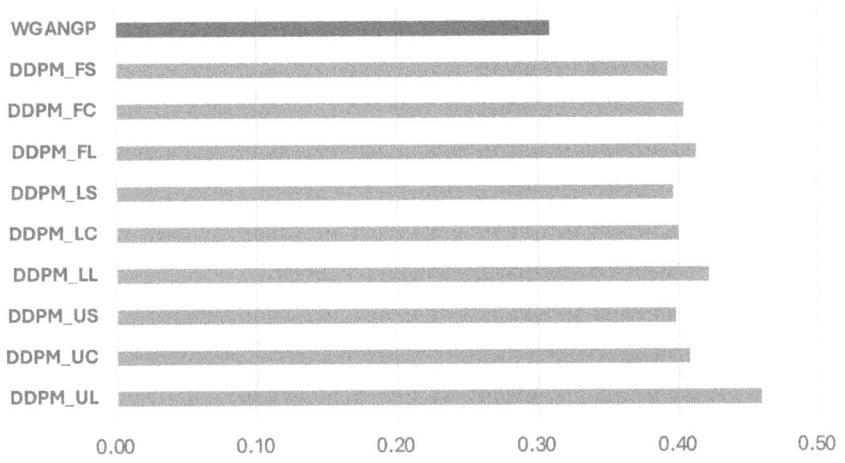

Fig. 6. Comparison of average path accuracy between DDPM and WGANGP

model generates covered branches.

$$precision = \frac{True\ positives}{True\ positives + False\ positives} \quad (5)$$

We also used "recall" to measure the proportion of successfully generated branches as 1 (True positives) to the total actual branches as 1 (True positives + False negatives), to understand whether the model's prediction of the branch with state 1 is comprehensive.

$$recall = \frac{True\ positives}{True\ positives + False\ negatives} \quad (6)$$

Tables 6, 7, and 8 represent the "accuracy", "precision" and "recall" of path information generated by WGANGP and DDPMs respectively. They are the average values calculated from the path information corresponding to 100 test

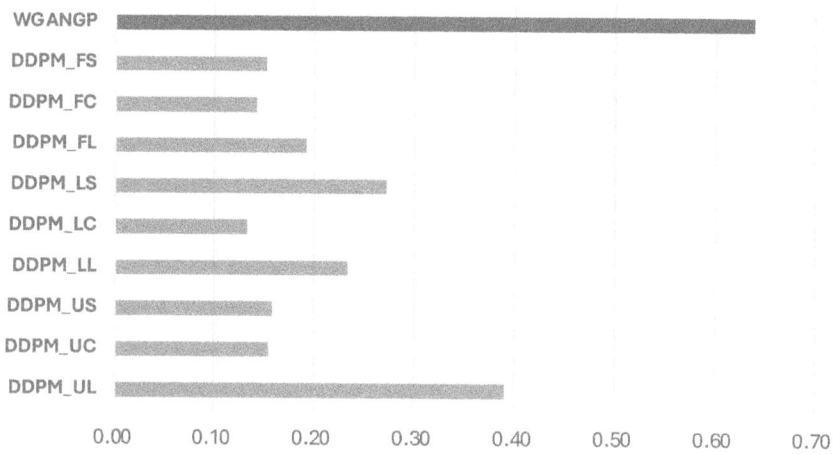

Fig. 7. Comparison of average path precision between DDPM and WGANGP

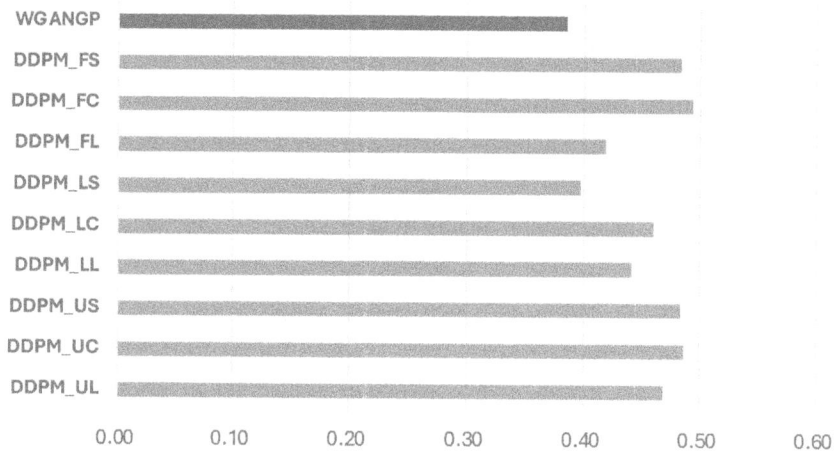

Fig. 8. Comparison of average path recall between DDPM and WGANGP

inputs generated by the model. We calculated the average value of each model under 8 functions for comparison.

Figures 6, 7, and 8 shows the comparisons of DDPMs and WGANGP. DDPMs demonstrates better accuracy in predicting overall path information and in capturing details of covered branches, as indicated by its higher "accuracy" and "recall" compared to WGANGP. This shows that compared with the WGANGP model, the path information generated by DDPMs is more similar to the real path data and captures a more important part of the actual path (branch state is 1). However, DDPMs exhibits lower "precision", indicating a tendency to produce false positives for path information with branch state 1. Although it captures more path information that may be covered (higher "recall"), it may also contain some unnecessary information, resulting in decreased "precision". In our approach, capturing path information with branch state 1 is more important than generating a lot of unnecessary information, so DDPMs is more suitable for our framework. Despite this, the overall accuracy of DDPMs still needs to be improved. In future work, we will make efforts to allow DDPMs to better understand the path information of the program.

5 Concluding Remark

In this paper, we proposed an automatic test input generation framework based on diffusion models to achieve high branch coverage. In the framework, the diffusion model is used to learn the distribution of input and path information of the program to automatically generate new test inputs for software testing, which can improve test coverage without detailed analysis of branch expressions.

Our proposed test coverage improvement strategy is highly dependent on the path information generated by DDPMs. Therefore, improving the accuracy of the paths generated by DDPMs is of great importance in future work. We will consider applying the internal structure information of the program, such as the control flow graph and other information, to DDPMs to better understand the behavior of the program. In addition, using DDPMs to generate test input has problems that make it difficult to cover some branches. These problems can be divided into three categories. The first is the "==" conditional branch. It is difficult for DDPMs to generate specific values, especially when the program input type is float. The second is the complex branches of conditional expressions. When the gap between the target data and the training data is large, it is difficult to cover it with the DDPMs method. In order to achieve full coverage of branches, we still need to solve this problem.

References

1. Lyu, C., Ji, S., Li, Y., Zhou, J., Chen, J., Chen, J.: Smartseed: smart seed generation for efficient fuzzing. arXiv preprint arXiv:1807.02606 (2018)
2. Joffe, L., Clark, D.J.: A generative neural network framework for automated software testing. arXiv preprint arXiv:2006.16335 (2020)
3. Li, Z., Zhao, H., Shi, J., Huang, Y., Xiong, J.: An intelligent fuzzing data generation method based on deep adversarial learning. IEEE Access **7**, 49327–49340 (2019)
4. Hu, Z., Shi, J., Huang, Y., Xiong, J., Bu, X.: Ganfuzz: a gan-based industrial network protocol fuzzing framework. In: Proceedings of the 15th ACM International Conference on Computing Frontiers, pp. 138–145 (2018)
5. Lv, W., Xiong, J., Shi, J., Huang, Y., Qin, S.: A deep convolution generative adversarial networks based fuzzing framework for industry control protocols. J. Intell. Manuf. **32**, 441–457 (2021)

6. Guo, X., Okamura, H., Dohi, T.: Automated software test data generation with generative adversarial networks. IEEE Access **10**, 20690–20700 (2022)
7. Zong, P., Lv, T., Wang, D., Deng, Z., Liang, R., Chen, K.: FuzzGuard: filtering out unreachable inputs in directed grey-box fuzzing through deep learning. In: 29th USENIX Security Symposium (USENIX Security 20), pp. 2255–2269 (2020)
8. Guo, X., Okamura, H., Dohi, T.: Towards high-quality test suite generation with ML-based boundary value analysis. In: 2023 10th International Conference on Dependable Systems and Their Applications (DSA), pp. 75–85. IEEE (2023)
9. Demir, S., Eniser, H.F., Sen, A.: Deepsmartfuzzer: reward guided test generation for deep learning. arXiv preprint arXiv:1911.10621 (2019)
10. Jiang, Z., Li, H., Wang, R.: Efficient generation of valid test inputs for deep neural networks via gradient search. J. Softw.: Evol. Process **36**(4), e2550 (2024)
11. Reddy, S., Lemieux, C., Padhye, R., Sen, K.: Quickly generating diverse valid test inputs with reinforcement learning. In: Proceedings of the ACM/IEEE 42nd International Conference on Software Engineering, pp. 1410–1421 (2020)
12. Kim, J., Kwon, M., Yoo, S.: Generating test input with deep reinforcement learning. In: Proceedings of the 11th International Workshop on Search-Based Software Testing, pp. 51–58 (2018)
13. Ferrer, J., Chicano, F., Alba, E.: Evolutionary algorithms for the multiobjective test data generation problem. Softw.: Pract. Exp. **42**(11), 1331–1362 (2012)
14. Suresh, Y., Rath, S.K.: Evolutionary algorithms for object-oriented test data generation. ACM SIGSOFT Softw. Eng. Notes **39**(4), 1–6 (2014)
15. Ho, J., Jain, A., Abbeel, P.: Denoising diffusion probabilistic models. Adv. Neural. Inf. Process. Syst. **33**, 6840–6851 (2020)
16. llvm-cov. https://llvm.org/docs/CommandGuide/llvm-cov.html
17. Lattner, C., Adve, V.: LLVM: a compilation framework for lifelong program analysis and transformation. In: Proceedings of the International Symposium on Code Generation and Optimization (CGO) (2004)
18. GSL. https://www.gnu.org/software/gsl/doc/html/intro.html

Blockchain Solutions for Cash-on-Delivery: Utilizing Encrypted NFTs, Smart Contracts, and IPFS Technology

Phan Hoang Tuan Trung[1], Tran Dang Khoa[1(✉)], Thanh Pham Nghiem[1],
Tran Ba Nam[1], Nguyen Thi Kim Ngan[2], Doan Minh Hieu[1],
and Van Cao Phu Loc[1]

[1] University, Can Tho City, Vietnam
trungpht@fe.edu.vn
[2] FPT Polytecnic, Can Tho City, Vietnam
khoatdce160367@fpt.edu.vn

Abstract. This paper explores the application of blockchain technology in Cash-on-Delivery (COD) systems, incorporating smart contracts, encrypted Non-Fungible Tokens (NFTs), and the InterPlanetary File System (IPFS) to enhance transaction security, data accessibility, and integrity. We review the functionality and efficiency of various encryption algorithms, including RSA, RC4, DES, ChaCha20, Blowfish, and AES, assessing their effectivenenm ss in safeguarding transaction data and enhancing system operations. By integrating these technologies into a COD framework, our study aims to address privacy concerns, improve transparency, and streamline transaction processes in e-commerce. We discuss our multi-platform blockchain deployment strategy, analyzing the strengths and weaknesses of different EVM-supported environments to determine their suitability for COD transactions. Our findings suggest that a well-implemented blockchain system could significantly improve the security and efficiency of COD transactions, providing a robust alternative to traditional delivery methods.

Keywords: Encrypted NFT · Blockchain · cash-on-delivery (COD) · NFT · Smart contract

1 Introduction

In the evolution of e-commerce strategies to overcome traditional challenges, the integration of blockchain technology has become crucial, particularly in how transactions are managed [14]. Notably, the use of smart contracts and decentralized frameworks is being employed to address several key issues in payment processes such as trust, transparency, and security [13]. Similarly, our proposed model enhances payment systems through blockchain-based methods and adds a layer of encrypted Non-Fungible Tokens (NFTs) to improve both security and efficiency in Cash-on-Delivery (COD) transactions. This approach is primarily a preparatory step aimed at addressing privacy concerns and operational hurdles on e-commerce platforms before the full-scale implementation of blockchain technology in a practical setting.

Our research builds upon previous efforts to create secure transactional ecosystems using blockchain technology, as initially developed by Son et al. [15] and Le et al. [9]. These frameworks have successfully enhanced transactional transparency and privacy by defining roles and responsibilities through smart contracts, particularly protecting the interests of sellers in Cash-on-Delivery (COD) transactions. However, these systems sometimes allow the unintended release of personal information to stakeholders. Our approach shifts the focus from merely ensuring transaction transparency among users, such as shippers and buyers, to enhancing the privacy of sensitive user data through the use of encrypted Non-Fungible Tokens (NFTs). This adjustment addresses a significant gap in previous frameworks by prioritizing the protection of personal information alongside the security of transactional details.

Our proposed framework utilizes the decentralized nature of blockchain technology to offer a secure alternative to conventional Cash-on-Delivery systems. Leveraging blockchain's inherent characteristics like immutability and transparency, our system employs a combination of RSA encryption and other algorithms including RC4, DES, ChaCha20, Blowfish, and AES, alongside Non-Fungible Tokens (NFTs). This setup ensures that only authorized participants can access transaction data, thereby safeguarding privacy and maintaining the uniqueness and integrity of each transaction record. Additionally, smart contracts are implemented to automate the processes of transaction creation, access, and data transfer. These contracts, programmed with specific terms, enhance the security and efficiency of operations within the delivery system, minimize errors, and provide a reliable mechanism for managing access to transactional information.

Our research builds on the foundational work of Ha et al. [5] and Quoc et al. [12], who have investigated decentralized marketplace mechanisms and the intricacies of cross-border e-commerce transactions. These studies have offered substantial solutions for maintaining the integrity and trust within transactions. Extending beyond their scope, our project implements a multi-platform blockchain deployment strategy to evaluate and compare the efficacy of various EVM-supported blockchain environments specifically for Cash-on-Delivery systems. This approach involves a detailed analysis of each platform's capabilities and limitations, enhancing our understanding of how blockchain technology can be optimized for Cash-on-Delivery services using encrypted Non-Fungible Tokens (NFTs), smart contracts, and IPFS technology. By doing so, we aim to identify the most suitable blockchain environment that aligns with the specific needs of secure and efficient transaction processing in e-commerce [3].

In conclusion, our study introduces a method that employs blockchain technology, smart contracts, encrypted Non-Fungible Tokens (NFTs), and the InterPlanetary File System (IPFS) to enhance Cash-on-Delivery systems. This approach addresses challenges related to transaction security, data accessibility, and integrity, setting a new standard for managing Cash-on-Delivery transactions securely and efficiently. By applying various encryption algorithms-RSA, RC4, DES, ChaCha20, Blowfish, and AES-our research assesses their suitability in terms of security and operational efficiency. We have thoroughly examined the integration of these technologies, demonstrating their potential to create a Cash-on-Delivery system that is secure and functional, meeting the needs of stakeholders in the logistics and retail sectors.

2 Background

The Traditional Approach Post-Office Transportation. The traditional approach to cash-on-delivery (COD) transactions follows a five-step, sequential process that starts with the seller preparing the package and culminates in the buyer receiving and paying for the delivery. This established model provides a baseline for incorporating encrypted Non-Fungible Tokens (NFTs) into blockchain technology, enhancing the existing framework.

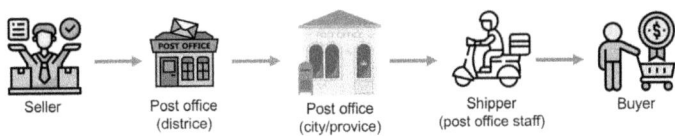

Fig. 1. The post-office case for transporting goods

Step 1 - Seller Preparation: The COD transaction starts with the seller preparing the item for shipment. This involves careful packaging and the preparation of necessary documents that detail security measures and delivery instructions. Proper initial preparation is crucial to avoid delays or issues in subsequent delivery stages.
Step 2 - District Post Office Handling: After the seller's preparation, the package is sent to the district post office. Here, postal workers take over, processing the package according to postal guidelines. This stage includes sorting the packages by destination, verifying addresses, and entering the package into the postal tracking system. The district post office serves as a transitional point, setting the stage for the next leg of the package's journey.
Step 3 - City/Provincial Post Office Processing: Once the package arrives at the city or provincial post office, it is sorted again. These larger facilities manage higher volumes and organize packages efficiently for the final delivery zones. During this phase, packages are grouped by destination, and plans are made for their final delivery to ensure they reach recipients promptly.
Step 4 - Delivery by Postal Staff: The next step involves the postal staff, responsible for the final delivery of the package. They load the packages onto

delivery vehicles and transport them to the respective recipients. This stage is vital for testing the postal system's efficiency and reliability, with delivery personnel navigating different routes to ensure safe and timely delivery.

Step 5 - Buyer Receives Package: The final stage of the delivery process occurs when the buyer receives the package. In COD transactions, the buyer pays the delivery amount due to the postal staff upon receipt of the package. This payment completes the transaction, with the buyer confirming that the package is in good condition and the seller's responsibility ending with the successful delivery and payment.

The conventional approach to cash-on-delivery transactions, when considered within the framework of a shipping company's operations, outlines a thorough and complex process. This method combines the detailed activities of seller preparation, postal handling, and the final steps of delivery with the logistical capabilities of a transportation firm. This blend ensures that each phase of the transaction is handled efficiently, from the initial seller actions to the ultimate delivery by the shipping company.

3 Related Work

3.1 Smart Contract-Based Solutions for Cash on Delivery (COD) and E-Commerce

Son et al. (2019) designed a blockchain-based payment system that ensures seller protection through smart contracts, which enforce transaction rules and improve transparency, reducing risks linked to delivery terms [15]. Le et al. (2019) developed a system that uses a multi-shipper approach combined with blockchain and smart contracts to enhance trust and reduce fraud in decentralized settings, validating their system with case studies and making their code available for public use [9]. They also proposed a dual smart contract framework to minimize fraud by requiring security deposits from buyers and shippers on the Ethereum blockchain, thereby increasing transaction security [10]. Furthermore, Ha et al. (2020) introduced DEM-COD, a decentralized marketplace mechanism that leverages smart contracts to strengthen the integrity and confidentiality of Cash-on-Delivery transactions, also providing implementation code [5]. Collectively, these studies highlight the effectiveness of blockchain and smart contracts in enhancing the dependability of COD transactions.

3.2 Security, Trust, and Transparency in E-Commerce and Delivery Systems

Ha et al. [6] examine current decentralized blockchain methodologies, pinpointing critical shortcomings in COD systems, particularly in fostering motivation for honest participation among all parties and the dependency on third-party arbitrators. They suggest a method using Hyperledger Composer and smart contracts to safeguard merchant rights and remove the need for arbitrators, aiming to improve trust and transparency while reducing risks associated with deception and disputes. Duong et al. [3] address the limitations in COD systems caused by the support for only single delivery sessions, which leads to inefficiencies if buyers are not present to receive their goods. They introduce a mechanism that supports multiple delivery sessions using blockchain technology and the hyperledger fabric platform, which enhances operational transparency and efficiency across decentralized markets. The publication of their source code invites further exploration and refinement in the sector.

3.3 Decentralized Marketplaces and Peer-to-Peer E-Commerce

Quoc et al. [12] developed the Safe Seller Safe Buyer (SSSB) system, utilizing blockchain technology and smart contracts to improve cross-border transactions by addressing transportation delays and information latency. This system employs a distributed ledger to store transaction data, simplifying access for buyers and sellers and reducing the need for intermediaries in dispute resolution. The SSSB system supports various blockchain platforms, including Ethereum, BNB Smart Chain, and Fantom, and includes a cost analysis for further research [12]. Dragomir et al. [2] addressed logistical challenges in online second-hand marketplaces by developing an adaptive strategy for the pickup and delivery problem, tested with an Austrian logistics provider, which showed potential savings for carriers of up to 30% [2]. The use of blockchain technology and smart contracts is being explored in various sectors to improve traditional processes, focusing on security, efficiency, and trust. For instance, Son et al. (2019) created a payment system using smart contracts on blockchain to protect sellers in cash-on-delivery transactions, employing Hyperledger to mitigate risks [15]. Le et al. (2019) used double smart contracts in their system to prevent fraud in similar contexts, ensuring secure transactions between shippers and buyers [10]. Hasan and Salah (2018) proposed a decentralized approach for proving the delivery of digital assets using Ethereum to create secure and unalterable logs [7]. Mohammed et al. (2023) developed a blockchain-based smart contract to prevent non-repudiation [11]. Ahmadieh and El Madhoun (2023) examined the use of NFTs in the digital art market, focusing on how smart contracts manage the lifecycle of digital artworks [1]. Jha et al. (2023) designed a blockchain system that removes the need for bank and third-party verification in financial transactions, enhancing the speed and security of these processes [8]. In the construction sector, Elghaish et al. (2020) implemented smart contracts for financial management in project delivery, which could improve outcomes significantly [4]. These studies demonstrate the application of blockchain and smart contracts to enhance transactional security and efficiency across various fields.

4 Approach

In the current digital transaction landscape, enhancing security, transparency, and efficiency is essential, particularly for cash-on-delivery (COD) systems. The architecture presented here is designed to improve COD operations by increasing security, verifying authenticity, and building trust among participants. As part of modern logistics and supply chain management, the use of encrypted Non-Fungible Tokens (NFTs) within blockchain frameworks marks a significant advancement in managing these transactions. This method integrates traditional logistics with blockchain technology in a stepwise process, ensuring heightened transparency and security while maintaining efficiency. This process is depicted in Fig. 2.

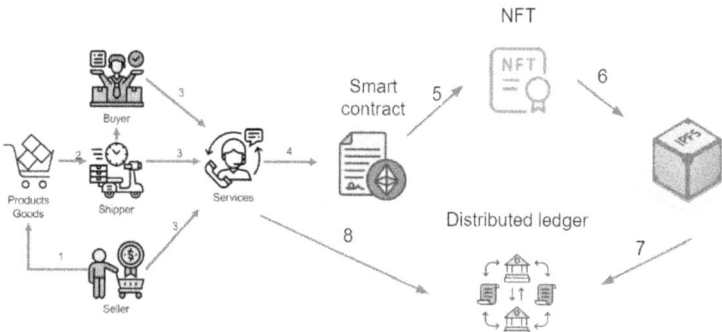

Fig. 2. The process of transporting goods based on blockchain technology, smart contract, NFT and IPFS

The Seller's Pivotal Role: The process starts with the seller, who uses a sophisticated service system not just to sell a product but to ensure it is recorded securely. By entering product details into the system, the seller converts these details into an encrypted Non-Fungible Token (NFT). This step not only digitizes the product information but also enhances its security and traceability. The initiation of a smart contract at this stage is crucial, as it triggers the delivery process, which is transparent and immutable.

The Journey of Products/Goods: After the transaction is finalized and the product information is embedded securely in the blockchain, the physical goods begin their journey. This phase bridges digital entries with physical logistics, using traditional shipping methods to ensure the product, linked to its digital counterpart, reaches the shipping personnel while maintaining a connection to its digital record.

The Interplay of Shipper and Buyer: The shipper is essential in this ecosystem. After receiving the product, the shipper updates the order status using the system interface. This update ensures that each phase of the delivery is transparently logged on the blockchain, which the buyer can monitor. When the goods are received, the buyer confirms this receipt through the interface, a vital step in cash-on-delivery transactions that enhances security and builds trust.

The Central Role of Smart Contracts and Encrypted NFTs: Smart contracts serve as the framework for automating the transaction terms, executing only when certain conditions, like the buyer's confirmation of receipt, are met. The representation of products as encrypted NFTs is critical as it verifies the uniqueness and non-replicability of each product, boosting the process's security and authenticity. These digital records also verify ownership, an important factor in cash-on-delivery transactions.

The Distributed Ledger: A Record of Transparency: Each action, from the issuance of the encrypted NFT to updates by the seller, shipper, or buyer, is meticulously documented on a distributed ledger. This ledger is immutable and transparent, recording every detail of the product delivery process. Once entered, the data in the ledger cannot be changed, ensuring a reliable and transparent record throughout the transaction.

The Service Interface: The Unifying Element: At the core of this system is the service interface, a critical component of the supply chain management system. It provides the tools needed to track, confirm, and manage order details. Through this interface, all parties-the seller, the buyer, and the shipper-interact. Whether it's updating order status or confirming delivery, each interaction is streamlined through this interface, facilitating a cohesive and efficient experience for all involved.

5 Implementation

In the implementation section of our study, we examine the use of different encryption algorithms to secure metadata within Non-Fungible Tokens (NFTs) in our blockchain-based Cash-on-Delivery transaction system. We evaluate six encryption methods-RSA, RC4, DES, ChaCha20, Blowfish, and AES-focusing on finding a balance between security and operational efficiency. Our assessment looks at encryption speed and security levels, specifically for encrypting NFTs and data on the InterPlanetary File System (IPFS). The results, presented in detailed tables, highlight performance metrics for encrypting both text and

Table 1. RSA Encryption and Decryption Performance for Image and text Data in Microseconds

RSA	1	2	3	4	5	6	7	8	9	10
Generating key	75356	95235	38750	78216	98703	95067	54002	301008	75905	98625
Encrypting image	10678	9685	8111	9330	9393	10638	11635	10350	10979	10646
Decrypting image	262878	265051	269676	255449	258359	265588	255306	258615	259331	260586
Generating key	109072	161201	58533	54586	24110	94431	168443	31826	46018	82341
Encrypting text	0	0	0	0	1367	0	0	0	0	998
Decrypting text	594	1413	1160	1274	501	1084	1378	1508	502	0

image data, which are critical for ensuring transaction integrity and transparency (Table 1).

In our analysis of encryption algorithms for blockchain-based Cash-on-Delivery systems, RSA, known for its asymmetric encryption, showed varying performance metrics that could affect system efficiency. The key generation time for RSA ranged from 75,356 to 301,008 microseconds, and the encryption and decryption times for image data were often over 250,000 microseconds for decryption. These findings suggest that while RSA provides strong security, its slower processing speeds may challenge computational efficiency and impact the overall performance of systems using encrypted NFTs, smart contracts, and IPFS technology (Table 2).

Table 2. RC4 Encryption and Decryption Performance for Image and text Data in Microseconds

RC4 (image)	1	2	3	4	5	6	7	8	9	10
Encrypting image	107	0	0	0	171	0	543	0	0	0
Decrypting image	0	0	664	0	0	0	0	0	1502	0
Encrypting text	0	0	0	0	0	0	0	0	0	0
Decrypting text	0	0	0	0	0	0	0	0	0	0

In our evaluation of encryption methods for a blockchain-based Cash-on-Delivery system, we found that the RC4 algorithm had very low encryption and decryption times for both image and text data, sometimes nearly zero microseconds. This indicates that RC4 could potentially enhance the speed of transaction processing within our system. However, RC4's security level is lower compared to more modern encryption algorithms, raising concerns about its ability to ensure data integrity and security. This discrepancy between RC4's speed and lower security may limit its use in systems utilizing encrypted NFTs, smart contracts, and IPFS technology, where maintaining secure and reliable transaction records is crucial (Table 3).

Table 3. DES Encryption and Decryption Performance for Image and text Data in Microseconds

DES (image)	1	2	3	4	5	6	7	8	9	10
Encrypting image	1073	540	820	1047	1091	708	1217	599	1121	1024
Decrypting image	1058	551	0	819	606	999	1005	1018	501	0
Encrypting text	0	0	0	0	0	0	0	0	0	0
Decrypting text	0	0	0	0	508	0	0	0	0	0

In our analysis of encryption algorithms for a blockchain-based Cash-on-Delivery system, DES exhibited moderate performance, with encryption times for image data between 540 and 1,217 microseconds and decryption times up to 1,058 microseconds. These times suggest that DES could improve operational efficiency due to its relatively fast processing. However, DES's well-documented security vulnerabilities are a significant concern. The risk of data integrity being compromised due to these vulnerabilities may outweigh the benefits of faster processing. This is similar to the issues seen with RC4's high speed but lower security and RSA's slower performance, both of which could impact the efficiency of systems using encrypted NFTs, smart contracts, and IPFS technology for secure and reliable transactions (Table 4).

Table 4. Chacha20 Encryption and Decryption Performance for Image and text Data in Microseconds

CHACHA20 (image)	1	2	3	4	5	6	7	8	9	10
Encrypting image	501	0	109	0	0	0	0	0	0	101
Decrypting image	0	584	511	0	0	668	0	634	0	0
Encrypting text	0	0	0	0	0	0	0	0	0	0
Decrypting text	0	0	0	0	0	508	0	0	0	0

In our analysis of encryption methods for a blockchain-based Cash-on-Delivery system, ChaCha20 showed a good balance between speed and security. It encrypted image data in 501 microseconds during tests, with decryption times also being efficient, though variable. This suggests that ChaCha20 could be suitable for securing metadata within systems using encrypted NFTs, smart contracts, and IPFS technology due to its fast data processing and robust security. This makes it a potentially better option compared to other algorithms like DES, which has security vulnerabilities, RC4, which has inadequate security, and RSA, which has slower operational speeds, particularly when maintaining the integrity and confidentiality of transaction records is a priority (Table 5).

Table 5. Blowfish Encryption and Decryption Performance for Image and text Data in Microseconds

blowfish (image)	1	2	3	4	5	6	7	8	9	10
Encrypting image	542	603	506	599	507	1145	608	1137	633	541
Decrypting image	0	0	508	512	501	501	1037	999	575	532
Encrypting text	0	0	537	520	0	533	91	0	0	0
Decrypting text	0	0	0	0	0	0	0	0	0	0

In our evaluation of encryption algorithms for blockchain-based Cash-on-Delivery systems, Blowfish showed moderate performance, with encryption times for image data ranging from 506 to 1,145 microseconds. While Blowfish has historically been known for balancing speed and security, newer encryption algorithms with superior security capabilities might reduce its applicability for modern uses. This brings into question Blowfish's ability to adequately protect transaction data within systems using encrypted NFTs, smart contracts, and IPFS technology, especially given evolving cybersecurity challenges. Similar concerns exist with other algorithms like DES due to security vulnerabilities and the trade-offs between speed and security observed in RC4, RSA, and ChaCha20 (Table 6).

Table 6. AES Encryption and Decryption Performance for Image and text Data in Microseconds

AES (image)	1	2	3	4	5	6	7	8	9	10
Encrypting image	0	360	0	82	592	608	502	541	510	513
Decrypting image	1332	0	1005	0	504	0	0	0	0	0
Encrypting text	0	0	0	0	0	0	0	507	0	0
Decrypting text	0	0	0	0	0	0	0	0	0	0

In our evaluation of encryption algorithms for blockchain-based Cash-on-Delivery systems, AES demonstrated strong performance and reliability. Data encryption sometimes occurred in nearly zero microseconds, and decryption times were as low as 504 microseconds in some trials. Known for its robust security, AES offers consistent and efficient performance, making it suitable for securing transaction data within systems using encrypted NFTs, smart contracts, and IPFS technology. This reliability is crucial for our system, which needs secure protection of transaction records and prompt data access, similar to challenges faced with algorithms like Blowfish, ChaCha20, and DES in balancing data integrity and adapting to evolving cybersecurity needs.

The data gathered provides insights into the suitability of various encryption algorithms for securing transaction records in a blockchain-based Cash-on-Delivery system. We are evaluating six encryption methods-RSA, RC4, DES, ChaCha20, Blowfish, and AES-to find the best balance of security and operational efficiency. Our system uses smart contracts and encrypted NFTs to manage transactions, requiring encryption that can handle frequent and diverse interactions typical of Cash-on-Delivery transactions. Through comprehensive testing and analysis, we aim to select an encryption method that ensures high security standards while supporting the rapid pace needed for efficient transaction management. This approach is essential for maintaining a reliable and transparent system for businesses and customers.

6 Evaluation

6.1 Exploring Encrypted NFTs Within Decentralized Storage Systems: An In-Depth Analysis

Figure 3 displays the results of benchmark tests on operations related to encrypted Non-Fungible Tokens (NFTs) within a testing setup (step 1). The figure specifically shows the time taken for two key processes: the minting of the encrypted NFT, completed in 2151 milliseconds, and the decryption of the encrypted NFT's URI, which requires 3329 milliseconds. These tests are crucial for evaluating the efficiency and dependability of the encrypted NFT creation and access processes. The overall duration of under seven seconds to complete all tests suggests that the operations are executed swiftly, making this approach suitable for environments where quick transaction processing is crucial.

In the second step, Fig. 4 provides a detailed look at the minting function's technical implementation through a JavaScript code snippet that uses asynchronous execution to manage the encrypted Non-Fungible Token (NFT) creation process. The code organizes the data into various fields, including product information, price, weight, and transaction details, which are critical for forming a detailed and informative encrypted NFT. Additionally, the metadata configuration is set to use a file named "COD_RSA.json," indicating that the encrypted NFT's metadata will adhere to the RSA encryption standard, thereby enhancing the security features of the NFT.

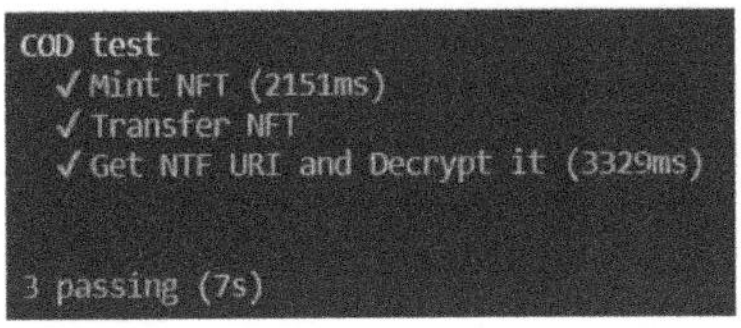

Fig. 3. NFT Minting and Decryption Test Benchmarks

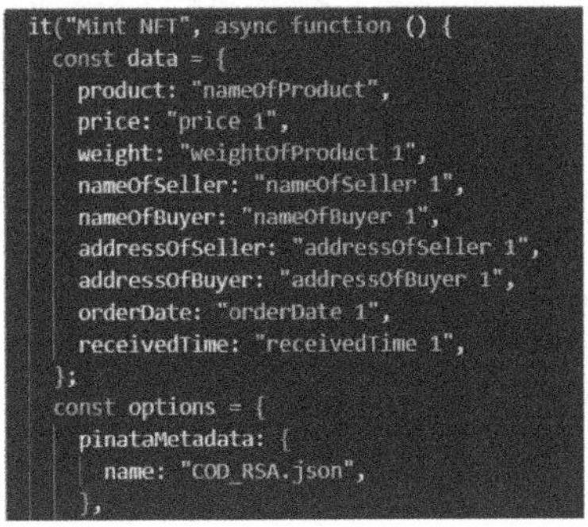

Fig. 4. Minting NFT Function Implementation

In Fig. 5, the Pinata cloud interface is displayed, showing its use for hosting encrypted Non-Fungible Token (NFT) data (step 3). The file "COD_RSA.json" is noted as successfully uploaded to the InterPlanetary File System (IPFS) via Pinata, as evidenced by its listing among the files. Employing Pinata for storing encrypted NFT metadata utilizes decentralized storage solutions, which are beneficial for their redundancy and persistence. This approach also matches the decentralized framework of blockchain technology, supporting the overall infrastructure of the system by maintaining metadata in a manner that enhances data availability and security.

Figure 6 illustrates how encrypted data is stored on the InterPlanetary File System (IPFS), accessed through a specific IPFS gateway. The data appears as an encrypted string, which secures the content of the encrypted Non-Fungible Token (NFT). This encryption level is essential for safeguarding sensitive transaction data against unauthorized access. To decrypt and access the transaction details, the corresponding private key is required, ensuring that only authorized individuals can view the information. This setup supports the security measures necessary for protecting transaction data within the blockchain framework.

Fig. 5. Pinata Cloud Storage Interface

Fig. 6. Encrypted NFT Data Retrieval from IPFS

The detailed analysis of the performance and the secure handling of data through encryption and storage reveals a system designed with security and efficiency at its core. The time taken for minting and decrypting NFTs demonstrates the feasibility of integrating such a system into real-world COD transactions, where the balance between security measures and performance is critical. The implementation of RSA encryption within this context not only safeguards against potential data breaches but also ensures the privacy and integrity of the transactions, thus addressing two of the most significant concerns in e-commerce today. This intricate process, from minting to encryption and secure storage, forms a comprehensive solution poised to enhance the COD payment landscape significantly.

6.2 Testing on EVM-Supported Platforms

The Ethereum Virtual Machine (EVM) is instrumental in our project for deploying smart contracts, providing a consistent runtime environment across various blockchain platforms. In our development of a blockchain-based Cash-on-Delivery system, we have chosen four EVM-compatible platforms: Binance Smart Chain, Polygon, Fantom, and Celo, to evaluate their capabilities in handling our operational needs. A key part of our analysis involves the process of recording transactions on the blockchain, a step crucial for determining how efficiently the system can process new orders. Additionally, we create encrypted Non-Fungible

Tokens (encrypted NFTs) for each transaction, which is critical for ensuring the security and uniqueness of each delivery record. We assess how these platforms manage the creation and transfer of encrypted NFTs, focusing on the speed, resource usage, and interface usability, as these factors are vital for regular use by shipping and logistics personnel. Furthermore, we examine the transferability of encrypted NFTs across networks, essential for enabling secure and efficient exchanges of transaction data between parties, ensuring smooth operation while maintaining strict security and data integrity.

Table 7. Transaction fee

	Transaction Creation	Create NFT	Transfer NFT
BNB Smart Chain	0.0273134 BNB ($8.27)	0.00109162 BNB ($0.33)	0.00057003 BNB ($0.17)
Fantom	0.00957754 FTM ($0.00)	0.000405167 FTM ($0.00)	0.0002380105 FTM ($0.00)
Polygon	0.006840710032835408 MATIC ($0.01)	0.000289405001852192 MATIC ($0.00)	0.000170007501088048 MATIC ($0.00)
Celo	0.007097844 CELO ($0.005)	0.0002840812 CELO ($0.000)	0.0001554878 CELO ($0.000)

Table 7 presents a comprehensive breakdown of the transaction fees involved in key operations necessary for a blockchain-based Cash-on-Delivery system. These operations include the recording of new transaction data, the minting of encrypted Non-Fungible Tokens (encrypted NFTs) that represent individual delivery records, and the transfer of these encrypted NFTs to reflect changes in access rights among authorized parties. Additionally, the table provides up-to-date information on the token prices for the platforms being evaluated as of March 27, 2024, at 7:00:00 AM UTC. This data is essential for understanding the economic factors that impact the cost-effectiveness and efficiency of these blockchain networks in managing delivery operations.

Starting with the BNB Smart Chain, transaction creation costs 0.0273134 BNB, approximately $8.27, while minting an encrypted Non-Fungible Token (encrypted NFT) is priced at 0.00109162 BNB, about $0.33, and transferring an encrypted NFT incurs a fee of 0.00057003 BNB, around $0.17. Despite these fees being higher than those on other networks, the BNB Smart Chain's robust functionality and high throughput could support systems that require efficient transaction processing. Conversely, the Fantom network offers significantly lower fees, with creating a transaction costing 0.00957754 FTM, minting an encrypted NFT at 0.000405167 FTM, and transferring an encrypted NFT at 0.0002380105 FTM, all virtually negligible, making it cost-effective for managing operations where minimizing expenses is crucial. Similarly, the Polygon network maintains low fees; creating a transaction costs roughly $0.01 in MATIC, with negligible costs for minting and transferring encrypted NFTs. This network's scalability and interoperability make it a viable option for systems prioritizing cost-effectiveness without sacrificing performance. Lastly, Celo's modest transaction fees-$0.005 for creating a transaction, with similarly low costs for NFT activities-may appeal to systems focused on accessibility and inclusivity, suitable for securely managing transactions in a decentralized and equitable framework.

In concluding the evaluation of blockchain solutions for Cash-on-Delivery systems using encrypted Non-Fungible Tokens (encrypted NFTs) and smart contracts, it is crucial to consider the transaction fees across different networks. While some platforms may offer lower transaction fees, others might provide additional features or benefits that could make higher costs reasonable. Therefore, a comprehensive analysis that includes both economic and technical aspects is essential to select the most suitable blockchain network for implementing an effective and efficient Cash-on-Delivery system. This approach ensures a balanced decision-making process, prioritizing both cost-effectiveness and functional requirements.

7 Conclusion

In conclusion, our research demonstrates the feasibility of using blockchain technology, encrypted NFTs, smart contracts, and IPFS to develop a more secure and efficient Cash-on-Delivery system. This system aims to address traditional e-commerce challenges such as transaction security, data accessibility, and privacy concerns. By evaluating various encryption algorithms and blockchain platforms, our study identifies practical solutions for improving transaction processes. Incorporating these technologies into a COD system ensures the security and integrity of data while enhancing the operational efficiency of delivery services. Future work should focus on integrating these blockchain solutions into existing e-commerce frameworks to further explore their impact on reducing transaction times and costs while maintaining high security and data privacy standards. Our findings provide a basis for e-commerce businesses to consider blockchain technology as a step toward optimizing their delivery processes and enhancing customer trust and satisfaction.

References

1. Ahmadieh, E., El Madhoun, N.: Artwork NFTs for online trading and transaction cancellation. In: 2023 Fifth International Conference on Blockchain Computing and Applications (BCCA), pp. 235–239 (2023)
2. Dragomir, et al.: The pickup and delivery problem with alternative locations and overlapping time windows. Comput. Oper. Res. **143**, 105758 (2022)
3. Duong-Trung, N., et al.: Multi-sessions mechanism for decentralized cash on delivery system. Int. J. Adv. Comput. Sci. Appl. **10**(9) (2019)
4. Elghaish, et al.: Integrated project delivery with blockchain: an automated financial system. Automat. Construct. **114**, 103182 (2020)
5. Ha, X.S., et al.: Dem-cod: novel access-control-based cash on delivery mechanism for decentralized marketplace. In: 2020 IEEE 19th International Conference on Trust, Security and Privacy in Computing and Communications (TrustCom), pp. 71–78. IEEE (2020)

6. Ha, X.S., et al.: Scrutinizing trust and transparency in cash on delivery systems. In: Security, Privacy, and Anonymity in Computation, Communication, and Storage: 13th International Conference, pp. 214–227. Springer (2021)
7. Hasan, H.R., Salah, K.: Proof of delivery of digital assets using blockchain and smart contracts. IEEE Access **6**, 65439–65448 (2018)
8. Jha, A., et al.: Transaction system based on blockchain technology using smart contract. Int. J. Sci. Res. Eng. Manag. (2023)
9. Le, H.T., et al.: Introducing multi shippers mechanism for decentralized cash on delivery system. Int. J. Adv. Comput. Sci. Appl. **10**(6) (2019)
10. Le, N.T.T., et al.: Assuring non-fraudulent transactions in cash on delivery by introducing double smart contracts. Int. J. Adv. Comput. Sci. Appl. **10**(5), 677–684 (2019)
11. Mohammed, et al.: Secure smart contract based on blockchain to prevent the non-repudiation phenomenon. Baghdad Sci. J. (2023)
12. Quoc, K.L., et al.: SSSB: an approach to insurance for cross-border exchange by using smart contracts. In: Mobile Web and Intelligent Information Systems: 18th International Conference, pp. 179–192. Springer (2022)
13. Raj, et al.: Procurement, traceability and advance cash credit payment transactions in supply chain using blockchain smart contracts. Comput. Indust. Eng. **167**, 108038 (2022)
14. Sikder, A.S.: Blockchain-empowered e-commerce: redefining trust, security, and efficiency in digital marketplaces in the context of Bangladesh: blockchain-empowered e-commerce. Int. J. Imminent Sci. Technol. **1**(1), 216–235 (2023)
15. Son, H.X., et al.: Towards a mechanism for protecting seller's interest of cash on delivery by using smart contract in hyperledger. Int. J. Adv. Comput. Sci. Appl. **10**(4) (2019)

Revolutionizing Animal Health Privacy: Blockchain and Encrypted NFTs

Phan Hoang Tuan Trung[1], Tran Dang Khoa[1(✉)], Thanh Pham Nghiem[1], Tran Ba Nam[1], Nguyen Thi Kim Ngan[2], Doan Minh Hieu[1], and Van Cao Phu Loc[1]

[1] FPT University, Can Tho City, Vietnam
trungpht@fe.edu.vn, khoatdce160367@fpt.edu.vn
[2] FPT Polytecnic, Can Tho City, Vietnam

Abstract. This paper explores the integration of blockchain technology, smart contracts, encrypted Non-Fungible Tokens (NFTs), and the InterPlanetary File System (IPFS) in enhancing the management of animal health data. Facing challenges such as the lack of traceability and the need for data security within the veterinary sector, our study proposes a novel approach that leverages advanced encryption algorithms-RSA, RC4, DES, ChaCha20, Blowfish, and AES-to ensure the confidentiality and integrity of health records. By conducting a comprehensive analysis of various EVM-compatible blockchain platforms, including Binance Smart Chain, Polygon, Fantom, and Celo, we assess the system's performance, operational efficiency, and economic feasibility. Our findings highlight the potential of our proposed framework to significantly improve transparency, reliability, and accessibility in the management of animal health data, providing a solid foundation for ethical practices and informed decision-making in veterinary care.

Keywords: Animals Healthcare · Blockchain · Data Management · Electronic Health Records (EHRs) · Non-Fungible Tokens (NFTs) · InterPlanetary File System (IPFS) · Decentralized Storage · Smart Contracts

1 Introduction

The impact of technological advancements on fields such as veterinary medicine is significant, especially regarding the management, analysis, and protection of animal health data. Traditional methods of handling animal health records often involved numerous manual processes, from initial data collection by veterinary staff to the prescription and treatment phases. This old approach, characterized by its step-by-step nature, depended greatly on the physical exchange of paperwork and manual data recording. Such dependency frequently introduced issues such as errors, data mismanagement, and delays, which could compromise the reliability and availability of vital health information. To address these challenges, our study introduces a framework that leverages blockchain technology and Non-Fungible Tokens (NFTs) encrypted with various algorithms-RSA, RC4, DES, ChaCha20, Blowfish, and AES. This framework aims to enhance the management of animal health data by exploring the optimal balance between ensuring data security and maintaining operational efficiency.

The adoption of Electronic Health Records (EHRs) has notably advanced the handling and analysis of animal health data, with research from Quintana et al. [12] and Hanauer et al. [7] leveraging EHRs to identify crucial health patterns and connections. These studies illustrate the capacity of digital records to streamline data management processes and improve health monitoring outcomes. Despite these advancements, issues related to the safeguarding of data privacy and maintaining the integrity of health information remain prevalent. Many conventional EHR systems are often inadequate in securing confidential health data.

In our research, we focus on improving the management of animal health data through the implementation of smart contracts, encrypted Non-Fungible Tokens (NFTs), and the InterPlanetary File System (IPFS). Our objective is to ensure that data related to animal health is managed with accuracy and transparency, from veterinary professionals to animal owners. To achieve this, we evaluate six encryption algorithms-RSA, RC4, DES, ChaCha20, Blowfish, and AES-to find a balance that optimizes both security and operational efficiency. Our method addresses the critical need for secure, traceable, and integral data within the veterinary field [4]. The integration of smart contracts facilitates the automated management of these health records, significantly reducing the need for manual input and thereby decreasing the chance of errors [8]. By conducting a comprehensive analysis to select the most suitable encryption algorithm, our blockchain-based approach aims to provide a dependable record-keeping system. This system ensures that all parties involved in the management of animal health data have access to information that is not only timely and accurate but also easily accessible.

Our approach was carefully tested across multiple EVM-compatible platforms, such as Binance Smart Chain, Polygon, Fantom, and Celo, to evaluate its suitability for enhancing the management of animal health data. The evaluation concentrated on critical capabilities such as recording health data activities, generating NFTs for the precise tracking of animal health records, and ensuring the secure transfer of these NFTs. This assessment provided in-depth understanding of the framework's performance, including aspects like transaction speeds, demand on resources, and system reliability. By examining the transaction costs associated with these blockchain platforms, we gained insight into the economic considerations of deploying blockchain technology in the veterinary sector. This analysis revealed opportunities for reducing expenses and improving operational effectiveness in animal health data management, leveraging the strengths of smart contracts and NFTs encrypted with algorithms including RSA, RC4, DES, ChaCha20, Blowfish, and AES, to achieve a harmonious balance between security measures and operational efficiency.

This research introduces a cohesive strategy that integrates blockchain technology, smart contracts, encrypted Non-Fungible Tokens (NFTs), and the InterPlanetary File System (IPFS) to address existing challenges in managing animal health data. Through a comprehensive review of the deployment process, thorough evaluations of performance on various blockchain platforms, and assessments of cost-effectiveness, this study underscores the crucial contribution of these technologies towards achieving a transparent, efficient, and trustworthy framework for animal health data management. By evaluating a range of encryption algorithms-RSA, RC4, DES, ChaCha20, Blowfish, and AES-the research aims to discover the most effective method for safeguarding data, while also facilitating efficient operations within the animal health data management ecosystem.

2 Related Work

2.1 Technological Advancements in Veterinary Health Records

The development of veterinary health records technology has made notable strides in improving animal health management and public safety. Quintana et al.'s study on using natural language processing to monitor animal bites for rabies surveillance demonstrates the efficiency of technology in extracting crucial epidemiological information from health records [12]. Similarly, Hanauer et al. investigated the link between cat bites and human depression, revealing gender differences in depression rates post-bite and suggesting areas for further research [7]. The quality and reliability of data in animal health records, as analyzed by Menendez et al. in the context of Swiss dairy farms, highlight the benefits of electronic systems in enhancing data traceability [11]. Moreover, Aigner's work on a prototype health record system for livestock management emphasizes the need for systems that are accessible and adhere to standards for various stakeholders [1]. Research by Willner on the requirements for an electronic veterinary patient file system and Krone's survey on the use of electronic veterinary medical records in practices reveal both the potential and the challenges in adopting such technologies for better health management and surveillance [10,18]. These studies underline the ongoing journey towards improving veterinary health record management and its pivotal role in the field.

2.2 Surveillance and Welfare Prioritization Using Health Records

The utility of health records in veterinary health, particularly in surveillance and welfare assessment, has seen significant advancements. Summers et al. utilized the VetCompass^{TM} Programme to analyze canine health data, identifying key welfare issues such as dental disorders, osteoarthritis, and obesity, which shed light on areas needing attention [16]. Anholt et al. highlighted the effectiveness of electronic health records (EHRs) in tracking companion animal enteric syndrome by pinpointing spatial-temporal clusters, thereby offering insights into environmental health hazards [2,3]. Further, Tulloch et al. and Kass et al. demonstrated the potential of EHRs in passive surveillance for monitoring ticks and developing syndromic surveillance systems to detect epidemics in pet populations, respectively, showcasing the role of EHRs in preventive health measures [8, 17]. Anholt's thesis further explores the challenges and capabilities of informatics in enhancing syndromic surveillance, underlining the critical role of EHRs in identifying and managing health threats [4]. These studies collectively emphasize the growing relevance of EHRs in advancing veterinary surveillance and animal welfare prioritization, contributing to a deeper understanding of disease dynamics and the early identification of health risks.

2.3 Data Analysis and Utilization in Veterinary Practices

Electronic health records (EHRs) in veterinary medicine have become integral for both patient-specific and broader health management decisions. Research by Singleton et al. on canine acute diarrhea treatments highlighted a mismatch between diagnostic testing rates and high levels of antimicrobial prescriptions, hinting at possible antimicrobial resistance issues [15]. Gray et al. delved into the emotional and complex decisions surrounding euthanasia, showing how EHRs document these challenging processes and the consideration of palliative care [6]. Studies by Kim et al. and Gates et al. demonstrated EHRs' role in identifying disease patterns across different breeds and life stages, and in monitoring prevalent health concerns like obesity, respectively, aiding in targeted care and prevention [5, 9]. Further, Salt and Sanchez et al. used EHR data to study pet demographics and life stage susceptibility to diseases, providing valuable insights into disease predisposition and the impact of socioeconomic factors on pet health [13, 14]. These examples collectively highlight the critical role EHRs play in veterinary medicine, facilitating informed care and broader health surveillance efforts.

3 Approach

3.1 Traditional Process for Managing Animal Health Records

The journey of managing animal health data traditionally starts at the grassroots level with animal caretakers who play a fundamental role in the health management cycle. Tasked with the day-to-day monitoring of animal well-being, these caretakers are crucial in identifying early signs of health concerns, prompting a visit to a veterinary clinic for further evaluation. At the clinic, the process of creating a foundational record begins, led by veterinary nurses who carefully compile the animal's medical history, noting current symptoms, and cataloging any past treatments or vaccinations. This initial record is essential, serving as the cornerstone for all future healthcare decisions regarding the animal. The precision of this data collection process is critical, as it directly influences the decisions made by veterinarians in the care and treatment of the animal, underscoring the importance of meticulous documentation in the traditional management of animal health data (Fig. 1).

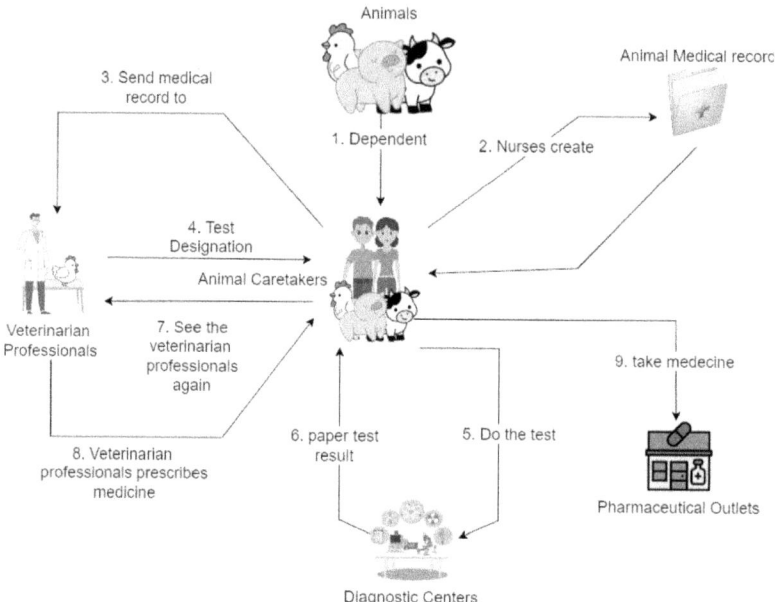

Fig. 1. Traditional Workflow of Animal Health Record Management

Following the initial documentation by veterinary nurses, the compiled animal health data is passed to veterinarians for detailed examination. The veterinarians assess the documented information to decide on the necessary diagnostic tests, a decision that is then relayed to both the animal caretakers and the diagnostic facilities capable of carrying out these tests. The allocation of diagnostic tests depends on the available resources and often requires careful scheduling, which can delay the treatment process. Diagnostic centers are pivotal in this stage, tasked with conducting the tests and consolidating the findings into comprehensive reports. These reports, typically in paper format, are physically delivered back to the veterinarians, a process that can slow down the communication flow due to logistical constraints in document transportation. Upon receipt of these results, veterinarians are required to analyze the data in light of the animal's comprehensive medical history. This analysis may lead to additional consultations or follow-up visits to the clinic, establishing a cycle of feedback that provides veterinarians with various insights to evaluate the animal's health more accurately, underlining the sequential and often manual nature of traditional animal health data management.

In the traditional management of animal health data, once a treatment plan is established, veterinarians issue prescriptions that are then passed to the animal caretakers. These caretakers are responsible for obtaining the prescribed medication from pharmacies, where they are also informed about the correct dosage and method of administration. This conventional process is sequential and compartmentalized, heavily reliant on the physical movement of documents and the manual entry of data at each stage. It operates on a system where the flow of information follows a strict chain of custody, critical for maintaining continuous care. Yet, this system's effectiveness is contingent upon the accuracy and promptness of each individual involved. Human errors, mismanagement of data, or logistical setbacks can introduce vulnerabilities, potentially compromising the integrity of the animal's medical records. The responsibility for maintaining the unbroken continuity of information, therefore, lies with each stakeholder in the process, from veterinarians to pharmacists, emphasizing the need for careful record-keeping and pointing towards areas where improvements could significantly bolster the security, precision, and ease of access to these essential records.

3.2 Building a Secure Framework for Animals Health Records Using Blockchain and NFTs Encrypted

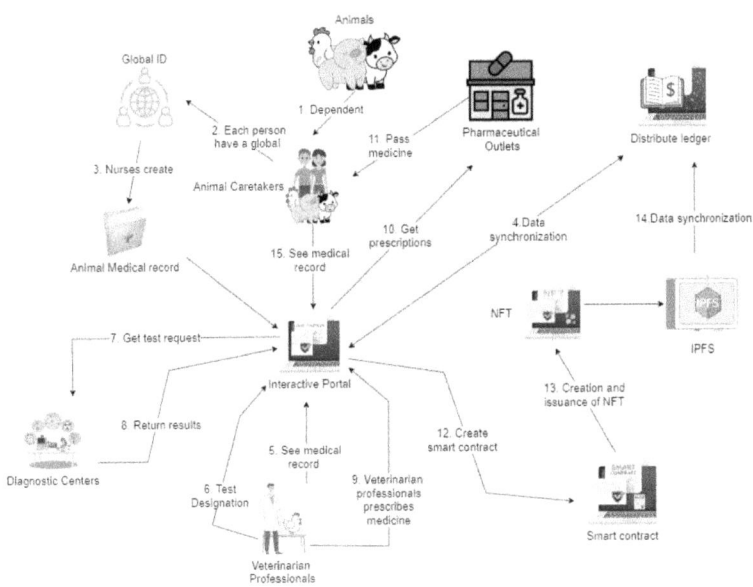

Fig. 2. Integrated Blockchain Model for Animal Health Record Management

The process of enhancing transparency in the management of animal health data is significantly advanced by the integration of blockchain technology. This integration brings into play a distributed ledger system that anchors the traceability and security of medical information throughout the various stages of veterinary care. With each animal assigned a global ID, a unique and verifiable identity is established within the system, facilitating a direct link to their health records. These records, meticulously compiled and regularly updated by veterinary professionals, are encrypted using a selection of cryptographic algorithms- RSA, RC4, DES, ChaCha20, Blowfish, and AES. This encryption process is crucial for assessing the balance between securing sensitive medical data and maintaining operational efficiency. As a dynamic component of a digital file system, these records are crafted for secure, efficient storage and retrieval, thereby enhancing the transparency of animal health data management (Fig. 2).

In the developed system, an interactive portal acts as the primary access point for medical records, serving both animal caretakers and veterinary professionals. This digital gateway enables veterinarians to send diagnostic requests directly to specialized centers via the portal. Following the completion of tests, the diagnostic results are returned through this portal, ensuring a rapid and secure exchange of medical information. Additionally, the prescription process is streamlined through the use of smart contracts on the blockchain, which automate the prescription issuance. This mechanism ensures that prescription activities are consistent and traceable across the network, allowing pharmacies to verify and dispense medications accurately. The application of encrypted Non-Fungible Tokens (NFTs), secured with one of the six cryptographic algorithms, plays a pivotal role in striking a balance between the rigorous security of medical records and the efficiency of veterinary operations.

Central to this architecture is the utilization of Non-Fungible Tokens (NFTs) as digital certificates on the blockchain, representing the ownership and authenticity of the animal health records. These NFTs, by their nature, are immutable and transparent, safeguarding the records from unauthorized changes or fraudulent duplication. The synchronization of data across the distributed ledger, coupled with the integration of the InterPlanetary File System (IPFS), ensures that all involved parties have access to the most current and authenticated information. This level of accessibility, supported by the decentralized storage of IPFS, enhances the resilience and availability of the records. Through the selective application of smart contracts and the strategic encryption of NFTs with advanced algorithms, the methodology aims to identify the optimal approach for safeguarding the integrity of animal health data while ensuring its transparent management within the veterinary care ecosystem.

4 Implementation

In the practical aspects of our research, we delve into the utilization of various encryption algorithms to protect the metadata of Non-Fungible Tokens (NFTs), a critical component in a blockchain-oriented strategy for improving transparency in the management of animal health data. Our aim is to assess these algorithms based on their security levels and time efficiency, factors that are essential for the seamless functioning of the system. By presenting comprehensive comparisons in our data tables, we highlight the effectiveness of each encryption method when applied to diverse data types, such as images and text, which play a significant role in ensuring the transparent handling of animal health information. This evaluation is particularly relevant in the framework of implementing blockchain technology and smart contracts, where the encryption times are crucial metrics, offering insight into the practicality and efficiency of employing encrypted NFTs and the InterPlanetary File System (IPFS) for the secure and efficient management of data within the animal health records system (Table 1).

Table 1. RSA Encryption and Decryption Performance for Image and text Data in Microseconds

RSA	1	2	3	4	5	6	7	8	9	10
Generating key	75356	95235	38750	78216	98703	95067	54002	301008	75905	98625
Encrypting image	10678	9685	8111	9330	9393	10638	11635	10350	10979	10646
Decrypting image	262878	265051	269676	255449	258359	265588	255306	258615	259331	260586
Generating key	109072	161201	58533	54586	24110	94431	168443	31826	46018	82341
Encrypting text	0	0	0	0	1367	0	0	0	0	998
Decrypting text	594	1413	1160	1274	501	1084	1378	1508	502	0

In our investigation into securing metadata for Non-Fungible Tokens (NFTs) associated with animal health data, the RSA encryption algorithm was scrutinized for its performance in operational speed. We observed that the time required for RSA key generation varied significantly, with durations ranging from 75,356 to 95,235 microseconds, and in some cases, stretching up to 301,008 microseconds. Additionally, the task of encrypting and decrypting image data under RSA was notably time-consuming, especially for decryption processes which frequently exceeded 250,000 microseconds. Despite RSA's high security reputation, these findings suggest that its operational efficiency may be hampered by substantial computational demands during our assessments (Table 2).

Table 2. RC4 Encryption and Decryption Performance for Image and text Data in Microseconds

RC4 (image)	1	2	3	4	5	6	7	8	9	10
Encrypting image	107	0	0	0	171	0	543	0	0	0
Decrypting image	0	0	664	0	0	0	0	0	1502	0
Encrypting text	0	0	0	0	0	0	0	0	0	0
Decrypting text	0	0	0	0	0	0	0	0	0	0

During our exploration of encryption techniques for NFT metadata in managing animal health data, we evaluated the RC4 algorithm and noted its exceptionally brief encryption and decryption times for both image and textual content, occasionally registering as minimal as zero microseconds. This performance indicates that RC4 could significantly expedite transaction processing. However, the comparative lack of security strength against more contemporary algorithms may limit RC4's application, despite its operational speed advantages. This discrepancy emphasizes the critical need for a careful balance between securing data effectively and maintaining transactional efficiency in managing animal health data (Table 3).

Table 3. DES Encryption and Decryption Performance for Image and text Data in Microseconds

DES (image)	1	2	3	4	5	6	7	8	9	10
Encrypting image	1073	540	820	1047	1091	708	1217	599	1121	1024
Decrypting image	1058	551	0	819	606	999	1005	1018	501	0
Encrypting text	0	0	0	0	0	0	0	0	0	0
Decrypting text	0	0	0	0	0	508	0	0	0	0

In our assessment of encryption algorithms for animal health data NFT metadata, the DES algorithm was analyzed for its processing efficiency. Encrypting image data with DES was found to require between 540 to 1,217 microseconds, while decryption times ranged from 0 to 1,058 microseconds, suggesting a moderate pace in operational terms. Despite these potentially acceptable processing speeds, DES's known vulnerabilities may detract from its utility for securing NFT metadata. These security concerns could overshadow the benefits of its processing efficiency, presenting a challenge in achieving the desired balance between security and operational speed in managing animal health data (Table 4).

Table 4. Chacha20 Encryption and Decryption Performance for Image and text Data in Microseconds

CHACHA20 (image)	1	2	3	4	5	6	7	8	9	10
Encrypting image	501	0	109	0	0	0	0	0	0	101
Decrypting image	0	584	511	0	0	668	0	634	0	0
Encrypting text	0	0	0	0	0	0	0	0	0	0
Decrypting text	0	0	0	0	0	508	0	0	0	0

Our study also examined ChaCha20's suitability for encrypting animal health data NFT metadata, with initial findings highlighting its promising combination of quick processing and security. Encryption times for image data with ChaCha20 were particularly low, around 501 microseconds, and decryption was efficient, albeit variable. These results suggest that ChaCha20 could be a viable candidate for securing NFT metadata, capable of fulfilling the dual requirements of robust

Table 5. Blowfish Encryption and Decryption Performance for Image and text Data in Microseconds

blowfish (image)	1	2	3	4	5	6	7	8	9	10
Encrypting image	542	603	506	599	507	1145	608	1137	633	541
Decrypting image	0	0	508	512	501	501	1037	999	575	532
Encrypting text	0	0	537	520	0	533	91	0	0	0
Decrypting text	0	0	0	0	0	0	0	0	0	0

security and operational efficiency needed for transparently managing animal health data (Table 5).

In our analysis focused on the management of animal health data, Blowfish's performance was evaluated, revealing encryption times for image data ranging from 506 to 1,145 microseconds. Historically, Blowfish has been recognized for balancing speed with security. However, with advancements in encryption technology introducing algorithms with enhanced security features, Blowfish's suitability for current applications, including securing NFT metadata for animal health data, warrants reassessment. This situation highlights the ongoing need to evaluate Blowfish's effectiveness in an evolving security landscape, particularly within contexts demanding high levels of data protection and efficiency (Table 6).

Table 6. AES Encryption and Decryption Performance for Image and text Data in Microseconds

AES (image)	1	2	3	4	5	6	7	8	9	10
Encrypting image	0	360	0	82	592	608	502	541	510	513
Decrypting image	1332	0	1005	0	504	0	0	0	0	0
Encrypting text	0	0	0	0	0	0	0	507	0	0
Decrypting text	0	0	0	0	0	0	0	0	0	0

Lastly, our research into optimizing the transparency of animal health data through NFTs included an assessment of the AES algorithm. AES is renowned for its robust security measures and was evaluated for its performance in encrypting and decrypting both textual and image data. The efficiency and security levels exhibited by AES suggest its strong potential for application in securing NFT metadata related to animal health records. This exploration underlines the importance of selecting an encryption method that not only safeguards data against unauthorized access but also supports the swift processing of transactions, which is essential for the effective management and transparency of animal health data.

Our research sheds light on the effectiveness of various encryption algorithms for securing Non-Fungible Token (NFT) metadata within a blockchain framework aimed at managing animal health data. This endeavor seeks to find an encryption solution that not only ensures the high security of NFT metadata but also complements the operational needs of managing animal health records, which involve regular and prompt updates. The critical balance between security and operational efficiency is underscored in our analysis, pointing towards the necessity of choosing an encryption method that fulfills stringent security demands while facilitating the smooth operation of the blockchain infrastructure. By conducting thorough comparisons and tests, our goal is to bolster the transparency and integrity of animal health data management, thereby fostering trust and dependability from the initial collection of data by veterinary professionals to its access and use by animal caretakers and other stakeholders.

5 Evaluation Scenarios

5.1 Analysis of NFTs Encrypted Integrated with Decentralized Storage Systems for Animal Health Record Management

The implementation of Non-Fungible Tokens (NFTs) encrypted, integrated with decentralized storage like the InterPlanetary File System (IPFS), outlines a methodical approach for the management of animal health records. This approach is detailed through both visual aids and code documentation, starting with the organization of critical data elements related to an animal's health history (Fig. 3). A specific segment of code is developed to accurately represent this data, including details such as types of tests conducted, their outcomes, and associated time stamps. This coding effort is instrumental in ensuring that the NFT accurately encapsulates every aspect of the health record, thereby contributing to the transparent management of animal health data.

Following the organization of the data, the creation of Non-Fungible Tokens (NFTs) for animal health records proceeds, demonstrated by terminal outputs that capture the time spent on minting and related processes (Fig. 4). This stage involves encrypting the health record with a selection of six cryptographic algorithms-RSA, RC4, DES, ChaCha20, Blowfish, and AES-and is carried out within specific time intervals, highlighting the system's capacity to manage encryption tasks with efficiency. This process is critical for ensuring the secure and transparent handling of animal health data, as it allows for the verification of operational effectiveness in the encryption and minting steps, essential for the system's overall performance in maintaining data integrity and accessibility.

Following the minting process, the NFT, which holds the encrypted metadata of the animal's health record, is stored on the InterPlanetary File System (IPFS), a platform known for its robustness and capability to ensure data remains distributed and redundant (Fig. 6). The successful storage of this information on IPFS is confirmed through visual cues in the IPFS interface, which display the stored file, signifying that the data transfer has been completed and the health record is now securely embedded within the network's distributed structure. This

Revolutionizing Animal Health Privacy   75

Fig. 3. Code Snippet Illustrating the Data Structure and Metadata for Encrypted NFT Creation

Fig. 4. Output Displaying the Performance Metrics of NFT Minting and Decryption Operations

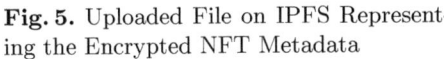

```
{"data":"6a0a7b746b157c651341dc9921f62b
2d18d94bbd1718280d38c0134ca761e3f9bcf2b
080a9162f10a9bf935d306e15e41fc5e5feec96
ffaf4675b0c123c90636c69496987402614bb00
fcb4346be0b281f0687a566cc606002c9e7d213
369f476358baee7054a26fbf53991c130cf3b19
505b1b36b580e38954524eaef146c5cd9e55a4d
432ae167a90b2e81efc6d4ccb8c6ab77d620215
6cb5e7133b14d633056861ac4585baf5e6514ed
8d2272431a05839e1c36168c87cf3ab6d86f587
a7c04f51c4de0df8d76a1e8610703413599e197
cb06fba7dd97e6fab7"}
```

Fig. 5. Uploaded File on IPFS Representing the Encrypted NFT Metadata

Fig. 6. Decrypted NFT Data Retrieved from IPFS, Demonstrating the Result of the Decryption Process

crucial step guarantees that the animal health data remains consistently available and accessible across various nodes, enhancing the system's dependability and the strength of the data management ecosystem.

The concluding step in the process involves the fetching and decrypting of NFT-based data from the IPFS, illustrated through a browser interface that displays the animal health record in a format understandable to humans (Fig. 5). This display allows for the necessary verification and examination, leading to the validation that the encrypted animal health data, once securely stored, is now readily accessible and decipherable by parties with the requisite authorization. Such a structured progression of actions highlights the deliberate and secure method adopted in the handling of animal health records, emphasizing the importance of both security and reliability within a framework that combines encrypted NFTs with decentralized storage solutions.

5.2 Testing on EVM-Supported Platforms

In our study, we examine the Ethereum Virtual Machine (EVM) alongside its interoperability with blockchain platforms like Binance Smart Chain, Polygon, Fantom, and Celo, for the deployment of smart contracts that are crucial in the management of animal health data. This exploration is aimed at evaluating the capability of each platform in documenting essential activities within the animal health data management process, generating Non-Fungible Tokens (NFTs) for the precise tracking of data origins and history, and ensuring the secure transfer of NFTs to maintain a verifiable data custody chain. Our assessment focuses on the transaction processing efficiency, cost considerations, and the ease of use of these platforms, which are critical for veterinarians and other animal health professionals in their routine tasks. The goal of this analysis is to pinpoint the platform that most effectively fosters a transparent environment for managing animal health data, highlighting the importance of secure and dependable transactions facilitated by NFTs, in the pursuit of achieving an equilibrium between stringent security protocols and operational efficiency.

Table 7. Transaction fee

	Transaction Creation	Create NFT	Transfer NFT
BNB	0.0273134 BNB ($8.27)	0.00109162 BNB ($0.33)	0.00057003 BNB ($0.17)
Fantom	0.00957754 FTM ($0.00)	0.000405167 FTM ($0.00)	0.0002380105 FTM ($0.00)
Polygon	0.006840710032835408 MATIC ($0.01)	0.000289405001852192 MATIC ($0.00)	0.000170007501088048 MATIC ($0.00)
Celo	0.007097844 CELO ($0.005)	0.0002840812 CELO ($0.000)	0.0001554878 CEL ($0.000)

Transaction Fee. The Table 7 we've included outlines the transaction fees across various blockchain platforms, an essential factor when considering the cost-effectiveness of incorporating blockchain technology into the management of animal health data. These transaction costs are a key component of the total operational expenses involved in running a blockchain framework for managing animal health records. It also captures the market values of the tokens for each blockchain as of March 27, 2024, at 7:00 AM UTC, providing a snapshot of the economic environment surrounding these technologies. This information serves to aid stakeholders in comprehending the financial implications of adopting blockchain networks to improve the transparency and security of animal health data management, with a focus on finding a middle ground between operational efficiency and the security enhancements offered through smart contracts and encrypted NFTs.

Transaction fees are essential in blockchain network operations, offsetting the computational energy required for processing and validating transactions. In the context of animal health record management, these fees appear during three main operations: transaction creation, NFT creation, and NFT transfer. On Binance Smart Chain, the cost for creating a transaction is 0.0273134 BNB, which is about $8.27. This fee covers the initiation and recording of new animal health records on the blockchain. NFT creation on this platform incurs a lower fee of 0.00109162 BNB ($0.33), representing the conversion of pet health records into unique digital assets. The transfer of an NFT, essential for sharing pet health information among parties, costs 0.00057003 BNB, approximately $0.17.

In contrast, Fantom offers significantly lower transaction fees. Transaction creation costs 0.00957754 FTM, which is effectively negligible in USD terms. The fee for creating an NFT on Fantom is 0.000405167 FTM, with the transfer fee even lower at 0.0002380105 FTM, both of which are also negligible in USD value. On the Polygon platform, transaction creation incurs a fee of 0.006840710032835408 MATIC ($0.01), while NFT creation and transfer fees are 0.000289405001852192 MATIC and 0.000170007501088048 MATIC, respectively, both less than a cent in USD terms. Similarly, Celo imposes transaction creation fees of 0.007097844 CELO ($0.005), with NFT creation and transfer fees at 0.0002840812 CELO and 0.0001554878 CELO, respectively, again less than a cent in USD value.

This comparison highlights the cost considerations for managing animal health records on various blockchain platforms. Each platform's fee structure varies, which is important to consider, especially in large-scale deployments where numerous transactions are expected. Therefore, accounting for these costs is crucial to maintaining the economic feasibility of veterinary practices or animal health record management systems that integrate RSA-encrypted NFTs and smart contracts.

6 Conclusion

In conclusion, our research demonstrates the viability of using blockchain technology, smart contracts, NFTs encrypted with various algorithms, and IPFS to address critical challenges in the management of animal health data. The study's examination across multiple blockchain platforms revealed a promising avenue for achieving greater transparency and security in veterinary health records. Our analysis indicates that the strategic application of selected encryption algorithms can offer an optimal balance between data protection and operational efficiency. This framework not only supports the ethical and transparent handling of animal health data but also streamlines the management processes, reducing costs and enhancing the overall efficacy of veterinary care practices. The adoption of this integrated approach could lead to significant advancements in the sector, fostering trust among all stakeholders and improving the quality of animal healthcare. Future work will focus on refining these technologies further and exploring their implementation in real-world veterinary settings to fully realize their potential benefits.

References

1. Aigner, C., et al.: Prototypical implementation of an animal health record (AHR) for livestock management. Ph.D. thesis (2014)
2. Anholt, R., et al.: Mining free-text medical records for companion animal enteric syndrome surveillance. Prevent. Vet. Med. **113**(4), 417–422 (2014)
3. Anholt, R., et al.: Spatial-temporal clustering of companion animal enteric syndrome: detection and investigation through the use of electronic medical records from participating private practices. Epidemiol. Infect. **143**(12), 2547–2558 (2015)
4. Anholt, R.: Informatics and the electronic medical record for syndromic surveillance in companion animals: development, application and utility. Ph.D. thesis, University of Calgary (2013)
5. Gates, M.C., et al.: Assessing obesity in adult dogs and cats presenting for routine vaccination appointments in the north island of New Zealand using electronic medical records data. New Zealand Vet. J. **67**(3), 126–133 (2019)
6. Gray, C., et al.: Using electronic health records to explore negotiations around euthanasia decision making for dogs and cats in the UK. Vet. Rec. **190**(9), e1379 (2022)
7. Hanauer, D.A., Ramakrishnan, N., Seyfried, L.S.: Describing the relationship between cat bites and human depression using data from an electronic health record. PLoS ONE **8**(8), e70585 (2013)
8. Kass, P.H., et al.: Syndromic surveillance in companion animals utilizing electronic medical records data: development and proof of concept. PeerJ **4**, e1940 (2016)
9. Kim, E., et al.: Major medical causes by breed and life stage for dogs presented at veterinary clinics in the Republic of Korea: a survey of electronic medical records. PeerJ **6**, e5161 (2018)
10. Krone, L.M., et al.: Survey of electronic veterinary medical record adoption and use by independent small animal veterinary medical practices in Massachusetts. J. Am. Vet. Med. Assoc. **245**(3), 324–332 (2014)
11. Menéndez, S., et al.: Data quality of animal health records on swiss dairy farms. Vet. Rec. **163**(8), 241–246 (2008)
12. Quintana, G.N., et al.: Exploratory analysis of animal bites events in the city of Buenos Aires using data from electronic health records. In: Digital Personalized Health and Medicine, pp. 1283–1284. IOS Press (2020)
13. Salt, C., et al.: Stratification of companion animal life stages from electronic medical record diagnosis data. J. Gerontol.: Ser. A **78**(4), 579–586 (2023)
14. Sánchez-Vizcaíno, F., et al.: Demographics of dogs, cats, and rabbits attending veterinary practices in Great Britain as recorded in their electronic health records. BMC Vet. Res. **13**, 1–13 (2017)
15. Singleton, D.A., et al.: Pharmaceutical prescription in canine acute diarrhoea: a longitudinal electronic health record analysis of first opinion veterinary practices. Front. Vet. Sci. 218 (2019)
16. Summers, J.F., et al.: Health-related welfare prioritisation of canine disorders using electronic health records in primary care practice in the UK. BMC Vet. Res. **15**, 1–20 (2019)
17. Tulloch, J.S.P., et al.: The passive surveillance of ticks using companion animal electronic health records. Epidemiol. Infect. **145**(10), 2020–2029 (2017)
18. Willner, V.: Erhebung und Analyse der Anforderungen an einen Animal Health Record (AHR) für Kleintiere. Ph.D. thesis (2011)

Improving and Evaluating Sparse Decision-Based Black-Box Attacks and Defenses

Jonas Brager Jacobsen⬤, Jingyue Li(✉)⬤, and Mathias Lundteigen Mohus⬤

Norwegian University of Science and Technology, Trondheim, Norway
{jingyue.li,mathias.l.mohus}@ntnu.no

Abstract. Decision-based black box attacks are rising concerns in adversarial machine learning, as they allow attackers to manipulate the outputs of machine learning models without having access to the model's internal architecture or hyperparameters. Sparse attacks, aiming to minimize the number of perturbed pixels, expose critical vulnerabilities in machine learning models, representing a considerable threat to real-world systems. A current limitation of sparse attacks is the need to query the target model in the range of thousands of queries to create imperceptible adversarial examples, which can be costly and easily detected. Our study demonstrates the potential of using the patch-wise adversarial removal (PAR) algorithm to improve the query efficiency of sparse attacks. To defend against sparse decision-based attackers, we find that adversarial training is an effective countermeasure, strengthened further by using median filtering and adversarial detection. We probe the possibility of enhancing the attacks with our modification of the PAR algorithm, blurring the adversarial example with the original unperturbed input, with results showing that the F1-score of the trained detector drops from 0.97 to 0.89. The study highlights the importance of continued research into understanding the potential severity of sparse attacks and optimizing related defenses.

Keywords: Sparse attacks · Adversarial Examples · Adversarial Training · Median Filtering · Deep Neural Network

1 Introduction

Deep Neural Networks (DNNs) have been increasingly popular with widespread application in real-world domains, such as software vulnerability detection [4], diagnosing diseases [1], autonomous driving [49], security and surveillance [8], and content moderation [3]. Failures in the classification models used in several systems can have severe consequences. Several DNN models are vulnerable to maliciously crafted perturbations [23,47], potentially having significant repercussions in applications, such as autonomous cars that rely on these models to navigate and read traffic signs. Therefore, continued research on adversarial attacks and defenses is essential to evaluate and improve the robustness of DNNs in critical systems.

Adversarial attacks are typically divided into two categories: white-box and black-box attacks. A white-box attack assumes access to internal information of the target model, such as the underlying architecture and the model gradients. In deployed real-world applications of DNNs, this information is usually unavailable to a potential attacker. In the black-box scenario, the adversarial input is crafted only from the model's output predictions. In this environment, some attackers exploit the transferability of DNNs [31,39,40] by training a surrogate model and then transferring these attacks to the target model. However, training a surrogate model is not always feasible or practical, limiting the available information to the output labels of the target model. Attacks restricted to only the output labels are called decision-based attacks, which separate into dense and sparse attacks. In dense attacks [6,9,11,28,29,43,51], L_2 and L_∞ norms measure the similarity between benign and perturbed inputs. Conversely, in sparse attacks [44,50,55], the L_0 norm is applied to measure the distortions. The few papers on sparse attacks give a limited understanding of the attacks' threats and defenses and warrant more research to improve the robustness of DNNs against sparse attacks. Existing sparse decision-based black box attacks need many queries to succeed [50]. Although the study [55] explores defensive methods against sparse attacks, it does not cover decision-based attacks nor consider the query efficiency of the attack. Thus, we investigate three research questions as follows.

- **RQ1:** How to create more query-efficient sparse decision-based black-box attacks?
- **RQ2:** How effective are existing defenses against sparse decision-based attacks?
- **RQ3:** Given the attacks can be defended by the defensive methods properly, are there other possibilities to enhance the sparse decision-based attacks further?

Our results show that the patch-wise adversarial removal (PAR) algorithm [46] can help improve the query efficiency of sparse attacks. The results also show that defenses, including adversarial training, median filtering, and adversarial detection, can help defend against the attack. However, our modification of the PAR algorithm may further defeat the defenses.

The rest of the paper is organized as follows. Section 2 introduces related work. Sections 3 to 5 present the research design and results of RQ1 to RQ3, respectively. Section 6 discusses the results, and Sect. 7 concludes the study.

2 Related Work

In a decision-based black-box attack, the adversary has access to the top predicted labels of the target network [10]. In the dense decision-based black-box attacks, the L_2 or the L_∞ distance measures the adversarial perturbations. The L_2, or Euclidean distance, is the distance between two vectors in an n-dimensional space. In contrast, the L_∞ distance is the largest distance between the original and the adversarial image. The adversarial perturbations of the sparse black-box attacks are measured by the L_0 distance, i.e., the number of changed elements. In the context of images, this translates to the number of changed pixels in an adversarial example. Unlike the dense attacks, measuring by the L_0-norm leads to an NP-hard problem where a global minimum cannot be guaranteed to be found [50].

2.1 Sparse Attacks

There exist two decision-based sparse attacks: PointWise [44] and SparseEvo [50].

PointWise was proposed by Schott et al. [44] to test the robustness of convolutional neural networks (CNN) [44]. They employ a simple search algorithm to minimize the L_0 distance, adding salt-and-pepper noise until the target model misclassifies the image. Every perturbed pixel is tested individually, checking if the image is misclassified. If the adversarial example still fools the classifier, the pixel is removed. The attack is complete when every perturbed pixel has been checked. In their experiments, Schott et al. [44] find that the accuracy of an unspecified CNN trained on the MNIST dataset is reduced from 99.1% to 19.9% when attacked. However, the primary objective of PointWise appears to test the resilience of CNNs, not necessarily to create an efficient sparse attack.

SparseEvo was proposed by [50] and uses a modified evolution strategy-based (ES) algorithm to create query-efficient attacks. SparseEvo works as a black-box optimization algorithm, making it well-suited for addressing the NP-hard problem inherent to sparse attacks. Vo et al. [50] disregard colors and treat the pixels as image coordinates that are either perturbed or original since exploring three color channels is both expensive and inefficient. They modify the evolution algorithm to evolve the binary representation of images and find this simplification very efficient at creating sparse attacks. Vo et al. [50] evaluated SparseEvo on the two datasets, CIFAR10 and ImageNet, and compared SparseEvo with PointWise. On the ImageNet dataset, PointWise struggled to produce efficient attacks with a 20k query budget, whereas SparseEvo generated very sparse adversarial examples. SparseEvo was also compared to the white-box attack PGD_0 [12], matching the ideal white-box attack in attack success rate on limited query budgets of 200 and 500 queries, especially as the sparsity threshold nears $L_\infty = 0.1$. However, the SparseEvo algorithm suffered from low query efficiency and slow convergence in the earlier stage of the evolution process.

2.2 Defenses

Most research on defending against adversarial attacks focuses on defenses against white-box attacks, but several defenses also apply to black-box attacks. Based on the survey papers [2,27,42,53], defensive techniques can be grouped into *Restricted Model Access*, *Input Transformation*, *Adversarial Training*, and *Adversarial Detection*.

Restricted Model Access includes masking or obfuscation of model gradients and restricted query access. Some techniques aim to obfuscate the gradients, including randomization of gradients [15], gradient regularization [33], adding masking layers [21], and feature squeezing [54]. However, the study [53] argued that gradient masking/obfuscation methods were unsafe, as they could only confuse or mislead adversaries. Studies, e.g., [5], also found that defenses relying on these techniques could be circumvented, suggesting adversarial training as a more robust defense.

Input Transformation is a defensive method that modifies the input to prevent or decrease the effect of adversarial attacks. Dziugaite et al. [16] and Das et al. [13] have found JPEG compression to be an effective way to increase robustness against some white-box attacks. Others try to use random resizing of images to improve robustness [52], or reduce the precision of the input data to minimize the effect of small perturbation, with techniques like median blur [30] or median filtering [54].

Adversarial Training is a defensive method where adversarial examples are introduced to the training data to create models that learn robustness to perturbations [5]. Szegedy et al. [47] introduced adversarial examples to their training data under a new label to enhance the resilience of their model. Goodfellow et al. [23] improved the accuracy of their model from 18% to 89% on perturbed MNIST images using an adversarially trained model. However, these adversarially trained models were trained on adversarial examples generated by non-iterative attacks. To address this limitation, Madry et al. [35] suggest training models using the iterative attack PGD [2], showing state-of-the-art robustness on MNIST and CIFAR-10 datasets. Vo et al. [50] tested their sparse attack, SparseEvo, against an adversarially trained ResNet-18 on the CIFAR10 dataset, finding that their algorithm performed comparably to the white-box attack PGD under 500 queries.

Adversarial Detection first considers inputs benign or adversarial. If the input is considered adversarial, the model can refuse to predict the class or give some random output to mislead the attacker. Grosse et al. [24] included an extra label for adversarial examples when training the classifier to check if two datasets were drawn from the same distribution to detect adversarial examples. Gong et al. [22] trained a separate binary classifier to filter adversarial examples before they reached the primary classifier. Metzen et al. [38] also used an external detection classifier but gave it the input of the hidden layers of the primary classifier instead of the input image.

3 Design and Results to Answer RQ1: Query-Efficient Attacks

While more research on sparse attacks may not necessarily lead to attacks that can outperform the dense attacks, their separation from the focus on the decision border and unique ways of generating adversarial solutions may give the family of attacks an advantage against defenses that focus on the techniques currently used for generating dense attacks. We believe this warrants further investigation into developing query-efficient sparse attacks and evaluating their response to defensive strategies.

A constraint for sparse decision-based attack methods is the need to query the target model with many queries to create sparse attacks. Previous state-of-the-art methods Pointwise [44] and SparseEvo [50] need thousands of queries to create sparse targeted attacks that are hard to detect with the human eye, which is especially true in the targeted setting where SparseEvo requires around ten thousand queries to create visually indistinguishable images from the starting image [50].

Based on the results in [46], we believe exploring their greedy initialization technique PAR [46] can significantly reduce the number of queries needed to create sparse attacks. PAR is a dense attack created by Shi and Han [46] investigating how different regions of an image are affected by noise. PAR operates by dividing the image into patches and gradually removing noise while maintaining the adversarial nature of the image. This reduction process starts with larger patches and progresses to smaller patches, prioritizing patches with higher noise magnitude. The modified image is queried against the target model, and if the image remains misclassified, the corresponding patch is discarded. This process repeats for all the patches. Once all patches have been processed, the remaining ones are halved in size, and this loop repeats. Shi and Han [46] only tested their algorithm in the dense attack setting. Unlike dense attacks, when creating sparse attacks, the distortions are measured directly by the number of adversarial pixels we can remove. As PAR is a noise removal algorithm, we believe PAR is even more suited to improve attacks in the sparse setting. We want the attack to apply to both targeted and untargeted settings as they provide distinct perspectives on the vulnerabilities of image classifiers. In the untargeted setting [27], the attacker aims to deceive the target classifier into predicting any label other than the original label. In the targeted setting [27], the attacker selects a target label and creates perturbations to an original image such that it is classified as the target label.

Figure 1 shows the targeted attack pipeline using PAR as the initialization method. A random image from the target class overlays the original image, after which patches from the random image are removed in iterations while keeping the image adversarial. When the initialization algorithm is unable to remove any more patches, we continue with the binary evolution strategy-based (ES) algorithm as in SparseEvo [50] on the reduced subgrid. All three images to the right of the original image of a hyena are classified as a honeycomb by the target model.

Some initial noise must be added to the image for the untargeted attacks to make it adversarial. PointWise developed salt-and-pepper noise [44], and Vo et al. [50] tested Gaussian and salt-and-pepper noise in their untargeted version of the SparseEvo algorithm and found that the salt-and-pepper noise was most effective. Salt and pepper noise is black-and-white, sometimes appearing

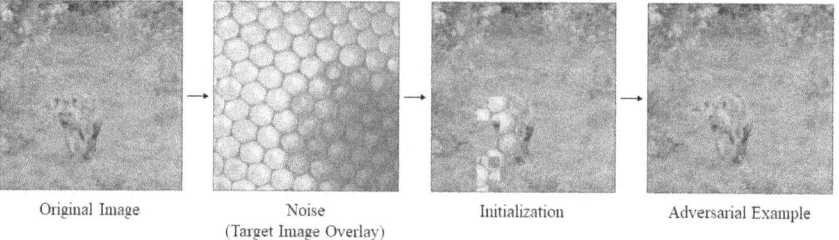

Fig. 1. Targeted attack pipeline, using PAR as the initialization method to reduce the noise overlay.

Table 1. Hyperparameters for the experiments in the targeted setting.

Parameters	Value
Population size (p)	10
Initialization rate (α)	0.0004
Mutation rate (μ)	$\begin{cases} \frac{1}{\text{num\_pixels}} & \text{if } t < 200 \\ \frac{3}{\text{num\_pixels}} & \text{if } 200 \leq t < 500 \\ 0.001, & \text{otherwise} \end{cases}$

Table 2. Hyperparameters for the experiments in the untargeted setting.

Parameters	Value
Population size (p)	10
Initialization rate (α)	0.004
Mutation rate (μ)	0.004

in digital images [48]. This noise is efficient at fooling classifiers and can occur naturally in input images, making it a relevant noise source for our studies.

In both targeted and untargeted settings, we use the same parameters for SparseEvo as described in [50], except parameters relating to the evolution. The parameters for the targeted setting are described in Table 1. The parameters for the untargeted setting are described in Table 2. The parameters for PAR are the same as described in [46].

We use the renowned computer vision dataset ImageNet to evaluate whether PAR can improve the query efficiency of the sparse attacks [14]. Regarding the target classifier, we use the state-of-the-art ResNet architecture [25]. Specifically, we use a version created for ImageNet called ResNet-50 that has a 76.15% accuracy in predicting the label of unperturbed images in the dataset. The model is provided by torchvision [36].

We found that PAR can be used to remove about 80% of the adversarial perturbations in the targeted setting and 95% in the untargeted setting. By combining it with the SparseEvo algorithm, we attempt to create a more query-efficient attack. In Fig. 2a and Fig. 2b, we see how adding the PAR initialization drastically improves the performance of the SparseEvo algorithm in the targeted and untargeted settings. The improved method reduces the L_0 distance quickly during the initialization, then converges steadily by reducing the grid for the subsequent thousand queries.

Table 3 shows the attack success rate (ASR) at different sparsity thresholds in the targeted setting. The methods are compared at four query budgets: 1k,

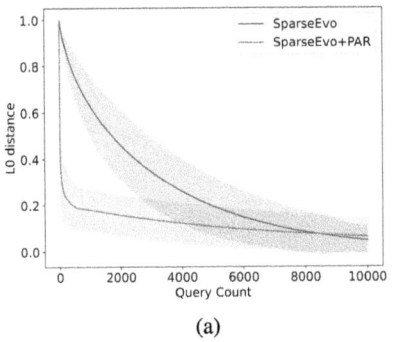 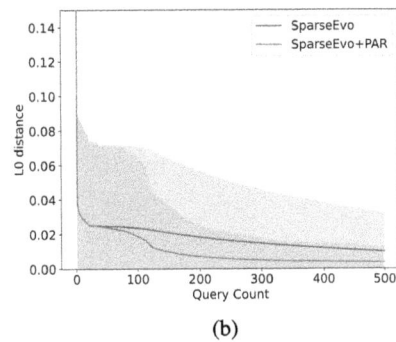

Fig. 2. The L_0 distance of targeted (a) and untargeted (b) perturbation created by SparseEvo and SparseEvo with PAR initialization, as an average of 200 runs. *Query Count* includes queries used for the PAR initialization.

2k, 5k, and 10k queries. The added initialization significantly improves the ASR at lower query budgets. At a budget of 1k queries, the version without PAR has no successful attacks, while the version with PAR is successful in 89% of the samples with a sparsity threshold of 0.3. Table 4 shows the attack success rate (ASR) at different sparsity thresholds in the untargeted setting. The versions with and without PAR are compared at four query budgets: 100, 300, and 500 queries.

Table 3. The ASR of SparseEvo with and without initialization using PAR in the targeted setting. The algorithm with initialization has higher success rates at all sparsity thresholds on query budgets 1k, 2k, 5k, and 10k.

Method \ Sparsity	0.05	0.10	0.15	0.20	0.30
SparseEvo - 1k	0%	0%	0%	0%	0%
SparseEvo+PAR - 1k	5%	20%	41%	65%	89%
SparseEvo - 2k	0%	0%	0%	0%	11%
SparseEvo+PAR - 2k	10%	31%	52%	72%	92%
SparseEvo - 5k	3%	21%	44%	63%	82%
SparseEvo+PAR - 5k	32%	58%	74%	85%	96%
SparseEvo - 10k	69%	89%	95%	98%	99%
SparseEvo+PAR - 10k	64%	78%	86%	91%	98%

In both the targeted and untargeted setting, we see that the L_0 distance is improved in the low-query setting when using the PAR initialization technique, with SparseEvo without PAR requiring a high amount of queries (above 8500 in the targeted setting, and at least above 500 in the untargeted setting).

Table 4. The ASR of SparseEvo with and without initialization using PAR in the untargeted setting. The algorithm with initialization has higher success rates at all sparsity thresholds on query budgets 100, 300, and 500.

Method \ Epsilon	0.001	0.002	0.005	0.010	0.020
SparseEvo - 100	28%	34%	49%	65%	76%
SparseEvo+PAR - 100	35%	48%	63%	75%	83%
SparseEvo - 300	40%	46%	58%	73%	83%
SparseEvo+PAR - 300	48%	62%	80%	91%	96%
SparseEvo - 500	47%	55%	68%	81%	88%
SparseEvo+PAR - 500	53%	69%	86%	95%	97%

We also see that the ASR improves in low-query settings, with PAR-initialized SparseEvo outperforming standard SparseEvo for every sparsity threshold and query count, except for the targeted setting with 10,000 queries, where the standard SparseEvo outperforms PAR-initialization.

4 Design and Results to Answer RQ2: Defenses

Restricted Model Access is irrelevant to the black-box attack setting as we already assume the gradients to be unavailable and that we have unrestricted query access. The relevant defensive techniques include adversarial training, input transformation, and adversarial detection.

Adversarial Training is, as a general defense, seen as the most robust defensive technique available [5,7]. Sparse adversarial examples often reduce to a minimal set of scattered pixels that throw off the model, especially in the untargeted setting. An adversarially trained model might give increased robustness for small but effective distortions. Instead of the vanilla ResNet-50 model provided by torchvision [36], we use an adversarially trained ResNet-50 model provided by Engstrom et al. [18]. Their model has a 57.90% accuracy on clean images, down from the 76.13% accuracy of the model without adversarial training, but shows impressive robustness to distortions created by the white-box attack PGD [35].

Input Transformation using a median filter is the second defense we consider. In the untargeted setting, random noise is added to the input image to create an adversarial attack before reducing the noise as much as possible to create a sparse attack. The effect of the attack can be reduced by running the input through a median filter before the target model labels it. This filter is especially effective against salt-and-pepper noise [17,19,20], which is the initialization used in SparseEvo. Figure 3 illustrates the effect of the median filter on an image distorted with salt-and-pepper noise. Firstly, we test the median filter's impact on the model on clean images to ensure the filtering will not considerably reduce the model's overall accuracy. In the following experiments, we test the efficiency of the median filter input transformation in untargeted attacks by measuring the sparsity after 500 queries and the attack success rate (ASR).

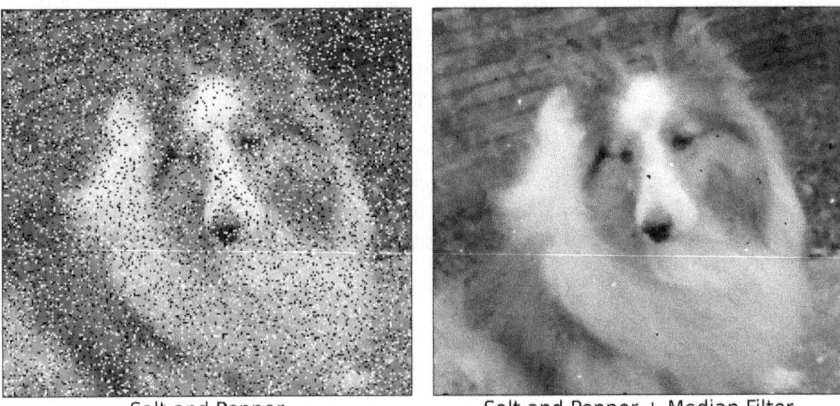

Salt and Pepper   Salt and Pepper + Median Filter

Fig. 3. To the left: An image from the ImageNet dataset distorted with salt and pepper noise. To the right: The same image after applying a median filter. The image to the right is visually less distorted to the human eye but slightly blurred.

Adversarial Detection is relevant because a downside to using PAR as an initialization technique is that it leaves distinct traces in the adversarial examples. Thus, we explore if these traces can be used to train a model for detecting perturbed images. The most promising techniques are two frameworks (SafetyNet [32] and Magnet [37]), defense-GAN [26,45], Network Invariant Checking (NIC) [34], and specific homemade detection classifiers [22,38]. The two frameworks (SafetyNet [32] and Magnet [37]) were developed and tested for much smaller datasets, so their efficiency and training time on the ImageNet dataset are uncertain [32,37]. We consider developing a separate GAN for adversarial detection too extensive for this scope. Instead, we create a ResNet-50 model for our ImageNet experiments, using transfer learning from a pre-trained ResNet-50. The training dataset consists of 2500 images divided into clean and PAR-distorted images (after 10, 30, and 50 queries of PAR). We evaluate the model's accuracy and F1-score on our new dataset and experiment with different prediction thresholds to find the best detection results.

The adversarially trained ResNet-50 model got an accuracy of 53.55% in our experiments on clean images (ImageNet validation set, 50k images), compared to the normal ResNet-50 provided by PyTorch with an accuracy of 76.13% [41].

Table 5 shows the ASR of the SparseEvo and SparseEvo, including PAR, against normal and adversarially trained models in the untargeted setting. We measure the ASR at different sparsity thresholds with a query budget of 500 queries. The ASR is heavily reduced for SparseEvo and SparseEvo with PAR.

At a sparsity threshold of 0.001, the ASR is about 16 times less without PAR and six times less with PAR. At a sparsity threshold of 0.020, where the version with PAR was almost 97% effective against the normally trained model, the adversarially trained model reduced the success rate to 58%. The sparsity threshold needs to be increased to 2000 perturbed pixels on a query budget of 500 queries before the version with PAR is above 90% ASR, showing how the adversarially trained defense reduces the query efficiency of the attacks but does not entirely prevent the attack at higher sparsity thresholds.

Table 5. Comparison of the ASR of SparseEvo with and without initialization against the normal- and the adversarially trained model. The ASR is measured with a query budget of 500 queries in the untargeted setting.

Method \ Sparsity	0.001	0.005	0.010	0.020	0.040
SparseEvo Not Adv. Trained	47%	68%	81%	88%	93%
SparseEvo Adv. Trained	3%	14%	25%	39%	63%
SparseEvo+PAR Not Adv. Trained	52%	86%	95%	97%	98%
SparseEvo+PAR Adv. Trained	8%	24%	39%	58%	91%

Adding the median filtering deteriorates the model's accuracy on benign images from 76.13% to 71.59% (ImageNet validation set, 50k images). The adversarially trained model with the median filter applied gives a 52.72% accuracy on clean images (ImageNet validation set, 50k images). This is very similar to the accuracy of the adversarially trained model without the filter, only 0.83% worse. In Fig. 4a, we compare four results: only median filter defense, only adversarial training defense, a combined median filter and adversarial training defense, and an attack without any defenses. The median filter significantly worsens the performance of the attack, proving to be an effective measure to reduce the effect of salt-and-pepper distortions at the cost of around a 5% drop in prediction accuracy. The graph shows a significant improvement in robustness for the combined defenses. Adding median filtering to the adversarially trained model increased the robustness of the model from around 0.03 sparsity to around 0.35 sparsity on a query budget of 500 queries. The robustness of the combined defenses is also persistent on larger query budgets, as shown in Fig. 4b, with average sparsity after 5000 queries no better than about 0.2.

Regarding adversarial detection, we trained a model to classify images as either benign or perturbed by PAR in the targeted setting. The trained model got an accuracy of 81.89% on our dataset after 50 epochs. In Fig. 5, we analyzed the model's predictions of 1000 benign and 1000 adversarial images after every iteration of PAR up to 50 queries. For each run with PAR, the model gets up to 50 different images, and we select the single highest confidence value that any of these images are adversarial to represent that run. We then compare this to the confidence predictions of the benign images. We assume that we do not care if

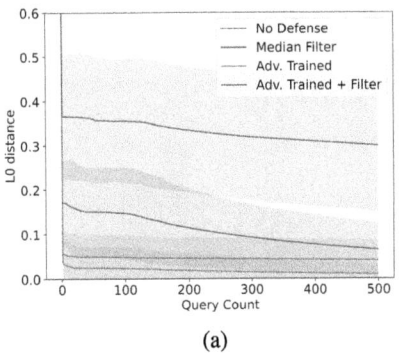 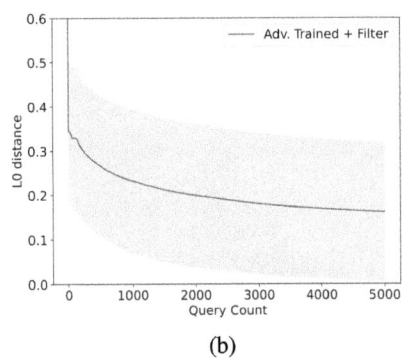

Fig. 4. (a): The performance of the SparseEvo+PAR algorithm against no defense, median filter defense, adversarially trained model, and median filter + adversarially trained model. (b): The adversarially trained model + median filter defense, left to run for 5k queries. The lines mark the average L0-distances across 200 runs. *Query Count* includes queries used for the PAR initialization.

some adversarial examples are allowed through the model as long as every single run of PAR is stopped somewhere along its 50 first queries.

By selecting the "worst" offenders out of the 50 queries in the 1000 PAR-generated adversarial runs, there are not a lot of misclassified examples. For this dataset, we can adjust the threshold for what we consider an adversarial example to find a balance between false positives and false negatives. Considering all model predictions above zero for the adversarial confidence, we misclassify 4.0% (40) benign images and correctly identify 97.5% (975) PAR runs. Adjusting this threshold to 1.6 means zero benign images are misclassified, while 83.1% of PAR runs are identified. If we use a combination of benign and adversarial prediction confidences, we can get even better predictions. We got adversarial confidence above one and benign confidence below zero. Only five benign images are misclassified, and 914 PAR runs are identified.

For the detection, discovering one adversarial example during the PAR run is considered to prevent the attack, which could be a too strong assumption. However, many adversarial examples are usually detected in the same run whenever one image is detected. For instance, if we set the adversarial confidence threshold to one, an average of 60.0% (69.23% median) of the adversarial images created during the first 50 PAR queries are detected in all the runs where at least one image was detected.

In a real-world scenario, the adversarial examples are most likely not 50% of the input a model receives. This distribution significantly affects the resulting F1-score. To give a more realistic example, we run the same numbers for 10k random benign examples from the ImageNet dataset, and the same PAR runs as before. Notably, 10% is still a very high estimate of adversarial input. With suitable thresholds, we achieve a very high F1-score of 0.99. However, it is essential to

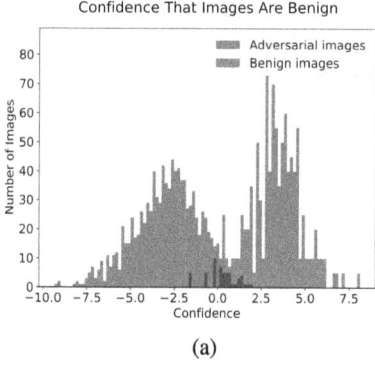
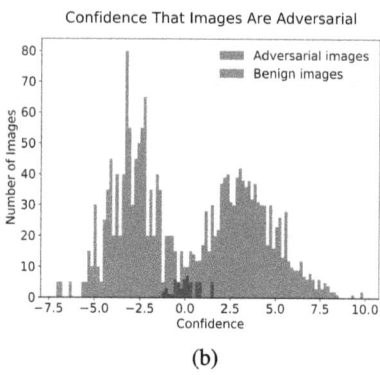

Fig. 5. The output predictions of a model trained to detect images perturbed by the PAR algorithm. The figure shows the prediction confidences of 1000 adversarial- (red) and 1000 benign images (blue). **(a)** (Color figure online): The model's confidence that the images are benign. **(b)**: The model's confidence that the images are adversarial.

note that the imbalance between benign and adversarial images favors setting a prediction threshold with a bias toward predicting an image as benign. With these thresholds, around 10% of the PAR runs are not detected.

5 Design and Results to Answer RQ3: Enhanced Attack

The results of RQ2 show that the model trained to detect the adversarial examples generated by PAR was highly effective on our created dataset. In an experiment to reduce the effectiveness of this defense, we propose a change to the PAR algorithm that blurs the adversarial patches together with the original image along the edges of the patches to make the edges less distinct. To achieve this purpose, we propose a change to the PAR algorithm that blurs the adversarial patches with the original image along the edges of the patches to make the PAR perturbations harder to detect. An example of an adversarial example created by the modified PAR algorithm is shown in Fig. 6.

The modified PAR algorithm works similarly to before, querying the target model with patches to check if they are necessary to keep the image adversarial and keeping track of a mask of the adversarial patches. In addition to this mask, the modified version of PAR tracks all edges the mask shares with the original image. Before passing the image to the target model, the target and original images are blurred along these edges.

The blurring is performed by gradually shifting from the original image to the target image along the edge of the mask. Thus, the pixels in between will be a blend of the two images. We chose to blur six pixels on either side of the edge to balance visually good-looking blends and keep the distortions to a minimum. To implement the blurring, we used a sigmoid function in the domain of $[-3, 3]$ to get an s-curve of values to blend the two images, i.e., using the values (0.047,

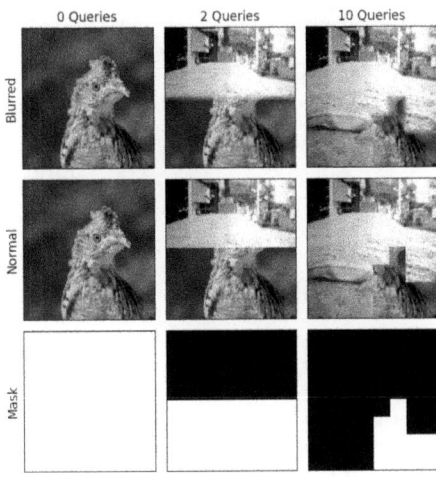

Fig. 6. Example of an adversarial example created by the modified version of PAR that blurs the images together along the edges.

0.076, 0.12, 0.18, 0.27, 0.38, 0.5, 0.62, 0.73, 0.82, 0.88, 0.92) to calculate the amount each image contributes to a single pixel.

We first evaluate the altered algorithm by checking how the blurring affects the distortion reduction compared to the normal PAR algorithm. Secondly, to test if the new algorithm is more challenging to detect by a trained model, we perform the same experimental setup and evaluation as done to answer RQ2, using the same base ResNet-50 model and dataset distribution.

If we measure the final L_0 distance by the adversarial patches tracked by PAR, the images are reduced to 16.7% of the original on average. When counting the blurred edges, the images are 26.6% reduced on average.

A new classifier is trained on the blurred PAR images to determine if an image is benign or adversarial, using the same setup as the adversarial detection model to answer RQ2. This model got an overall accuracy of 89.3% on the test set. We run the same experiment in answering RQ2 by combining the model's predictions of 1000 PAR runs, selecting the maximum confidence that a single image is adversarial across the 50 queries in the same run. We compare this to 1000 benign images. As we can see in Fig. 7, there is more overlap in the prediction confidences of the model between the two classes than in Fig. 5.

With the new detection model, no thresholds can be set, which would boost the F1-score of the model significantly. The best configuration found was a benign threshold of 0 and an adversarial threshold of -1. With this setting, 8.3% (83) benign images are misclassified, and 84.8% (848) PAR runs are correctly identified, giving an F1-score of 88.64%, significantly worse than the F1-scores of 97% of the model that trained on non-blurred pictures. Our results show that adversarial examples created from the blurred version of the PAR algorithm

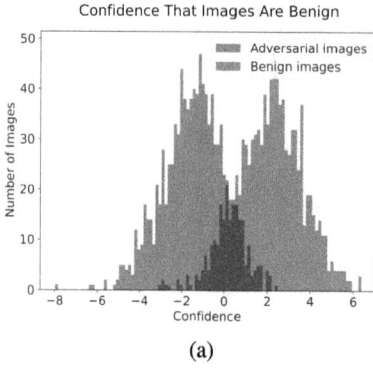 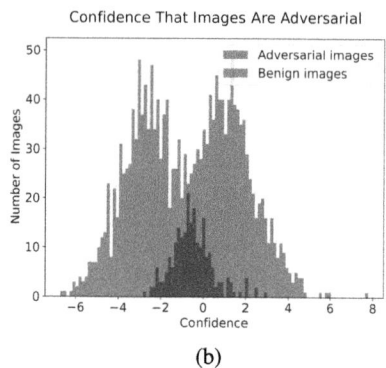

Fig. 7. The output predictions of a model trained to detect images perturbed by the blurred PAR algorithm. The figure shows the prediction confidences of 1000 adversarial- (red) and 1000 benign images (blue). **(a)** (Color figure online): The model's confidence that the images are benign. **(b)**: The model's confidence that the images are adversarial.

are more challenging to separate from benign images with this dataset for this experiment.

6 Discussion

The results of RQ1 demonstrate that the PAR algorithm can be used as an initialization method to improve the query efficiency of the best sparse attack SparseEvo. Using PAR significantly improved the image sparsity and attack success rate of the attack on query budgets for both targeted and untargeted attacks. The implications of our findings are important for future research because sparse attacks can create barely noticeable adversarial examples using less than a thousand queries. Improving the query efficiency of the attacks complicates the challenge of distinguishing between benign inputs and attacks, which could have severe repercussions for safety-critical classification models.

The results of the adversarial detection are promising and are the only tested defense that appears to prevent the attack entirely. With suitable prediction thresholds, the trained classifier can detect most adversarial examples created by the PAR algorithm while keeping the false positive rate low, suggesting that adversarial detection can be a viable defensive option against techniques similar to PAR. However, the results are highly dependent on the balance between benign and adversarial examples, and the thresholds used for the limited dataset in our experiment may not necessarily transfer to other distributions. We also demonstrated that the adversary can modify the attack algorithm to decrease the effectiveness of adversarial detection, possibly making the false negative rate of the detector too high.

As previously discussed, sparse attacks are more challenging to optimize than dense attacks. From a security standpoint, sparse attacks can be as severe as dense attacks. However, we have not seen any direct comparisons between the performance of SparseEvo and the best dense attacks since L_0, L_2, and L_∞ can't be used interchangeably to make the comparison, also making it hard to compare the efficiency of defenses.

7 Conclusion and Future Work

The work presented in this paper provides improvements and evaluations in sparse decision-based black-box attacks, demonstrating the potential of using the PAR algorithm as initialization to the state-of-the-art sparse attack SparseEvo. Moreover, we evaluated various defensive techniques against PAR and SparseEvo. Our study underlines the potential security threat posed by sparse attacks. Given some hundred queries to a target classifier, an attacker can create visually unperturbed adversarial examples. We have also demonstrated the effect of several defensive countermeasures and how they can help reduce the query efficiency of sparse attacks. Future work should focus on investigating the other detectors that may be able to detect the attacks with the PAR variations.

References

1. Ahmadian, S., Jalali, S.M.J., Islam, S.M.S., Khosravi, A., Fazli, E., Nahavandi, S.: A novel deep neuroevolution-based image classification method to diagnose coronavirus disease (covid-19). Comput. Biol. Medi. **139**, 104994 (2021), ISSN 0010-4825, https://doi.org/10.1016/j.compbiomed.2021.104994, https://www.sciencedirect.com/science/article/pii/S0010482521007885
2. Akhtar, N., Mian, A.: Threat of adversarial attacks on deep learning in computer vision: A survey (2018). https://doi.org/10.48550/arxiv.1801.00553
3. Akyon, F.C., Temizel, A.: Deep architectures for content moderation and movie content rating (2022). https://doi.org/10.48550/arxiv.2212.04533
4. An, J.H., Wang, Z., Joe, I.: A CNN-based automatic vulnerability detection. EURASIP J. Wireless Commun. Netw. **2023**(1), 41 (May 2023), ISSN 1687-149https://doi.org/10.1186/s13638-023-02255-2
5. Athalye, A., Carlini, N., Wagner, D.: Obfuscated gradients give a false sense of security: circumventing defenses to adversarial examples (2018). https://doi.org/10.48550/arxiv.1802.00420
6. Brendel, W., Rauber, J., Bethge, M.: Decision-based adversarial attacks: Reliable attacks against black-box machine learning models (2017). https://doi.org/10.48550/ARXIV.1712.04248
7. Carlini, N., Wagner, D.: Adversarial examples are not easily detected: bypassing ten detection methods (2017). https://doi.org/10.48550/arxiv.1705.07263
8. Chawla, D., Trivedi, M.C.: A comparative study on face detection techniques for security surveillance. In: Advances in Computer and Computational Sciences: Proceedings of ICCCCS 2016, vol. 2, pp. 531–541, Springer (2018)
9. Chen, J., Gu, Q.: Rays: A ray searching method for hard-label adversarial attack (2020). https://doi.org/10.48550/arxiv.2006.12792
10. Chen, J., Jordan, M.I.: Boundary attack++: Query-efficient decision-based adversarial attack. CoRR **1904.02144** (2019). https://doi.org/10.48550/arxiv.1904.02144

11. Chen, J., Jordan, M.I., Wainwright, M.J.: Hopskipjumpattack: A query-efficient decision-based attack (2020). https://doi.org/10.48550/arxiv.1904.02144
12. Croce, F., Hein, M.: Sparse and imperceivable adversarial attacks. CoRR **abs/1909.05040** (2019). https://doi.org/10.48550/arxiv.1909.05040
13. Das, N., Shanbhogue, M., Chen, S.T., Hohman, F., Chen, L., Kounavis, M.E., Chau, D.H.: Keeping the bad guys out: Protecting and vaccinating deep learning with jpeg compression (2017). https://doi.org/10.48550/arxiv.1705.02900
14. Deng, J., Dong, W., Socher, R., Li, L.J., Li, K., Fei-Fei, L.: Imagenet: A large-scale hierarchical image database. In: 2009 IEEE Conference on Computer Vision and Pattern Recognition, pp. 248–255 (2009). https://doi.org/10.1109/CVPR.2009.5206848
15. Dhillon, G.S., et al.: Stochastic activation pruning for robust adversarial defense (2018). https://doi.org/10.48550/arxiv.1803.01442
16. Dziugaite, G.K., Ghahramani, Z., Roy, D.M.: A study of the effect of jpg compression on adversarial images (2016). https://doi.org/10.48550/arxiv.1608.00853
17. E Woods, R., C Gonzalez, R.: Digital image processing (2008)
18. Engstrom, L., Ilyas, A., Salman, H., Santurkar, S., Tsipras, D.: Robustness (python library) (2019). https://github.com/MadryLab/robustness
19. Erkan, U., Enginoğlu, S., Thanh, D.N., Hieu, L.M.: Adaptive frequency median filter for the salt and pepper denoising problem. IET Image Proc. **14**(7), 1291–1302 (2020). https://doi.org/10.1049/iet-ipr.2019.0398
20. Erkan, U., Gökrem, L., Enginoğlu, S.: Different applied median filter in salt and pepper noise. Comput. Electr. Eng. **70**, 789–798 (2018). ISSN 0045-790https://doi.org/10.1016/j.compeleceng.2018.01.019, https://www.sciencedirect.com/science/article/pii/S0045790617320244
21. Gao, J., Wang, B., Lin, Z., Xu, W., Qi, Y.: Deepcloak: masking deep neural network models for robustness against adversarial samples (2017). https://doi.org/10.48550/arxiv.1702.06763
22. Gong, Z., Wang, W., Ku, W.S.: Adversarial and clean data are not twins (2017).https://doi.org/10.48550/arxiv.1704.04960
23. Goodfellow, I.J., Shlens, J., Szegedy, C.: Explaining and harnessing adversarial examples (2015). https://doi.org/10.48550/arxiv.1412.6572
24. Grosse, K., Manoharan, P., Papernot, N., Backes, M., McDaniel, P.: On the (statistical) detection of adversarial examples (2017). https://doi.org/10.48550/arxiv.1702.06280
25. He, K., Zhang, X., Ren, S., Sun, J.: Deep residual learning for image recognition. In: Proceedings of 2016 IEEE Conference on Computer Vision and Pattern Recognition, pp. 770–778, CVPR '16, IEEE, Las Vegas, NV, USA (2016). ISSN 1063-691https://doi.org/10.1109/CVPR.2016.90, http://ieeexplore.ieee.org/document/7780459
26. Lee, H., Han, S., Lee, J.: Generative adversarial trainer: defense to adversarial perturbations with gan (2017),. https://doi.org/10.48550/arxiv.1705.03387
27. Li, G., Zhu, P., Li, J., Yang, Z., Cao, N., Chen, Z.: Security matters: A survey on adversarial machine learning (2018). https://doi.org/10.48550/arxiv.1810.07339
28. Li, H., Li, L., Xu, X., Zhang, X., Yang, S., Li, B.: Nonlinear projection based gradient estimation for query efficient blackbox attacks (2021). https://doi.org/10.48550/arxiv.2102.13184
29. Li, H., Xu, X., Zhang, X., Yang, S., Li, B.: QEBA: query-efficient boundary-based blackbox attack. CoRR **abs/2005.14137** (2020). https://doi.org/10.48550/arxiv.2005.14137

30. Li, X., Li, F.: Adversarial examples detection in deep networks with convolutional filter statistics (2017). https://doi.org/10.48550/arxiv.1612.07767
31. Liu, Y., Chen, X., Liu, C., Song, D.: Delving into transferable adversarial examples and black-box attacks (2017). https://doi.org/10.48550/arxiv.1611.02770
32. Lu, J., Issaranon, T., Forsyth, D.: Safetynet: Detecting and rejecting adversarial examples robustly (2017). https://doi.org/10.48550/arxiv.1704.00103
33. Lyu, C., Huang, K., Liang, H.N.: A unified gradient regularization family for adversarial examples (2015). https://doi.org/10.48550/arxiv.1511.06385
34. Ma, S., Liu, Y., Tao, G., Lee, W.C., Zhang, X.: Nic: detecting adversarial samples with neural network invariant checking. In: 26th Annual Network And Distributed System Security Symposium (NDSS 2019), Internet Soc (2019)
35. Madry, A., Makelov, A., Schmidt, L., Tsipras, D., Vladu, A.: Towards deep learning models resistant to adversarial attacks (2019). https://doi.org/10.48550/arxiv.1706.06083
36. Marcel, S., Rodriguez, Y.: Torchvision the machine-vision package of torch. In: Proceedings of the 18th ACM International Conference on Multimedia, p. 1485-1488, MM '10, Association for Computing Machinery, New York, NY, USA (2010). ISBN 978160558933 https://doi.org/10.1145/1873951.1874254
37. Meng, D., Chen, H.: Magnet: a two-pronged defense against adversarial examples (2017). https://doi.org/10.48550/arxiv.1705.09064
38. Metzen, J.H., Genewein, T., Fischer, V., Bischoff, B.: On detecting adversarial perturbations (2017). https://doi.org/10.48550/arxiv.1702.04267
39. Papernot, N., McDaniel, P., Goodfellow, I.: Transferability in machine learning: from phenomena to black-box attacks using adversarial samples (2016). https://doi.org/10.48550/arxiv.1605.07277
40. Papernot, N., McDaniel, P., Goodfellow, I., Jha, S., Celik, Z.B., Swami, A.: Practical black-box attacks against machine learning (2017). https://doi.org/10.48550/arxiv.1602.02697
41. PyTorch: Pytorch, resnet50. https://pytorch.org/ (2017). Accessed 06 May 2023
42. Qiu, S., Liu, Q., Zhou, S., Wu, C.: Review of artificial intelligence adversarial attack and defense technologies. Appl. Sci. **9**(5) (2019). ISSN 2076-341https://doi.org/10.3390/app9050909, https://www.mdpi.com/2076-3417/9/5/909
43. Rahmati, A., Moosavi-Dezfooli, S.M., Frossard, P., Dai, H.: Geoda: a geometric framework for black-box adversarial attacks (2020). https://doi.org/10.48550/arxiv.2003.06468
44. Schott, L., Rauber, J., Brendel, W., Bethge, M.: Robust perception through analysis by synthesis. CoRR **abs/1805.09190** (2018). https://doi.org/10.48550/arxiv.1805.09190
45. Shen, S., Jin, G., Gao, K., Zhang, Y.: Ape-gan: adversarial perturbation elimination with gan (2017). https://doi.org/10.48550/arxiv.1707.05474
46. Shi, Y., Han, Y.: Decision-based black-box attack against vision transformers via patch-wise adversarial removal. CoRR **abs/2112.03492** (2021). https://doi.org/10.48550/arxiv.2112.03492
47. Szegedy, C., Zaremba, W., Sutskever, I., Bruna, J., Erhan, D., Goodfellow, I., Fergus, R.: Intriguing properties of neural networks (2014). https://doi.org/10.48550/arxiv.1312.6199
48. Thanh, D.N., Prasath, V., Phung, T.K., Hung, N.Q.: Impulse denoising based on noise accumulation and harmonic analysis techniques. Optik **241**, 166163 (2021), ISSN 0030-402 https://doi.org/10.1016/j.ijleo.2020.166163, https://www.sciencedirect.com/science/article/pii/S0030402620319690

49. Turay, T., Vladimirova, T.: Toward performing image classification and object detection with convolutional neural networks in autonomous driving systems: a survey. IEEE Access **10**, 14076–14119 (2022). https://doi.org/10.1109/ACCESS.2022.3147495
50. Vo, V.Q., Abbasnejad, E., Ranasinghe, D.C.: Query efficient decision based sparse attacks against black-box deep learning models. CoRR **abs/2202.00091** (2022). https://doi.org/10.48550/arxiv.2202.00091
51. Wang, X., Zhang, Z., Tong, K., Gong, D., He, K., Li, Z., Liu, W.: Triangle attack: A query-efficient decision-based adversarial attack. CoRR **abs/2112.06569** (2021). https://doi.org/10.48550/arxiv.2112.06569
52. Xie, C., Wang, J., Zhang, Z., Zhou, Y., Xie, L., Yuille, A.: Adversarial examples for semantic segmentation and object detection (2017). https://doi.org/10.48550/arxiv.1703.08603
53. Xu, H., Ma, Y., Liu, H., Deb, D., Liu, H., Tang, J., Jain, A.K.: Adversarial attacks and defenses in images, graphs and text: a review (2019). https://doi.org/10.48550/arxiv.1909.08072
54. Xu, W., Evans, D., Qi, Y.: Feature squeezing: Detecting adversarial examples in deep neural networks. In: Proceedings 2018 Network and Distributed System Security Symposium, Internet Society (2018). https://doi.org/10.14722/ndss.2018.23198
55. Zuo, F., Yang, B., Li, X., Zeng, Q.: Exploiting the inherent limitation of l0 adversarial examples. In: 22nd International Symposium on Research in Attacks, Intrusions and Defenses (RAID 2019), pp. 293–307 (2019)

Recovery of Trace Links Between a SOFL Formal Specification and Its Corresponding Incomplete Java Code

Jiandong Li[1,2], Shaoying Liu[3(✉)], and Zhi Jin[1,2(✉)]

[1] School of Computer Science, Peking University, Beijing, China
{jiandong.li,zhijin}@pku.edu.cn
[2] Key Laboratory of High-Confidence Software Technologies (PKU), Ministry of Education, Beijing, China
[3] Graduate School of Advanced Science and Engineering, Hiroshima University, Higashihiroshima, Japan
sliu@hiroshima-u.ac.jp

Abstract. Formal specification-based inspection is a practical program verification technique for detecting requirement-related faults and can be applied at any time before or after the code is completed. A high level of automated support for specification-based inspection is desirable as it will help to enhance efficiency and reduce human errors during inspection. To achieve this goal, the open problem of how to link the components in a formal specification to those in the corresponding program must be addressed first, since it is a prerequisite for inspection. By taking advantage of the multi-dimensional attributes of the components in a SOFL formal specification, which are mostly remained in their implementation, we have proposed an approach to establishing trace links between a SOFL formal specification and its corresponding complete code after programming in our previous work. This paper solves the challenge of establishing trace links between a SOFL specification and the incomplete code during programming. The method is comprised of four steps: preprocessing the formal specification, extracting the intermediate states and final states of the multidimensional attributes for components in the specification and the current state of those in its corresponding programs, calculating the similarity, and predicting traceability links through filtering and ranking. A comparative evaluation of the proposed method, using two selected modules of the SOFL formal specification of an ATM system and its Java implementation, demonstrates an improvement in precision than existing latent semantic indexing (LSI) that is an information retrieval-based method.

Keywords: Formal-Specification-to-Code Trace Links · SOFL · Traceability

1 Introduction

Formal specification-based program inspection is a static analysis technique that is used to find the discrepancies between the requirements and its corresponding programs [1, 2]. The essence of formal specification-based program inspection is that human inspector reads programs and checks whether each component in the formal specification describing requirements is implemented correctly in the programs.

The inspection process of formal specification-based methods is usually comprised of the following steps: linking the components in a formal specification to those in the corresponding programs, generating a checklist based on the inspection targets (the components in a formal specification) [1], analyzing related programs, and producing an inspection report. It is widely recognized that formal specification-based program inspection suffers from limited automation due to the human participation in some steps of the whole inspection process. For example, the inspection of Darlington project took 60 people and a period of nearly one year [2]. A high level of automated support for specification-based inspection is desirable as it will help to enhance efficiency and reduce human error during inspections.

Since it would be not easy to achieve the automation of each step in the inspection process one time, we first focus on solving the problem of how to link the components in a formal specification to those in the corresponding programs [9], which is a prerequisite for inspection, to support automatic formal specification-based inspection.

Formal specifications specify software requirements through available well-established mathematical notations, such as SOFL [3], Z, and B-Method. We choose SOFL notation among available formal notations for discussion in this paper mainly based on our expertise and familiarity with it and its successful applications in practice. A SOFL formal specification is comprised of multiple levels of components like modules, operations, and data flows in a high-to-low level order which are usually implemented as Java classes, methods of Java classes, fields of Java classes respectively in Java programs (with some exceptions). The research in this paper focuses on the establishment of fine-grained traceability links that connect a "high-level" SOFL formal specification artifact to the corresponding "low-level" code artifact written in Java programing language (SOFL-to-Java), specifically module-to-class, operation-to-method, and data-flow-to-field trace links.

Even though many researchers have contributed to the development of automatically building traceability links between other types of software artifacts such as informal requirements to source codes [4–6], few works have been seen to automatically build traceability links between a formal specification and its corresponding program implementation. In our previous work, we proposed a systematic method to build the trace links between a SOFL formal specification and its corresponding completed code after programming by taking advantage of the multi-dimensional attributes of the components in a SOFL formal specification [7]. The multi-dimensional attributes including semantic, structural, functional, and relational ones are mostly remained in their implementation by using a programming language like Java, which offers a firm basis to calculate components' similarity and predict the true traceability links. However, the proposed trace links recovery method in our previous work does not perform well in when facing incomplete code during programming.

In this paper, we present a new method for SOFL-specification-to-incomplete-Java-code trace links establishment during programming, aiming to overcome the weakness of existing approaches and support formal specification-based program inspection before the code is completed. The proposed method is comprised of the following steps: (1) preprocessing the formal specification, (2) extracting the intermediate states of the multidimensional attributes for each component in the preprocessed formal specification, (3) extracting the multidimensional attributes for each component in the corresponding Java code under development, (4) calculating similarity scores between all possible pairs of components formed from the formal specification and its corresponding code under development, and (5) ranking and filtering the similarity scores to predict true trace links.

An experiment is conducted to evaluate the proposed SOFL-to-Java traceability links approach by comparing it with two existing and common traceability links methods called naming conventions [8] and latent semantic indexing [9]. The experiment data is two selected modules of the SOFL formal specification of a critical ATM system [10] with 36 specification components and its corresponding Java implementation. The experiment results for 5 incomplete programs implementing 2, 5, 9, 17, 28 components respectively demonstrate that our proposed method could attain 100%, 100%, 100%, 100%, 89.2% precision respectively and is better than latent semantic indexing technique with 100%, 80%, 88.9%, 82.3%, 75% precision respectively in the situation of partially consistent identifiers. Further, the proposed method could also solve traceability links problem for 5 incomplete programs with the 50%, 80%, 66.7%, 82.3% and 71.4% precision without taking identifiers into account.

We make two main contributions in this paper. First, we propose an approach to establish traceability links between a whole formal specification and its corresponding incomplete code. Second, a comparative evaluation for the proposed approach is conducted.

2 SOFL-to-Java Trace Links Recovery Problem

2.1 Transformation from SOFL to Java

SOFL, standing for Structured Object-oriented Formal Language, is a formal specification language [3, 11, 13]. As illustrated in Fig. 1, a SOFL formal specification is a set of modules. Each module is functional abstract and encapsulates a set of process specifications and necessary constant declarations, type declarations, variable (var) declarations, function definitions. The data types provided in SOFL for type declaration include basic type, product type, composite type, enumeration type, map type, sequence type, and set type. State variables are data stores that hold data in rest for use by processes. The constant declarations, type declarations, variable (var) declarations aim to offer data items that need to be taken in or produced by processes or functions (equivalent to operations in general term). A process or a function can be expressed as a 4 tuple $< IV, OV, Pre, Post >$, where IV denotes the set of its input variables, OV denotes the set of its output variables, Pre and $Post$ are its pre-condition and post-condition respectively. Processes P describe the functional requirements or services via pre-condition and post-condition based on predicate logic.

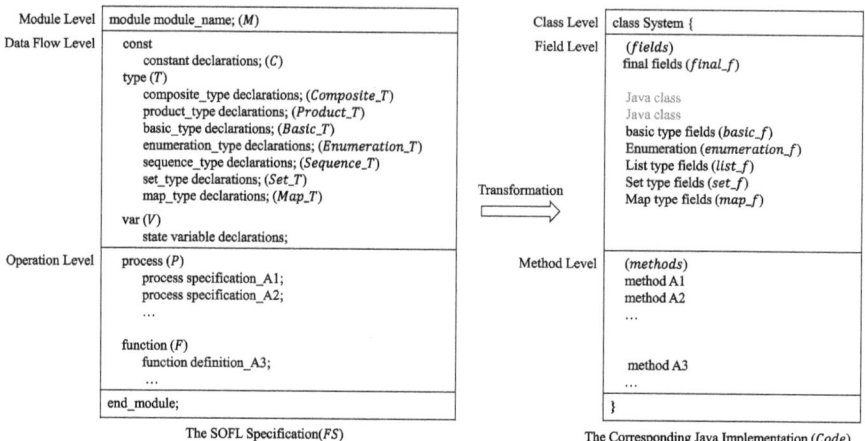

Fig. 1. An illustration of the transformation from SOFL formal specification to Java programs.

Figure 1 also shows various components' corresponding relationships in their transformation from a SOFL specification to its corresponding Java implementation. Data-flow-level components except composite type declarations and product type declarations in the specification are implemented as fields of Java classes. Specifically, in a module, the constant type declarations are transformed to final fields in a Java class; basic type declarations with basic type such as nat0, nat, int, real, bool, char are implemented as fields of basic types in a Java class with int, int, int, double, boolean, char data type respectively; enumeration type declarations are implemented as fields of enumeration data type in a Java class; set type declarations are usually implemented as fields of Set type in a Java class; sequence type declaration are usually implemented as fields of List type in a Java class; map type declarations are usually implemented as fields of Map type in a Java class; compositive type declarations and product type declarations should be implemented as the Java classes. Operation-level components including processes and functions are implemented as methods in Java classes. Module-level components, which are modules, are implemented as Java classes.

2.2 Problem Statement

When formal specification-based inspection is applied before the code is completed, we need to make a solution to the link mapping from the components of a whole formal specification to the ones in the incomplete code. By incomplete code, we mean the current version of the program under construction, which only implements parts of the components describing requirements in the SOFL specification. A precise description is given through the Definition 1 below.

Definition 1. SOFL-Specification-to-Java-Code Traceability Links. Given a SOFL formal specification FS and its corresponding incomplete Java code $Code$, we let $L = \{(s\_c, p\_c) | s\_c \in Component_{FS}, p\_c \in Component_{Code}, s\_c \leftrightarrow p\_c\}$ denote a trace link between $Component_{FS}$, and $Component_{Code}$, where $Component_{Code}$ denotes the set of components of Code and each pair of components s_c and p_c is called the transformative link represented by ↔.

3 The Approach for SOFL-to-Java Trace Links Recovery

In this section, we present the proposed SOFL-to-Java trace links establishment approach for incomplete code from the following aspects including the supported principle, the proposed workflow, the detailed introduction of trace links establishment process.

3.1 The Principle Supporting Trace Links Establishment between a Whole SOFL Specification and an Incomplete Java Code

SOFL formal specifications are different from other artefacts such as the informal requirements written in natural language. We find that every component in a formal specification has its own attributes concerned with its semantics, structure, function, and relationships with other components in the same specification during their interactions, as shown Table 1. Table 2 classifies the 33 attributes into 4 categories of semantic, structure, function and relation based on the designed dimension. Different types of components in a SOFL specification own different attributes as shown in Table 3. We call such attributes *multi-dimensional attributes*. Despite some variants referring to syntactical changes during the transformation from specifications to programs, these four different kinds of attributes of each component in a SOFL specification are remained in their implementation by using a programming language like Java. This is the first principle that supports the proposed SOFL-to-Java trace links recovery method.

In addition, the feature of *from part to whole* construction of a formal specification inspires us to have an idea of breaking this imbalance caused by information asymmetry and establish correspondence between incomplete information derived from a whole specification and the one from incomplete programs. The is the second principle that supports our solution to build SOFL-to- Java traceability links for incomplete programs.

To ensure the comprehensibility of the following discussion, a money-box example is given in Fig. 2. The money-box has three required functions: *save money*, *check money* and *purchase toy* with a fixed price of 1500 Japanese yen.

The *part-to-whole* construction means that the formal specification can be split into pieces, which can be used to extract their multi-dimensional attributes in Table 1. Figure 3 illustrated the feature from part to whole construction of the *Money_Box* module.

In step 1 of Fig. 3, the module *Money_Box* only contains its identifier. The attribute set that is extracted for the piece corresponding to step 1 of the module "Money_Box" is as follows:

{ *'identifier'*: *'Money_Box'*, 'type': 'class', 'data-type': 'class', *'fields-type'*: '', *'fields-amount'*: *0*, *'fields-identifier'*: '', 'identifier-of-interacted-field': '', 'type-of-interacted-field': '', 'amount-of-interacted-field': 0, 'identifier-of-interacted-method-with-parameter': '', 'amount-of-interacted-method-with-parameter': 0, 'identifier-of-interacted-method-with-return-type-part': '',

Table 1. Designed Attributes for Components of SOFL Specification and Java Code.

ID	Attribute Name and Explanation	Value Type
1	**identifier** – What is its identifier?	String
2	**type** – Will it be transformed into class or field or method in Java programs?	String
3	**dataType** – What is its type? < basic, set, map, etc.. >	String
4	**constantValue** – What is its constant value?	String
5	**enumerationValue** – What is the enumeration value?	String
6	**elementType** – What is the data type of its element?	String
7	**domainType** – What is the domain type of a map type field?	String
8	**rangeType** – What is the range type of a map type field?	String
9	**parameterAmount** – How many parameters does a method have?	Integer
10	**parameterType** – What types are the input parameters of a method?	String
11	**returnValueType** – What is the return type of a method?	String
12	**feildType** – What are the types of constitutive fields of a class?	String
13	**fieldIdentifier** – What are the identifiers of constitutive fields of a class?	String
14	**fieldAmount** – What is the number of constitutive fields of a class?	Integer
15	**methodAmount** – How many methods does a class have?	Integer
16	**methodIdentifier** – What are the identifiers of methods that a class have?	String
17	**methodParameterType** – What are the types of the parameters of methods that a class have?	String
18	**methodReturnType** – What are the return types of methods that a class have?	String
19	**interactedFieldType** – What are the types of other components interacting with this component?	String
20	**interactedFieldAmount** – How many other field-level components interact with it?	Integer
21	**amountOfInteractedMethodWithInputParamters** – How many methods use this component as the input parameter?	Integer
22	**identifierOfInteractedMethodWithInputParamters** – What are the identifiers of the methods using this component as the input parameter?	String
23	**amountOfInteractedMehodWithReturnType** – How many methods use this component as the return type?	Integer
24	**identifierOf InteractedMehodWithReturnType** – What are the identifiers of the methods using this component as the return type?	String
25	**amountOfInteractedMethodWithBody** –What are their identifiers of those methods using this component in their method bodies?	Integer

(continued)

Table 1. (*continued*)

ID	Attribute Name and Explanation	Value Type
26	**identifierOfInteractedMethodWithBody** – How many methods use this component in their method bodies?	String
27	**amountOfInteractedMethodInTheSameClass** – How many local class's methods use this component?	Integer
28	**amountOfInteractedMethodInOtherClass** – How many other classes' methods use this component?	Integer
29	**interactedClassType** – What are the types of interacted classes?	String
30	**interactedClassIdentifier** – What are the identifiers of interacted classes?	String
31	**interactedClassAmount** – How many classes does it interact?	Integer
32	**interactedCallMethodIdentifier** – What are the identifiers of other methods calling the method?	String
33	**interactedCallMethodAmount** – How many methods call the method?	String

Table 2. Attributes Classification.

Classification	Attribute Combination	Attribute Amount
Semantical Attributes	1	1
Structural Attributes	2 - 18	17
Functional Attributes		0
Relational Attributes	19 - 33	15

'amount-of-interacted-method-with-return-part': 0, 'identifier-of-interacted-method-with-body-part': '', 'amount-of-interacted-method-with-body-part': 0, 'amount-of-interacted-method-in-class': 0, 'amount-of-interacted-method-outside-class': 0, 'identifier-of-interacted-class': '', 'method_amount': 0, 'method_identifier': '', 'method-parameter-type': '', 'return-type-of-method': '', 'amount-of-interacted-class': 0}.

In step *i* of Fig. 3, *i* refers to some time during specification development, the module *Money_Box* grows by adding the constant declaration and variable declaration. The attribute set that is extracted for the piece corresponding to step *i* of the module "Money_Box" is as follows:

{'identifier': 'Money_Box', 'type': 'class', 'data-type': 'class', *'fields-type'*: *'1500 int'*, *'fields-amount'*: *2*, *'fields-identifier'*: *'toy_price money_box'*, 'identifier-of-interacted-field': '', 'type-of-interacted-field': '', 'amount-of-interacted-field': 0,

Table 3. Attributes For Various Components in SOFL Specification and Java Code.

Type of Component	Attribute Combination	Attribute Amount
constant type declaration in SOFL/ final field in Java	1 – 4, 25 - 31	11
basic type declaration in SOFL / basic type field in Java	1 – 3, 19, 20, 25 – 31	12
set type declaration in SOFL / Set type field in Java	1 – 3, 6, 19 – 31	17
sequence type declaration in SOFL / List type field in Java	1 – 3, 6, 19 – 31	17
map type declaration in SOFL / Map type field in Java	1 – 3, 7, 8, 19 – 31	18
enumeration type declaration in SOFL / Enumeration type field in Java	1 – 3, 5, 19 – 31	17
composite type declaration or product type declaration in SOFL	1 – 3, 12 – 14, 19 – 31	19
process or function in SOFL / method in Java	1 – 3, 9 – 11, 19, 20, 29 – 33,	13
module in SOFL / Class in Java	1 – 3, 12 – 31	23

'identifier-of-interacted-method-with-parameter': '', 'amount-of-interacted-method-with-parameter': 0, 'identifier-of-interacted-method-with-return-type-part': '', 'amount-of-interacted-method-with-return-part': 0, 'identifier-of-interacted-method-with-body-part': '', 'amount-of-interacted-method-with-body-part': 0, 'amount-of-interacted-method-in-class': 0, 'amount-of-interacted-method-outside-class': 0, 'identifier-of-interacted-class': '', 'method_amount': 0, 'method_identifier': '', 'method-parameter-type': '', 'return-type-of-method': '', 'amount-of-interacted-class': 0}.

In step j of Fig. 3, j refers to the time when the development of the specification is finished, the module *Money_Box* grows by adding process specifications. The attribute set that is extracted for the piece corresponding to step j of the module "Money_Box" is as follows:

{*'identifier'*: *'Money_Box'*, 'type': 'class', 'data-type': 'class', *'fields-type'*: *'1500 int'*, *'fields-amount'*: 2, *'fields-identifier'*: *'toy_price money_box'*, 'identifier-of-interacted-field': '', 'type-of-interacted-field': '', 'amount-of-interacted-field': 0, 'identifier-of-interacted-method-with-parameter': '', 'amount-of-interacted-method-with-parameter': 0, 'identifier-of-interacted-method-with-return-type-part': '', 'amount-of-interacted-method-with-return-part': 0, 'identifier-of-interacted-method-with-body-part': '', 'amount-of-interacted-method-with-body-part': 0, 'amount-of-interacted-method-in-class': 0, 'amount-of-interacted-method-outside-class': 0, 'identifier-of-interacted-class': '', *'method_amount'*: 3, *'method_identifier'*: *'Save_Money Check_Money Purchase_Toy'*, *'method-parameter-type'*: *'int void void'*, *'return-type-of-method'*: *'void int int string'*, 'amount-of-interacted-class': 0}.

Recovery of Trace Links Between a SOFL Formal Specification

```
module Money_Box                              public class Money_Box {
    const                                         public static final int toy_price = 1500;
        toy_price = 1500                          private int money_box = 0;
    var                                           void save_money(int amount) {
        money_box: int                                if (amount >0) {
    process Save_Money(amount: int)                       money_box += amount;
        ext wr money_box                          }}
        pre amount > 0.0                          int check_money() {
        post money_box = ~money_box + amount          return money_box; }
    end_process;                                  int purchase_toy() {
    process Check_Money() total: int                  int expense;
        ext rd money_box                              if (money_box >= toy_price) {
        post total = money_box                            money_box -= toy_price;
    end_process;                                          expense = toy_price;
    process Purchase_Toy() expense: int | warning: string     return expense;
        ext wr money_box
        post ~money_box >= toy_price and expense =    } else {
toy_price and money_box = ~money_box – toy_price              System.out.println("the shortage of the money in the
        or                                        money_box, failed transaction");
        ~money_box < toy_price and warning = "the shortage        expense = 0;
of the money in the money_box, failed transaction"            return expense;
    end_process;                                  }}
end_module;                                       public static void main(String args[]) {
                                                      Money_Box ljd = new Money_Box();
                                                      System.out.println(ljd.check_money());
                                                      ljd.save_money(2000);
                                                      int cost = ljd.purchase_toy();
                                                      System.out.println("cost is " + cost);
                                                      System.out.println(ljd.money_box);
                                                  }
                                              }
```

Fig. 2. A money-box example of the transformation from a SOFL specification to its Java implementation.

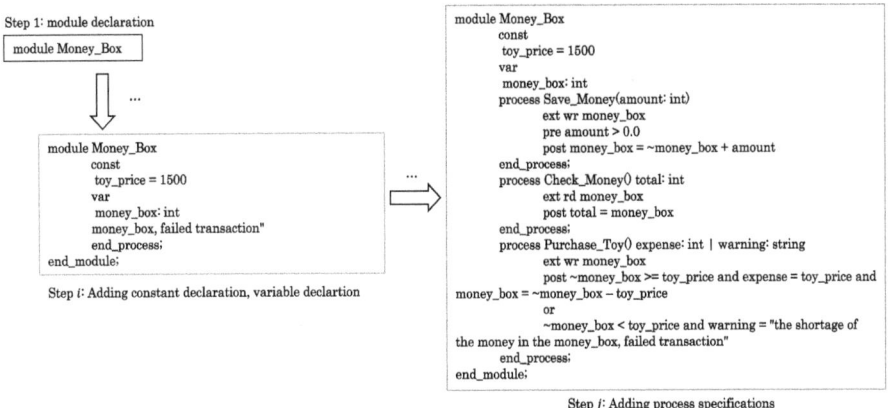

Fig. 3. An illustration of part-to-whole construction in SOFL specification development.

During the construction of the module *Money-Box* from step 1 to step i, we could see the change of the values of the multi-dimensional attributes. Here we call the values of the multi-dimensional attributes extracted for each component before the specification is completed **states**. The values of the attribute set, which is extracted from a component when it is declared, is called ***initial state***, such as the state of step 1. The values of the attribute set, which is extracted from component when the construction of the specification is completed, is called ***final state***, such as the state of step j. ***Intermediate states*** are the values of the attribute set that is extracted at any time from the declaration of a component itself and the construction process of the whole specification, such as the state of step i. The intermediate state for each component is dynamically changing during the construction of the formal specification. Each component in the formal specification has an intermediate state set.

The value of the multi-dimensional attribute set extracted from components in the incomplete programs (current version of program under construction) is called *current state*. Each component in the incomplete program has only one current state. The current state of a component from the incomplete programs is usually corresponding to an intermediate state of a component from the formal specification. We could capture the transformative relationships between components of formal specifications and the ones in incomplete programs by calculating the similarity between the current state representing a component in Java programs and each intermediate state representing a component in a SOFL formal specification.

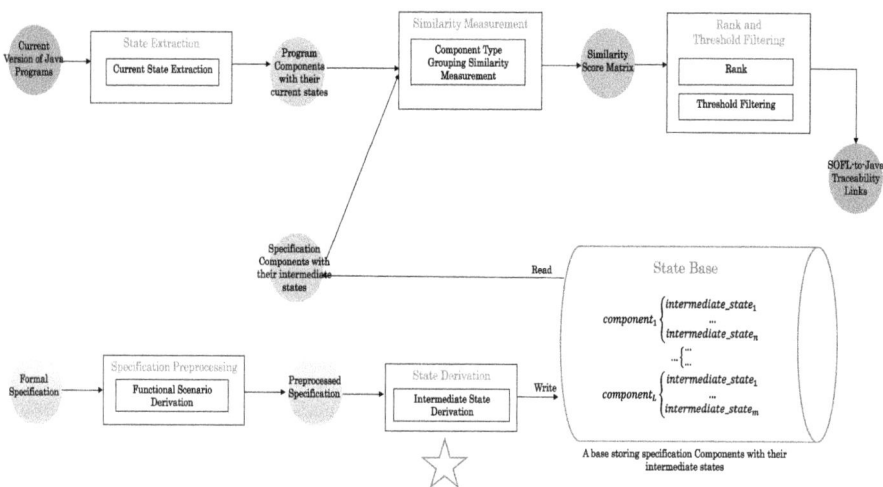

Fig. 4. The proposed workflow of establishing SOFL-to-Java traceability links for incomplete programs.

3.2 The Workflow of Establishing Trace Links for Incomplete Code

The workflow for establishing trace links for incomplete programs is presented in Fig. 4. The proposed method is comprised of the following steps: (1) preprocessing formal specification, (2) extracting the intermediate states for each specification component, (3) extracting the current state for each component in the incomplete Java code, (4) calculating similarity scores between all possible pairs of components formed from the formal specification and its corresponding programs, and (5) ranking the similarity scores to predict true trace links.

Based on Table 1 and Table 3, the component identification and attribute extraction in the formal specification are done statically, using lexical analysis, syntax analysis and rules to analyse the specification [12]. Given the incomplete code implementing a specification, the tokens of each component could be obtained by lexical analysis and the abstract syntactical tree (AST) of code could be built by syntactical analysis, which can be traversed and analysed to extract different information about the multi-dimensional attributes as shown in Table 1 and Table 3. The extracted attribute sets for multilevel components of both SOFL specifications and Java codes are the basis to measure their similarity. To calculate the similarity score or trace link score, we select three existing similarity measurement techniques including longest common subsequence-both (LCS-B), cosine similarity, and the similarity measurement between two numbers. A matrix of similarity scores is generated or constructed after the similarity calculation by the integrated application of above similarity measurement technique. Steps (1), (4), (5) are detailed in [7] and we omit the explanation here. The point in this workflow is to derive the intermediate state set for each component from the whole formal specification.

3.2.1 Derive Intermediate States for Each Component in SOFL Specification

Given a formal specification *FS* and the set of its components $Component_{FS}$, we need to derive a set of intermediate states $component\_inermediate\_state_i = \{intermediate\_state_{i1}, intermediate\_state_{i2}, \cdots, intermediate\_state_{in}\}$ for any component $component_i \in Component_{FS}$.

The intermediate state for each component in a formal specification is characterized by its changeability. We find that three conditions trigger the generation and the change of intermediate states for each component. These three conditions are as follows.

Condition 1. *For each component in a SOFL specification, the declaration of itself leads to the generation of an intermediate state (initial state).*

Condition 2. *For each component, which is a module or a composite or product type declaration in a SOFL specification, the addition of its element leads to the generation and the change of an intermediate state. The types of elements in a module contains type declaration, process specification, function definition, etc. The elements in a composite type declaration or a product type declaration refer to their fields.*

Condition 3. *For each component in a SOFL specification, its interaction with other components leads to the generation of an intermediate state. The interaction refers to the relationships between components, which are shown in Table 2 of reference* [11].

Based on the three intermediate state generation and change conditions, we propose the following 5 steps to derive the set of intermediate states for components from a whole formal specification. To ensure the comprehensibility of our discussion, we also use the money-box example in Fig. 2 to explain it.

(1) Identify and extract all components $Component_{FS}$ from the given completed formal specification *FS*.

As shown in Fig. 5, after step (1), 6 constitutive components are extracted from the *money-box* specification. Their identifiers are *Money_Box, toy_price, money_box, Save_Money, Check_Money,* and *Purchase_Toy* respectively. The constitutive components of a formal specification are recognized by rules based on the general syntactical structures and modifiers of various components. For example, the part starting from modifier "*module*" and ending with "*end_module*" in a formal specification is an identified module component. In essence, the rule-based component recognition is the syntactical analysis of formal specifications.

(2) Build a dependence graph for each component $component_i \in Component_{FS}$.

The dependence graphs built for each constitutive component of the *money-box* specification are presented as an example in Fig. 6. There are two kinds of relationships in the constructed dependence graph. One is called *"depend on"* and another one is call *"be dependent on"*. It should be pointed that each component, which is not a module or composite type declaration or product declaration, depends on the declaration of the module that encapsulates the component. For example, the constant type declaration *toy_price* depends on the declaration of the module *Money_Box*. This is because *toy_price* is part of *Money_Box*. In other words, the *Money_Box* must be declared before the declaration of *toy_price*.

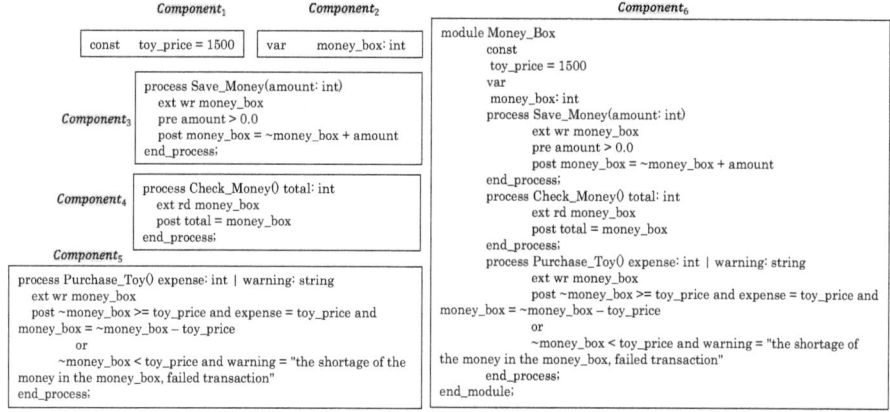

Fig. 5. Six components extracted from the money-box specification.

(3) Based on the dependence graph for each component $component_i \in Component_{FS}$, reorganize the related components to generate a new specification $spec_{component_i}$ for $component_i$;

A set of new specifications $\{spec_{component_1}, \cdots, spec_{component_n}\}$ are generated in step (3). After reorganizing the specification based on the dependence graphs, the generate new specifications $spec_{toy\_price}$, $spec_{money\_box}$ and $spec_{save\_money}$ that are specific to the components *toy_price, money_box* and *Save_Money* respectively are illustrated in Fig. 7. The new specifications $spec_{toy\_price}$, $spec_{money\_box}$ and $spec_{save\_money}$ are meaningful for components *toy_price, money_box* and *Save_Money*, even though they are not right and incomplete in terms of the syntactic norms of SOFL formal language.

(4) Based on the corresponding new specification $spec_{component_i}$ for the component $component_i \in Component_{FS}$, slice the reorganized specification $spec_{component_i}$ to get a set of slices $slice_i = \{slice_i\_1, slice_i\_2, \cdots, slice_i\_N\}$ based on the above

mentioned three conditions, Condition 1, 2 and 3, which are actually the slicing criterions.

Figure 8 shows the slicing result for the reorganized specification $spec_{toy\_price}$ corresponding to the component *toy_price*. Two slices in $slice_{toy\_price}$ are generated when *toy_price* component is declared, and it is used in the body of process *Purchase_Toy*.

(5) For each component $component_i \in Component_{FS}$, extract intermediate state $intermediate\_state_{ij}$ from each slice $slice_i\_j$ in the corresponding slice set $slice_i$;

Only one intermediate state could be extracted from one slice. For a component $component_i \in Component_{FS}$, the number of its intermediate states is equal to the cardinality of the corresponding slice set $slice_i$. The cardinality of $slice_i$ is the number of elements in $slice_i$. To extract the multi-dimensional attributes from each slice $slice_i\_j$ in the corresponding slice set $slice_i$ is based on Table 1 and Table 3.

For instance, all the attributes that are extracted for constant type declaration "toy_price" of the *money-box* example from $slice_{toy\_price}\_1$ in Fig. 8 are as follows:

{'identifier': 'toy_price', 'type': 'field', 'data-type': 'final', 'constant-value': 1500, 'identifier-of-interacted-method-with-body: '', 'amount-of-interacted-method-with-body': 0, 'amount-of-interacted-method-in-class': 0, 'amount-of-interacted-outside- class': 0, 'identifier-of-interacted-class': 'Money_Box', 'amount-of-interacted-class': 1}.

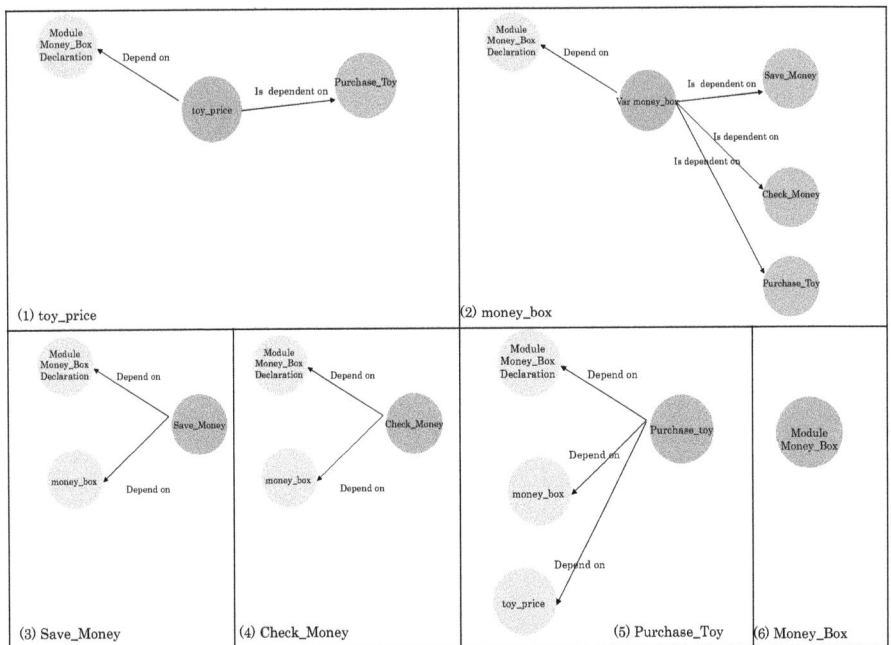

Fig. 6. The dependence graphs for the components in the money-box specification.

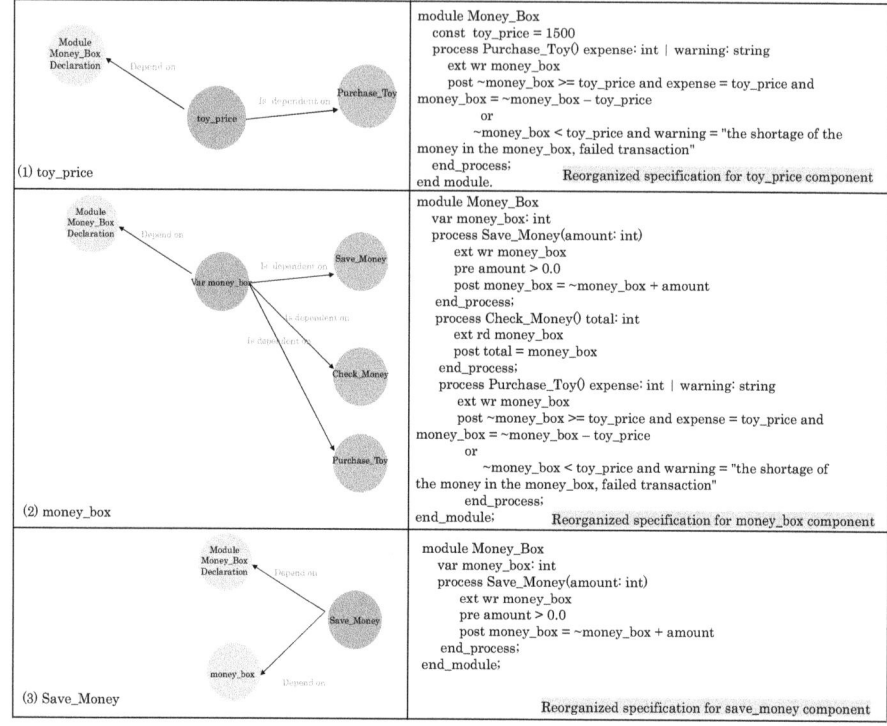

Fig. 7. Part of the reorganized specifications generated in Step (3) for the components in money-box specification.

The attribute set that is extracted for constant type declaration "toy_price" from $slice_{toy\_price}\_2$ in Fig. 8 are as follows:

{'identifier': 'toy_price', 'type': 'field', 'data-type': 'final', 'constant-value': 1500, *'identifier-of-interacted-method-with-body': 'Purchase_Toy', 'amount-of-interacted-method-with-body': 1, 'amount-of-interacted-method-in-class': 1,* 'amount-of-interacted-outside-class': 0, 'identifier-of-interacted-class': 'Money_Box', 'amount-of-interacted-class': 1}.

3.2.2 The Number of Intermediate States

In step (4) of Sect. 3.2.1, there is a subproblem, which is how many intermediate states could be derived for each component $component_i \in Component_{FS}$. We provide a solution for it by using permutations and combinations that are part of a branch of mathematics [38]. Given a component $component_i$ and a dependence graph DG built for $component_i$, we could get three sets from DG, which are set of its declaration $declaration_i$, set of its elements $element_i$, set of its interactions $interaction_i$. The number of elements in the set $declaration_i$ is always 1. Let M and N denote the number of elements in $element_i$ and $interaction_i$ respectively. Selections of element from the three sets $declaration_i$, $element_i$, $interaction_i$ follow the following rule that is the element in $declaration_i$ must be select first. Theoretically, the number of the intermediate states of *component*$_i$ is the total number of combinations to choose 1 element from *declaration*$_i$, *m* elements from *element*$_i$ and *n* elements from *interaction*$_i$, where $m = 0, \cdots, M$ and $n = 0, \cdots, N$. It can be expresses as following:

$$\text{the number of intermediate states of } component_i = 1 + \sum_{\substack{m = 0, \cdots, M \\ n = 0, \cdots, N}} C_M^m C_N^n$$

Let us take the state variable declaration *money_box* as the example. The number of elements in *declaration*$_{money\_box}$, *element*$_{money\_box}$, *interaction*$_{money\_box}$ are 1, 0, and 3 respectively. Then the number of intermediate states of *component*$_{money\_box}$ is $1 + C_0^0 \times C_3^1 + C_0^0 \times C_3^2 + C_0^0 \times C_3^3 = 8$.

When the size of a formal specification becomes big, the number of intermediate states extracted for all the components in the formal specification will be huge too. We suggest a breadth-first traversal method of the dependence graph to reduce the intermediate states. For example, only 4 intermediate states will be extracted for the component.

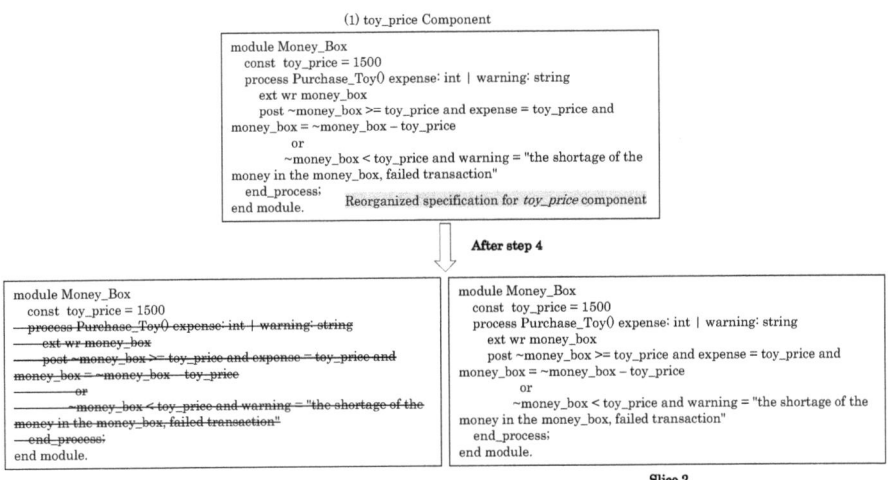

Fig. 8. The slices after slicing *spec*$_{toy\_price}$ based on the slicing criterions.

money_box by using breadth-first traversal method. The breadth-first traversal result of the dependence graph of state variable declaration *money_box* could be "*var money_box, Save_Money, Check_Money, Purchase_Toy*". The "*var money_box*", "*var money_box, Save_Money*", "*var money_box, Save_Money, Check_Money*", and "*var money_box, Save_Money, Check_Money, Purchase_Toy*" are corresponding to the 4 slices from which the 4 intermediate states are extracted.

4 A Controlled Experiment and Evaluation

This section describes a controlled experiment used to evaluate the performance of the proposed method, presents the results obtained, and discuss the findings.

4.1 Research Questions

To evaluate our proposed method about incomplete programs, we are concerned about the following research questions:

- How effective is our proposed method in establishing SOFL-to-Java traceability links for incomplete programs in the situation of partially consistent identifiers during implementation? (RQ1)
- How effective is our proposed method in establishing SOFL-to-Java traceability links for incomplete programs in the situation of inconsistent identifiers during implementation? (RQ2)
- Is the performance of proposed method better than existing LSI method? (RQ3)

4.2 Experiment Result

To answer these questions, we use 5 incomplete Java programs, *breakpoint 2, breakpoint 5, breakpoint 9, breakpoint 17, breakpoint 28*, from the complete Java programs implementing the SOFL specification of the ATM system that contains 36 components in total as the experiment data [7, 10]. The number like 2 after "*breakpoint*" refers to the number of components in the SOFL specification that have been implemented or are implementing by the incomplete Java programs. 170 intermediate states are derived and extracted for the total 36 components in the SOFL formal specification of an ATM system by using the simplified breadth-first traverse method. To answer RQ1 and RQ2, we use 0.7 as the similarity threshold in the situation of partially consistent identifiers and 0.8 as the similarity threshold in the situation of inconsistent identifiers. The similarity thresholds 0.7 and 0.8 are selected based on our previous work [7].

Table 4 illustrates the result for RQ1. We see that, our proposed method can solve the problem effectively. However, performance like the recall and precision tends to degrade with the increase of component types. Table 5 shows the result for RQ2. We see that, the recall of proposed method is good while its precision decreases compared to the situation of partially consistent identifiers taking the identifiers (semantic attribute) into account. Table 6 presents the performance comparison result between our proposed method and the existing LSI technique. We see that our proposed method is better in precision than LSI technique.

Table 4. Experiment Result for RQ1.

Incomplete program ID	Situation	Number of components in the incomplete program	Recall	Precision
Breakpoint 2	partially consistent identifiers	2	100%(2/2)	100%(2/2)
Breakpoint 5		5	100%(5/5)	100%(5/5)
Breakpoint 9		9	100%(9/9)	100%(9/9)
Breakpoint 17		17	100%(17/17)	100%(17/17)
Breakpoint 28		28	82.1%(23/28)	92%(23/25)

Table 5. Experiment Result for RQ2.

Incomplete program ID	Situation	Number of components in the incomplete program	Recall	Precision
Breakpoint 2	inconsistent identifiers	2	50%(1/2)	50%(1/2)
Breakpoint 5		5	80%(4/5)	80%(4/5)
Breakpoint 9		9	66.7%(6/9)	66.7%(6/9)
Breakpoint 17		17	82.3%(14/17)	82.3%(14/17)
Breakpoint 28		28	71.4%(20/28)	71.4%(20/28)

Table 6. Experiment Result for RQ3.

Situation	Incomplete program ID	Number of components in the incomplete program	Method	Precision
partially consistent identifiers	Breakpoint 2	2	Proposed method	100%(2/2)
			LSI	100%(2/2)
	Breakpoint 5	5	Proposed method	100%(5/5)
			LSI	80%(4/5)
	Breakpoint 9	9	Proposed method	100%(9/9)
			LSI	88.9%(8/9)
	Breakpoint 17	17	Proposed method	100%(17/17)
			LSI	82.3%(14/17)
	Breakpoint 28	28	Proposed method	89.2%(25/28)
			LSI	75%(21/28)

5 Conclusion

We have described an approach for establishing multilevel SOFL-to-Java traceability links for incomplete programs. The underlying principle of the method is based on the semantic, structural, functional, and relational attributes of components in the formal specification that should be remained in their corresponding code implementations. The establishment process could be carried out step by step, includes four activities: the preprocess of the formal specification, multi-dimensional attributes extraction for the components of both specification and codes, similarity measurement, trace links prediction by ranking and threshold filtering. Specific techniques for each of these activities are discussed. Further, we have conducted a comparative evaluation of the proposed approach and present our findings, experience and lessons learned. The results show that our proposed method gives an accurate and fine-grained view of the relationships between the SOFL specification and Java code artefacts.

References

1. Liu, S., Chen, Y., Nagoya, F., McDermid, J.A.: Formal specification-based inspection for verification of programs. IEEE Trans. software Eng. SE-**38**(5), 1100–1122 (2012)
2. Parnas, D.L., Asmis, G., Madey, J.: Assessment of safety-critical software in nuclear power plants. Nuclear Safety **32**(2), 189–198 (1991)
3. Liu, S.: Formal engineering for industrial software development using the sofl method, (Springer Science & Business Media, 2013)
4. Cleland-Huang, J., Gotel, O.C., Huffman Hayes, J., Mäder, P., Zisman, A.: Software traceability: trends and future directions. In: Future of Software Engineering Proceedings, (pp. 55–69), 2014
5. Winkler, S., Von Pilgrim, J.: A survey of traceability in requirements engineering and model-driven development. Softw. Syst. Model. **9**(4), 529–565 (2010)
6. Lin, J., Liu, Y., Zeng, Q., Jiang, M., Cleland-Huang, J.: traceability transformed: generating more accurate links with pre-trained BERT models. In: Proceedings of the 43rd International Conference on Sofware Engineering, pp. 324–335 (2021)
7. Li, J., Liu, S., Liu, A., Huang, R.: Multilevel traceability links establishments between SOFL formal specifications and java codes using multi-dimensional similarity measures. In: Proceedings of 2021 IEEE International Conference on Quality, Reliability and Security (QRS 2021), IEEE Press, Hainan Island, China, December, pp. 6–10 (2021)
8. White, R., Krinke J., Tan, R..: Establishing multilevel test-to-code traceability links. In Proceedings of the ACM/IEEE 42nd International Conference on Software Engineering, pp. 861–872 (2020)
9. Marcus, A., Maletic, J.I.: Recovering documentation-to-source-code traceability links using latent semantic indexing. In: 25th International Conference on Software Engineering, pp. 125–135 (2003)
10. Liu, S.: A case study of modeling an ATM using SOFL. Tech.l Report (2013)
11. Li, J., Liu, S., Liu, A., Huang, R.: Knowledge graph construction for SOFL formal specifications. Int. J. Software Eng. Knowl. Eng. **32**(04), 605–644 (2022)
12. Zhu, S., Liu, S.: A supporting tool for syntactic analysis of SOFL formal specifications and SOFL formal specifications and automatic generation of functional scenarios. In: SOFL+MSVL 2013. Lecture Notes in Computer Science, vol 8332. Springer, Cham (2014)
13. Li, J., Liu, S.: Requirements-related fault prevention during the transformation from formal specifications to programs. IET Software **17**(3), 316–332 (2023)

S3DA: A 3D Point Cloud Based PCB Solder Defect Detection Algorithm

Yilongfei Xu, Zhewei Wang, Jinhao Liang, Yueling Zhang[✉], Jincao Feng[✉], Weikai Miao[✉], Jiangtao Wang, and Geguang Pu

East China Normal University, Shanghai, China
{ylzhang,wkmiao}@sei.ecnu.edu.cn, jincaofeng@foxmail.com

Abstract. Surface Mount Technology (SMT) is prevalent in Printed Circuit Board (PCB) assembly, mainly using solder printing to connect the components and the board. During the process of solder printing, solder defects due to machine failure and environmental factors are widespread. Existing defect detection methods mainly use computer vision to detect solder defects. The main idea of this type of method is to obtain the image information and defect features of the PCB and use the machine learning model to identify the solder defects of the PCB. In actual industrial PCB assembly, the lack of illumination and the occlusion caused by other workpieces leads to incomplete input images for machine learning models, which makes existing methods unable to detect such occluded defects. In order to solve the above problems, this paper proposes a new algorithm for solder defect detection using 3D point cloud data. First, the point cloud data is obtained by scanning the 3D point cloud camera. Next, the point cloud data is denoised and filtered, and the area of interest is further screened to obtain the solder area to be calculated. Finally, using the idea based on integral summation, solder defects are identified by calculating the solder volume. This algorithm can automatically assist manual judgment and effectively identify possible defects in solder processing.

Keywords: Automatic Optical Inspection (AOI) · Defect detection · Solder joint · Point cloud

1 Introduction

SMT technology, where electronic components like resistors and ICs are attached to PCBs using solder, is vital in making various electronic devices, from smartphones to automotive electronics [1]. Despite its prevalence, the soldering process can face challenges such as uncontrollable solder flow due to environmental factors [2], leading to defects like solder accumulation or loss. These defects can make PCBs brittle or cause failures, and fixing them later in production is costly due to the *10X Rule*, emphasizing the need for early defect detection. "Solder paste volume is key to quality [3]." The leading cause of solder defects is mainly that the solder volume is not within the normal volume threshold range. Early detection of solder defects in PCB produced on the assembly line was through visual identification and basic electrical inspection by experienced production line workers [4,5]. This traditional method is extraordinarily time-consuming and limited by the experience of operators. If defects can be detected automatically, then the cost of rework and cycle time can be greatly reduced [3].

At present, Automatic Optical Inspection is the mainstream method in the industry [6]. AOI uses a high-precision camera to obtain PCB images and then applies image processing, machine learning, or geometric methods to locate and detect solder defects. For AOI methods, the image accuracy achieved in the initial step ensures the integrity of all subsequent analyses. In other words, the detection accuracy is constrained by the image quality of the PCB. Insufficient lighting or occlusion can result in blurred or incomplete image features, thereby compromising the ability to detect defects. To overcome this challenge, researchers have proposed novel image acquisition methods to extract diverse information for detection, such as 3D point cloud [7]. The proposed method takes into account the dimensional information of the image and addresses the issue of incomplete information caused by viewing angle problems or occlusions. This approach enriches the image information from multiple perspectives, allowing for the extraction of higher-dimensional information and a greater number of image features. As a result, it provides a foundation for incorporating new technologies to further analyze images. However, it is important to acknowledge that working with 3D point cloud data presents both benefits and challenges. On one hand, it enables the extraction of richer information, enhancing the analysis capabilities. On the other hand, the presence of noise and complex features within 3D point cloud data introduces difficulties in obtaining reliable and high-quality data.

In order to solve the shortcomings of the existing technology, this paper proposes a novel solder defect detection algorithm based on the integral calculation of volume. By leveraging 3D point cloud data instead of traditional 2D PCB images, the algorithm effectively captures the volumetric characteristics of solder defects. Notably, this paper pioneers the use of integral summation method to calculate the volume of PCB solder parts within 3D point cloud data and utilizes this metric as the criterion for defect classification.

Overall, the main contributions of this paper are as follows:

1. Based on the idea of integral summation, a novel method for calculating the volume of PCB solder in the 3D point cloud is proposed.
2. A novel PCB solder defect detection algorithm based on that volume calculation algorithm is proposed, which solves the problem that defects cannot be detected due to inadequate lighting or occlusion.
3. A specialized dataset consisting of point clouds obtained from a binocular lidar system is introduced to evaluate the performance of the algorithm.

The remaining sections of this paper are structured as follows: Sect. 2 provides an overview of related works in the field. Section 3 outlines the fundamental methodology of the algorithm. Section 4 presents the experimental setup designed to validate the algorithm's effectiveness. Section 5 summarizes the key findings of this study and provides suggestions for future enhancements.

2 Related Work

2.1 Automatic Optical Inspection

Automatic Optical Inspection (AOI) has emerged as the prevailing methodology for automatic inspection of solder defects in the contemporary era. AOI principally employs high-resolution imaging devices to procure superior quality images of Printed Circuit Boards (PCBs), followed by the integration of detection algorithms into industrial control computer platforms for the identification of PCB anomalies [8]. The AOI process typically encompasses three stages: (1) Image Acquisition, (2) Solder Joint Localization, and (3) Classification. The latter two stages are frequently the subject of rigorous scholarly investigation [9].

Solder Joint Localization. Solder joint positioning is the basis of the entire solder defect detection. The required position of the solder is called the Region Of Interest (ROI), there are three prevalent methods to realize the localization of solder joints: template matching, image histogram, and deep neural networks.

Template matching is a feature-based method, which always includes position prior knowledge or explicit template information, and extracts ROI by calculating the similarity between the part to be tested and the template. For example, Gaidhane et al. [10] use the rank of the symmetric matrix as a measure of similarity and obtain the position of the ROI by measuring the similarity between the scene image and the PCB surface reference image. Specifically they computed a symmetric matrix using the companion matrices of the two compared images without computing image features such as eigenvalues and eigenvectors, which simplifies the computational complexity of pattern matching and achieves better performance. When the region of interest (ROI) is known a priori, the method based on pattern matching eliminates the necessity for training intricate models and assembling labeled datasets. Yet, this advantage may concurrently lead to a diminished capacity for generalization inherent in this approach.

Histogram-based methodologies primarily determine a global threshold by leveraging the specific interrelations between pixels within the PCB image, which then serves as the benchmark for identifying the ROI. Such methods may include employing the mean and variance of pixel values to compute the threshold [11, 12]. While exploiting pixel-based global thresholds can maximize the application of human experience, the computational process associated with this method remains highly time-intensive [13]. Furthermore, the performance of histogram-based strategies diminishes significantly when presented with the challenge of other salient components in the image.

The method of using neural networks is a wildly popular trend at the moment. A variety of neural network research with excellent performance continues to emerge [14–17]. Among these machine learning-based methods, models based on deep learning have an overwhelming performance. [18] proposed a pyramid pooling module for efficiently extracting features over a wide range of resolutions. The accuracy of the model can reach 98.6%. In [19], the authors proposed a

YOLOv4-based PCB defect detection framework and optimized the deep learning model through the Intel OpenVINO toolkit. While ensuring the accuracy of the model, the execution speed of the model is greatly improved. Machine learning-based methods have shown exceptional recognition rates and accuracy. However, it is crucial to note that such methods require a significant amount of labeled data to train their models effectively. Furthermore, retraining the model is necessary when migrating to new problems, which can be a time-consuming process. Therefore, the use of machine learning-based methods may not always be the most practical or cost-effective solution.

Classification. Classification tasks are currently most commonly performed using machine learning-based algorithms. Vafeiadis et al. [20] implement and compare common machine learning classification algorithms, including decision trees(DTs), random forest (RF), multi-layer perceptron (MLP), logistic regression (LR), gradient boosting (GB), naive-Bayes (NB), Support Vector Machine (SVM) and its variants. The accuracy of the algorithm can reach up to 81%. Ye et al. [21] build a deep learning-based generic solder defect detection system (GSDD) to classify defects into seven types and solve the data imbalance problem with fewer defect data and the problem of color difference. Its recognition accuracy rate reaches 96%.

2.2 3D Point Clouds

The AOI method has high accuracy under the conditions of high image precision and good lighting effect, but when the parts in the workpiece overlap or are blocked by other parts, the efficiency may be greatly reduced. 3D point clouds provide a proven alternative to poor image accuracy caused by poor lighting conditions or overlapping components. Point cloud is a form of 3D data produced by depth sensors due to its complex hierarchical structure and rich data characteristics. Many researchers are studying the feature engineering of point clouds, and by combining it with deep learning, a lot of breathtaking results have been obtained [22]. In the related work of point clouds, the object classification of 3D point clouds is the most commonly used. It can also be applied to PCB defect detection. The goal of 3D object classification is to identify objects from 3D point clouds and label the corresponding point cloud objects with specific semantic labels. It has numerous applications in the area of robotics, virtual reality, and automation. Classification of 3D objects can be done through surface matching, which compares the perceived surface of the object with the surface of the object stored in memory to identify the object in the scene. There are few related studies on analyzing 3D point cloud data of PCB for solder defect detection. Hu, Qiming, et al. [23] first applied 3D point clouds to solder joint inspection. They designed a binocular lidar system to acquire point clouds, and proposed a neural network called DoubleRAN, which obtains ROI through backpropagation, and can effectively identify solder joint locations in point cloud data.

Solder joint inspection based on 3D point cloud still has great potential. There are already many effective deep learning methods based on point cloud, which can be further migrated to solder joint inspection.

3 Methodology

The framework of the algorithm is shown in Fig. 1, The proposed soldering defect detection algorithm consists of the following steps, as follows:

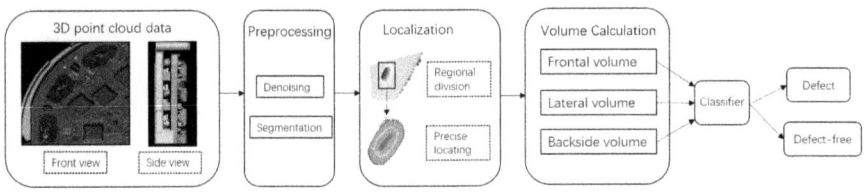

Fig. 1. Framework of our approach, including the specific process of the method.

1. Data preprocessing: First, the 3D point cloud data is preprocessed to remove noise and filter out invalid data points, and then perform preliminary segmentation to rough segment the positions of the three pins in the PCB board. This step is essential as it reduces the amount of data used in subsequent steps and improves the accuracy of the detection algorithm.
2. Solder joint localization: The algorithm performs regional division and precise localization to determine the position of the solder joint to be detected. This step is crucial as it helps to focus the detection algorithm on the specific area of interest, thereby reducing the computational burden and improving the detection accuracy.
3. Volume calculation: The proposed method calculates the volume of the solder joint using the integral summation method. This is a novel approach that enables the detection algorithm to use the 3D information of the point cloud data and overcome the limitations of 2D image processing techniques.
4. Defect classification: Finally, the PCBs are classified into defective and non-defective based on a given empirical threshold. If the calculated solder volume is outside the normal threshold range, the PCB is classified as defective, otherwise, it is classified as non-defective.

3.1 Preprocessing

The pivotal role of preprocessing in the analysis of 3D point cloud data is well-established. Due to the complexity of 3D point cloud data, there are often individual specific abnormal points in the data collection process. Therefore, it is necessary to perform data preprocessing on the PCB 3D point cloud data before inputting it into the subsequent volume calculation method. The preprocessing can be divided into two steps: denoising and segmentation.

Denoising. Denoising constitutes the procedure of purging noise elements from the dataset. In this particular algorithm, the employed denoising method is a discrete point removal strategy, underpinned by statistical radius considerations. The discrete point removal technique involves inscribing a sphere around each point within the point cloud, the radius of which is defined by a pre-set value. If the tally of additional points located within the sphere falls short of a predetermined point cloud number threshold, that specific point is classified as noise and subsequently excised. This discrete point removal algorithm has widespread application in 3D point cloud processing, demonstrating efficacy in the elimination of noise and outliers present within the dataset. Figure 2 illustrates the comprehensive process encompassed by this discrete point removal algorithm.

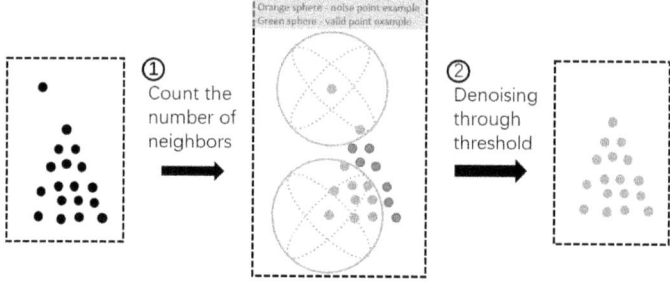

Fig. 2. Visualization of the Radius-Based Discrete Point Removal Algorithm.

Segmentation. Solder defects often occur in the regions where pins are connected to the PCB through the process of soldering. If the soldering process is flawed, it may lead to various soldering defects such as bridging, cold soldering, insufficient or excessive solder, among others. To detect such potential defects, it is imperative to accurately isolate and analyze the areas surrounding the pins. Given this context, we deploy pre-defined positional information to accurately separate the desired pin section from the complete set of point cloud data. This pre-defined positional information serves as an a priori knowledge about the relative positioning and orientation of the PCB and pins during each scan session. The segmentation of pin-specific data delivers dual advantages. Firstly, it provides a focused dataset, allowing for precise volumetric calculations and reducing noise from unrelated data points. Secondly, it simplifies the solder defect detection process, as we can directly investigate the areas of primary interest without distractions. This meticulous pin-focused segmentation significantly enhances the effectiveness and accuracy of the subsequent stages in our PCB inspection process, most notably in solder volume calculation.

3.2 Solder Joint Localization

The accurate positioning of the solder joint is a sufficient condition for the subsequent calculation of the solder volume to be correct or not. In the algorithm proposed in this paper, the positioning of solder joints is mainly based on the depth features of the point cloud in the 3D point cloud image and the prior position knowledge of the PCB solder point. The specific localization can be divided into two steps: regional division and precise locating. The 3D rendering of the solder joint localization is shown in Fig. 3.

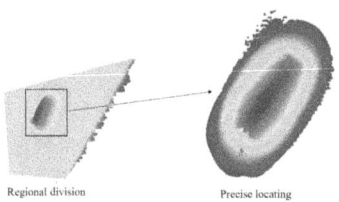

Fig. 3. Solder joint localization via regional division and precise locating.

Regional Division. The ROI is first roughly determined by the regional division. The regional division here is based on the prior location information: the design drawing of the PCB workpiece. The position distribution of the point cloud conforms to the layout in the design drawing, so the approximate position of the ROI can be quickly obtained. The rough division method used in this part is mainly to roughly divide the relevant positions in the 3D point cloud image according to the position information of the corresponding solder points in the design drawing of the PCB board, and obtain the solder positions that need to be calculated later.

Precise Locating. The ROI obtained by the regional division is much larger than the real ROI, so it needs to be further refined. In order to precisely locate the ROI in each PCB, this paper proposes a novel point cloud mutation-checking method based on the feature of point cloud data. The core idea of this method is to separate the PCB from the solder point by finding the interface between the PCB and the solder point, to obtain the actual position of the solder point.

Specifically, after the first step of area division and screening, in the obtained ROI area, only the solder joint exists in the remaining approximate area on the PCB. Therefore, in the depth image, it can be found that only the height of the solder point is significantly different from that of the PCB. In other words, the position of the solder point can be extracted through the difference in height. When the PCB is regarded as the horizontal plane, the surface with the largest change in height information is the interface between the solder point and the

PCB. When this idea is applied to the 3D point cloud, the interface between the solder point and the PCB is the surface with the largest change in the number of point clouds between horizontal planes. Finding this interface separates the solder point from the PCB and allows better localization of the ROI area. Furthermore, determining the location of the interface is essential for calculating the solder volume, as it provides the relative height of the point cloud with respect to the PCB.

The detailed calculation process of this method is explained in detail below.

1. We regard the plane formed by the point cloud of the PCB board as the horizontal plane of the point cloud data and calculate the number of point clouds of the plane.
2. We continuously calculate the number of point clouds at the current height according to the specified height step in the vertical direction. Subtract the number of point clouds calculated last time from the number of point clouds calculated by the current calculation, and calculate the difference in the number of point clouds between different point cloud heights.
3. When the difference suddenly changes significantly, which is 100 times different from the previous point cloud number difference, then we found the interface between the PCB and the solder point.
4. After the interface is obtained, the area composed of all point clouds above the height of the interface is the real ROI.

After the solder joint localization is completed, re-use denoising and filtering to further obtain a more accurate ROI.

3.3 Volume Calculation

The innovation of this paper is to use 3D point cloud data to calculate the volume of solder. The algorithm is based on the characteristics of 3D point clouds and the concept of integration. The main concept involves treating each point in the ROI as a cuboid with the reference surface of the PCB as its base. The sum of these cuboids constitutes the solder volume. In detail, to collect 3D point cloud data from the PCB, a laser line scan camera is used to perform point sampling in each beam while scanning from the front and side of the board at a particular step size. Given the camera's 12um resolution, each sampling point represents a small rectangular area, leading to the idea of integration. The product of the line scan step length and the sampling interval yields the area of the rectangle, with the area multiplied by the height representing the volume of the small cuboid. Summing the volumes of each cuboid, which is the sum of all point heights multiplied by the area of the small rectangle, provides the solder volume.

According to the definition formula of double integral to calculate volume:

$$V = \iint f(x,y)d\sigma = \lim_{\lambda \to 0} \sum_{i=0}^{n} f(\xi_i, \eta_i) \Delta \sigma_i \tag{1}$$

Here, x and y represent the horizontal and vertical coordinates of the bottom plane, $f(x, y)$ represents the height coordinates under this coordinate, and σ

represents the area of the bottom plane. Since the interval between the point cloud data is only $12\,\mu$, the bottom surface can be divided into square area elements $\Delta\sigma_i$ with a side length of $12\,\mu$. Each point on $\Delta\sigma_i$ has its horizontal and vertical coordinates (ξ_i, η_i) and the corresponding height $f(\xi_i, \eta_i)$, which are the height coordinates of each point cloud. As a result, the volume is transformed into small cuboids, with the bottom surface of each cuboid being a square with a side length of $12\,\mu$. The height of each cuboid is the height difference between the point cloud and the PCB reference surface. Thus, the process of calculating the volume by integration is transformed into the calculation of the sum of the point cloud heights. Figure 4 provides a clear understanding of these ideas.

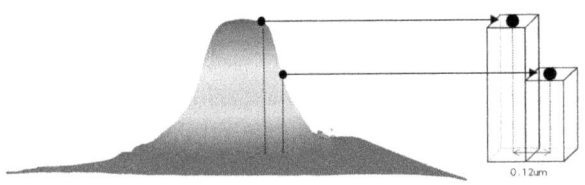

Fig. 4. Using the idea of integral, the solder volume is converted into the sum of the relative height of the point cloud data.

3.4 Classification

The key criterion for classifying solder defects is the volume calculated by the integral-based volume calculation algorithm. For solder joints, the volume is a crucial factor in determining their defect. In cases where any of the tripartite sections of the solder joint, namely the frontal, lateral, or backside volume, strays from the conventional volume threshold range, the solder joint is deemed likely defective. Consequently, the proposed classifier primarily ascertains whether the tripartite volume of the solder joint surpasses our pre-established threshold bounds. Should the volume of any solder joint segment derived from the 3D point cloud of the workpiece exceed or undercut the threshold volume range, it is classified as defective; otherwise, it is considered non-defective.

In the overall defect detection algorithm, the classifier's task is to determine whether the workpiece has a solder defect by checking if the volume of the solder joint falls within the threshold range. In order to determine the specific threshold range, we analyzed and compared a large number of good and defective workpiece samples, and worked with the factory to determine the threshold range of frontal volume, lateral volume, and backside volume through experiments. Overall, this classification process effectively identifies defects in the solder joint by analyzing the volume of each part and provides an accurate and reliable approach to solder joint defect detection in the electronics manufacturing industry.

Algorithm 1. Solder Defect Classification Procedure

Require: Integral-based Volumes V_f, V_l, V_b
Ensure: Defect indicator $defect$
1: $D_f \leftarrow max(0, V_{f\_min} - V_f, V_f - V_{f\_max})$
2: $D_l \leftarrow max(0, V_{l\_min} - V_l, V_l - V_{l\_max})$
3: $D_b \leftarrow max(0, V_{b\_min} - V_b, V_b - V_{b\_max})$
4: **if** $D_f > D_{threshold}$ or $D_l > D_{threshold}$ or $D_b > D_{threshold}$ **then**
5:    $defect \leftarrow 1$
6: **else**
7:    $defect \leftarrow 0$
8: **end if**
9: **return** $defect$
---

4 Experiment

In this study, the experiment is divided into two parts in total. The first part is to verify the accuracy of the algorithm using the integral summation of the 3D point cloud to calculate the volume. The second part is to verify the accuracy of the solder defect detection algorithm designed based on the above algorithm. Experiments are conducted on a 3D point cloud dataset of PCB which is collected by an electronics factory. In order to evaluate the result of the experiment and verify the performance of the algorithm, this paper introduces four commonly used statistical metrics: Accuracy, Precision, Recall, and F-measure.

4.1 Validation of the Volume Algorithm

The point cloud dataset utilized to validate the volume calculation algorithm is divided into three batches, each containing point cloud data of 50 individual PCBs. Notably, each PCB is furnished with three pins with pre-established volumes. Our algorithm is developed to compute the volume of these three pins for each PCB and juxtapose the calculated volumes with their corresponding ground truth volumes. Detailed data results are tabulated in Table 1, and the performance of our algorithm is demonstrated in Fig. 5. Our algorithm's performance is scrutinized using various statistical metrics such as:

1. **Mean Absolute Error (MAE):** This metric estimates the average absolute difference between the calculated volumes (predicted values) and the actual volumes (ground truth). The formula for MAE is defined as:

$$MAE = \frac{1}{n}\sum_{i=1}^{n}\left|Y_i - \hat{Y}_i\right| \quad (2)$$

2. **Mean Squared Error (MSE):** The MSE squares the difference between the predicted and actual volumes before computing the average. The formula for MSE is:

$$MSE = \frac{1}{n}\sum_{i=1}^{n}(Y_i - \hat{Y}_i)^2 \quad (3)$$

3. **Relative Error (RE)**: The relative error signifies the ratio of the mean absolute error to the actual value. The formula for Relative Error is:

$$RE = \frac{1}{n}\sum_{i=1}^{n}\left|\frac{Y_i - \hat{Y}_i}{Y_i}\right| \qquad (4)$$

In these formulas, Y_i signifies the actual values, $\hat{Y}_i$ represents the predicted values, and n is the total number of observations or data points. These metrics enable an empirical and rigorous evaluation of our algorithm's performance, ensuring the effectiveness and accuracy of the volume calculation process.

Table 1. Comparison of the Algorithm Calculated Volume and the True Volume for Each MSA

Group	Pin	True Volume	Calculated Volume	Relative Error (%)	MAE	MSE
MSA#1	v1	62.5	61.466	1.65	0.93	1.07
	v2	32	31.031	3.03		
	v3	18.375	19.161	4.28		
MSA#2	v1	30	29.838	0.73	0.67	0.94
	v2	30	31.443	4.81		
	v3	30	29.677	1.14		
MSA#3	v1	30	29.441	1.86	1.740	3.616
	v2	30	30.061	0.20		
	v3	30	29.050	3.17		

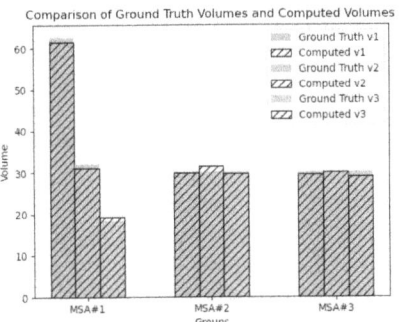
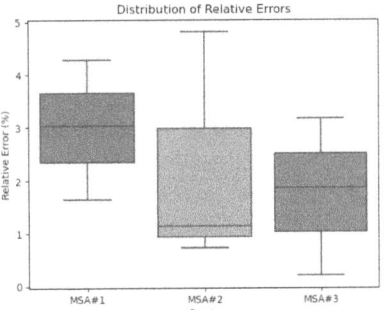

(a) Comparison of Ground Truth Volumes and Computed Volumes

(b) The relative error of the volume calculation algorithm for each group

Fig. 5. The performance of each group on the volume Algorithm

4.2 Validation of the Defect Detection Algorithm

In order to verify the accuracy of the defect detection algorithm based on solder volume detection, we designed the following experiments.

1. We used KEYENCE's LJ-X8000A camera to collect 3D point cloud data of 144 workpieces.
2. We detected whether there are solder defects on each workpiece through manual electrical inspection and used the detection results as the annotation information of the point cloud data.
3. We divided 144 workpieces into three groups by random sampling. In these three test groups, each group contains 48 workpieces, 28 of which are PCB data without defects, and 20 PCB data with defects.
4. We applied our proposed algorithm to detect solder defects for the three test groups and documented the experimental results.

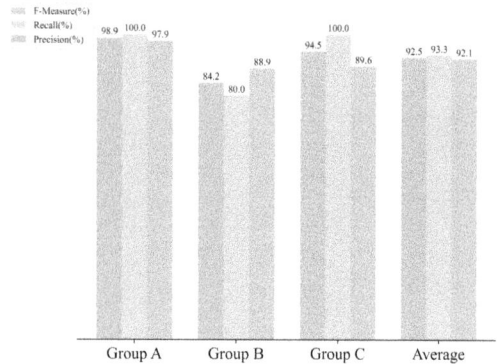

Fig. 6. The performance of each group on the defect detection algorithm.

Figure 6 illustrates the performance of each group using our defect detection algorithm, where we precisely define the normal volume range for solder joints through a systematic experiment. This range is determined to be the mean volume of standard solder joints plus or minus 'n' standard deviations. We meticulously explored various 'n' values to optimize the algorithm's effectiveness, as shown in Fig. 7. The optimal 'n' value, found to be approximately 0.3, achieves the highest F1 score, balancing precision and recall effectively. Thus, the normal volume range in our classifier is set based on this data-driven approach, ensuring superior performance in processing solder joint volume data.

4.3 Experiment Analysis

We conducted two experiments to authenticate the efficacy of the volume calculation algorithm and the solder defect detection algorithm. Our results substantiate that both algorithms exhibit commendable performance on the dataset,

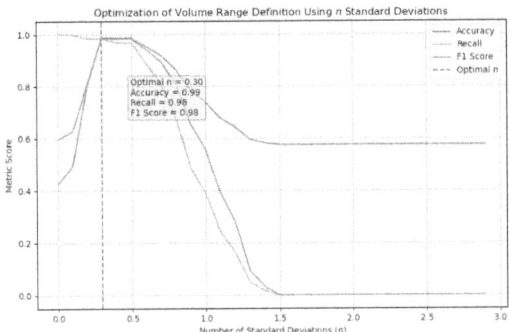

Fig. 7. Optimization of volume range definition using n standard deviations. The red dashed line indicates the optimal value of n. The text box shows the accuracy, recall, and F1 score at the optimal value of n. (Color figure online)

suggesting that the volume of solder joints can serve as a potential indicator for solder defect detection. In the validation process for the volume calculation algorithm, our experiment's outcomes were predominantly accurate. The Relative Error did not exceed 5%, and other indicators such as MAE and MSE were also considerably low, substantiating that the integral summation method for volume calculation is a viable method. However, it's crucial to note that due to the inherent nature of the integral summation approach in calculating the volume of 3D point clouds, there are specific constraints for the object whose volume is being calculated. Firstly, the ROI must has a relatively fixed, large horizontal plane that serves as the boundary of the ROI. Secondly, the object's interior must be solid for accurate computation.

Regarding the defect detection algorithm, the total dataset included 84 normal workpieces and 60 defective PCBs, making a total of 144 workpieces. The algorithm has an average accuracy rate of 91.7% for identifying non-defective workpieces and an average accuracy rate of 83.3% for identifying defective workpieces. The algorithm shows excellent performance in the three test groups, and the average of the three indicators (Precision, Recall, F-Measure) can exceed 90%, indicating the stability and feasibility of the algorithm. We observed that the algorithm's accuracy in identifying defective workpieces is lower than that of non-defective workpieces. This difference in identification is due to the classification threshold set when designing the algorithm. The motivation behind this threshold setting lies in the cost comparison of misclassifications. The cost of falsely identifying a non-defective workpiece as defective is deemed less significant than misclassifying a defective workpiece as non-defective. Therefore, we widened the standard threshold of the solder joint volume when designing the algorithm. The algorithm's overall performance met the acceptance criteria of the workpiece manufacturer, affirming the stability and feasibility of our approach.

To summarize, the experiments have shown that both the volume calculation algorithm and the defect detection algorithm are feasible and effective. The proposed approach of using integral summation for calculating the volume of point cloud data has proven accurate, particularly for standard shapes. The defect detection algorithm exhibits reliable and stable performance, but it is crucial to consider the influence of classification thresholds on the identification accuracy of defective workpieces. Overall, these algorithms can potentially enhance the efficiency and accuracy of solder defect detection in the electronics manufacturing industry. However, it is essential to acknowledge the limitations of these algorithms. For instance, the volume calculation algorithm is less accurate when dealing with complex, irregular shapes. Similarly, the defect detection algorithm's performance is sensitive to the chosen threshold for classification, which may affect the identification accuracy of defective workpieces. Nonetheless, the results of these experiments show that the proposed algorithms are a promising approach to improving the efficiency and accuracy of solder defect detection. Further research and development can be conducted to address these limitations and enhance the algorithms' robustness and accuracy.

5 Conclusion

We have presented a new algorithm for solder defect detection: to identify solder defects by calculating the solder volume based on 3D point data. The algorithm detects PCB solder defects through preprocessing, solder joint localization, and volume calculation. The experiment results show that this integral-based point cloud volume algorithm has a high accuracy rate, and the calculated volume can be effectively used for the automatic inspection of PCB solder defects. This conclusion proves that solder defects are affected by solder volume to a certain extent. This conclusion fully proves that solder defects are affected by the solder volume to a certain extent, and using 3D point cloud data can more comprehensively obtain the relevant feature of PCB solder volume to detect PCB solder defects better. In the future, we will further extract more features of the point cloud data by combining deep learning methods to improve the performance of the solder defect detection algorithm and field test the algorithm proposed in this paper on the actual industrial assembly line to verify the accuracy of the algorithm further.

Acknowledgement. This work is supported by the National Natural Science Foundation of China for Young Scientists (Grant 62202166, NSFC), the Shanghai Pujiang Program (Category D) (Grant 22PJD021), the CCF-Huawei Populus Grove Fund (Grant CCF-HuaweiTC202304, CCF-Huawei), National Trusted Embedded Software Engineering Technology Research Center (East China Normal University).

References

1. Acciani, G., Brunetti, G., Fornarelli, G.: Automatic detection of solder joint defects on integrated circuits. In: IEEE International Symposium on Circuits and Systems. IEEE **2007**, 1021–1024 (2007)

2. Dai, W., Mujeeb, A., Erdt, M., Sourin, A.: 2018 International Conference on Cyberworlds (CW). In: Towards Automatic Optical Inspection Of Soldering Defects, pp. 375–382. IEEE (2018)
3. Burr, D.: Proceedings International Test Conference 1997. In: Solder Paste Inspection: Process Control For Defect Reduction, p. 1036. IEEE (1997)
4. Mak, C.W., Afzulpurkar, N.V., Dailey, M.N., Saram, P.B.: A Bayesian approach to automated optical inspection for solder jet ball joint defects in the head gimbal assembly process. IEEE Trans. Autom. Sci. Eng. **11**(4), 1155–1162 (2014)
5. Kim, J., Ko, J., Choi, H., Kim, H.: Printed circuit board defect detection using deep learning via a skip-connected convolutional autoencoder. Sensors **21**(15), 4968 (2021)
6. Taha, E.M., Emary, E., Moustafa, K.: Automatic optical inspection for pcb manufacturing: A survey. Int. J. Sci. Eng. Res. **5**(7), 1095–1102 (2014)
7. Shao, Z., Hao, K., Wei, B., Tang, X.-S., Solder joint defect detection based on depth image cnn for 3d shape classification, in,: CAA Symposium on Fault Detection, Supervision, and Safety for Technical Processes (SAFEPROCESS). IEEE **2021**, 1–6 (2021)
8. Lu, Z., He, Q., Xiang, X., Liu, H.: Defect detection of PCB based on Bayes feature fusion. J. Eng. **2018**(16), 1741–1745 (2018)
9. Dai, W., Mujeeb, A., Erdt, M., Sourin, A.: Soldering defect detection in automatic optical inspection. Adv. Eng. Inform. **43**, 101004 (2020)
10. Gaidhane, V.H., Hote, Y.V., Singh, V.: An efficient similarity measure approach for pcb surface defect detection. Pattern Anal. Appl. **21**(1), 277–289 (2018)
11. Gao, H., Jin, W., Yang, X., Kaynak, O.: A line-based-clustering approach for ball grid array component inspection in surface-mount technology. IEEE Trans. Industr. Electron. **64**(4), 3030–3038 (2016)
12. Sa-nguannam, A., Srinonchat, J.: 2008 9th International Conference on Signal Processing. In: Analysis Ball Grid Array Defects By Using New Image Technique, pp. 785–788. IEEE (2008)
13. Abdelhameed, M.M., Awad, M.A., Abd El-Aziz, H.M.: 2013 8th International Conference on Computer Engineering & Systems (ICCES). In: A Robust Methodology For Solder Joints Extraction, pp. 268–273. IEEE (2013)
14. Ma, H., Zhang, H.: PCB component rotation detection based on polarity identifier attention. In: Iliadis, L., Papaleonidas, A., Angelov, P., Jayne, C. (eds.) Artificial Neural Networks and Machine Learning – ICANN 2023: 32nd International Conference on Artificial Neural Networks, Heraklion, Crete, Greece, September 26–29, 2023, Proceedings, Part IX, pp. 140–151. Springer Nature Switzerland, Cham (2023). https://doi.org/10.1007/978-3-031-44201-8_12
15. Liu, W., et al.: SSD: single shot multibox detector. In: Leibe, B., Matas, J., Sebe, N., Welling, M. (eds.) Computer Vision – ECCV 2016: 14th European Conference, Amsterdam, The Netherlands, October 11–14, 2016, Proceedings, Part I, pp. 21–37. Springer International Publishing, Cham (2016). https://doi.org/10.1007/978-3-319-46448-0_2
16. Redmon, J., Divvala, S., Girshick, R., Farhadi, A.: You only look once: unified, real-time object detection. In: Proceedings of the IEEE Conference on Computer Vision And Pattern Recognition, pp. 779–788 (2016)
17. Tsan, T.-C., Shih, T.-F., Fuh, C.-S.: Tsankit: artificial intelligence for solder ball head-in-pillow defect inspection. Mach. Vis. Appl. **32**(3), 1–17 (2021)
18. Tang, S., He, F., Huang, X., Yang, J.: Online pcb defect detector on a new pcb defect dataset, arXiv preprint arXiv:1902.06197 (2019)

19. Tham, M.-L., Chong, B.Y., Tan, Y.H., Wong, Y.K., Chean, S.L., Tan, W.K.: 2022 IEEE International Conference on Artificial Intelligence in Engineering and Technology (IICAIET). In: Optimizing Deep Learning Inference to Detect PCB Soldering Defects, pp. 1–5. IEEE (2022)
20. Vafeiadis, T., Dimitriou, N., Ioannidis, D., Wotherspoon, T., Tinker, G., Tzovaras, D.: A framework for inspection of dies attachment on PCB utilizing machine learning techniques. J. Manage. Analy. **5**(2), 81–94 (2018)
21. Ye, S.-Q., Xue, C.-S., Jian, C.-Y., Chen, Y.-Z., Gung, J.-J., Lin, C.-Y.: A Deep Learning-based Generic Solder Defect Detection System. In: 2022 IEEE International Conference on Consumer Electronics-Taiwan, pp. 99–100. IEEE (2022)
22. Liu, W., Sun, J., Li, W., Hu, T., Wang, P.: Deep learning on point clouds and its application: a survey. Sensors **19**(19), 4188 (2019)
23. Hu, Q., Hao, K., Wei, B., Li, H.: An efficient solder joint defects method for 3d point clouds with double-flow region attention network. Adv. Eng. Inform. **52**, 101608 (2022)

Consistency Naming Between Requirements Analysis and Specifications

Fumiko Nagoya[1,2(✉)]

[1] Nihon University College of Commerce, Tokyo, Japan
nagoya.fumiko@nihon-u.ac.jp
[2] Institute for Integrated and Intelligent Systems, Griffith University, Brisbane, Australia

Abstract. Many studies on software development have made it clear that naming identifiers consistently and concisely is challenging. Verification of software using consistency seems possible by ensuring that each name refers to only one concept throughout the entire software development. This should be based on naming concepts in the application domain, not the implementation domain. This paper presents a case study on the naming of identifiers in the description of software application domains, specifically in requirements analysis and specifications. The case study evaluated the similarity of the textual information of the identifier names in requirements analysis and the specifications, and analyzed the reasons for the lack of consistency from the answers to questions asked to the designers. The results show that the lack of consistency arises from the recognition of data structures and response to changes in the external environment.

Keywords: Identifier Naming · Requirements Analysis · Specifications

1 Introduction

Identifiers represent entities by names, which serve as labels used to uniquely determine useful names for properties or behavior in software development. Much of the research on identifier naming focused on how to construct names to improve program maintainability and understandability [1, 2]. Unfortunately, consistent identifier naming [5] from requirements analysis to implementation does not yet exist as a practical best practice [6]. However, the situation is increasingly likely to change because Large Language Models (LLMs) have emerged as a game changer. LLMs, such as OpenAI's ChatGPT and Google's Bard, have shown remarkable progress in text summarization, translation into different languages, automatic question and answer generation, and more. The implementation of these techniques has already started to exert a profound influence on both society and the economy. Particularly noteworthy, McKinsey reports that software development can improve speed and productivity by treating computer languages as just another language and using LLMs as coding assistants [7]. According to [8], research papers on software engineering using LLMs have already been published on requirements analysis, software design, development, quality assurance, and maintenance, with a focus on automatic code generation, test generation, and code repair.

Software developers may expect that LLMs will contribute to improving software quality. Indeed, because identifier names are textual information, their text can be easily extracted from artifacts produced in requirements analysis, which we call "*requirements artifacts*," and the implemented source code using LLMs. An artifact refers to a human-produced object, document, or image. If the names of entities defined in *requirements artifacts* can be mapped to identifiers in the implemented source code, it will contribute to verifying that the functions and services defined in requirements analysis are implemented in the source code. Therefore, it is necessary to clarify who will perform the verification of the mapping between entity names originated in *requirements artifacts* and identifier names defined in source code, as well as what and how this verification will be conducted: First, the developer or designer must decide who should verify internal consistency. As mentioned above, there are no best practices for consistent identifier naming from system requirements analysis to implementation, the programmer performs the verification because the naming convention is specified in the programming language style guide in practice. We need to wait for future empirical research using LLMs as coding assistants to determine who is best suited to verify software quality by mapping entity names in *requirements artifacts* to identifier names in source code. Next, *requirements artifacts* include use cases and user stories that describe the interaction between users and the system in various scenarios. However, we believe that prototypes and use case diagrams should also be included. The reason is that prototypes and use case diagrams are used in many development sites to allow stakeholders to intuitively understand what is realized by scenarios described in natural language. Research has already been conducted [10] using multimodal technology to generate prototypes from image data repositories of similar applications and adjust them to meet client requirements. With the progress of these subsequent studies, it is expected that requirements analysis using multimodal technology to extract text information from graphics will continue to evolve in the future. Finally, it is still unclear how closely the entity names originated in the *requirements artifacts* and the identifier names in the source code must match to determine whether the implemented source code meets the system requirements. Additionally, it is not necessarily a failure if entity name concepts are created in the *requirements artifacts* but not used in the implemented source code. It is necessary to clarify the factors causing this mismatch, in other words, why entity names in the *requirements artifacts* are removed or changed during the subsequent development process.

We designed and conducted a case study to understand why entity names are removed or changed during requirements analysis and subsequent specifications. The case study was conducted with 18 undergraduate students trained in requirements analysis and specification writing acting as designers, and the author acting as an advisor. Each designer analyzed requirements for the application software domain of their choice and then wrote the specifications. The *requirements artifacts* and specifications were refined through iterations by the team. The advisor then inquired about the sources and nature of the data (concept names) of the entities defined in the specifications as input data, output data, and data stores, as found among the artifacts from the requirements analysis. The advisor also asked why concept names had been removed or changed during the specification phase. Based on the designers' answers, the advisor analyzed the similarity of textual information between the concept names in *requirements artifacts* and the entity names in the specifications, and considered the reasons for the inconsistencies. The main reason for these inconsistencies was that many designers only came to a clear understanding of the data structures when they wrote the specifications. Additionally, some designers discovered and adapted to various changes in the external environment based on feedback from team members.

The results of the case study suggest that additional elements should be incorporated into the verification process rather than simply extracting and comparing identifier name information mechanically. Further research is expected to contribute to the development of software verification techniques by tracing concept names in *requirements artifacts*, entity names in specifications, and identifier names in source code. Section 2 introduces related work on identifier naming. Section 3 describes the case study. Section 4 presents the results and discussion, and Sect 5 provides conclusions and outlines future research.

2 Related Work

This chapter discusses related work on identifier naming. While certain programming languages publish naming conventions within their style guides, software development practitioners often face significant challenges in devising naming schemes that are meaningful and consistent throughout the development process. Programmers are typically responsible only for naming identifiers in the implementation domain, while system designers handle naming for entities in the application domain. Ideally, meaningful and consistent identifier names should be used throughout the system. However, in practice, this is difficult to achieve.

Researchers mentioned the following reasons why it is difficult to use meaningful and consistent identifier names: First, [3] found that the probability that two people would spontaneously choose the same term for the same object was less than 0.2 in the experiments, and pointed out that this property of vocabulary selection in communication limits the success of various design methods for vocabulary-driven interaction. Second, [5] derived a formal description of concise and consistent naming of identifiers based on a formal analysis of the properties of identifiers, names, concepts, and codes, and their interrelationships, and argued that names need to be meaningful in the application domain, not the implementation domain. Third, [4] pointed out the lack of an established mechanism for systematically constructing names that are meaningful to programmers. Their proposed mechanism involves three steps: (i) discovering the concept to include in the name, (ii) selecting words to represent that concept, and (iii) determining the structure of the name.

Several studies have also proposed approaches and tools to improve program maintainability and understandability. For example, [2] stated that identifier names are one of the most important sources of information about program entities, and proposed an approach to extract identifier names from source code and semi-automate their reconstruction. The paper described a mechanism to semi-automate identifier replacement for program maintenance. Finally, given the mechanism for systematically constructing identifier naming described above, a precise set of rules for creating concise and consistent names, Remo Gresta et al. conducted an empirical study of identifier naming in Java programs [6].

These studies mainly focused on the implementation domain, specifically the names of identifiers that exist in both old and new source code [1]. In contrast, this paper differs from the mentioned studies by focusing on the application domain, namely requirements analysis and specifications. Unfortunately, this paper does not include the scope of tracing identifier names in source code from entity names in specification descriptions. However, in the case study, the formal engineering method SOFL [11] was used to write the specifications. As a result, since the definitions of data resources, functions, and constraints required for implementation are more clearly defined than in natural language descriptions, it is expected that it will not be difficult to consistently apply the same identifier names from the entity names in the specifications to the implementation domain.

3 Case Study

This chapter describes a case study that we conducted to clarify why some names of data concepts in *requirements artifacts* are removed or changed during the specification phase. The case study consists of three parts: (1) requirements analysis of the application domain selected by 18 designers, (2) specifications based on the *requirements artifacts* by each designer, and (3) questions and answers from the advisor to the designers about the names of data entities defined in the specifications and the concepts inspired by the *requirements artifacts* that are their origin. We provide an overview of the case study and then describe each component part.

3.1 Outline

Eighteen third- and fourth-year students majoring in commerce and business participated as designers after receiving pre-training in requirements analysis and specification writing. Figure 1 shows an overview of the requirements analysis deliverables and specifications performed in the case study. The pre-training period for requirements analysis and specification writing was six months. The case studies themselves were conducted for six months each, from October 2020 to August 2021, October 2021 to August 2022, and October 2022 to August 2023.

In the case studies, one designer served as a team leader and organized a team of five to nine people. The team members were other designers who had received pre-training. The team leader refined the *requirements artifacts* and specifications through iterations [18], making corrections within one to two weeks based on the feedback of the team members. These *requirements artifacts*, specifications, and feedback comments were written in their native language, Japanese. Feedback was provided face-to-face or through online meetings. In face-to-face meetings, as well as online meetings, the team members' opinions were recorded using recording and chat functions. Based on the feedback received from team members, the designer decided which opinions to adopt and which ones to reject, and wrote down the reasons for their decisions. Each designer submitted documentation in response to two questions made by the advisor concerning the data entities defined in the specifications.

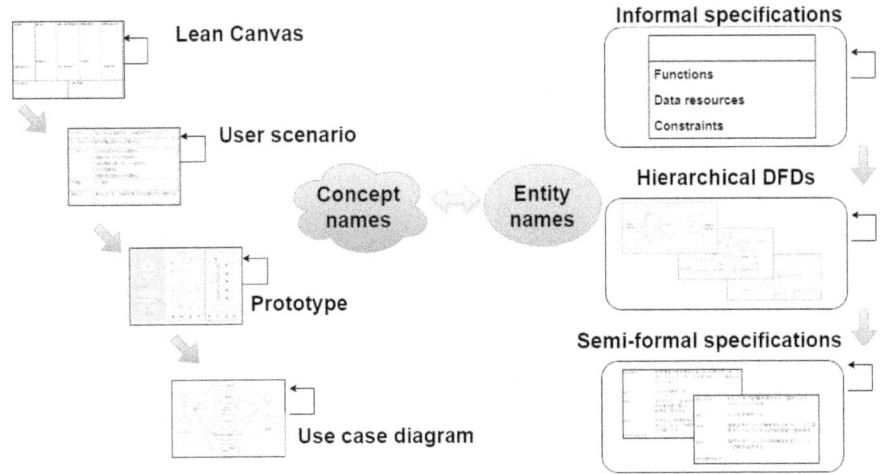

Fig. 1. Overview of requirements analysis and specifications

3.2 Requirements Artifacts

This part explains the contents of *requirements artifacts* and the designers' behavior in the case study. The *requirements artifacts* generated by the designers were a business idea template, a description of user scenarios in natural language, a prototype, and a use case diagram.

We adopted the Lean Canvas for the business idea template. Lean is a method of agile development, and the Lean Canvas is a one-page modeling tool proposed by Ash Maurya [13] that consists of 12 building blocks necessary for business modeling. This Lean Canvas breaks down the business idea in terms of Customer Segments, Early Adopters, Problem, Existing Alternatives, Unique Value Proposition, High-Level Concept, Solution, Channels, Revenue Streams, Cost Structure, Key Metrics, and Unfair Advantage, allowing for analysis suitable for products in the early stages. The designers of the case study had specialized lessons on the Lean Canvas from an expert, but since they originally specialized in commerce and business, they had no difficulty writing the business idea template.

A user scenario description in natural language is a set of scenarios written from the user's point of view. Commonly, use cases and user stories are sentences that describe the behavior of a system provided to the user. However, the user scenario descriptions in the case study included not only main scenarios (use cases) but also a short overview of functions, a definition of the target user, limitations and exclusions, and screen transitions. In particular, as [9] mentioned, a short overview of functions, a one-line description of what the system does, facilitates the team's understanding of the system throughout the case study. Furthermore, the sentences about screen transitions contributed to the subsequent prototype and use case diagram.

Prototypes and use case diagrams are visual representations that include actual human users, the system itself, and external stakeholders. Prototypes serve to present the mockup user interface that sketches the product idea to stakeholders and obtains alternatives and complements to the idea through feedback. In the case study, we used a prototyping tool that allows team members to enter and record feedback comments online. On the other hand, use case diagrams are graphical representations that represent the interactions of system actors with the system, with the aim of showing how some valuable result can be achieved [14]. We selected use case diagrams that represent an idea selected from the prototype alternatives as a series of scenarios in the case study.

3.3 Specifications

We employed the SOFL three-step approach [12] for specification generation. SOFL stands for Structured Object-Oriented Formal Language, a formal engineering method that integrates data flow diagrams (DFDs) [15], Petri nets [17], and VDM-SL [16]. This three-step approach goes from a well-organized informal specification, through a semi-formal specification, to a formal specification. The formal specifications integrate textual module definitions and a graphical representation of the relationships between the modules [11]. The application domains in this case study are not safety-critical or security-critical, for which formal methods are required, so the designers did not define them using formal specifications. Instead, they produced hierarchical DFDs, after well-organized informal specifications and prior to semi-formal specifications.

Well-organized informal specifications are clearly and precisely written in natural language, consisting of the functions to be implemented, the data resources to be used, and the constraints required on these functions and data resources. However, it is not necessary to describe the relationships between the functions, data resources, and constraints. In the case study, the functions to be implemented are identified in the artifacts of the requirements analysis, but the designers performed decomposition to break down one function into several processes to achieve some valuable result. Data resources are analyzed to include the fact that one data resource has multiple attributes, for example, vital data consists of body temperature, pulse rate, blood pressure, and respiration. Constraints specify the properties of the environment that may limit what the system can do. The environment includes not only people, organizations, and devices, but also the influence of relevant laws and regulations and external APIs.

Hierarchical DFDs in the case study are composed of three layers: a top-level data flow diagram (also called a context diagram), a middle-level data flow diagram, and a bottom-level data flow diagram. The DFDs are designed to hierarchically decompose several processes that represent the functions to be implemented, based on a well-organized informal specification. They also clarify the input data, output data, and data store entities, as well as their relationships to the processes. In the case study, the designers began with the middle-level data flow diagram, followed by the context diagram and the bottom-level data flow diagram. Unfortunately, due to a lack of experience in drawing DFDs, the process was challenging. Many designers and team members had to return to a 'short overview of functions' perspective, as they were too focused on creating the entire picture and tended to overlook the core functions.

Semi-formal specifications clearly defined the process names, input data, output data and data stores, and the pre and postconditions were specified in natural language. Even though the hierarchical DFDs already declared the process names, the associated input data, the output data generated by the process, and the involved data stores, many reworks occurred because designers found missing data and had to return to the hierarchical DFDs and/or well-organized informal specifications.

3.4 Questions to Designers

The 18 designers answered the following questions provided by the advisor. The questions were related to the entity names of data resources, input data, output data, and data stores, as defined in well-organized informal specifications, hierarchical DFDs, and semi-formal specifications. All questions and answers were provided after the *requirements artifacts* and specifications had been generated and refined based on feedback.

- Q1: Where and what data origins (concept names) did you find in the *requirements artifacts*, such as business idea templates, natural language user scenario descriptions, prototypes, and use case diagrams?
- Q2: For what reasons did you change the entity names defined in the well-organized informal specification, hierarchical DFDs, and semi-formal specification from the concept names?

The designers submitted their answers to these questions in the specified format.

4 Results and Discussion

We analyzed the results using the following process. First, the entity name tokens were extracted from the data attached to the data resources, input data, output data, and data stores, and duplicate data of the entity name tokens were cleaned up to obtain ET_j for each designer. ET means a set of entity names derived from the specifications, and j represents the jth designer. We counted the number of ET_j respectively and obtained a total of 465 samples from a collection of specifications defined by 18 designers. Second, the concept name tokens were extracted from the data based on the answers to Q1, and duplicate data of the concept name tokens were cleaned up to obtain CN_j. CN means a set of concept names derived from the *requirements artifacts*, and j represents the jth designer, as mentioned above. We found a total of 270 samples from the related *requirements artifacts*. Thirdly, we extracted common tokens between ET_j and CN_j if j matched, and obtained CT_j. CT_j represents the common tokens based on the data extracted from the jth specifications and the jth *requirements artifacts*. Throughout the case study, we identified a total of 82 samples as intersections. Finally, the similarity between each designer's entity names and concept names was calculated using the Jaccard coefficient. The Jaccard coefficient of set A and set B is expressed by the following formula:

$$J(A, B) = |A \cap B|/|A \cup B|$$

For example, if set A and set B have the following values:

A = {height, weight, vision, blood pressure}.
B = {height, weight, age}.

Then, the Jaccard coefficient between set A and set B is calculated as:

$$J(A, B) = |A \cap B|/|A \cup B| = 2/5 = 0.4$$

We calculated the Jaccard coefficient for each designer. The formula applied to this case study is as follows:

$$J(ET\_j, CN\_j) = |ET\_j \cap CN\_j|/|ET\_j \cup CN\_j| = CT\_j/|ET\_j \cup CN\_j|$$

Table 1 shows the Jaccard coefficient over the case study: mean 13.1%, median 8.0%, minimum 0, and maximum 43.6%.

Table 1. Jaccard coefficient over the case study.

Basic Static	Jaccard coefficient
Mean	13.1%
Median	8.0%
Minimum	0
Maximum	43.6%

This result may not be surprising given the difficulty of naming consistent and concise identifiers, as discussed in the related work. More importantly, why do concept names and entity names not match, even though they are written by the same designer? Therefore, we used the answers to Q2 to explore why concept names recognized in *requirements artifacts* were removed or changed in the specification phase. The following factors were identified based on the responses of 18 designers.

1. Eleven designers defined compound data, including data attributes, in well-organized informal specifications, which required them to change concept names to different entity names.
2. Five designers added and changed entity names because they recognized security, privacy, and related regulations as constraints in the well-organized informal specifications.
3. Three designers removed entity names of data related to unnecessary functions because they switched to using external APIs, such as Google Maps.

The second and third factors can be rephrased as arising from responses to environments external to the system. In short, the case studies showed that there are two main reasons why data concept names originating from *requirements artifacts* had to be removed or changed to entity names: (1) recognition of data objects defined in data resources, and (2) response to the environment outside the system. Moreover, it became clear from the designers' comments in Q2 that the feedback comments influenced the recognition of these data objects and the response to the external environment that was later identified.

5 Conclusion and Future Research

This case study evaluated the textual similarity between the concept names for data formed in the *requirements artifacts* and the entity names related to the data in the subsequent specifications. It analyzed the factors behind the inconsistent names based on the designers' response comments. The main factors were the recognition of data objects and the response to the external environment. It was also found that the influence of feedback in iterative team development was significantly related to the inconsistency. Unfortunately, at the time of conducting this case study, it was difficult to mechanically extract accurate text information from prototypes and use case diagrams using multimodal technology, so it was not possible to extract it fully automatically, and some text information had to be extracted from the graphics manually, which was very time-consuming and labor-intensive. However, future advances in multimodal technology are expected to improve the accuracy of text information extraction from graphics and facilitate comparison of specifications written in natural language with the associated prototypes and use case diagrams. We believe that this will encourage empirical research on traceability that focuses on consistency between specifications at different layers used in actual development. In the future, we would like to further investigate these traceability studies and consider proposing automated techniques to track and verify the use of concept, entity, and identifier names using LLMs.

Acknowledgments. We would like to thank Hiroyuki Ogura for teaching us about Lean Canvas, and the students of our seminar at Nihon University College of Commerce, who participated as designers in the case study. Special thanks are due to the Institute for Integrated and Intelligent Systems, Griffith University, for providing an excellent environment for a visiting research fellow. Finally, we gratefully acknowledge the support of the Nihon University Research Grant for 2024 Overseas Researchers.

References

1. Anquetil, N., Lethbridge, T.: Extracting concepts from file names: a new file clustering criterion. In: Proceedings of the 20th International Conference on Software Engineering (ICSE '98). IEEE Computer Society, USA, pp. 84–93 (1998)
2. Caprile, B., Tonella, P.: Restructuring Program Identifier Names. In: Proceedings of the International Conference on Software Maintenance (ICSM'00) (ICSM '00). IEEE Computer Society, USA, 97 (2000)
3. Furnas, G.W., Landauer, T.K., Gomez, L.M., Dumais, S.T.: The vocabulary problem in human-system communication. Commun. ACM 30, **11**(1987), 964–971 (1987)
4. Feitelson, D.G., Mizrahi, A., Noy, N., Shabat, A.B., Eliyahu, O., Sheffer, R.: How Developers Choose Names. IEEE Trans. Software Eng. **48**(01), 37–52 (2022)
5. Deissenboeck, F., Pizka, M.: Concise and consistent naming. Software Quality J. **14**(3), 261–282 (2006)
6. Gresta, R., Durelli, V., Cirilo, E.: Naming Practices in Java Projects: An Empirical Study. In Proceedings of the XX Brazilian Symposium on Software Quality. Association for Computing Machinery, New York, NY, USA, Article 10, pp. 1–10 (2021)

7. McKinsey & Company, Economic potential of generative AI: The next productivity frontier, June 14, 2023 Report, https://www.mckinsey.com/capabilities/mckinsey-digital/our-insights/the-economic-potential-of-generative-ai-the-next-productivity-frontier. Accessed 5 Aug 2024
8. Hou, X., et al.: Large Language Models for Software Engineering: A Systematic Literature Review, arXiv preprint arXiv.2308.10620 (2024)
9. Meyer, B.: Handbook of Requirements and Business Analysis, Springer, 277 (2022)
10. Kolthoff, K., Bartelt, C., Ponzetto, S.P.: Data-driven prototyping via natural-language-based GUI retrieval. Automated Software Engg. **30**, 1 (2023)
11. Liu, S.: Formal Engineering for Industrial Software Development. SpringerVerlag (2004)
12. Liu, S.: Agile-SOFL: Agile Formal Engineering Method Springer Singapore (2024)
13. Maurya, A.: Running Lean: Iterate from Plan A to a Plan That Works (2nd. ed.). O'Reilly Media, Inc. (2012)
14. Wiegers, K.E., Beatty, J.: Software Requirements 3. Microsoft Press, USA (2013)
15. DeMarco, T.: Structured analysis and system specification, pp. 409–424. Classics in software engineering. Yourdon Press, USA (1979)
16. Jones, C.B.: Systematic software development using VDM. Prentice Hall International (UK) Ltd., GBR (1986)
17. Reisig, W., Rozenberg, G.: Informal Introduction to Petri Nets. In: Lectures on Petri Nets I: Basic Models, Advances in Petri Nets, the volumes are based on the Advanced Course on Petri Nets, pp. 1–11. Springer-Verlag, Berlin, Heidelberg (1996)
18. Nagoya, F.: A Case Study on Combining Agile Requirements Development and SOFL. In: Structured Object-Oriented Formal Language and Method: 10th International Workshop, SOFL+MSVL 2020, Singapore, March 1, 2021, pp. 23–33. Revised Selected Papers. Springer-Verlag, Berlin, Heidelberg (2020)

A Framework for Standardized Partitioning Analysis in Integrated Modular Avionics Systems

Jilu Zhang[1], Yong Cai[1(✉)], Weikai Miao[1], and Zhouyang Wang[2]

[1] East China Normal University, Shanghai, China
ycai@sei.ecnu.edu.cn
[2] Queen's University, Kingston, Canada

Abstract. With the increasing adoption of the Integrated Modular Avionics (IMA) architecture, ensuring robust partitioning, a fundamental technique of this architecture, is crucial. Additionally, the benefits of reduced verification costs that robust partitioning provides for software verification on multicore processor platform are undeniable. However, robust partitioning faces various challenges posed by the time partitioning and space/resource partitioning of shared and dedicated resources, which can compromise robust partitioning. Although DO-297 describes what a partitioning analysis should contain, there is still no systematic and complete guide available for organizing and addressing partitioning analysis activities in public research. We propose a systematic framework to guide the performance of specific tasks within partitioning analysis, including identifying top-level partitioning properties, decomposing these properties, extracting all potential error sources, combining potential error sources with robust partitioning properties to identify vulnerabilities and verifying mitigation means.

Keywords: partitioning analysis · multicore processor platform · time partitioning · space/resource partitioning

1 Introduction

Since the late 1990 s, partitioning has become a common technique in avionics with the gradual popularity of Integrated Modular Avionics (IMA). IMA serves as an architectural solution alternative to federated architecture, primarily addressing the latter's limitation where each function necessitates an independent computer system. However, federated architecture inherently excels at fault isolation. In contrast, any realization of IMA must provide partitioning to provide protection against fault propagation from one function to another [1]. Moreover, since 2010, with further research of multicore processors, the European Union Aviation Safety Agency (EASA) in Europe and the Federal Aviation Administration (FAA) in the US have proposed distinct software verification guidelines for different types of MCP platforms, based on their support for robust partitioning, in A(M)C 20–193. Software applications can be verified independently on MCPs with robust partitioning and their worst-case execution time (WCET) can be determined separately [2,3]. The significance of partitioning is clear, hence implementing a system with robust partitioning requires extreme care and caution.

DO-297 advocates for an activity known as partitioning analysis. A partitioning analysis should demonstrate that no application or sub-function in a partition could affect the behavior of a sub-function or application in any other partition in an adverse manner [4]. Partitioning analysis is necessary to establish robust partitioning for the IMA system. Current research in this area is often fragmented and lacks a unified guiding method or framework. Consequently, this paper introduces a systematic and thorough general framework for partitioning analysis. In this section, we introduce an overview of our topic, clarifying the importance of proposing a partitioning analysis framework. In Sect. 2, fundamental concepts related to partitioning and multicore interference are introduced. Section 3 introduces the content of our partitioning analysis framework in detail. Finally, Sect. 4 offers a brief summary and outlines future research directions.

2 Background

In this section, we provide relevant background knowledge, including definitions of robust partitioning in both unicore and multicore contexts, the hardware mechanisms that affect robust partitioning, and the concept of multicore interference.

2.1 Robust Partitioning for Unicore and Multicore

The integration of multiple federated systems into a single system within the IMA platform reduces hardware costs, but increases the complexity and expenses related to safety certification. Certification costs of IMA systems can be contained by use of partitioning, isolating each application to minimize interaction, and thus simplifying safety analysis [5]. Additionally, achieving a level of isolation comparable to federated architectures requires robust partitioning within the IMA systems.

Various aviation standards provide guidelines for designing and analyzing robust partitioning. DO-297 details the considerations and objectives necessary for robust partitioning design and specifies the essential components of partitioning analysis. DO-248C [6] offers mechanism recommendations for robust partitioning, while ARINC 653 [7] establishes standards for interface definitions and related requirements for robust partitioning.

Robust partitioning typically relies on both time and space/resource partitioning.

Time Partitioning. ARINC 653 [7] enforces time partitioning through a two-level scheduling system, featuring mandatory round-robin scheduling between partitions. This involves a periodically repeating major time frame that allocates one or more minor time frames for each partition, as illustrated in Fig 1.

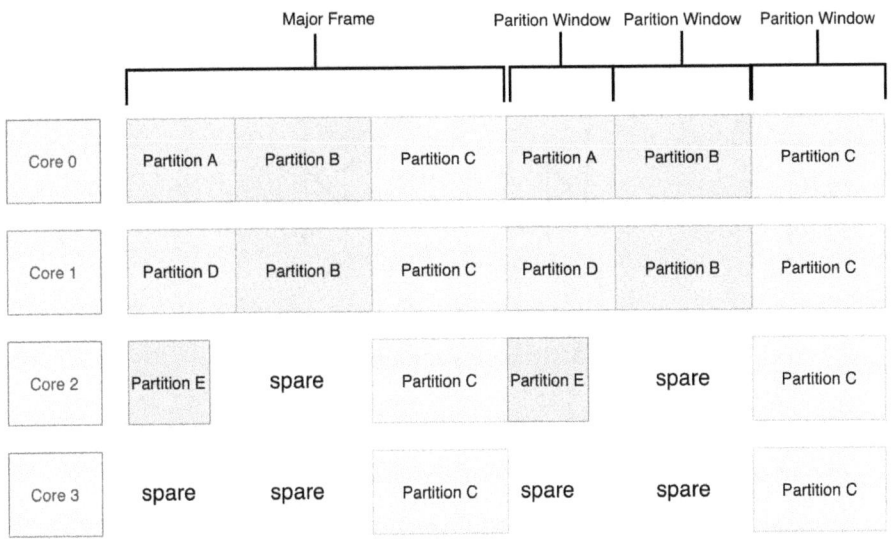

Fig. 1. Time Partitioning

In unicore systems, time partitioning prevents one partition from impacting another partition's access to shared resources.

While in multicore systems, robust time partitioning is achieved when, as a result of mitigating the time interference between partitions hosted on different cores, no software partition consumes more than its allocation of execution time on the core(s) on which it executes, irrespective of whether partitions are executing on none of the other active cores or on one, more than one, or all of the other active cores [3].

Space/Resource Partitioning. In unicore systems, it is generally referred to as space partitioning, while in multicore systems, it is known as resource partitioning. The objectives of both are essentially the same. Space/Resource partitioning is achieved when [3]:

- Software partitions cannot contaminate the storage areas for the code, I/O, or data of other partitions.
- Software partitions cannot consume more than their allocations of shared resources.
- Failures of hardware unique to a software partition cannot cause adverse effects on other software partitions.

Space/Resource partitioning, whether implemented via Memory Management Unit (MMU) or Software Fault Isolation (SFI), is predominantly ensured by restricting memory access (especially write access) to only the areas defined by the partition, as illustrated in Fig 2.

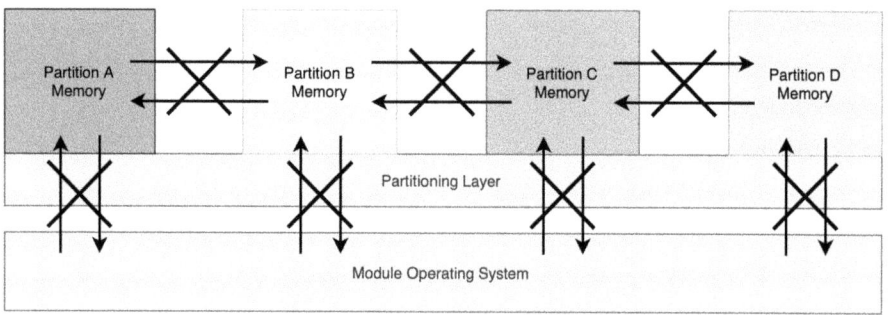

Fig. 2. Space/Resource Partitioning

2.2 Hardware Mechanisms that Affect Partitioning

Many hardware mechanisms influence robust partitioning by impacting the usage of shared and dedicated resources. The following description outlines some hardware mechanisms that may potentially compromise robust partitioning.

Interrupt. An interrupt is a signal that triggers asynchronous events, typically classified into two types: timer interrupts and external interrupts. When an external device triggers an interrupt, it diverts the processor from the current task to an interrupt service routine. This routine's execution time is generally accounted for within the active partition's allotted time. If the duration of this routine exceeds what is scheduled for the partition, it could disrupt time partitioning. As aforementioned, the only interrupt typically found in a robustly partitioned IMA system is the system clock, and this is for good reason [8].

In order to receive interrupts from external devices without compromising robust partitioning, several specialized techniques can be employed to mitigate potential partition violations. These include using software to continuously poll data related to interrupt signals, designing a function to verify whether the execution time of the requested interrupt service routine will fit within the allotted time of the current partition, and restricting application access to the hardware responsible for triggering interrupts [8]. While these strategies are promising, their effectiveness must be carefully evaluated to ensure they do not adversely affect the partition. This evaluation should consider factors such as the additional processing overhead introduced by polling methods and the potential for reduced system responsiveness due to restricted hardware access.

Modes of Operation. Power PC defines three different levels of instruction set architecture: User Instruction Set Architecture (UISA), Virtual Environment Architecture (VEA) and Operating Environment Architecture (OEA), as illustrated in Fig. 3. To efficiently build systems that provide partitioning, virtualization environments, and protection, the processor typically defines different levels of privilege modes (user mode, guest supervisor mode and hypervisor mode) to execute these different levels of instructions and access different levels of resources [11].

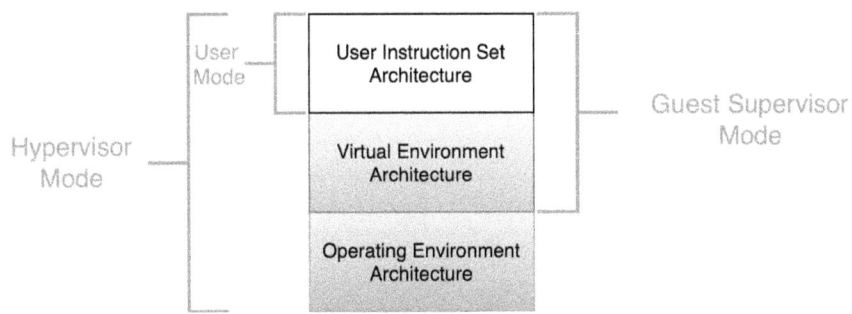

Fig. 3. Instruction Set Architecture and Privilege Modes in Power PC

UISA. defines the basic user-level instruction set, user-level registers, data types, floating-point storage conventions, and interrupt models seen by user programs, as well as memory and programming models. Correspondingly, in user mode, software can only execute these user-level instructions, access certain control registers, and access user storage space. No privileged operations can be performed.

VEA describes the memory model for an environment in which multiple devices can access memory, defines aspects of the cache model, defines cache control instructions, and defines the time-base facility from a user-level perspective. Correspondingly, at the guest supervisor mode, several privileged operations can be performed and resources that are not hypervisor privileged can be accessed.

OEA describes the memory management model, supervisor-level registers, synchronization requirements, and the interrupt model. It also defines the time-base feature from a supervisor-level perspective. Correspondingly, the hypervisor mode is used to provide partitioning and virtualization for operating systems software, which runs as a guest to the hypervisor software. All control registers and the supervisor memory space can be accessed.

Pipeline. Modern processors are equipped with pipeline mechanisms, including branch prediction capabilities, which are designed to minimize disruptions caused by branch instructions. This mechanism has a dual impact: it generally speeds up program execution, but it also introduces a degree of uncertainty and interference. When different partitions use the branch prediction unit (BPU), its state is changed, thereby affecting the execution time of these partitions.

Avoiding interference due to retained state in the BPU requires flushing the BPU, but not all processors provide such a feature [5].

MMU. The MMU is used to map virtual addresses to physical addresses and provide control of memory access. All of the RTOSs investigated that provide support for multiple partitions use the MMU of the processor and its underlying architecture to implement the memory protection mechanism [9].

Several aspects generally need to be considered for the MMU: 1) the need to check for memory overlaps or other configuration errors in the MMU configuration table, 2) consistency checks from the configuration table to the internal address translation tables, 3) preventing users from gaining permissions to alter MMU access controls.

Interconnect. Interconnect is a hardware infrastructure that enables the implementation of coherent, multicore systems. Interconnect acts as a central interconnect for cores, memory subsystems, peripheral devices, and I/O host bridges in the system.

The CAST-32A position paper mentions that most MCPs have internal mechanisms such as "interconnects" to handle and arbitrate the demands for MCP resources, but the contention for shared resources between applications usually causes delays in access to the resources. These delays are a form of time interference between applications, which can cause applications to take much longer to execute than when executing on their own [12].

Cache. Cache, a hardware device positioned between the Central Processing Unit (CPU) and main memory, is designed to improve memory access performance. In the IMA system, Cache serves as a shared resource and is subject to thorough review.

Concerns in a common (unicore or multicore) environment focus on the impact of cache jitter on time partitioning. Cache jitter arises because the current partition's use of the cache inevitably changes the state of the cache. When the subsequent partition switches in, this change affects the next partition's cache hit rate, which in turn impacts its performance characteristics. Consequently, these changes can disrupt time partitioning, as each partition's execution time depends on the predictability and consistency of cache behavior. Several strategies mentioned in a FAA research report for mitigating cache jitter include [9]:

- Disabling the Cache: Avoids uncertainty associated with Cache usage at the cost of significant performance loss; recommended for cautious use.

- Setting a Large Jitter Margin: Compensates for cache misses by adjusting the timing of partition switch, though this may reduce the available processor time for partitions.
- Cache Flushing: Applicable with a write-back policy, this involves copying all cached data back to main memory during partition switches, ensuring a clear cache for incoming partitions.
- Cache Invalidation: When using a write-through policy, cache invalidation instructions during partition switching help clear the cache.

These strategies ensure more predictable Cache behavior, thereby minimizing the impact of cache jitter on time partitioning.

In multicore environments, snooping protocols that implement cache coherence may create interfering channels between cores affecting execution time and thus time partitioning [10].

I/O. "The RTOS in an IMA system must effectively control access to shared I/O ports, devices, and channels. As with other shared resources, I/O operations should be partitioned or protected in some fashion" [13]. Given that I/O operations can influence both time and space aspects of partitioning, I/O resources need to be partitioned. And for each I/O devices, time and space issues for partitioning must both be considered.

ARINC 653 specifies two modes for inter-partition I/O communication: sampling ports and queuing ports. However, it does not establish a message transmission mechanism (protocol), leaving application designers and system integrators to select mechanisms that must guarantee minimal message delays and required reliability. Steven H. VanderLeest highlights the necessity of managing all critical features of the I/O subsystem- "The partitioning environment must manage all the salient features of the I/O subsystem (such as bandwidth, latency, semaphores, control registers, buffer space) so that partitions cannot affect one another by unauthorized means." [14] The primary concerns include data delays, data loss, data integrity, and potential protocol halts, which are influenced by factors such as bandwidth, latency, buffer size and transmission protocol.

Moreover, I/O interrupts represent a significant risk to robust partitioning. These interrupts can disrupt partition scheduling and compromise time partitioning, necessitating cautious management of I/O interrupts within IMA systems.

DMA. Direct Memory Access (DMA) is a hardware mechanism that allows specific hardware subsystems to read from and write to system memory directly, without passing through the CPU.

According to reference [8], the process of transferring PCIe device data to memory via DMA, controlled by the DMA engine, follows the pattern shown in Fig. 4: The processor requests bus access to post transaction parameters to the DMA controller. Once granted, the DMA engine requests and receives memory access from the arbitrator, transfers data from the reference to the target location while controlling the bus, and then notifies the processor upon completion of the transfer.

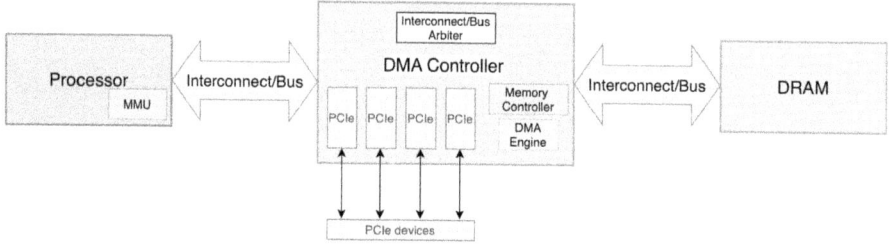

Fig. 4. DMA Transfer Process

DMA provides a mechanism for transferring large blocks of memory within the system, significantly enhancing efficiency. However, it poses potential challenges to robust partitioning. Since the DMA engine is granted exclusive access to the memory bus for block transfers, and because the memory bus is a shared resource within the entire IMA system, a vulnerability arises: one partition using DMA transfers could monopolize the memory bus, thereby depriving other partitions of this resource and compromising time partitioning.

2.3 Multicore Interference

A multicore processor chip comprises several processing cores, with each core potentially managing one or more partitions. These partitions are deployed on cores that share the majority of hardware resources, such as memory and I/O. As a result, partition applications operating on different cores often compete for these shared resources, leading to inter-core interference. This type of interference is typically more direct and significant than what is observed with inter-partition interference on unicore systems. This can result in partition applications taking much longer to execute than if they were run independently, thereby compromising robust partitioning. Therefore, conducting a partitioning analysis on MCP platforms necessitates a thorough consideration of the challenges posed by multicore interference.

3 Framework for Standardized Partitioning Analysis

This section proposes a systematic and comprehensive framework for partitioning analysis based on the content requirements of the partitioning analysis activity in DO-297, including the steps of partitioning analysis, the tasks to be performed in each step, and the key considerations for each task.

3.1 Overview

As shown in Fig. 5, this framework consists of the following five steps.

- Step 1 Identifying Top-level Partitioning Property: Identifies the essential top-level properties for establishing robust partitioning.
- Step 2 Decomposition of Partitioning Properties: Breaks down these properties into necessary lower-level properties.
- Step 3 Extracting Potential Error Sources: Analyzes resources including shared resources and dedicated resources to extract all potential error sources impacting robust partitioning properties.
- Step 4 Identifying Vulnerabilities: For each partitioning property, assesses whether and how all the potential error sources could affect robust partitioning property.
- Step 5 Verifying mitigation means: Verify whether there are appropriate mitigation means for vulnerability

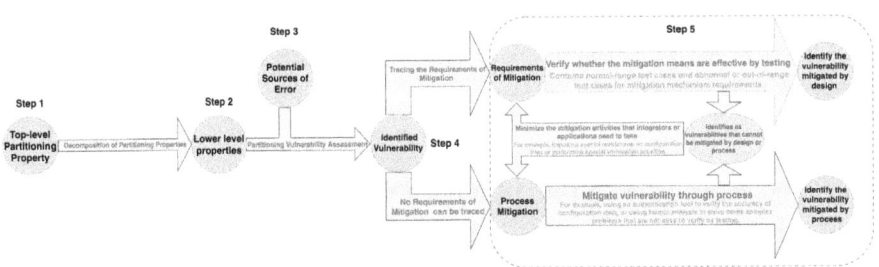

Fig. 5. Framework for Standardized Partitioning Analysis

3.2 Identifying Top-Level Partitioning Property

DO-297 mentions that partitioning analysis and design should conform to two principles. First, the dedicated resources assigned to one partition can never be affected by or affect the operation of an application or application function in any other partition. Second, the use of shared resources by one partition cannot unacceptably affect, as shown by a safety assessment, the operation of an application or application function in any other partition sharing that resource [4].

Based on this, we believe that robust partitioning arises from the isolation and protection of shared resources between partitions and isolation of dedicated resources unique to a partition. As illustrated in Fig 6, In a standard IMA architecture, shared resources are generally considered to be three types: Central Processing Unit (CPU), Memory, and I/O. The top-level properties of robust partitions are also centered around these three shared resources and dedicated resources.

In accordance with the robust partitioning guidelines outlined in Sect. 2.3.3 of DO-297 [4], we have identified the top-level properties for robust partitioning. This identification is also guided by the classification of shared resources and dedicated resources we mentioned before. The first three top-level properties focus on the isolation of shared resources, while the last top-level property focuses on the protection of shared resources and isolation of dedicated resources. The following are the essential top-level properties for establishing robust partitioning:

- CPU
  A software partition should be allowed to consume shared processor resources only during its allocated time.
- Memory
  A software partition should not be allowed to contaminate the code, I/O, or data storage areas of another partition.
- I/O
  A software partition should be allowed to consume only its allocation of shared I/O resources.
- Partition-specific Hardware
  Failures of hardware unique to a software partition should not cause adverse effects on other software partitions.

3.3 Decomposition of Partitioning Properties

According to the description of the decomposition of partitioning properties in Sect. 3.5.2.2 of DO-297 [4] and recommendations for robust partitioning mechanisms in Sect. 4.14.5 of DO-248C [6], we decompose the top-level properties into lower level properties. The decomposition on different platforms can be based on platform features, broken down into the lowest-level properties that are satisfied by one or more design features of the platform. The following is an example of the decomposition of top-level properties, with the top-level properties and their decomposed lower-level properties shown as follows:

- CPU - A software partition should be allowed to consume shared processor resources only during its allocated time.
  ○ Deterministic Scheduling of Processor.
- Memory - A software partition should not be allowed to contaminate the code, I/O, or data storage areas of another partition.
  ○ Persistent storage locations (for example, data memory), assigned to a software partition, write-able only by that partition.
  ○ Context data (for example, processor registers, CPU-caches) used by a task preserved or flushed, as appropriate, when control is transferred to another partition.
  ○ Data flow and communications between partitions.

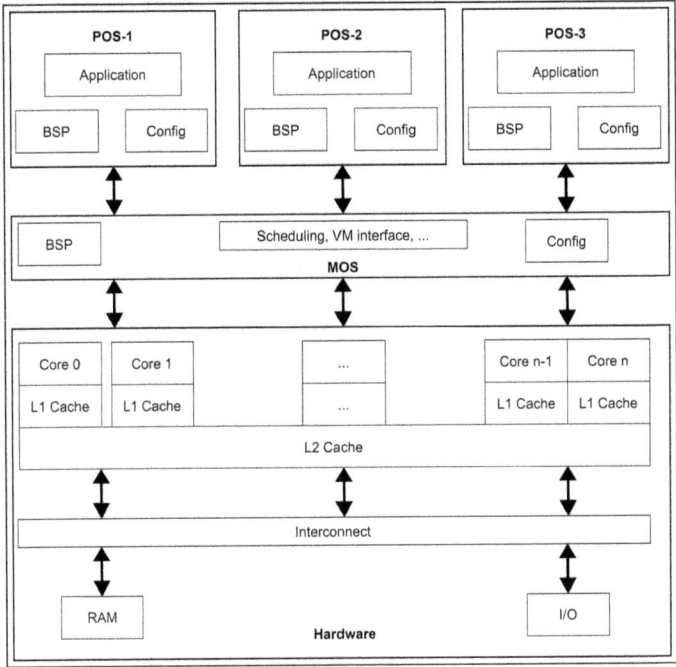

Fig. 6. Architecture of IMA System on Multicore Processor

- I/O - A software partition should be allowed to consume only its allocation of shared I/O resources.
    ○ Deterministic scheduling of communication.
    ○ Guaranteed access for each software partition to a prescribed set of hardware resources for a prescribed period of time and at a prescribed rate and, if necessary, at a prescribed point in time.
- Dedicated Resources - Failures of hardware unique to a software partition should not cause adverse effects on other software partitions.
    ○ Protection of code memory, data memory, registers, and input/output buffers.
    ○ Protection of the processing and communication assigned to a partition.
    ○ The consistent order of execution between communicating partitions.

3.4 Extracting Potential Sources of Error

Robust partitioning occurs across the three basic subsystems of any computing platform: memory, central processing unit (CPU), and I/O [14]. Continuing our framework, we need to analyze and extract all the potential sources of error that may impact the isolation and protection of shared resources and isolation of dedicated resources, thus affecting time partitioning and space/resource partitioning. The extracted potential sources of error will provide input for identifying partitioning vulnerabilities. The potential sources of error are unique to the system we analyze, and the following lists some aspects that need to be considered in general cases.

CPU. For time partitioning, many issues need consideration, and no single mechanism can ensure its integrity alone. Ensuring time partitioning requires an analysis of the impacts from CPU internal mechanisms as well as how partitions utilize the CPU. Initially, from the CPU's own mechanisms, the following aspects should be considered: 1) Interrupts, 2) Modes of operation, 3) Pipeline. Additionally, abnormal operations or instructions by partition applications, along with other issues, also need thorough examination.

- Interrupt

  External interrupts, with the exception of the system clock, can cause partitions to exceed their allocated execution times, thereby disrupting time partitioning.

- Modes of operation

  Partition applications should operate in user mode. Operating in a privileged mode, such as guest-supervisor mode, may allow users to execute privileged instructions or modify critical register values (such as altering MMU access controls), thereby compromising robust partitioning.

- Pipeline

  In pipeline mechanisms, the Branch Prediction Unit (BPU) is used by different partitions, resulting in changes to its internal state, which can affect the BPU's behavior when subsequently accessed by other partitions, thereby potentially causing interference with partition execution times.

- Other considerations

Several pertinent issues should be considered like "a partition to fail to relinquish the CPU on time include simple schedule overruns, where particular parameter values cause a computation to take longer than its allotted time, and runaway executions, where a program gets stuck in a loop" [1]. And the CAST-2 position paper identifies several items need to be considered when analyzing time partitioning, such as interrupts and interrupt inhibits (software and hardware), loops (e.g., infinite loops), frame overrun, interference with real time clock, counter or timer corruption, pipelining and caching, control flow defects, memory or I/O contention, data flags, software traps (such as divide by zero), recursion termination, etc. [15].

Memory

Space/Resource Partitioning Issues in Memory. Just as the CPU is closely related to time partitioning, memory and space partitioning are inseparable. "Space partitioning must ensure that software in one partition cannot change the software or private data of another partition (either in memory or in transit) nor command the private devices or actuators of other partitions." [1]

Real-Time Operating Systems (RTOS) supporting multiple partitions typically utilize the processor's MMU for memory protection. This system requires a memory configuration table that must be validated to confirm its accuracy and completeness. As the MMU is a commercial off-the-shelf (COTS) device, its accuracy is usually verified through rigorous testing during RTOS testing periods.

Additionally, Software Fault Isolation (SFI) provides another approach to memory protection. This software-based method incorporates logic checks at each memory access point within the code, ensuring that the destination of memory references and jumps are correct by examining the machine code of the partition.

The CAST-2 position paper identifies items need to be considered when analyzing space partitioning, like loss, corruption, or delay of input or output data, corruption of internal data, external device interaction (e.g., protocol halts), program overlays, buffer sequences, control flow defects (e.g., corruption of a jump table), etc. [15].

Time Partitioning Issues in Memory. Several issues in memory that affect time partitioning include the following:

- Interconnect
  Different partitions running on multiple cores may attempt to access main memory, cache, or external devices simultaneously, which can lead to contention for these shared resources. Typically, the interconnect mechanism on MCP arbitrates these access requests, which may result in delayed access to resources for some partitions.
- Cache

When a partition uses the cache, it alters its state, which can subsequently affect the performance of the next partition accessing this cache. VanderLeest mentions that although Level 1 caches are often provided for each core with exclusive access, often the larger cache layers are shared between two or more cores and thus partitions running simultaneously on those cores can impact one another's performance - and in this case flushing the cache does not solve the issue [5].

I/O

Space/Resource Partitioning Issues in I/O. Space partitioning of I/O is also generally ensured by the Memory Management Unit (MMU), especially for shared I/O resources. Therefore, the correct configuration of the MMU is crucial.

Time Partitioning Issues in I/O. Several issues in I/O that affect time partitioning include the following:

- I/O Interrupt
  The issues related to time partitioning due to I/O interrupts have been thoroughly discussed previously; therefore, we will not reiterate those details here.
- I/O With DMA

  Under the control of DMA, I/O devices can directly interact with system memory, bypassing the CPU. This mechanism can lead to scenarios where, even after a partition has completed its allocated CPU time, it may still engage in DMA operations to transfer data between I/O and memory. As a result, this prevents the current partition from using the bus and delays its execution.

Dedicated Resources. Dedicated resources are allocated to specific partitions and need to be protected from influences from other partitions. One of the FAA's research studies mentions that "Other sources of error include the effect of IMA system hardware failures on shared and non-shared hardware components [16]."

Other Considerations.

Interpartition Communication. Inter-partition communication poses a challenge when designing and analyzing robust partitioning systems. Ensuring robust partitioning would be considerably simpler if the only requirement were to maintain functional isolation between partitions, without the need for communication across them. However, given that partitions often require the capability to communicate, both the design and analysis processes must incorporate this aspect. There are two dimensions to inter-partition communication: the space dimension is concerned with where and how data is transferred from one partition to another, and the time dimension is concerned with whether and how synchronization is performed and how one partition invokes services from another [1]. FAA report's research report mentions one potential error scenario in which if a servicing partition fails to respond, another partition might wait indefinitely for the data or service from the servicing partition.

Configuration Data. Configuration data not only offers a flexible approach to system setup but also plays a crucial role in managing shared resources like memory, CPU, and I/O, thereby influencing robust partitioning. Consequently, it is essential to verify the accuracy of this configuration data and ensure its consistency with the corresponding transformed binary data during the partitioning analysis.

ARINC 653 specifies several types of configuration data [7]:

- System_HM_Table: A table that maps system states and error IDs to error levels.

- Module_HM_Table: Actions to be taken when module-level errors occur.
- Partition: Application space and its ports.
- Partition_Memory: Partition memory requirements.
- Module_Schedule: Scheduling requirements for modules.
- Partition_HM_Table: Actions to be taken when partition-level errors occur.
- Connection_Table: Channel and its port mapping table.

Potential configuration errors include overlapping memory settings in Partition_Memory, overlapping schedule times in Module_Schedule, and misconfigurations in Partition_HM_Table, which may result in unaddressed partition-level errors. IMA system integrators must provide evidence that the configuration data is correct and consistent with the transformed binary data to prevent any compromise to robust partitioning.

BSP. The Board Support Package (BSP) serves as the interface between the operating system and hardware resources, encompassing both boot firmware and device drivers. The BSP initializes the processor, memory, performs various memory checks, and initializes devices, load and run OS from flash, and so on. After initialization, the BSP returns control to the RTOS, but its functions are still available to execute hardware-related features. When the device driver's processes are placed in the MOS, it is important to consider whether the execution of its process will affect scheduling such as partition switch, thereby disrupting time partitioning.

3.5 Identifying Vulnerabilities

DO-297 requires that a vulnerability assessment be conducted for each partition property. In the vulnerability assessment, all potential sources of error need to be considered [4]. Based on all identified potential sources of error, we need to conduct a detailed examination to compare the properties required for establishing robust partitioning with these sources of error, determining whether and how these sources of error could compromise the partitioning properties.

3.6 Verifying Mitigation Means

Most vulnerabilities are typically addressed during the development stage of robust partitioning through specific design features aimed at mitigation. Consequently, it is essential to construct detailed vulnerability scenarios based on the vulnerabilities identified in the previous step to test the effectiveness of these mitigation means in practice, as shown in Fig 5. If any vulnerability lacks appropriate mitigation (whether through design features or process-based solutions such as using verification tools to check configuration data accuracy), integrators and application developers must implement additional strategies to ensure all vulnerabilities are adequately addressed. This might include imposing extra restrictions on configuration files to mitigate vulnerabilities.

4 Conclusion and Future Work

Partitioning has been a crucial technique in the field of avionics for decades, yet no systematic and comprehensive framework for partitioning analysis has been publicly proposed. We believe that by following the framework for partitioning analysis we propose, researchers can gain a clear understanding of partitioning analysis activity and systematically conduct thorough analyses of specific platform partition schemes. In the future, we will focus on the widespread application of this framework in practical platforms to identify vulnerabilities, classify them, and create a standardized test suite for verifying the robustness of partitioning.

Acknowledgments. This paper is funded by Shanghai Trusted Industry Internet Software Collaborative Innovation Center.

References

1. Rushby, J.: Partitioning in avionics architectures: Requirements, mechanisms, and assurance, DOT/FAA/AR-99/58 (Washington, DC: Office of Aviation Research, March 2000). Also published as NASA/CR-1999-209347, Hampton, VA: Langley Research Center (March 2000)
2. AMC 20-193, Use of multi-core processors, EASA (January 2022)
3. AC 20-193, Use of Multi-Core Processors, FAA (January 2024)
4. RTCA DO-297, Integrated Modular Avionics (IMA) Development Guidance and Certification Considerations,Washington, DC: RTCA, Inc. (November 2005)
5. VanderLeest, S.H., Millwood, J., Guikema, C.: A framework for analyzing shared resource interference in a multicore system. In: 2018 AIAA/IEEE 37th Digital Avionics Systems Conference (DASC). IEEE (2018)
6. RTCA DO-248C, Supporting Information for DO-178Cand DO-278A, Washington, DC: RTCA, Inc., (December 2011)
7. ARINC Specification 653P1-2, "Avionics Application Software Standard Interface Part 1 Required Services." 1 Dec (2005). http://www.arinc.com
8. Littlefield-Lawwill, J., Kinnan, L.: System considerations for robust time and space partitioning in integrated modular avionics. In: IEEE Digital Avionics Systems Conference, Orlando, FL (2008)
9. Krodel, J.: Commercial off-the-shelf real-time operating system and architectural considerations, DOT/FAA/ AR-03/77. Office of Aviation Research, Washington, DC (2004)
10. VanderLeest, S.H., Matthews, D.C.: Incremental assurance of multicore integrated modular avionics (IMA). In: 2021 IEEE/AIAA 40th Digital Avionics Systems Conference (DASC). IEEE (2021)
11. Freescale Semiconductor, EREF: A Programmer's Reference Manual for Freescale Power Architecture Processors (June 2014)
12. FAA, "Certification Authorities Software Team (CAST) Position Paper: Multi-core Processors" CAST-32A (November 2016), Rev 0
13. Krodel, J., Romanski, G.: Real-time operating systems and component integration considerations in integrated modular avionics systems report, DOT/ FAA/AR-07/39. Hampton, VA, Langley Research Center (2007)
14. VanderLeest, S.H.: ARINC 653 hypervisor. In: IEEE Digital Avionics Systems Conference, Salt Lake City, UT, pp. 5.E.2-1-5.E.2-20 (2010)

15. Certification Authorities Software Team (CAST), Guidelines for assessing software partitioning/protection schemes, Position Paper CAST-2 (February 2001)
16. Krodel, J., Romanski, G.: Handbookfor Real-Time Operating Systems Integration and Component Integration Considerations in Integrated Modular Avionics Systems, DOT/FAA/AR-07/48. Office of Aviation Research, Washington, DC (2008)

A Common Declarative Language for UML State Machine Representation, Model Transformation, and Interoperability of Visualization Tools

Ali Jannatpour(✉) and Constantinos Constantinides

Department of Computer Science and Software Engineering, Concordia University,
Montreal, Canada
{ali.jannatpour,constantinos.constantinides}@concordia.ca

Abstract. Originally presented in previous work to capture the set of fundamental elements of the UML state machine specification, Common Declarative Language (CDL) provides a model that can aid in the validation and verification of requirements. In this paper we target two objectives: First, we extend CDL by addressing one of the advanced concepts of the UML state machine specification, namely the notion of orthogonality which allows complex machine behavior through parallel state configurations. Second, we complement previous work by focusing on how CDL can serve as a platform for the representation of a state machine, how the language can be deployed for a model transformation where the initial machine (containing composite and/or orthogonal states) can be flattened into a model whose formal definition we provide, and finally how the CDL can be deployed to support interoperability among text-to-UML drawing tools [11].

Keywords: UML · State Machine · EFSM · Declarative Representation

1 Introduction and Background

The Unified Modeling Language (UML) adopted and extended Harel's statechart specification to provide an elaborated state machine specification [2,9]. A UML state machine is part of the dynamic model of the UML specification and it can be deployed to model the behavior of a software system at any level of abstraction [7]. We can view the state machine as a cyclic directed multigraph where the elements in the tuple representation of the state machine map to an ordered pair that represents the equivalent graph, namely $Graph(G) = (V, A)$, where V is a set of nodes, and A is a set of ordered pairs of nodes called (directed) edges.

In discrete mathematics, a state machine may be represented as a graph, consisting of labelled edges, where each label represents an event that triggers the transition. In an extended form, a state machine may be represented using an Extended Finite State Machine (EFSM) where each label is a triplet $\langle e, g, a \rangle$, representing the corresponding event, guard, and the post-transition action. It must be noted that EFSM representation does not allow the inclusion of most UML features such as nested states, parallel regions, state behaviors, and pseudostates. Hence, only a *flat* UML state machine, that does not include such features, can be represented using an EFSM.

Various textual representations of UML diagrams may be found in the literature. While UML is a graphical language, elements of a UML diagram may be represented in a textual format. Balasubramanian et al. [1] introduce Polyglot, a comprehensive framework for analyzing models described using multiple statechart formalisms. Their approach involves translating statechart models into Java and analyzing them using pluggable semantics for different variants. The translation process captures the structure of the statechart model, while behavior is defined in separate Java modules. They also provide an implementation of their framework and present a case study where interacting components are modeled using different statechart formalisms. Sheng et al. [3] present a Prolog-based consistency checking for UML class diagram and object diagram. They formalize the elements of a model and then convert the model into Prolog clauses (facts). Consistency rules are also defined in Prolog, along with interfaces that enable querying of properties, elements, and submodels of the model. Khai et al. [4] propose an Prolog-based approach for consistency checking of class and sequence diagrams. Mens et al. [5] introduce a technique to improve statechart design supported by tools for test-driven development, behavior-driven development, design by contract, and property statecharts to facilitate the testing and validation process.

1.1 Motivation

In previous work, we presented the definition of Common Declarative Language (CDL) over the set of fundamental elements of the UML state machine specification while focusing on two applicabilities: 1) the provision of a query platform and 2) the simulation of state machine behavior. In this paper, we extend the CDL definition to capture one of the advanced elements of the UML specification, namely orthogonal states, while complementing the previous discussion by focusing on 1) how CDL can serve as a platform for the representation of a state machine, 2) how the language can be used for model transformation where the initial machine (with composite and orthogonal states) can be flattened into a model which we define, and finally 3) how the CDL can be deployed in an additional applicability: the interoperability among text-to-UML drawing tools [11].

The Common Declarative Language serves as a platform that can support a number of activities in the aid of requirements analysis and verification. It has several applicabilities: State machine presentation, UML state machine representation, a queryable database for model verification, transformation, and simulation. We map the graph's elements into a set of clauses, maintained in a declarative model as a set of facts in the Prolog language. We refer to such a set of clauses as the *Common Declarative Language as a Database*. While there exist many platform independent descriptive languages i.e. JSON, YAML, XML, etc. We view the Prolog representation as a common queryable and language-independent platform, since Prolog's querying platform can efficiently used in model transformation.

1.2 Organization of the Rest of the Paper

The formalism of the EFSM and the state machine presentation including the clause signatures is discussed in Sect. 2. The transformation of the (initial) state machine model into a flattened model into an EFSM format is discussed in Sect. 3. The deployment of the visualization tools (text-to-UML drawing tools) and their interoperabilty issues are discussed in Sect. 4. Both the initial and the flattened models can function as databases where developers can execute queries to obtain knowledge on three aspects: Behavior, Complexity and Measurements, and Wellformedness (to ensure the validation of the machine). Even though the focus of the paper is not on the query system (as discussed in previous works), in Sect. 5, we discuss how CDL can be deployed in such a platform.

2 A Formalism for an Extended Finite State Machine

An EFSM is formally defined as a 7-tuple [6]. Our redefinition of an EFSM adopts this 7-tuple, with a slight modification on the transition inputs to address ϵ-transitions, *guard lists* and *action lists*. The formal definition of EFSM is given in Sect. 2.1. The Common Declarative Language (CDL) clauses signatures are listed in Sect. 2.2. The set of *selection* and *manipulation* primitives for model transformation are defined in Sect. 2.3. These operations are applied on CDL clauses.

2.1 A Modified Definition of an Extended Finite State Machine

We define an EFSM M, as a 7-tuple $\langle Q, \Sigma_1, \Sigma_2, q_0, V, \Gamma, \rangle$, where

Q is a finite set of *states*.
$\Sigma_1 = \{e_i : i \in \mathbb{Z}\}$, is a non-empty finite set of *events*.
$\Sigma_2 = \{a_i : i \in \mathbb{Z}\}$, is a finite set of *actions*.
$q_0 \in Q$, is the *initial state*.
$V = \{v_i : i \in \mathbb{Z}\}$, is a finite set of *mutable* global *variables*.
$\Gamma = \{g_i : i \in \mathbb{Z}\}$, is a finite set of *guards*.
$\Lambda = \{\lambda : q \xrightarrow{e_i[g_j]/a_k} q'$, where $i, j, k \in \mathbb{Z}\}$, is a finite set of *deterministic* transitions defined on $Q \times (\{\epsilon\} \cup \Sigma_1) \times 2^\Gamma \to Q \times \Sigma_2{}^\star$, where ϵ denotes *null*, $q, q' \in Q$, $e_i \in \{\epsilon\} \cup \Sigma_1$, $g_j \subseteq \Gamma$, is a set of guards, and $a_k \in \Sigma_2{}^\star$ (the Kleene closure of Σ_2), is a sequence of actions.

A guarded ϵ-transition is represented by $\lambda : q \xrightarrow{\epsilon[g_j]/a_k} q'$. In the case $g_j = \emptyset$, the transition becomes ϵ-transition. In order for Λ to be deterministic, for every state $q \in Q$, at most one possible transition must exist. While this property holds for all EFSMs, we enforce the following additional restrictions: i) If state q has an outgoing ϵ-transition, no other outgoing transitions are allowed on q. ii) If state q has an outgoing guarded ϵ-transition, all other transitions on the state must also be guarded ϵ-transitions.

2.2 The Common Declarative Language

The clause signatures of the common declarative language are compatible with Unified Modeling Language (UML) 2.5 [8] (currently the most recent version) and are shown in Tables 1 and 2. Table 1 lists the core (common clauses in both the initial and the flattened model) while Table 2a to 2b list the clause signatures to support UML features related to the composite states and state behaviors, pseudostates, and parallel regions. The core signatures essentially describe an EFSM model, where the events (including their types) are explicitly specified.

Table 1. Core common clause signatures for UML state machines/EFSMs.

CLAUSE	DESCRIPTION
state/1	state(?Name) implies that ?Name is a state.
alias/2	alias(?Name, ?Alias) implies that ?Alias is a new name for ?Name.
initial/1	initial(?Name) implies that ?Name is the initial state of the state machine.
final/1	final(?Name) implies that ?Name is the exit (final) state of the state machine.
event/2	event(?Type, ?Argument) indicates an event where ?Type shows event type and ?Argument is a literal.
action/2	action(?Type, ?Argument) indicates an action where ?Type shows action type and ?Argument is a literal.
transition/5	transition(?Source, ?Destination, ?Event, ?Guard, ?Action) indicates that while the system is in state ?Source, should ?Event occur and with ?Guard being true, the system performs a transition to state ?Destination while performing ?Action.

2.3 Signatures of Transformation Operations

EFSMs do not support advanced UML features. To transform a UML state machine into an EFSM, we use tagging to attach and detach attributes to states and transitions. Examples of tagging are: attached by a 'do' tag to implement a *do* behavior, linking a sub-graph to a particular state to implement a *composite* state, etc. The following primitives are used in the transformations:

new-id([prefix]): creates and returns a new global unique identifier.
match(*s*, clause/arity [, condition = **true**]): selects all clauses matching *clause/arity* in *s* that satisfies given *condition*.
add(clause/arity, args): adds a new clause to the database.
remove(*s*): removes clause(es) denoted by the selector *s* from the database.
replace(*s*, args): replaces a single clause denoted by selector *s* with new arguments.

Table 2. The Common Declarative Language: Additional Clause Signatures.

CLAUSE	DESCRIPTION
substate/2	substate(?Superstate, ?Substate) implies that ?Superstate is a composite state with ?Substate being a nested state.
onentry_action/2	onentry_action(?Name, ?Action) implies that ?Name defines ?Action as an entry behavior.
onexit_action/2	onexit_action(?Name, ?Action) implies that ?Name defines ?Action as an exit behavior.
do_action/2	do_action(?Name, ?Proc) implies that ?Name defines ?Proc as a do behavior.
proc/1	proc(?Procedure) implies that ?Procedure is a process in do behavior.
internal_transition/4	internal_transition(?State, ?Event, ?Guard, ?Action) indicates that while the system is in ?State, should ?Event occur and with ?Guard being true, the system performs ?Action. In the triplet (?Event, ?Guard, ?Action), only ?Guard is optional, the absence of which is codified as nil.

(a) Clause signatures for composite states and state behaviors.

CLAUSE	DESCRIPTION
entry_pseudostate/2	entry_pseudostate(?Entry, ?Substate) implies that ?Substate is the target inner-state whose superstate is already defined by substate(?Superstate, ?Substate).
exit_pseudostate/2	exit_pseudostate(?Exit, ?Superstate) implies that ?Exit is an exit state within the superstate ?Superstate.
choice/1	choice(?Name) defines a choice pseudostate.
junction/1	junction(?Name) defines a junction pseudostate.
history/1	history(?State) implies that history of the incoming transitions to state ?State is captured.
deep_history/1	deep_history(?State) implies that history of the incoming transitions to state ?State as well as all its substates are captured.

(b) Clause signatures for pseudostates.

CLAUSE	DESCRIPTION
region/2	region(?State, ?Region) implies that ?State contains a autonomous region ?Region with substates, defined by substate(?Region, ?Substate).
fork/1	fork(?State) implies that ?State is a fork pseudostate.
join/1	join(?State) implies that ?State is a join pseudostate.
forking/2	forking(?Fork, ?State) implies a forked-transition to the ?State.
joining/2	joining(?Join, ?State) implies a joining-transition from the ?State to the join point ?Join.
par/2	par(?PState, ?List), used in the flattening process, keeps the list of all corresponding parallel [sub]-states that are handled by the state ?PState.

(c) Clause signatures for parallel regions and parallel states.

select(s, condition = **true**): selects all items from selector s that satisfy a given condition.
exists(s [, condition = **true**]): returns **true** if selector s contains elements that satisfy condition, otherwise **false**.
exists(s, clause/arity, [, condition = **true**]): ≡ match(x, clause/arity); return exists(x, condition); x may be referenced in condition.
bind(x, selector): binds x to the selector.
insert(e, place): inserts element e to the beginning of the list represented by place. If place is **nil**, a new list containing e is created, where place is pointing to. If place is singular, it is converted to a list that contains the element place.
append(e, place): same as ***insert()***, except e is appended to the end of the list represented by place.
remove(e, col): removes e from the collection represented by col. If col is singular, it is converted to a list that contains the element col itself.
pop(col): removes and returns the first element of col.
diff(s_1, s_2): returns the set difference $s_1 - s_2$. Both s_1 and s_2 are converted to a set if they are not.
concat(ℓ_1, ℓ_2): concatenates/appends ℓ_1 and ℓ_2 in a newly constructed list, as return value. If either arguments are singular they are converted to lists.

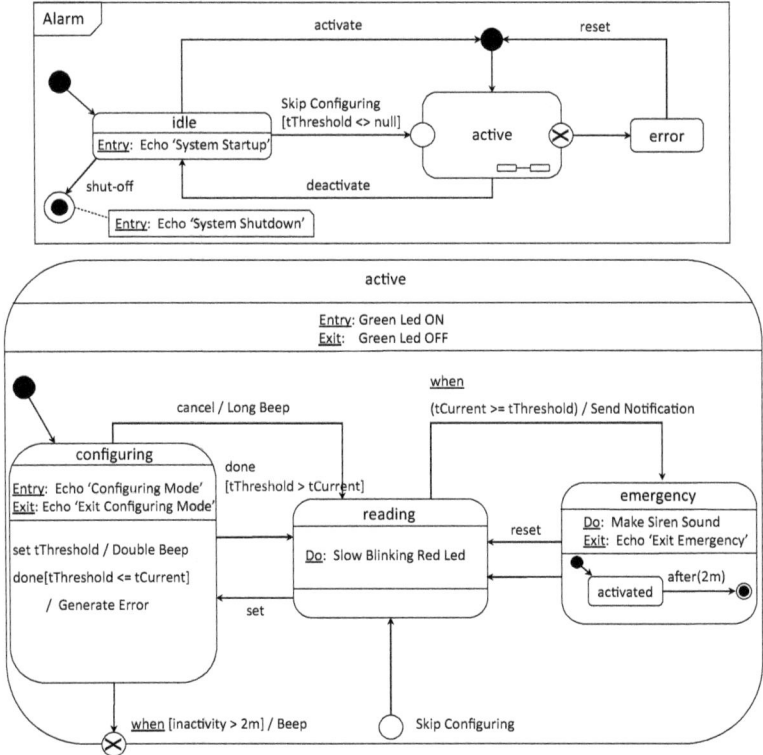

Fig. 1. A sample case-study representing complex UML features.

3 Flattening of a UML State Machine

In previous work, we presented an algorithm that flattens a state machine which is defined at a high level of abstraction (i.e. with superstates). The algorithm takes the UML representation of the machine and produces a flat state machine (with no composite states) which is a version of an EFSM (see Fig. 2). In this paper, we extend the algorithm to support parallelism through the provision of orthogonal states. The algorithm covers the following UML features: parallel regions, join and fork pseudostates, and nested state behaviors. It also addresses the implicit completion transitions in parallel regions, that are triggered by reaching inner final states in all branches.

In UML, completion events are represented as ϵ-transitions. An ϵ-transition is a transition whose *event* and *guard* are empty. Other examples of ϵ-transitions are those in pseudostates (i.e. entry and exit), as well as region completion (i.e. in the case of completion of a do action, or reaching a final substate). The flattened model is analogous to a bytecode platform for languages such as Java and Clojure, which is a seamless virtual machine. We believe that such a model can provide a platform for deeper analysis as well as a simulation of behavior. The flattening procedure is fully automated. The specification of the EFSM and the flattening procedure is given in the subsequent sections.

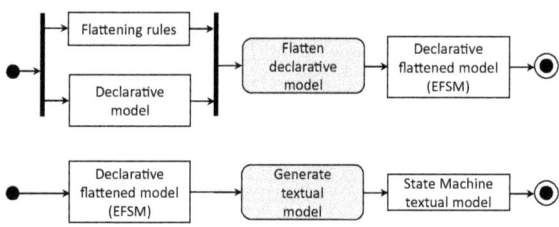

Fig. 2. Flattening activities.

3.1 The Flattening Process

In previous work, we presented a flattening algorithm that converts an input UML state machine into an EFSM. It was demonstrated that the process simplifies the complexity of a general UML diagram by resolving major features such composite states, state behaviors, exit- and entry-point pseudostates, choice and merge pseudostates into a flat EFSM machine with simple event-action-guard labels. The outline of the Flattening algorithm, namely procedure *Flatten* is given in the following.

Procedure *Flatten* (outline)
Input: The UML machine in CDL.
Output: The EFSM machine in CDL.

Pass 0 involves pre-processing that handles *completion*, *choice* and *junction* pseudostates.

Pass 1 resolves the pseudostates, *entry* behaviors. It also expands the *do* behaviors.

Pass 2 performs full top-to-bottom *full state resolution*, by which top level states are removed and their *exit* behaviors are handled. It also processes the *exit* behaviors for non-composite states as well as the internal transitions.

Pass 3 involves post processing, in which a) *stop* logs for *do* processes are resolved, and b) compound actions are converted into separate transitions. The *stop* event logs are produced in two phases: book-marked in Pass 1 and resolved in Pass 3.

In **Pass** 4, the resulting EFSM is minimized.
END Flatten.

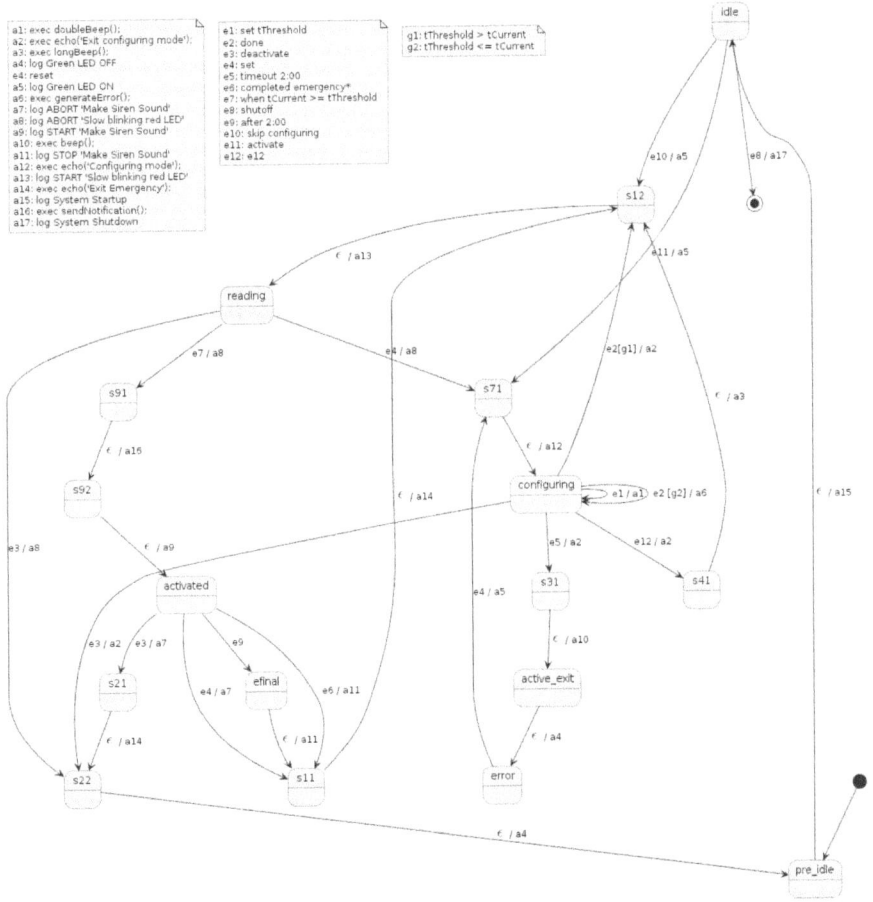

Fig. 3. Uncollapsed flattened ESFM.

A sample case-study (see Fig. 1) is used to demonstrate the conversion process. The output is illustrated in Fig. 3.

In UML, the completion events are presented using an unlabeled transitions which should not be confused with ϵ-transitions in the EFSM model. As a result, all unlabeled transitions are converted into explicit completion event, and remain as such.

Each pass in the flattening procedure, processes the input using clause selectors and incrementally transforms the input model into a resolved model by pipelining the output to the next pass. Pass 0 essentially ensures that the input UML does not contain any implicit completion event. All `nil`-transitions implying a region completion must therefore be converted into an explicit completion event. Hence, we assume all `nil`-transitions imply region completion, except for the outgoing transitions in *choice* and *junction* pseudostates, which are essentially event-free. In our model, regions are represented using state names (see state `pr` and `completed pr` event in Figs. 5 vs. 7, for instance). Passes 1-3 resolve state behaviors. We convert all state behaviors into actions. Handling the do behaviors in general is challenging. We treat do behaviors as processes that are being executed while the machine is *in* the corresponding state. Such process may be normally finished, in which case, it triggers a region completion even. We use the state name as a reference to the region. Alternatively, the process may be aborted, if there is an external event that triggers a transition from the state with the do behavior to another state. Such behavior may be analogous to the concept of processes and sub-processes in operating systems, where a process may be finished normally, or aborted by an external event. Hence, a do behavior representing a process 'P' is expanded into pairs of *start-stop* or *start-abort* action logs depending on whether the state/region is completed or aborted by an external event. We extend Pass 4 to further minimize the number of states of the resulting graph by collapsing the `nil`-transitions, as explained Sect. 3.2. The original algorithm did not address the resolution of the orthogonal states and their behaviors. This is discussed in Sect. 3.3.

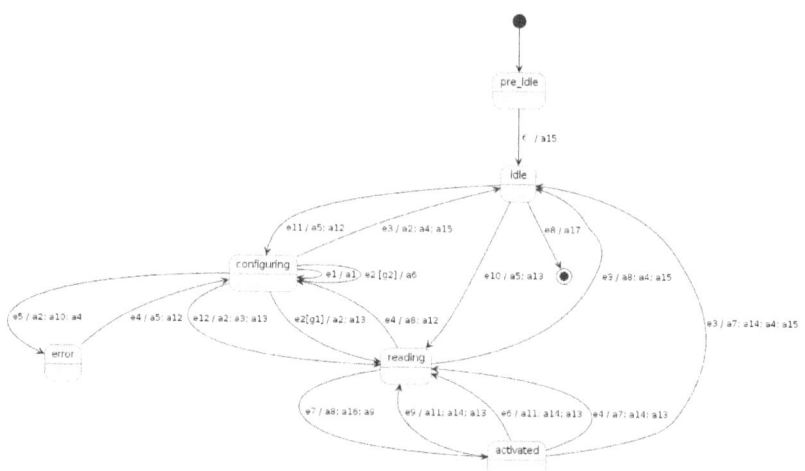

Fig. 4. Minimized collapsed flattened ESFM.

3.2 Minimization of nil-Transitions

The minimization of the flatten algorithm reduces the number of states by merging equivalent states and transitions. The original EFSM model did not support array of actions. That resulted in creating many (as well as) reduntant ϵ-transitions. By redefining the EFSM in Sect. 2.1, we suggest that a transition can contain a sequence of actions. Thus, we add a post-process minimization step by which, all sequences of ϵ-transitions are followed and merged into a single transition and the intermediary states are removed. Compare the resulting machines in Figs. 3 and 4. The post-processing step is implemented by procedure *Collapse*.

Procedure *Collapse*
Input: The EFSM machine in CDL.
Output: The EFSM machine in CDL.
    1. Set $l_s \leftarrow \emptyset$.
        Set $l_t \leftarrow$ all t in $match(t, \texttt{transition/5}, t.\text{event} \neq \textbf{nil})$.
    2. For each t_1 in l_t do:
    2.1. $bind(q, t_1.\text{destination})$; $remove(t_1, l_t)$.
    2.2. While $exits(t_2, \texttt{transition/5},$
                     $t_2[.\text{source},.\text{event},.\text{guard}] = \langle q, \textbf{nil}, \textbf{nil} \rangle$:
    2.2.1. $match(t, \texttt{transition/5}, t.\text{source} = t_2.\text{source}$ and $t.\text{event} \neq \textbf{nil})$;
          If $exists(t)$ return **ERR**.
    2.2.2. $replace(t_1, \langle\, t_1.\text{source}, t_2.\text{destination}, t_1.\text{event}, t_1.\text{guard},$
                 $concat(t_1.\text{action}, t_2.\text{action})\, \rangle)$.
    2.2.3. $append(t_1, l_t)$.
    2.2.4. $match(m, \texttt{initial/1}, m.\text{state} = q)$; If **not** $exists(m)$: $append(q, l_s)$.
    3. For each s in l_s do:
    3.1. $match(t, \texttt{transition/5}, t.\text{destination} = s)$; If $exists(t)$ return **ERR**.
    3.2. $remove(t)$; $remove(s)$.
END Collapse.

Note that in step 2, the list l_t includes all transitions whose source is a candidate state that is to be eliminated. The list is dynamic and newly added items are revisited in the iteration (see step 2.2.3.).

3.3 Parallel State Configurations Through Parallel Regions

Our declarative model is extended to support UML parallel regions using fork and join pseudostates. A sample abstract case study with corresponding declarative models are given in Fig. 5. An equivalent join-fork version of the above model is given in Fig. 6 with the corresponding changes in the declarative model. The two models are automatically convertible to one another.

3.4 Extending the Flattening Process

We extend the flattening algorithm to resolve the parallel states by simulating the parallel regions in an equivalent machine. The simulation is done by generating an equivalent UML state machine whose states are the Cartesian product of the set of states in parallel regions. The algorithm detail is given in procedure *PExpand*. The output of the algorithm on the input model in Fig. 5 is given in the Fig. 7 which illustrates that the flattened model correctly captures the handling of state behaviors in parallel states, in particular with parallel do behaviors, and with regards to the normal completion or aborted externally. The result is a UML state machine without parallel states. As illustrated, the initial entry behaviors are kept to keep the number of states to minimum. Once the parallel states are eliminated, the resulting machine may be fully flattened by applying the process Flatten to it. Note that the state entry and exit are covered in steps 3.3.3 to 3.3.6 in subroutine PStateBahavior.

Here we assume that the states in the parallel regions are not composite. All junctions and choice pseudostates are converted into regular states whose outgoing events are nil. The process expects explicit events. Hence, all nil-transitions are collapsed using procedure *Collapse*, as specified in Sect. 3.2.

Procedure *PExpand*
Input: The UML machine in CDL.
Output: The expanded UML machine in CDL.
   0. For all t in match(t, transition/5, t.event = nil):
       Set t.event = 'event(completed, $\{t.\text{source}\}$)'.
   1. Execute PCartesian.
   2. Execute PStateBahavior.
END PExpand.

Subroutine *PStateBehavior*
  0. Set $\ell \leftarrow$ all ℓ.state in $match(x, \text{par}/2)$s.
     Set $s \leftarrow x$.state in $match(x, \text{initial}/1, x \in \ell)$.
  1. For each $x \in \ell_2$.list in $match(\ell_2, \text{par}/2, \ell_2.\text{state} = s)$ do:
  1.1. $match(e, \text{onentry\_action}/2, e.\text{name} = s)$;
  1.2 $match(\alpha, \text{onentry\_action}/2, e.\text{name} = x)$;
     if $exits(\alpha)$ $append(\alpha.\text{action}, e.\text{action})$.
  1.3 $match(\alpha, \text{do\_action}/2, e.\text{name} = x)$;
     if $exits(\alpha)$ $append(\text{'action(log, "START } \{\alpha.\text{name}\}\text{"))'}, e.\text{action})$.
  2. Save ℓ in ℓ_{save}.
  3. While ℓ is not empty do:
  3.1. $\text{remove}(s, \ell)$.
  3.2. $l_{\text{from}} \leftarrow x$.list where $\text{match}(x, \text{par}/2, x.\text{state} = s)$.
  3.3. For each t in $match(t, \text{transition}, t.\text{source} = s)$ do:
  3.3.1. $\ell_{\text{to}} \leftarrow p$.list where $match(p, \text{par}/2, p.state = t.\text{destination})$.
  3.3.2. $s_{\text{leave}} \leftarrow \textit{diff}(\ell_{\text{to}}, \ell_{\text{from}})$; $s_{\text{enter}} \leftarrow \textit{diff}(\ell_{\text{from}}, \ell_{\text{to}})$.
  3.3.3. $match(\alpha, \text{onentry\_action}/2, \alpha.\text{name} = s_{\text{enter}})$;
     if $exits(\alpha)$ $append(\alpha.\text{action}, t.\text{action})$.
  3.3.4. $match(\alpha, \text{onexit\_action}/2, \alpha.\text{name} = s_{\text{leave}})$;
     if $exits(\alpha)$ $insert(\alpha.\text{action}, t.\text{action})$.
  3.3.5. $match(\alpha, \text{do\_action}/2, \alpha.\text{name} = s_{\text{leave}})$;
     if $exits(\alpha)$ and $t.\text{event} = $ 'event(completed, $\{s_{\text{leave}}\})$'
        $insert(\text{'action(log, "STOP } \{\alpha.\text{name}\}\text{"))'}, t.\text{action})$,
     otherwise $insert(\text{'action(log, "ABORT } \{\alpha.\text{name}\}\text{"))'}, t.\text{action})$.
  3.3.6. $match(\alpha, \text{do\_action}/2, \alpha.\text{name} = s_{\text{enter}})$;
     if $exits(\alpha)$ $append(\text{'action(log, "START } \{\alpha.\text{name}\}\text{"))'}, t.\text{action})$.
  4. Restore ℓ from ℓ_{save}.
  5. For all $p \in \ell$, For all x in $match(x, \text{par}/2, x.\text{state} = p)$,
     For all s in x.list do:
  5.1. $remove(e)$ where $match(e, \text{onentry\_action}/2, e.\text{name} = s)$.
  5.2. $remove(e)$ where $match(e, \text{do\_action}/2, e.\text{name} = s)$.
  5.3. $remove(e)$ where $match(e, \text{onexit\_action}/2, e.\text{name} = s)$.
END PStateBehavior.

Subroutine *PCartesian*
For each s_{top} in $match(s, \text{state/1}, exists(r, \text{region/1}, r.\text{state} = s))$ do:
1. $s_{\text{new}} = \text{new-id}(\text{'s'}); add(\text{substate/2}, \langle s_{\text{top}}, s_{\text{new}}\rangle); add(\text{par/2}, \langle s_{\text{new}}, \{\}\rangle)$.
2. For each r in $match(r, \text{region/2}, r.\text{state} = s_{\text{top}}$ and
   $exists(x, \text{substate/2}, x.\text{superstate} = r.\text{state}$ and
   $exists(y, \text{initial/1}, y.\text{state} = x.\text{substate}))$ do:
   $match(\ell, \text{par/2}, \ell.\text{state} = s_{\text{new}}); append(y.\text{state}, \ell.\text{list})$.
3. Set $l \leftarrow \{s_{\text{new}}\}$.
4. While l is not empty do:
4.1. $s \leftarrow pop(l)$.
4.2. $match(x, \text{par/2}, x.\text{state} = s); bind(p, x.\text{list})$.
4.3. For each t in $match(t, \text{transition/5}, t.\text{source} \in p)$:
4.3.1. Set $p' \leftarrow p - \{\ t.\text{source}\ \} + \{\ t.\text{destination}\ \}$.
4.3.2. If not $exists(x, \text{state/1}, x.\text{list} = p')$:
   $s_{\text{new}} = \text{new-id}(\text{'s'}); add(\text{substate/2}, \langle s_{\text{top}}, s_{\text{new}}\rangle);$
   $add(\text{par/2}, \langle s_{\text{new}}, p'\rangle); append(s_{\text{new}}, l)$.
4.3.3. $match(x, \text{state/1}, x.\text{list} = p')$.
4.3.4. If $\forall x_i \in p' : exists(f, \text{final/1}, f.\text{state} = x_i)$, then
   $add(\text{final/1}, \langle s_{\text{new}}\rangle)$.
4.3.5. $add(\text{transition/5}, \langle s, x.\text{state}, t.\text{event}, t.\text{guard}, t.\text{action}\rangle)$.
5. For all q in $match(r, \text{region/2}, r.\text{state} = s_{\text{top}})$,
   $match(q, \text{substate/2}, q.\text{region} = r.\text{region})$ do:
5.1. $remove(t)$ in $match(t, \text{transition/5}, t.\text{source} = q$ or
   $t.\text{destination} = q)$;
5.2. $remove(x)$ in $match(x, \text{substate/2}, x.\text{substate} = q)$.
5.3. $remove(x)$ in $match(x, \text{initial/1}, x.\text{state} = q)$, if any.
5.4. $remove(x)$ in $match(x, \text{final/1}, x.\text{state} = q)$, if any.
6. $remove(r)$ in $match(r, \text{region/2}, r.\text{state} = s_{\text{top}})$.
END PCartesian.

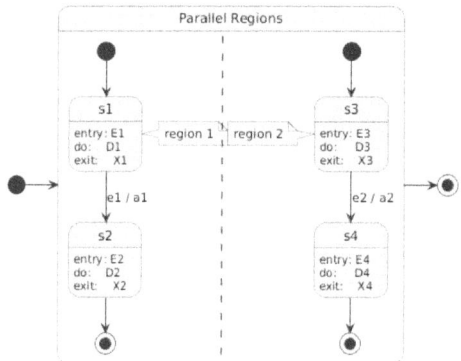

Fig. 5. An abstract UML state machine with parallel regions.

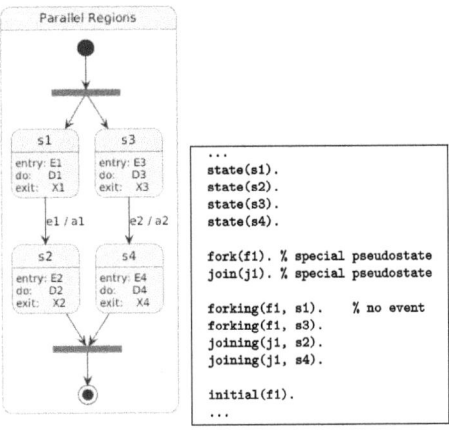

Fig. 6. Equivalent UML inner-states using join/fork pseudostates.

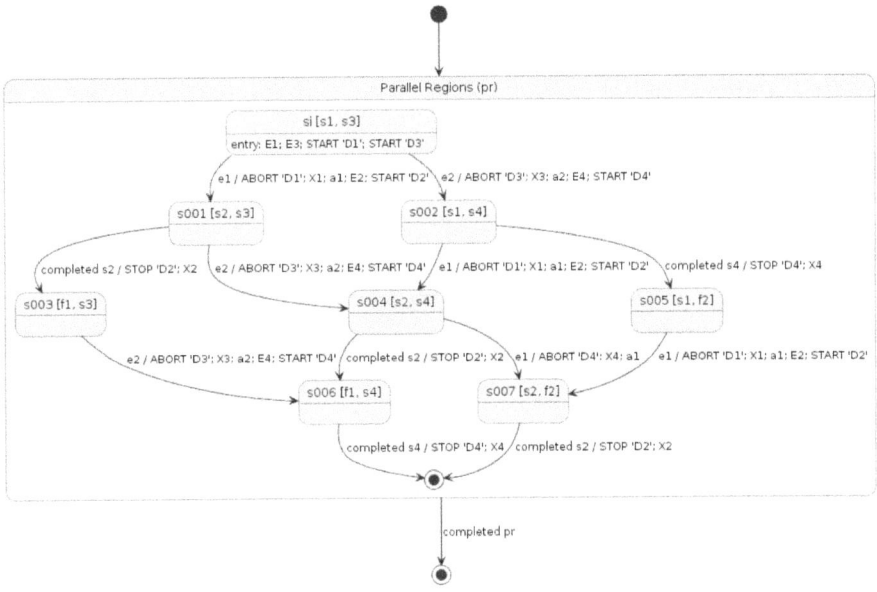

Fig. 7. Generated equivalent expanded machine without parallel regions.

3.5 Complexity and Correctness of the Flattening Process

We verified the correctness of the algorithm by using a database of case-studies with nested composite states, with both implicit and explicit events. We used complex behaviors to verify the resulting sequence of actions [10]. For simplicity, we did not include an external event in the complex region.

The flattened model though at a low level of abstraction, serves as a tool to aid in the behavior analysis of the state machines. While the resulting EFSM includes more vertices compared to the number of states in the original UML state machine, it makes all transitions explicit. This can aid in behavior analysis of the initial machine (correctness, complexity, and welformedness). The formal proof of correctness may be provided by using formal definition of UML state machines. We plan to address this in future.

4 Interoperability Among Text-to-UML Drawing Tools

There exist, currently, a number of industrial tools that allow developers to provide a textual description of UML diagrams, which are subsequently visualized. Examples include PlantUML, Mermaid, and others, that normally support a number of different diagrams [11]. One of the problems we have identified is that there does not exist any interoperability between these tools, e.g. a visual representation created by one cannot be backward (i.e. visual-to-text) mapped to a different specification (and subsequently extended or modified). The lack of interoperability is mainly caused by missing and/or custom implementation of certain UML features (i.e. pseudostates, junctions, and region completion). Our approach to resolving the interoperability issue is to use our declarative model as a common descriptive language among the different visualization tools. There are two types of model transformation, as shown in Fig. 8.

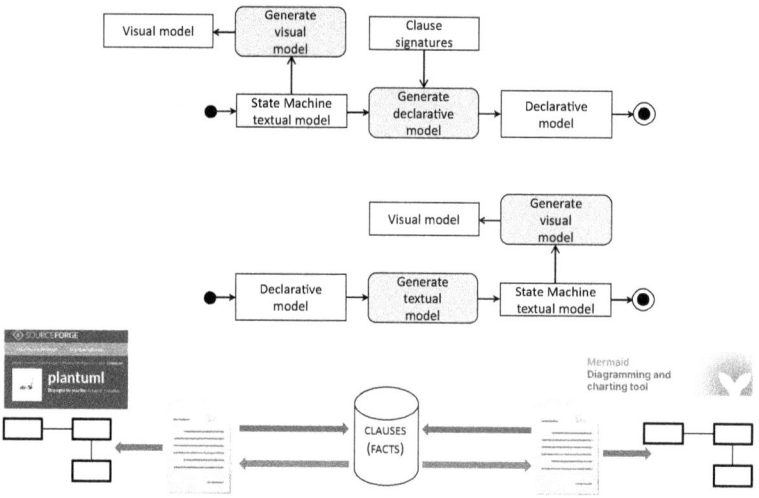

Fig. 8. Transformation activities to support visualization tool interoperability.

A state machine is initially represented as a textual model in some text-to-UML drawing package like e.g. PlantUML. The package can provide a visualization of the machine as a state transition diagram. Our first model transformation is to represent the machine in a declarative model, as shown in Fig. 8.

Utilizing Prolog to establish a declarative representation of state machines offers an simple and powerful method to depict the diverse constituents of a state machine, encompassing states and transitions. State machines often encompass intricate and diverging behavior, introducing complexity in ensuring exhaustive testing of all conceivable paths. Prolog's functionalities such as pattern matching and backtracking render it particularly apt for simulating the intricate behavior of complex systems. Furthermore, Prolog offers the valuable assets of a query engine and a query interface, which play a pivotal role in streamlining the process of flattening a state machine. This technology enables us to seamlessly navigate the intricacies of state machines by formulating and executing queries that extract essential information about states and transitions. Additionally, Prolog's declarative nature provides the flexibility to expand the model's capabilities. By introducing custom Prolog rules, we gain the ability to delve into the study of behavioral patterns, complexity analysis, and overall design intricacies inherent in the underlying state machine. This strategic incorporation of Prolog not only facilitates our immediate goals but also lays a solid foundation for comprehensive exploration and understanding of the state machine's behavior and structure.

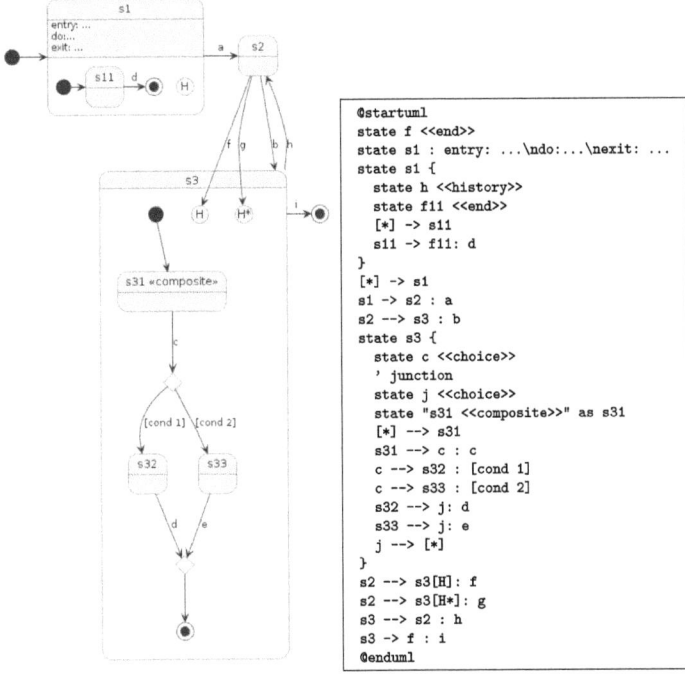

Fig. 9. A sample diagram in PlantUML, illustrating various UML features.

The transformation from the declarative model to a visualization tool deploys a template-based approach. Every clause is mapped into certain annotated code-blocks with placeholders, in which the element name, id, and underlying attributes are codified. The full diagram is then embedded in a top level template with an appropriate header and footer. Visualization tools would not necessarily support the most recent of the UML specifications in their entirety.

A sample diagram in PlantUML highlighting the above features is given in Fig. 9. Indicatively, we can refer to PlantUML where a number of elements are not supported such as History annotated state (see state s1, as opposed to the History entry pseudostate in s3), the composite annotated state (state s31), state behavior (state s1), junction pseudostates (state s3). As illustrated, missing features are implemented using mock states, as alternative notations, to be replaced by proper notation when the feature is supported by the tool. The transformation from the visualization tool to the common declarative model is challenging, as we need to identify and detect any and all alternative notations which will have to be properly codified in the declarative model. To achieve this, our UML parser searches for certain keywords in the textual description and when it finds a match, it automatically puts the detected element (i.e. the state behavior) in the declarative model. Furthermore, since the declarative model requires specific event types, certain assumptions are made. For instance, we assume all event types are call events, all do behaviors are processes, and all actions (including the actions in the state behaviors) are log actions. In general, it is desirable to have unique element IDs in the diagram. However, this is not enforced by the tools. To address this, we define an alias clause (see Table 1). Another example of using the alias clause is in the process of flattening parallel states, in which the link between the newly generated states and the expanded states is maintained (see Fig. 7).

5 The Common Declarative Language as a Database

State machine can be deployed during requirements analysis to capture functional requirements such as a use case and thus can provide a helpful tool for the validation of the requirements. The machine can also serve as a tool further down the line of the development during testing for the verification of the requirements. With the declarative model as is, we can execute simple (ground and non-ground) queries that can give us some basic knowledge of the machine. We extend the database with rules that reason about graph navigation and graph complexity. These two aspects would correspond to the observable behavior and the properties of the underlying machine, which can be subsequently mapped to the functional and non-functional requirements respectively. Available rules include in_degree/2 that succeeds by returning the in-degree of a state, and get_all_internals/1 that succeeds by finding all state-event-action triplets over internal transitions whose definitions and sample execution are shown below:

```
in_degree(State, N) :-
    findall([Source, State],
        (initial(State); transition(Source, State, _, _, _);
        (entry_pseudostate(Entry, Substate),
            transition(_, Entry, _, _, _),
            superstate(State, Substate));
        entry_pseudostate(Source, State)), Lst), length(Lst, N).

get_all_internals(Lst) :-
    findall([Source, [EType, Event], [AType, Action]],
        internal_transition(Source, event(EType, Event), _,
        action(AType, Action)), Lst).

?- in_degree(configuring, N).   %% N = 2
?- in_degree(reading, N).       %% N = 5
?- in_degree(active, N).        %% N = 3

?- get_all_internals(Lst).
%% Lst = [[configuring, [set, tThreshold], [exec, "doubleBeep();"]],
%%        [configuring, [call, done], [exec, "generateError();"]]]
```

When we study the observable behavior of the machine, we want rules that reason about elements such as the exposed interface and legal event sequences. When we study the properties of the machine, we want rules that reason about elements such as connectivity and measurements. A third aspect of analysis is the well-formedness of the machine. Example issues include the presence of infinite loops, dead ends, or conflicts with the UML specification, such as e.g. the existence of an internal transition without an action association. If an issue is present in a machine, then there are two issues to consider: If the machine faithfully maps requirements, then the conflict originates in requirements and the discovery of such conflict aids in requirements validation where developers pose the following question: "Are we building the right product?" Otherwise, if the machine does not faithfully map requirements, then the discovery of such conflict aids in the proper construction of the machine.

6 Conclusion and Future Work

The common declarative language of a UML state machine serves initially as a textual representation. Text-to-UML drawing tools can deploy this language in a model transformation to create a repository of representation as well as to support tool interoperability, as a machine produced by one tool can then be represented declaratively and read by another tool. A possible challenge and limitation to this is the fact that not participants (UML specification, visualization tools and declarative language) may support the exact same set of UML elements, so compatibility may not always be full, while at the same time it is never static as all participants constantly evolve. Our extended finite state machine definition allows a UML state machine to be flattened, whereby composite and orthogonal states collapse into a single level of abstraction. In previous work we deployed the flattened model as the basis of simulation. Both the initial and the flattened representations can serve as declarative databases, where one can execute queries in order to extract more knowledge about the machine and consequently on the corresponding functional and non-functional requirements of the component that the machine represents, whether the system in its entirety, a case study, or other. In previous work, we concentrated on the fundamental features of the UML specification, where the common declarative language was deployed mainly as a database and the basis for simulation. In this paper we addressed one of the major advanced features of the UML specification, namely the presence of orthogonality, while complementing on previous work concentrating on representation, model transformation (flattening) and visualization tool interoperability. Future work should address the second major advanced feature of a UML state machine, namely the presence of the History pseudostate.

References

1. Balasubramanian, D., Păsăreanu, C.S., Karsai, G., Lowry, M.R.: Polyglot: systematic analysis for multiple statechart formalisms. In: Piterman, N., Smolka, S.A. (Eds.) Tools and Algorithms for the Construction and Analysis of Systems. TACAS 2013. Lecture Notes in Computer Science, vol. 7795. Springer, Berlin, Heidelberg (2013)
2. Beckert, B.: UML State Machines, Lecture notes, Universität Koblenz-Landau
3. Sheng, F., Zhu, H., Yang, Z., Yin, J., Lu, G.: Verifying static aspects of UML models using Prolog. In: Proceedings of the 31st International Conference on Software Engineering and Knowledge Engineering, SEKE 2019, Portugal (2019)
4. Khai, Z., Nadeem, A., Lee, G.S.: A Prolog based approach to consistency checking of UML class and sequence diagrams. In: Th, K. et al. Software Engineering, Business Continuity, and Education. Communications in Computer and Information Science, vol. 257. Springer, Berlin, Heidelberg (2011)
5. Mens, T., Decan, A., Spanoudakis, N.I.: A method for testing and validating executable statechart models. In: Software and Systems Modeling, vol. 18, pp. 837–863. Springer-Verlag (2019)
6. Cheng, K.T., Krishnakumar, A.S.: Automatic generation of functional vectors using the extended finite state machine model. ACM Trans. Des. Autom. Electron. Syst. 1(1), 57–59 (1996)
7. Friedenthal, S., Moore A., Steiner, R.: A Practical Guide to SysML (Third Edition), Kaufmann M. (ed.) (2015)
8. Object Management Group: Unified Modeling Language (UML) Version 2.5.1 (2017)
9. Alagar, V.S., Periyasamy, K.: Specification of Software Systems (2011)
10. Podeski, A.: Hierarchical State Machines. Albert-Ludwigs-Universität Freiburg, Lecture notes (2015)
11. https://modeling-languages.com/text-uml-tools-complete-list/

The Three-Point Optimization Algorithm: A Novel Physics-Based Metaheuristic Approach

Xiong Deng[1,2](✉), Shaoying Liu[1], and Yanli Liu[2]

[1] Hiroshima University, Higashi-Hiroshima City, Hiroshima 739-8511, Japan
{d204465,sliu}@hiroshima-u.ac.jp
[2] Anyang Normal University, Anyang City, Henan 455000, China
dx801216@163.com

Abstract. In this paper, a novel metaheuristic approach called The Three-point Optimization Algorithm (TPOA) is proposed. TPOA is inspired by the principle of three point positioning. Three point positioning is a geometric based positioning method that determines the position of a target by measuring the distance between the target point and a known point. This method has a wide range of applications in multiple fields, including geological surveying, satellite navigation systems, and WeChat positioning. TPOAs performance is demonstrated by benchmarking with 10 well-known test functions (including unimodal, multimodal, fixed-dimension multimodal, and composite functions). Moreover, TPOAs results are verified by comparison to 5 other metaheuristics. In this study, the experimental results for the above 6 methods on the 10 testing functions in terms of the Mean (mean value), Std (standard deviation), the Best(the best value), the Worst(the worst value), and Burden(cost time), and it suggest that TPOAs results are competitive and, in many instances, outperform the aforementioned well-known metaheuristics.

Keywords: TPOA · Three-point positioning · Target point · Known point

1 Introduction

Optimisation has been ubiquitous since ancient times, and the search for maximising or minimising the solution of a problem has pervaded every aspect, from the daily lives of individuals to the practice of financial markets, from scientific research to engineering design applications [1]. In terms of system design, the goal of optimisation is to find a system whose output is the optimal value given the constraints [2]. There are a large number of complex system problems that need to be solved by optimisation in the real world, such as engineering structural design [3], communication networking [4], energy scheduling [5], and various unmanned systems [6,7]. Traditional optimisation algorithms such as gradient descent, linear programming, Newton's method and conjugate gradient, etc., usually take the approach of constructing an exact mathematical model to solve, these classical algorithms have high theoretical thresholds, are computationally complex, and are generally only suitable for solving small-scale problems in specific scenarios [8]. With the increasing complexity of optimisation problems in various fields such as science and technology engineering, financial market and social environment, it is difficult to establish accurate mathematical models, and traditional optimisation algorithms are increasingly difficult to meet the demand, especially when some problems have complex constraints, multiple objective functions, and variables with high dimensionality and high order, which make it impossible to complete the solution even if the problem can be modelled.

There are two important search strategies for metaheuristic optimisation algorithms: (1) exploration/diversification and (2) exploitation/reinforcement [9,10]. Exploration refers to the ability to explore the search space in a global context. This ability is related to avoiding local optima and solving local optima traps. Conversely, exploration is the ability to explore nearby promising solutions to improve their local quality [11]. Superior performance of an algorithm requires a proper balance between these two strategies [12–14]. All population-based algorithms use these features, but with different operators and mechanisms. A popular classification of meta-heuristic algorithms is based on the inspiration of evolutionary algorithms [15,16], swarm intelligence algorithms [17,18], physically-based approaches [19,20] and human-based approaches [21,22].

The theoretical research published in the literature can be divided into three sections: modifying existing algorithms, mixing various algorithms, and proposing new algorithms. The reason why researchers do not use a single algorithm is because, according to the no free lunch theorem [23], no single optimisation algorithm can solve all optimisation problems. Therefore, we need to modify existing algorithms or propose new algorithms to better solve the current problem or provide solutions for new problems. This motivates us to try to propose a new optimisation algorithm, namely the three-point optimisation algorithm (TPOA). The rest of the paper is structured as follows.

The particular implementation of the proposed TPOA is illustrated in Sect. 2. The results of the proposed TPOA in solving various benchmark test functions in Sect. 3. Finally, the conclusion and potential future research directions are presented in Sect. 4.

2 The Three-Point Optimisation Algorithm(TPOA)

2.1 The Principle of Three-Point Positioning

The formulation of the three-point localisation principle primarily involves measuring the distance from an unknown point to a known point and then determining the position of the unknown point by solving a system of equations. Specifically, suppose there are three known points AP1 (x_1, y_1), AP2(x_2, y_2), AP3 (x_3, y_3) and an unknown point S(x, y). In order to obtain the coordinates

(x, y) of the unknown point S, it is necessary to measure the distances r_1, r_2, and r_3 from S to the three known points AP1, AP2, and AP3. Then, using the three known points as the centre of the circle, and the measured distances as the radius, draw three circles, which should theoretically intersect at one point, the unknown point. According to this principle, a system of binary quadratic equations can be established, and the x-value and y-value of the unknown point can be obtained by solving this system of equations.

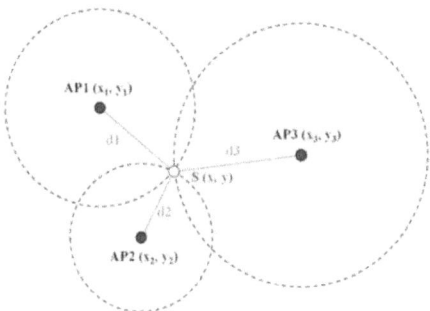

Fig. 1. The principle of three-point positioning

The process of calculating the coordinates of the unknown point based on the coordinates of the three known points is shown below.

Step 1: Construct the system of equations shown below.

$$(X - X_1)^2 + (Y - Y_1)^2 = r_1^2 \tag{1}$$

$$(X - X_2)^2 + (Y - Y_2)^2 = r_2^2 \tag{2}$$

$$(X - X_3)^2 + (Y - Y_3)^2 = r_3^2 \tag{3}$$

Step 2: The system of equations from step 1 is deformed.

$$-2(-X_1 + X_2)X + 2(-Y_1 + Y_2)X = r_1^2 - r_2^2 - X_1^2 + X_2^2 - Y_1^2 + Y_2^2 \tag{4}$$

$$-2(-X_2 + X_3)X + 2(-Y_2 + Y_3)X = r_2^2 - r_3^2 - X_2^2 + X_3^2 - Y_2^2 + Y_3^2 \tag{5}$$

Step 3: Rewrite expression (4) as (6) and (5) as (7) respectively.

$$AX + BY = C \tag{6}$$

$$DX + EY = F \tag{7}$$

where A, B, C, D, E, and F stand for the following expressions respectively.

$$A = -2(-X_1 + X_2) \tag{8}$$

$$B = -2(-Y_1 + Y_2) \tag{9}$$

$$C = r_1^2 - r_2^2 - X_1^2 + X_2^2 - Y_1^2 + Y_2^2 \tag{10}$$

$$D = -2(-X_2 + X_3) \tag{11}$$

$$E = -2(-Y_2 + Y_3) \tag{12}$$

$$F = r_2^2 - r_3^2 - X_2^2 + X_3^2 - Y_2^2 + Y_3^2 \tag{13}$$

v**Step 4**: Solve for the horizontal coordinate value X and vertical coordinate value Y of the unknown point.

$$X = \frac{CE - BF}{AE - BD} \tag{14}$$

$$Y = \frac{CD - AF}{BD - AE} \tag{15}$$

2.2 The Procedures for TPOA

Inspired by the principle of three-point localisation positioning, the Three-point Optimization Algorithm (TPOA) provides a new physics-based intelligence optimization algorithm. This algorithm allows a simple optimization mechanism, few control variables, easy programming, and good converging effect. Following the principle of three-point localisation positioning, the procedures for TPOA can be outlined below.

Step 1: Initialise the values of the horizontal X and vertical coordinates Y of the three random reference points.

$$X_i^R = LB + (UB - LB) \times rand() \quad (i = 1, 2, 3) \tag{16}$$

$$Y_i^R = LB + (UB - LB) \times rand() \quad (i = 1, 2, 3) \tag{17}$$

where $rand()$ is a function which returns a value from the uniform distribution [0,1], and LB and UB are the lower and upper bounds of the search space, respectively.

Step 2: Randomly generate distances D_{ij} between jth unknown points and three reference points.

$$D_{ij} = (UB - LB)rand() \quad (i = 1, 2, 3; j = 1, 2, ..., N) \tag{18}$$

where N is the number of unknown points.

Step 3: Calculate the horizontal axis value X_{Iter} and vertical axis value Y_{Iter} of the unknown point using formulas (19) and (20), respectively.

$$X_{Iter}^j = \frac{C_{Iter}^j E_{Iter}^j - B_{Iter}^j F_{Iter}^j}{A_{Iter}^j E_{Iter}^j - B_{Iter}^j D_{Iter}^j} \quad (Iter = 1, 2, ..., Max\_Iter; j = 1, 2, ..., N) \tag{19}$$

$$Y_{Iter}^j = \frac{C_{Iter}^j D_{Iter}^j - A_{Iter}^j F_{Iter}^j}{B_{Iter}^j D_{Iter}^j - A_{Iter}^j E_{Iter}^j} \quad (Iter = 1, 2, ..., Max\_Iter; j = 1, 2, ..., N) \tag{20}$$

Step 4: Calculate the local optimum for all unknown points in the *Iter* iteration.

$$Local\_Best_{Iter} = min(f(X_{Iter}, Y_{Iter}))(Iter = 1, 2, ..., Max\_Iter) \tag{21}$$

Step 5: Calculate the global optimum for the previous *Iter* iterations

$$Global\_Best_{Iter} = min(f(X_{Iter}, Y_{Iter}))(Iter = 1, 2, ..., Max\_Iter) \tag{22}$$

Step 6: Update the horizontal axis value X_{Iter} and vertical axis value Y_{Iter} of the unknown point using formulas (23) and (24), respectively.

$$X_{Iter+1}^j = \begin{cases} X_{Iter}^j + Local\_Best_{Iter}rand(-1.0, 1.0) & \text{if } \frac{Iter}{Max\_Iter} < rand(0.0, 1.0) \\ X_{Iter}^j + Global\_Best_{Iter}rand(0.0, 1.0) & \text{otherwise} \end{cases} \tag{23}$$

$$Y_{Iter+1}^j = \begin{cases} Y_{Iter}^j + Local\_Best_{Iter}rand(-1.0, 1.0) & \text{if } \frac{Iter}{Max\_Iter} < rand(0.0, 1.0) \\ Y_{Iter}^j + Global\_Best_{Iter}rand(0.0, 1.0) & \text{otherwise} \end{cases} \tag{24}$$

Step 7: Start the iterative optimizing loop, repeating the implementation of steps 3 to 6, and evaluate whether the best function value exceeds that of the previous iteration. In case the function value improves on the previous iterative function value or the present iterations are under the maximal iterations, proceed to step 6.

$$Global\_Best(X*,Y*) = min(Global\_Best_{Iter})) \quad (Iter = 1, 2, ..., Max\_Iter) \tag{25}$$

where $Global\_Best(X*,Y*)$ is the global optimum after the end of the iteration.

The TPOA algorithm flow is shown as follows.

Algorithm:TPOA

Input: $N, Iter, Max\_Iter, LB$ and UB
Output: $Global\_Best\_Solution$ (X^*,Y^*)
1: Generate three random reference points using the Eq. (16) and (17).
2: Randomly generate distances using the Eq.(18).
3: Calculate the axis value of the unknown point using Eq. (19) and (20).
4:     for $1 \leq j \leq N$ do
5:        if $X_0^j < LB$ then
6:           $X_0^j = LB$
7:        if $X_0^j > UB$ then
8:           $X_0^j = UB$
9:    **end**
10: **Repeat**
11:     for $1 \leq Iter \leq Max\_Iter$ **do**
12:        for $1 \leq j \leq N$ **do**
13:           Calculate the local optimum in the Iter iteration using Eq. (21).
14:           Calculate the global optimum for the previous Iter iterations using Eq. (22).
15:           Update the axis value of the unknown point using Eq.(23) and (24).
16:           if $X_{Iter+1}^j < LB$ then
17:             $X_{Iter+1}^j = LB$
18:           if $X_{Iter+1}^j > UB$ then
19:             $X_{Iter+1}^j = UB$
20:        **end**
21:     **end**
22: Iter=Iter+1
23: **Until** $Iter > Max\_Iter$
24: Return the global best solution(X^*,Y^*) using Eq.(25).

3 Experiments and Analysis

As a test of TPOA's performance, the following ten typical optimization operations will be used for experimental simulations, including test functions from IEEE CEC (Congress on Evolutionary Computation) 2014 and IEEE CEC2017, as well as variants of these functions, which have the following properties: Unimodal, Multimodal, Continuous, Nondifferentiable, Differentiable, Nonseparable, Nonscalable, Separable and Scalable. The testing system adopted in this article is Windows XP with Intel Core i4, the processor speed and working memory are 2.0 GHz and 1 GB respectively, and the programming environment is VC + + 6.0. Testing operations performed are listed below Table 1.

Table 1. Benchmark functions.

Function	Range	Optimum
$f_1(x) = -200 \times e^{-0.02\sqrt{x_1^2+x_2^2}}$	[-32,32]	-200.00
$f_2(x) = cos(x_1)sin(x_2) - \frac{x_1}{x_2^2+1}$	[-2,2]	-2.0218
$f_3(x) = |x_1^2 + x_2^2 + x_1x_2| + |sin(x_1)| + |cos(x_2)|$	[-500,500]	1.0
$f_4(x) = 100x_2^2 + 0.01|x_1 + 10|$	[-15,15]	0.0
$f_5(x) = x_1^2 + 2x_2^2 - 0.3cos(3\pi x_1) - 0.4cos(4\pi x_2) + 0.7$	[-100,100]	0.0
$f_6(x) = x_1^2 + 2x_2^2 - 0.12cos(3\pi x_1)cos(4\pi x_2) + 0.3$	[-100,100]	0.0
$f_7(x) = x_1^2 + 2x_2^2 - 0.3cos(3\pi x_1 + 4\pi x_2) + 0.3$	[-100,100]	0.0
$f_8(x) = (x_1 + 2x_2 - 7)^2 + (2x_1 + x_1x_2 - 5)^2$	[-10,10]	0.0
$f_9(x) = (x_2 - \frac{5.1x_1^2}{4\pi^2} + \frac{5.1x_1}{\pi} - 6)^2 + 10(1 - \frac{1}{8\pi})cos(x_1) + 10$	[-15,15]	0.397887
$f_{10}(x) = sin(x_1)e^{[1-cos(x_2)]^2} + cos(x_2)e^{[1-sin(x_2)]^2} + (x_1 - x_2)^2$	[-2, 2]	-106.764537

To comprehensively compare the performance of the above six algorithms, we set a fixed number of 100 individuals and a fixed population iteration number of 100, calculate the optimal, worst, average, standard deviation(STD), and running time(measured in seconds) of the six optimization algorithms on the 10 test functions mentioned above, then added the ranking values of each algorithm separately to obtain the comprehensive ranking value, and finally evaluated the grade of algorithm performance according to the comprehensive ranking value as shown in Table- 4 (Integrated rankings and grades are in bold).

Table 2 reports the experimental results for the above 6 methods on the 10 benchmark functions in terms of Best,-Worst, Average,-STD,-and Burden (running time), which are obtained from 100 repeated simulations and 100 population size.

According to the results in Table 2, to compare further the performance, we ranked each models score from low to high in each testing function and the corresponding results are shown in Table 3.

Table 2. Performance of TPOA, TSA, DE, GA, PSO and AOA on 10 benchmark functions.

Function	Measure	Algorithm					
		TPOA	TSA	DE	GA	PSO	AOA
f1	Best	−199.9628	−199.9476	−199.9498	−199.8401	−199.9837	−200.0000
	Worst	−163.8188	−165.0204	−92.3865	−81.1576	−86.9886	−81.48815
	Average	−191.6423	−192.1039	−191.5251	−195.2029	−99.36751	−199.3148
	STD	0.389213	0.275726	0.226009	0.289027	26.28078	6.606275
	Burden	0.015000	0.022000	0.047000	0.166000	0.018000	0.077000
f2	Best	−2.02055	−2.004488	−2.019738	−1.959848	−2.021807	−1.919563
	Worst	1.209679	1.159996	1.995383	1.969890	1.87411	3.743286
	Average	−0.243742	−0.378005	−0.155040	−0.030436	−1.820430	−1.091731
	STD	0.084591	0.032814	0.044223	0.077731	0.260760	0.454695
	Burden	0.029000	0.033000	0.041000	0.167000	0.019000	0.058000
f3	Best	1.009384	1.00243	1.003441	1.005570	1.033381	1.000000
	Worst	45.22743	173.0845	165081.2	44748.29	652236.3	588096.3
	Average	8.419661	7.285355	281.9989	3.139297	137804.8	1953.996
	STD	0.89715	0.529019	128.6702	0.219824	12340.33	19062.68
	Burden	0.024000	0.024000	0.050000	0.170000	0.020000	0.065000
f4	Best	0.003422	0.000511	0.000427	0.002373	0.000010	8.13E-06
	Worst	14555.18	36911.87	156078.2	71972.16	174813.4	132525.8
	Average	9948.618	429.1499	2622.567	11506.95	163.0953	105.6254
	STD	22327.32	362.5316	914.7296	3851.472	948.5031	992.6208
	Burden	0.019000	0.0310000	0.050000	0.171000	0.024000	0.102000
f5	Best	0.001238	0.00564	0.002937	0.122638	0.002171	0.000000
	Worst	136.0254	184.5851	22924.43	29847.95	24039.58	28002.49
	Average	9.658123	7.958843	9.737037	18.18223	4811.181	96.87483
	STD	1.35944	0.715506	0.528676	1.929574	2562.337	970.8589
	Burden	0.016000	0.032000	0.047000	0.175000	0.019000	0.063000
f6	Best	0.000547	0.00038	0.001177	0.035187	0.000280	0.000000
	Worst	135.7864	184.2057	22924.10	29847.86	25112.18	25187.22
	Average	9.092502	7.417229	9.160994	17.47957	624.8872	94.0199
	STD	1.359858	0.734583	0.529982	1.872914	733.4546	938.2461
	Burden	0.026000	0.020000	0.045000	0.173000	0.020000	0.050000
f7	Best	0.001294	0.00019	0.000324	0.003107	0.000234	0.000000
	Worst	135.9819	184.6414	22924.25	29847.87	26657.85	27176.27
	Average	9.270464	7.510249	9.339694	17.63677	644.7738	105.1979
	STD	1.358277	0.705502	0.531668	1.865210	728.9435	1041.889
	Burden	0.01400	0.020000	0.045000	0.165000	0.015000	0.050000
f8	Best	0.000607	0.000023	0.002088	0.001332	0.001196	0.014176
	Worst	218.0311	216.0864	2545.057	206.3633	2497.941	5719.266
	Average	32.12598	28.05810	61.77510	56.31615	133.7728	34.74786
	STD	6.699201	4.015184	5.080083	33.08554	17.97098	44.62457
	Burden	0.017000	0.022000	0.040000	0.061000	0.160000	0.092000
f9	Best	0.413739	0.398112	0.400624	0.463444	0.403582	0.417827
	Worst	105.4683	306.7957	3552.924	460.7176	5164.66	5149.848
	Average	29.30604	27.76077	43.86936	28.33846	77.38122	70.97459
	STD	4.209889	2.343116	2.566398	17.57861	7.919740	65.51272
	Burden	0.018000	0.022000	0.044000	0.061000	0.168000	0.050000
f10	Best	−82.294626	−106.69629	−106.47959	−106.76062	−106.34746	−106.7645
	Worst	103.6044	42.23410	170.0963	87.80018	170.7344	126.7963
	Average	7.232617	6.269218	6.731247	−5.736507	11.98133	−30.58109
	STD	1.311856	1.036712	0.990560	9.793921	2.581613	35.54652
	Burden	0.022000	0.027000	0.061000	0.083000	0.187000	0.061000

According to the results in Table 3, we add the ranking values of each algorithm separately to obtain the comprehensive ranking value, and finally evaluate

Table 3. Rankings of TPOA, TSA, DE, GA, PSO and AOA according to 10 benchmark functions.

Function	Measure	Algorithm					
		TPOA	TSA	DE	GA	PSO	AOA
f1	Best	1	4	1	3	2	1
	Worst	2	3	6	5	1	4
	Average	2	5	4	3	6	1
	STD	3	4	5	1	6	2
	Burden	3	2	6	5	1	4
f2	Best	3	4	1	5	2	6
	Worst	2	5	1	4	3	6
	Average	3	6	1	5	2	4
	STD	6	2	4	1	3	5
	Burden	5	1	3	6	2	4
f3	Best	1	2	1	3	4	1
	Worst	1	2	6	3	5	4
	Average	1	3	5	2	6	4
	STD	2	3	6	1	4	5
	Burden	2	3	6	5	1	4
f4	Best	1	6	3	5	4	2
	Worst	3	6	1	2	5	4
	Average	2	5	1	6	4	3
	STD	4	5	1	6	2	3
	Burden	2	3	4	6	1	5
f5	Best	1	5	1	6	3	1
	Worst	1	5	6	4	2	3
	Average	2	6	4	1	5	4
	STD	2	4	6	1	5	3
	Burden	2	4	5	6	1	3
f6	Best	1	3	1	4	2	1
	Worst	1	4	6	5	2	3
	Average	1	6	5	2	4	3
	STD	2	5	6	1	3	4
	Burden	2	5	4	6	1	3
f7	Best	1	4	1	3	2	1
	Worst	1	4	6	5	2	3
	Average	1	6	5	2	4	3
	STD	2	5	6	1	3	4
	Burden	2	5	4	6	1	3
f8	Best	2	6	1	4	3	5
	Worst	2	5	1	4	3	6
	Average	4	6	1	5	2	3
	STD	6	5	1	2	4	3
	Burden	6	3	2	5	1	4
f9	Best	1	3	4	5	2	6
	Worst	1	5	2	4	6	3
	Average	4	6	1	5	2	4
	STD	6	5	2	1	4	3
	Burden	6	5	3	4	1	2
f10	Best	1	3	1	4	2	1
	Worst	1	3	2	5	6	4
	Average	1	5	2	6	3	4
	STD	4	2	6	1	3	5
	Burden	3	1	5	6	2	4

Table 4. Grades of TPOA, TSA, DE, GA, PSO and AOA according to 10 benchmark functions.

SUM, ranking and grades	Algorithm					
	TPOA	TSA	DE	GA	PSO	AOA
SUM- Best	13	40	15	42	26	25
Ranking-Best	**1**	**5**	**2**	**6**	**4**	**3**
SUM- Worst	15	42	37	41	35	40
Ranking-Worst	**1**	**6**	**3**	**5**	**2**	**4**
SUM- Average	21	54	29	37	38	33
Ranking-Average	**1**	**6**	**2**	**4**	**5**	**3**
SUM- STD	37	40	43	16	37	37
Ranking-STD	**2**	**3**	**4**	**1**	**2**	**2**
SUM- Burden	33	32	42	55	12	36
Ranking-Burden	**3**	**2**	**5**	**6**	**1**	**4**
Integrated -Ranking	**8**	**22**	**16**	**22**	**14**	**16**
Grades	<u>1</u>	<u>4</u>	<u>3</u>	<u>4</u>	<u>2</u>	<u>3</u>

the grade of algorithm performance according to the comprehensive ranking value, as shown in Table 4.

Besides the given evaluation metrics (i.e., best, average and standard deviation), Worst ranking test and Burden ranking test have been carried for conducting ranking comparisons for the above mentioned algorithms in a statistical way, as shown in Table 2, Table 3 and Table 4. The obtained results show that the proposed TPOA is ranked first compared to other comparative algorithms, followed by PSO is ranked second, DE and AOA are ranked third simultaneously, and finally TSA and GA are ranked twelfth. According to this test, the proposed TPOA algorithm proved its ability to get the optimal solution by getting the first rank in different test functions compared to other comparative optimization algorithms.

4 Conclusions

The Three-point Optimization Algorithm (TPOA) proposed in this paper is a revolutionary metaheuristic algorithm. It draws inspiration from the principle of three point positioning, which vary greatly depending on the three reference points. TPOA was tested utilizing 10 commonly used benchmark test functions, including Unimodal, Multimodal, Continuous, Nondifferentiable, Differentiable, Nonseparable, Nonscalable, Separable and Scalable functions. The evaluation comprised assessments of Burden ranking test, STD ranking test, Best ranking test, Worst ranking test, Average ranking test, and Grades analysis.

We have proposed the TPOA algorithm with a simple yet effective framework and a minimum number operators to build the foundations of this algorithm. It does not need to adjust many parameters except the population size and stopping criterion, which are standard parameters in all optimization algorithms. We will leave exploring other arithmetic and evolutionary operators (e.g.mutation and crossover, and multi-swarm composition) to future works.

In addition, other improved versions of the proposed TPOA can be proposed to solve optimization problems with discrete, and multiple objectives, respectively. The TPOA algorithm can be hybridized with other stochastic components, including local search or global search methods, in the area of optimization to enhance its performance. Finally, the investigation of the utilization of TPOA in other various disciplines would be a valuable contribution, such as in neural networks, image processing, feature selection, task scheduling, data mining, other benchmark test functions, other real-world problems.

References

1. Yang, X.: Engineering Optimization: An Introduction with Metaheuristic Applications. John Wiley and Sons (2010)
2. Mykel, J., Tim, A.: Algorithms for Optimization. The MIT Press (2019)
3. Ying, Y.: Application of particle swarm optimization in the engineering optimization design. J. Mech. Eng. (2008)
4. Wieselthier, J.E., Nguyen, G.D., Ephremides, A., et al.: Application of optimization techniques to a nonlinear problem of communication network design with nonlinear constraints. IEEE Trans. Autom. Control **47**(6), 1033-1038 (2002)
5. Zhang, J., Yu, Y., Li, Y.: Optimal scheduling of integrated energy system based on improved gray wolf algorithm. J. Science Technol. Eng. **21**(19), 8048–8056 (2021)
6. Ramezanlou, M., Azimirad, V., Zakeri, M.: Hybrid path planning of robots through optimal control and PSO algorithm. In: 7th International Conference on Robotics and Mechatronics (ICRoM) (2019). https://doi.org/10.1109/ICRoM48714.2019.9071893
7. Yue, W., Xi, Y., Guan, X.: A new searching approach using improved multi-ant colony scheme for multi-UA Vs in unknown environments. IEEE Access (2019)
8. Boyd, S., Vandenberghem L.: Convex optimization. Cambridge University Press (2004)
9. Abualigah, L., Diabat, A.: A comprehensive survey of the Grasshopper optimization algorithm: results, variants, and applications. Neural Comput. Appli. (2020)
10. Abualigah, L., Diabat, A., Geem, Z.: A comprehensive survey of the harmony search algorithm in clustering applications. Appli. Sci. **10**(11), 3827 (2020)
11. Abualigah, L.: Group search optimizer: a nature-inspired meta-heuristic optimization algorithm with its results, variants, and applications. Neural Comput. Appli. (2020)
12. Faramarzi, A., et al.: Equilibrium optimizer: a novel optimization algorithm. Knowl.-Based Syst. **191**
13. Sadollah, A., et al.: Mine blast harmony search: a new hybrid optimization method for improving exploration and exploitation capabilities. Appli. Soft Comput. (2018)
14. Gholizadeh, S., Danesh, M., Gheyratmand, C.: A new Newton metaheuristic algorithm for discrete performance-based design optimization of steel moment frames. Comput. Struct. **234**, 106250 (2020)

15. Mitchell, M., Holland, J.: When Will a Genetic Algorithm Outperform Hill-Climbing? (1993)
16. Feoktistov, V.: Differential evolution C in search of solutions. New York NT Am. Soc. Civil Eng. (2006)
17. Van Der Merwe, D.W., Engelbrecht, A.P.: Data clustering using particle swarm optimization. IEEE (2004)
18. Mirjalili, S., et al.: Salp swarm algorithm: a bio-inspired optimizer for engineering design problems. Adv. Eng. Softw. **114**, 163–191 (2017)
19. Abualigah, L., et al.: The arithmetic optimization algorithm. Comput. Methods Appli. Mech. Eng.**376**(2021)
20. Layeb, A.: The Tangent Search Algorithm for Solving Optimization Problems (2021). https://doi.org/10.48550/arXiv.2104.02559
21. Talatahari, S., Bayzidi, H., Saraee, M.: Social network search for global optimization. IEEE Access **99**, 1–1 (2021)
22. Oladejo, S.O., Ekwe, S.O., Mirjalili., S.: The hiking optimization algorithm: a novel human-based metaheuristic approach. Knowl.-Based Syst. **296**(2024)
23. Wolpert, D.H, Macready, W.G.: Optimizer.: no free lunch theorems for optimization. IEEE Trans. Evolutionary Comput. (1997)

Generating Simulink Models from Hybridised Event-B Models

Neeraj Kumar Singh(✉), Guillaume Dupont(✉), Yamine Aït Ameur(✉), and Marc Pantel(✉)

INPT-ENSEEIHT/IRIT, University of Toulouse, Toulouse, France
{nsingh,guillaume.dupont,yamine,marc.pantel}@enseeiht.fr

Abstract. Verifying hybrid system designs is complex due to the integration of discrete and continuous features, requiring formal verification, simulation, and testing. This paper presents a strategy for generating Simulink models from verified hybridised Event-B models, which use a correct-by-construction approach to progressively build both types of behaviours. A key challenge in simulating these models is synchronising the discrete and continuous elements. Our objective is to translate hybridised Event-B models into Simulink, with Stateflow representing the discrete components and MATLAB function blocks for the continuous ones. We illustrate this process through a water tank case study, demonstrating formal modelling, verification, and subsequent simulation of the generated Simulink model.

Keywords: Hybrid systems · Proof-based verification · Animation and Simulation · Event-B · Simulink

1 Introduction

Hybrid systems are used in our daily lives to build a variety of sophisticated safety critical systems that incorporate both discrete and continuous behaviours. Verifying such systems is an open challenge to ensure functional correctness under all conditions. However, formal methods have shown some interesting results [7] to address some of these challenges. One key challenge for modelling hybrid systems is that the physical plants exhibit continuous behaviours, whereas the software controller defines discrete computations. Recently, hybridised Event-B [11,12] has been successfully applied for designing complex hybrid systems using a correct-by-constriction approach in order to define dual discrete and continuous natures. The desired properties are specified in form of invariants and proofs are done. However, there is a lack of tools for doing animation or simulation of the built system to ensure its correct behaviour.

In this study, we show the translation of hybridised Event-B models (used for verification) to MathWorks Simulink/Stateflow models [15,16]. Our approach is useful for animating and validating the verified hybrid systems at different level of abstractions. The hybridised Event-B models consist of an abstract model and a chain of refined models, where different system components are introduced progressively to model a system controller with the required safety properties. Furthermore, all of the controller components of the concrete model are realised using Simulink blocks such as Stateflow for modelling discrete components and Matlab function blocks for modelling continuous components. Several formal analysis tools have been proposed, such as SpaceEx [13], Flow* [10], and Keymaera [17]. The majority of these tools do not include refining mechanism to support correctness by construction. In our proposed approach, a designer may develop a complex controller using a correct-by-construction approach and then the final model can be transformed into a Simulink model. We propose an approach to transform a hybridised Event-B model into a trajectory-equivalent Stateflow model and Matlab functions. Trajectory-equivalence entails that the discrete behaviours of the translated Stateflow model match the original discrete behaviours of the hybridised Event-B model. It is important to note that the semantics of hybridised Event-B models differs from Stateflow models. For example, the transitions of the discrete model of the hybridised Event-B model are based on guard predicates as long as the safety invariants are not violated, whereas the transitions of the discrete model of Stateflow are based on given transition guards, which can be enabled based on numerical aspects with zero-crossing detection.

This paper presents two main contributions. (a) To the best of our knowledge, this is the first study to provide a translation mechanism from hybridised Event-B models to Simulnk models that can be easily used in the main stream MBD (Model-Based Design) process. (b) We demonstrate the applicability of our approach in many case studies in which hybridised Event-B models are translated into Simulink models for simulation.

The paper is organised as follows. Section 2 discusses related work. Section 3 summarises the Event-B and hybridised Event-B methods, as well as MathWorks' Simulink and Stateflow tools. Section 4 describes how to generate the Simulink model from the hybridised Event-B model. Section 5 describes a water tank case study to illustrate our approach. Section 6 provides an assessment, and Sect. 7 concludes the paper along with future work.

2 Related Work

In [5], the authors discuss an approach for investigating how the behaviour of a B model can be represented in finite labelled transition systems (LTS). In this work, all B model states are represented in several disjunctive predicates, which are then used to identify LTS states and transitions. This strategy is demonstrated by developing an interface system for a small computer. Further, in [6], the authors describe methods and tools to build symbolic labelled transition systems from B specifications, handling refinement and visualising the decomposition of abstract states into concrete hierarchical states. In a similar vein, [9] proposes a methodology for generating Hierarchical State Transition Machines (HASTM), based on partitioning predicates, of a system for visualising Event-B models.

In [4], the authors propose an approach for designing cyber-physical systems by embedding hybrid automata into Simulink models. The verified hybrid automata are used to elaborate a Simulink model, transferring all of the necessary safety properties. The primary contribution of this work is to provide a flexible and expressive framework for hybrid automata, specifically a translation for handling both deterministic and non-deterministic models by generating trajectory-equivalent Simulink models. Several examples of translation and simulation are demonstrated, and these modes are then used to deploy on a hardware platform. In [21], the authors present an algorithmic implementation of a subset of a hybrid systems modelling language (HSML) within the Matlab simulation environment. The research emphasises state-based management of both continuous-time and discrete-time components. The authors illustrate the effectiveness of their proposed methodology through a practical example.

In [18], the authors introduce a hybrid methodology where control and software engineers collaborate in developing controller designs. The central idea involves the use of Requirement, Refinement, and Modelling (RRM) diagrams. This leads to a concrete model featuring discrete components designed by software engineers, alongside placeholder components for continuous elements crafted by control engineers. The final model integrates both discrete and continuous parts, with the concrete RRM model producing SL/SF components, while controller engineers approximate the continuous components manually. This mixed approach yields high-quality designs for modulation controllers. To illustrate this method, the authors present a simplified Adaptive Cruise Controller (ACC), including a manual conversion of the SL/SF model derived from the RRM model.

In [20], the authors explore the development of hybrid systems using Event-B and the Rodin Platform, presenting several examples that highlight the effectiveness of this methodology. They use the core Event-B modelling language for the discrete components of hybrid systems, while employing Matlab Simulink to simulate the continuous aspects. Note that the Event-B models do not incorporate differential equations, operating with fixed discrete time jumps instead. The authors advocate for the integration of Matlab for verification purposes, which provides insights into potential system failures when operating beyond intended domains. Additionally, most Event-B models are manually converted to Matlab for experimental validation. Similarly, the paper [3] presents a method for reachability analysis and simulation by generating JuliaReach and Simulink models from hybrid Event-B models.

The previously discussed approaches encounter various challenges, including the translation of B/Event-B into Labelled Transition Systems (LTS), the generation of Simulink models from hybrid automata, and the use of Simulink for simulating simple Event-B models. Nonetheless, the primary contribution of these studies lies in addressing the specific challenge of designing complex systems for both discrete and continuous features. To our knowledge, there is currently no translation mechanism for generating Simulink models from hybridised Event-B models, nor is there a simulation framework for simulating or animating hybridised Event-B models. This paper describes the first translation mechanism that produces Simulink models from hybridised Event-B models.

3 Preliminaries

This section offers an overview of the Event-B method [1] and its extension for addressing the continuous aspects of hybrid systems, with a specific focus on formalising differential equations. Additionally, we will discuss background information on the Simulink and Stateflow modelling toolboxes [16] in MATLAB for simulating hybrid systems.

3.1 Event-B and Hybridised Event-B

Event-B is a mathematical language grounded in first-order logic (FOL) and set theory, supporting a correct-by-construction methodology for modelling complex systems. An Event-B model comprises two essential components: *context*, which captures the static properties of a system (see Listing 1a), and *machine*, which delineates the dynamic properties of the system (see Listing 1b).

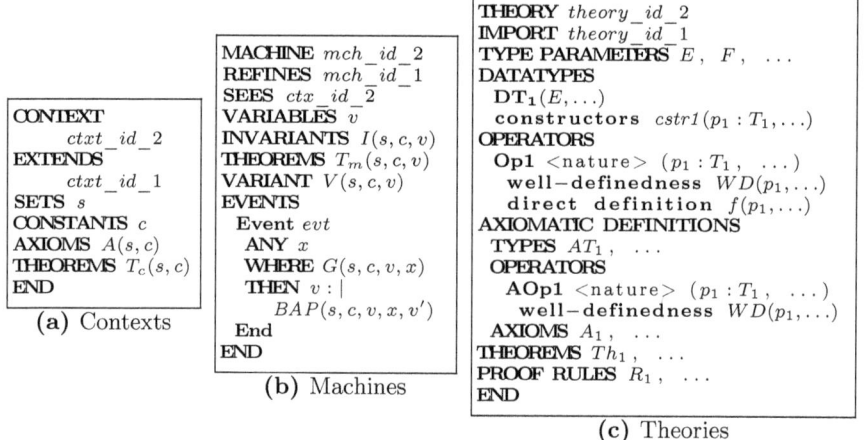

Listing 1.1. Event-B model structure

The primarily modelling key components of a context model include sets (s), constants (c), axioms ($A(s,c)$), and theorems ($T_c(s,c)$). Other modelling key components of a machine model are variables (v) to represent states, invariants ($I(s,c,v)$) to represent in predicate form on states to define typing as well as safety properties, guarded events (evt) to describe the evolution of states using before-after predicates (BAP). A set of proof obligations is generated in association with an Event-B model, that must be discharged to ensure the correctness of the modelled system.

Refinement operations are important for modelling and designing complex systems. Initially, an abstract model can be created, which can be progressively refined to incorporate additional details while maintaining the system's soundness. These refinement operations can be applied iteratively to develop a final concrete model that is closely aligned with the system's implementation.

The core of Event-B's modelling language is based on FOL and set theory, which is very expressive for modelling complex systems using refinement; however, it does not natively support higher-level structures. In order to mitigate this issue, the *theory plugin* was proposed [2,8], that enables the definition of theory components (see Listing 1c). These components include new type-generic datatypes as well as constructive and axiomatic operators, theorems, axioms, and proof rules. Once established, the elements of a theory can be seamlessly integrated into an Event-B model and its associated proofs.

Hybridised Event-B. In [11,12], the authors introduced a methodology that incorporates Event-B theories to integrate continuous features, such as real and differential equations, for modelling continuous behaviours. This proposed approach offers a generic model suitable for designing and verifying a variety of simple and distributed controllers, accommodating both continuous and discrete modelling elements.

Discrete and Continuous Variables. In hybrid systems, variables are categorised into two types to capture the discrete and continuous states of the system. The discrete variables are associated with instantaneous, point-wise assignments, represented by a Before-After Predicate (BAP). In contrast, the continuous variables are expressed as functions of time and can be updated through the defined Continuous Before-After Predicate (CBAP) operator.

$$x_p :|_{t \to t'} \mathcal{P}(x_p, x'_p) \ \& \ H \equiv [0, t[\triangleleft x'_p = [0, t[\triangleleft x_p \quad (PP)$$
$$\wedge \ \mathcal{P}([0, t] \triangleleft x_p, [t, t'] \triangleleft x'_p) \quad (PR)$$
$$\wedge \ \forall t^* \in [t, t'], x_p(t^*) \in H \quad (LI)$$

The introduced CBAP operator modifies the continuous variable x_p by adding a segment of a function over the interval $[t, t']$, while maintaining its value on the interval $[0, t]$. This ensures the preservation of its "past" (past preservation, *PP*). The additional segment is defined using the predicate $\mathcal{P}$ (*PR*) and must stay within the specified evolution domain or local invariant H (*LI*).

Modelling hybrid systems in Event-B. In [12], we introduced key generic patterns that encapsulate all necessary components for modelling controllers in hybrid systems. These defined patterns can be instantiated to create an initial abstract model, which can then be refined to enhance both discrete and continuous behaviours, enabling the specification and verification of the desired controller behaviour.

```
MACHINE Generic
VARIABLES t, x_s, x_p
INVARIANTS
  inv_1 : t ∈ ℝ⁺
  inv_2 : x_s ∈ STATES
  inv_3 : x_p ∈ ℝ ⇸ S
  inv_4 : [0, t] ⊆ dom(x_p)
```

Listing 1.2. Generic pattern header

In the generic model, we have two state variables: x_s for expressing discrete states, and x_p for expressing continuous states, as a function of time (valued in the vector state space S). Additionally, the model includes a read-only real variable for dense time, denoted as t, which can be employed in the modelling and proving processes.

```
Sense
ANY  s , p
WHERE
    grd₁ :  s ∈ ℙ1(STATES)
    grd₂ :  p ∈ ℙ(STATES × ℝ × S)
    grd₃ :  (xₛ ↦ t ↦ xₚ(t)) ∈ p
THEN
    act₁ :  xₛ :∈ s
END
```
(a) Sense event

```
Actuate
ANY  eq , s , H , t'
WHERE
    grd1 :  eq ∈ DE(S)
    grd2 :  Solvable([t, t'], eq, H)
    grd3 :  s ⊆ STATES
    grd4 :  xₛ ∈ s
    grd5 :  H ⊆ S
    grd6 :  xₚ(t) ∈ H
THEN
    act1 :  t, xₚ :∼_{t→t'} eq & H
END
```
(b) Actuate event

```
Behave
ANY  eq , t'
WHERE
    grd1 :  eq ∈ DE(S)
    grd2 :  Solvable([t, t'], eq, ⊤)
THEN
    act1 :  t, xₚ :∼_{t→t'} eq & ⊤
END
```
(c) Behave event

```
Transition
ANY  s
WHERE
    grd₁ :  s ∈ ℙ1(STATES)
THEN
    act₁ :  xₛ :∈ s
END
```
(d) Transition event

Listing 1.3. Generic pattern events

In the generic model, there are two categories of events: *discrete* and *continuous*. These events facilitate updates to discrete and continuous state variables via the BAP and CBAP operators, respectively. For instance, Listing 1.3 specifies a generic discrete event called **Sense**, which updates concrete states by acquiring a value from the plant. Similarly, another generic continuous event named **Actuate** is provided to update the continuous variable x_p according to a **Solvable** differential equation eq (guards $grd1$ and $grd2$) given as the parameter of the event. This **Solvable** predicate ensures that eq admits solutions, and thus that it describes feasible dynamic behaviours for the plant. Each of these generic events defines a set of parameters that can be instantiated through refinement using witnesses, as well as a set of guards that establish the necessary conditions for modelling the evolution of both discrete and continuous variables. In a similar vein, two additional categories of generic events have been introduced: **Behave** and **Transition**. The **Behave** events model the anticipated behaviour of the system under environmental stress (e.g., perturbations), while the **Transition** events signify discrete internal changes within the controller or user commands.

Proving process. The defined generic patterns are associated with specific proof obligations to ensure that the defined operators are used correctly when designing hybrid controllers. For the discrete part, classical POs can be generated, while for the continuous part, CFIS and CINV associated with CBAP can be generated.

$$\Gamma \vdash \exists t' \cdot t' \in \mathbb{R}^+ \wedge t' > t \wedge \textbf{Feasible}([t,t'], x_p, \mathcal{P}, \mathcal{H}_{saf}) \quad \text{(CFIS)}$$

$$\Gamma, \mathcal{I}([0,t] \lhd x_p), CBAP(t,t',x_p,x'_p,\mathcal{P},\mathcal{H}) \vdash \mathcal{I}([t,t'] \lhd x'_p) \quad \text{(CINV)}$$

Feasibility (CFIS) ensures the continuous behaviour described in the CBAP operator is valid and sound. To prove this, we need to show that there exists a time t' where the predicate $\mathcal{P}$ is feasible. In other words, we must show that there exists a x'_p defined over the interval $[t,t']$ for which the condition $\mathcal{P}(x_p, x'_p)$ is true. Another property, Continuous invariant preservation (CINV), is a particular instance of invariant preservation. It ensures that if x_p meets the invariant criteria on the interval $[0,t]$, it will continue to satisfy them on the interval $[t,t']$ as well. The syntactic representation of hybrid Event-B is described below as Labelled Transition Systems (LTS), which establish a direct correspondence with the Stateflow model.

Definition 1 (Hybridised Event-B as Labelled Transition Systems). For an Event-B model M_B, a syntactic representation of the Labelled Transition System (LTS) for M_B, is a tuple $\mathcal{H} \triangleq (\Sigma_h, I_h, V_h, L_h, T_h)$, where Σ is a set of states, I_h is the initial state ($I_h \in \Sigma_h$), V_h is a set of continuous and discrete variables of states Σ_h, L_h is a set of labels of the form (G_h, A_h, e_h), where G_h is the guard predicates, A_h is the action predicates and e_h is an event name, and T_h is a transition relation $T_h \subseteq \Sigma_h \times L_h \times \Sigma_h$.

A transition $(e_{h1}, (G_h, A_h, e_h), e_{h2})$, where $e_{h1} \in \Sigma_h$, and $e_{h2} \in \Sigma_h$, entails that the target state e_{h2} is reachable from the source state e_{h1}, if guard predicates G_h and action predicate A_h hold for the event e_h. If guard predicates G_h hold, the event e_h is enabled in the source state e_{h1}, and reaches the target state e_{h2} if action predicates A_h hold.

3.2 Simulink and Stateflow

Simulink [15] is a Matlab add-on that provides a graphical environment to model, simulate, and analyse complex dynamic hybrid systems. It can model both linear and nonlinear systems, with continuous and discrete time representations. The software has a user-friendly graphical interface (GUI) that allows for the design of complex models using block diagrams. Simulink includes a large number of pre-defined libraries for different modelling elements, such as sources, sinks, linear and nonlinear components, and connectors. Additionally, it provides support for specialised toolboxes in different areas such as neural networks, signal processing, communication, and HDL, among others. In addition, a unique component known as S-Functions allows for the customisation and creation of user-defined blocks in MATLAB, C, C++, Ada, and Fortran. All of these blocks work together by transmitting data over connecting wires. Each elementary block processes input signals and produces output signals based on specific parameters and defined functionalities.

Simulink models can be organised hierarchically using both top-down and bottom-up approaches. A defined Simulink model can be simulated with various parameters that can be changed in real time. While the simulation is running, key results can be viewed using the scope and other display blocks. Furthermore, the results can be saved in a workspace or file for future analysis.

One effective interactive simulator for modelling and simulating reactive system behaviour is Stateflow [15]. Users can build intricate system models that replicate real-world behaviour by adding a Stateflow block to a Simulink model. The Stateflow syntax is reminiscent of Statecharts [14], with a similar hierarchical structure and visual representation. Stateflow also supports advanced features, including hierarchical state modelling, concurrency (where multiple states can be executed simultaneously), and communication (through a broadcast mechanism). Additionally, it offers more sophisticated features, such as inter-level transitions, complex transitions through junctions, and event broadcasting. These features enable users to design complex systems in an efficient manner. A Stateflow model is composed of a network of interconnected states, linked by transitions. Each state has a unique name and can be used to create a hierarchical state diagram, allowing for detailed modelling and simulation of complex systems.

There are two different types of states: 1) AND-states and 2) OR-states. In each state, we may invoke the following actions in sequential order: *entry, exit, during*, and *on event_name*. An arc known as a transition connects two states, with one being the source state and the other the destination state. Each transition is characterised by a label that may encompass event triggers, conditions, conditional actions, and transition actions. A general format for a transition label can be expressed as *event [condition] condition_ action/transition_ action* [19].

Definition 2 (Stateflow Model). A Stateflow model (M_s) is a tuple $\mathcal{S} \triangleq (\Theta_s, V_s, T_s, A_s)$, where Θ_s is the finite set of states, V_s is a finite set of variables, T_s is a set of transitions and A_s is a set of actions defined for each state. In the transition T_s, every transition $\tau_s \in T_s$ is formally defined as a tuple $(\theta_{s1}, G_s, U_s, \theta_{s2})$, where θ_{s1} is a source state, G_s is the guard must be satisfied for a transition to be taken, U_s is a set of mapping actions to modify a set of variables in V_s, and θ_{s2} is the target state. The actions A_s are subdivided into entry, during and exit actions, where entry actions are executed only once when entering the state, during actions perform the continuous-time evolution of the variables of V_s according to a differential equation, and exit actions are executed only once when the state is exited.

In our work, we use Stateflow to express the discrete controller behaviour and Simulink blocks to model the plant dynamics of a hybrid system.

4 Translating Hybridised Event-B Model to Simulink

We present our key contribution, which is the process for translating a hybridised Event-B model to a Simulink model. We primarily work with deterministic models. Furthermore, we intend to compare the simulation trajectories of the Stateflow model to those of the Event-B model. To facilitate this comparison, we describe the concepts of *correspondence* and *trajectory-equivalence* [4] used in our translation process.

Definition 3 (Correspondence). A trajectory (α) of a hybridised Event-B model M_B and a simulation trajectory (β) of a Simulink model M_S correspond to each other if the discrete states, transitions, variables and transition times are encountered same in both models, and there is a direct correspondence between the trajectory's continuous points and the simulation trajectory.

Definition 4 (Trajectory-Equivalence). A Simulink model M_S is trajectory-equivalent to a Hybridised Event-B M_B if, for every trajectory α of $\mathcal{H}$, there exists a corresponding (Definition 3) simulation trajectory β of $\mathcal{S}$, and for every simulation trajectory β of $\mathcal{S}$, there exists a corresponding trajectory α of $\mathcal{H}$.

Translating a hybridised Event-B model to Simulink is a straightforward process. However, it is important to acknowledge that any numerical challenges related to Simulink fall outside the scope of this work. For example, the integration of differential equations in the Simulink model may lack precision, which can lead to variations in the observed behaviour. While the generated Simulink model reflects the behaviour of the Event-B model, more accurate simulation results can be achieved by selecting different simulation time steps, albeit at a higher computational cost.

4.1 Translating Hybridised Event-B Model

In order to generate a Simulink model from a hybridised Event-B model, we proceed as follows: let $\mathcal{H} = (\Sigma_h, I_h, V_h, L_h, T_h)$ be the hybridised Event-B model, and $\mathcal{S} = (\Theta_s, V_s, T_s, A_s)$ be the Simulink model. Instantiate $\Theta_s = \mathcal{H}.\Sigma_h$, $V_s = \mathcal{H}.V_h$, and $T_s = \mathcal{H}.T_h$. The generated Simulink model consists mainly two components: a Stateflow model and a plant model. For generating the Stateflow model, we proceed as follows: for each state $e_h \in \Sigma_h$, there is a corresponding state $\theta_s \in \Theta_s$ in $\mathcal{S}$, and for each variable $v_h \in V_h$, there is a corresponding variable $v_s \in V_s$ in $\mathcal{S}$.

In the Stateflow model, based on states and variables, we instantiate the during, entry and exit actions as $A_s(\theta_s, v_s)$ for the variable v_s to be equal for variable v_h. These actions express an ordinary differential equation for variables in continuous-time Stateflow models to copy the flow from hybrid Event-B model $\mathcal{H}$ to Simulink model $\mathcal{S}$ for each state and variable. Furthermore, we instantiate the Event-B transitions as follows: for each Event-B state $e_{h1} \in \Sigma_h$ and $e_{h2} \in \Sigma_h$ with their corresponding state $\theta_{s1} \in \Theta_s$ and $\theta_{s2} \in \Theta_s$ (respectively) in the Stateflow model, for each transition $(e_{h1}, (G_h, A_h, e_h), e_{h2}) \in T_h$, we instantiate a transition $\gamma_s \in T_s$ as the tuple $(\theta_{s1}, G_s, U_s, \theta_{s2})$, where $\gamma_s.\theta_{s1} = e_{h1}, \gamma_s.G_s = G_h, \gamma_s.U_S = A_h$, and $\gamma_s.'\theta_{s2} = e_{h2}$. Since our Event-B model ($\mathcal{H}$) is deterministic, only one transition is enabled at a time. Moreover, the guarded predicates are directly translated to transition conditions for each given transitions. In Fact, the stateflow model is derived from the hybridised Event-B's

Labelled Transition Systems (LTS). We consider stateflow model results for creating the plant model. These outputs are Simulink model variables that have been modified. Furthermore, these results are used as input for describing the plant model. The plant model is directly derived from the original Event-B models. We generate this plant model block using Matlab Simuink and an integrator block to depict the plant evolution with regard to time. Finally, the output signal is connected to the stateflow model as a feedback loop, as well as to a scope to display the simulation results.

There are some additional minor syntactic translations to consider, for example the variables updates in Simulink are evaluated sequentially, while they are evaluated in a single shot in Event-B. For example, we have used extra temporary variables to perform the variable updates, such as the Event-B updates $a' := a + 1 \wedge b' := a$ is rewritten to the Simulink update as $a'_{tmp} = a; a' = a_{tmp}+1; b' := a_{tmp}$, where a_{tmp} is a new variable to support the one shot update. Another key issue is to describe how Simulink recognizes events during simulation in order to have correct event detection, which is mostly handled by the zero-crossing detection techniques natively provided by the Simulink routines.

It is important to recognise that if a single guard activates at a specific moment, the zero-crossing mechanism may fail to detect it, resulting in a missed transition and causing unpredictable behaviour. To systematically capture all necessary behaviour, we implement an ϵ-relaxation for each guard constraint. For example, an Event-B guard $a == c \wedge b \leq a$ is transformed into $c - \epsilon \leq a \leq c + \epsilon \wedge b \leq a - \epsilon$. Additionally, the simulation time must be sufficiently small in relation to ϵ and the Lipschitz constant of the system's dynamics to ensure that no transitions are overlooked.

In fact, when compared to the original Event-B model, this approach facilitates a broader range of behaviours and ensures that no transitions are overlooked, which is essential for achieving trajectory equivalence. However, this additional behaviour can be minimised by selecting a smaller value for ϵ, necessitating a smaller simulation time step. While opting for a shorter time step guarantees that all transitions are captured and maintains trajectory equivalence, it can also be expensive in terms of increased simulation time.

5 Case Study: A Water Tank

In this section, we describe the water tank case study taken from [12] to demonstrate the use of hybrid modelling and the subsequent transformation of the Event-B model into a Simulink model. The goal of this exercise is to demonstrate the transformation approach and run simulations. This example demonstrates the feasibility of translating Event-B models into Simulink models, allowing for the seamless integration of formal methods and simulation-based analysis.

5.1 Informal Requirements

The water tank system is a controlled plant that can store a maximum volume of water, denoted by $V_{\max}$. This system is equipped with two pumps for filling and emptying water in the tank. The actual water volume, V, in the tank is regulated by switching between the filling and emptying water pumps, which respectively control the input flow rates δ_{in} and output flow rates δ_{out}. The primary goal of the water tank controller is to maintain the water level within a specified range, namely, $V_{\min} \leq V \leq V_{\max}$. The two pumps can operate simultaneously or independently, which can be summarised as follows:

- When both pumps are turned off, the water volume remains constant.
- When only the input water pump is running, the water volume will increase.
- When only the output water pump is running, the water volume will decrease.
- When both pumps are running, the water volume will change depending on the difference in flow rates between the two pumps.

The primary objective of the water tank controller is to manage the input and output pumps to fill and empty the tank, which can be categorised into three operating modes:

1. *Normal:* In this default mode, the water volume ($V(t)$) can change arbitrarily in response to input and output flow rates when both pumps are running simultaneously.
2. *Emptying:* During this mode, the water volume decreases. The water tank controller may operate in this mode if $V(t) > V_{low}$ or switch to this mode automatically when $V(t) = V_{high}$.
3. *Filling:* During this mode, the water volume increases. The water tank controller may operate in this mode if $V(t) < V_{high}$ or switch to this mode automatically when $V(t) = V_{low}$.

In summary, the water tank system requirements can be described as follows:

- **Fun_Req1:** The tank's water volume varies according to its operating mode: it decreases as it empties, increases as it fills, and remains under controlled variations when in normal mode;
- **Env_Req2:** The water volume is physically bounded between 0 and V_{max}: $\forall t \in \mathbb{R}^+, 0 \leq V(t) \land V(t) \leq V_{max}$;
- **Saf_Req3:** The water volume must always be within the set bounds, V_{low} and V_{high}: $\forall t \in \mathbb{R}^+, V_{low} \leq V(t) \land V(t) \leq V_{high}$;
- **Saf_Req4:** the variation of the volume ($\dot{V}(t)$) is always below the maximum allowed variation ΔV_{max}: $\forall t \in \mathbb{R}^+, |\dot{V}(t)| \leq \Delta V_{max}$.

5.2 Event-B Development

This section describes the step-by-step development of the water tank model. The initial water tank model is obtained by refining the generic model presented in Sect. 3.1. In this development, we begin with a generic abstract model, which is then refined to formally specify the water tank behaviour.

Listing 1.4 shows the context model obtained through instantiating the generic context. This context model defines a set of constants (axm1-4) and

```
CONTEXT AbstractTankCtx EXTENDS GenericCtx
CONSTANTS $V_{max}$, $V_{low}$, $V_{high}$, $\Delta V_{max}$, $V_0$
AXIOMS
    axm1-4:  $V_{max}, V_{low}, V_{high}, \Delta V_{max} \in \mathbb{R}$
    axm5:    $0 \leq V_{low} \leq V_{high} \leq V_{max}$
    axm6:    $\Delta V_{max} > 0$
    axm7-9:  $V_0 \in \mathbb{R} \wedge V_{low} \leq V_0 \wedge V_0 \leq V_{high}$
    axm10:   $S = \mathbb{R}$
    axm11:   $partition(STATES, \{Normal\}, \{Emptying\}, \{Filling\})$
END
```

Listing 1.4. Abstract Tank – Context

the required system specific constraints in axioms (axm5-9). The system's state space ($\mathbb{R}$) is defined in axm10, and the possible controller modes of the water tank are defined as an enumerated set in axm11.

An abstract model of the water tank hybrid controller is developed by refining the generic machine outlined in Sect. 3.1. Listing 1.5 shows a set of invariants and the initial model of the water tank controller. In this model, we introduce a continuous state variable, V, to represent the volume of water in the tank and its corresponding properties (invariants inv1-2). A gluing invariant, inv3, is defined to establish a link between the generic abstract continuous variable x_p and the water tank volume V. The next invariant, inv4, contains the environmental property **Env_Req2** from the requirements section. Finally, invariants inv5 and inv6 are developed to address the safety requirements **Saf_Req3** and **Saf_Req4** for the water tank controller, respectively.

```
MACHINE AbstractTank REFINES Generic
SEES AbstractTankCtx
VARIABLES $t$, $x_s$, $V$
INVARIANTS
    inv1:  $V \in \mathbb{R} \nrightarrow S$
    inv2:  $[0,t] \subseteq dom(V)$
    inv3:  $V = x_p$
    inv4:  $\forall t^* \cdot t^* \in [0,t] \Rightarrow 0 \leq V(t) \wedge V(t) \leq V_{max}$
    inv5:  $\forall t^* \cdot t^* \in [0,t] \Rightarrow V_{low} \leq V(t^*) \wedge V(t^*) \leq V_{high}$
    inv6:  $\forall t^* \cdot t^* \in [0,t] \Rightarrow |\dot{V}(t^*)| \leq \Delta V_{max}$
```

```
INITIALISATION
WITH
    $x'_p$:  $V' = x'_p$
THEN
    act1:  $t := 0$
    act2:  $x_s := Normal$
    act3:  $V := \{0 \mapsto V_0\}$
END
```

Listing 1.5. Abstract Tank – Machine Header

In the abstract model, an initialisation event assigns a default value to each specified variable. The controller begins in *Normal* mode, with the volume set to a constant value of V_0, which represents the initial volume in the tank.

```
ctrl_transition_normal REFINES
     Transition
WHERE
    grd1: V(t) < V_high
    grd2: V_low < V(t)
WITH
    s: s = {Normal}
THEN
    act1: x_s := Normal
END
```

```
ctrl_sense_too_high REFINES Sense
WHERE
    grd1: V_high ≤ V(t)
WITH
    s: s = {Emptying}
    p: p = STATES × ℝ × {V* | V_high ≤ V*}
THEN
    act1: x_s := Emptying
END
```

Listing 1.6. Abstract Tank – Transition and Sensing

In the water tank machine model, we introduce 8 events that refine the abstract generic events (Actuate, Behave, Sense, and Transition). Listing 1.6 presents the transition and sensing events associated with the water tank controller. The transition event ctrl_transition_normal refines the generic event Transition, enabling the controller to operate in Normal mode when the current water volume $V(t)$ exceeds V_{low} and remains below V_{high}. Note that for the abstract discrete variable s, a witness is represented by one of the controller modes (Normal). The sensing event ctrl_sensing_too_high refines the generic event Sense, allowing the controller to operate in Emptying mode when the current water volume $V(t)$ is higher than or equal to V_{high}. Witnesses are provided for the abstract discrete variable s and continuous variable p in the form of a controller mode (Emptying) and vector state space for the water tank. The remaining four transition and sense events are defined in a similar manner.

```
EVENT ctrl_actuate_pumps REFINES Actuate
ANY eq, s, t'
WHERE
    grd0: t' ∈ ℝ ∧ t < t'
    grd1: eq ∈ DE(S)
    grd2: Solvable([t, t'], eq, {V* | V_low ≤ V* ∧ V* ≤ V_high})
    grd3: isFlowEq(s, [t, t'], eq, 0, V_max)
    grd4: s ∈ STATES
    grd5: x_s = s
    grd6: V_low ≤ V(t) ∧ V(t) ≤ V_high
WITH
    x'_p: x'_p = V'
    H: H = {V* | V_low ≤ V* ∧ V* ≤ V_high}
THEN
    act1: V :∼_{t→t'} eq & {V* | V_low ≤ V* ∧ V* ≤ V_high}
END
```

Listing 1.7. Abstract Tank – Actuation Event

Listing 1.7 illustrates the actuation process of the water tank, which is a refinement of the abstract generic event Actuate. For instantiation, the WITH clause replaces x_p with V using the gluing invariant, and a concrete evolution domain H is provided to ensure that the volume V remains within specified limits, V_{low} and V_{high}. The differential equation remains undefined but is constrained by the pumps' desired behaviour. The *isFlowEq* predicate captures these constraints defined in the water tank theory. Thus, based on the shape of the concrete tank, any differential equation that models the liquid dynamics of this tank and satisfies the conditions imposed by guards grd2 and grd3 can be used as a witness for the parameter eq during instantiation. Similarly, the event Behave is refined to model the liquid dynamics of the water tank that satisfy the given constraints.

Proofs. The developed Event-B model of the water tank yields relatively straightforward proofs. A total of 64 proof obligations (POs) are generated, with 30% pertaining to well-definedness. The remaining 44% are associated with simulation and guard strengthening, arising from the substitution of generic discrete and continuous variables, as well as abstract event parameters. All these POs are simple and can be easily discharged. By successfully discharging all of them, we ensure the correct refinement necessary to derive an accurate water tank model from the generic Event-B model.

Additionally, 23% of the proof obligations (POs) pertain to invariants (excluding trivial type-related invariants). These generated POs depend on the model's specific constraints, such as the values of H and the use of the $isFlowEq$ predicate. These constraints, along with the characteristics outlined in the tank theories, play an important role in the proofs. The remaining 3% of the POs are generated in relation to feasibility. Due to a limitation in the Rodin proving tool with the *Theory plugin*, most of these POs require manual intervention to be discharged. All these POs are addressed to ensure that the required safety properties and continuous behaviours are valid within the evolution domain H under the specified constraints.

5.3 Hybrid Water Tank Event-B Model Simulation

This section describes the hybrid Event-B model transformation of the water tank model to Simulink/Stateflow representations, as described in Sect. 4. Figure 1 shows the Simulink model of the water tank system. In our approach, the discrete components are implemented using Stateflow, while the continuous components are realised using a MATLAB user-defined function. It is important to note that our method clearly distinguishes between the discrete and continuous components of the water tank's hybrid Event-B model.

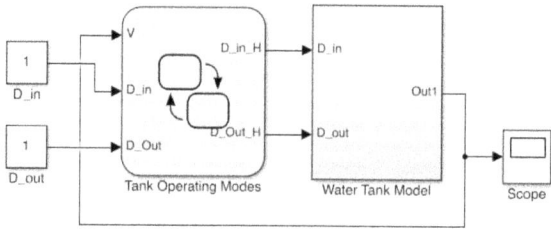

Fig. 1. Simulink model of water tank

As outlined in Sect. 5.1, the water tank model operates in three discrete modes: Normal, Emptying, and Filling. The stateflow model comprises three distinct states, as depicted in Fig. 2, which are derived from the defined enumerated set in the context model. These modes facilitate transitions between different states, governed by the water level in the tank. The water volume must be maintained within the range of $Vlow$ and $Vhigh$. All of these stateflow transitions correspond to the hybrid water tank Event-B model. Transitions between these discrete states are defined by conditions that align with respective guards of the transition events of the hybrid Event-B model. For instance, the system may enter filling mode when the water volume is at or below the minimum threshold ($Vlow$). The discrete variables in each state can be modified by utilising *entry*, *exist*, and *during* actions, as defined in the hybrid Event-B model. In this context, we will only employ *during* actions to regulate the incoming and outgoing water flow for different modes. Finally, we choose an initial state corresponding to the initial state of the hybrid Event-B model of water tank.

For instance, the normal operation of the water tank serves as the initial state for the Stateflow model, with the inflow and outflow designated as D_in and D_out, respectively. The dynamics of the water flows are governed by a differential equation linked to each state, which describes how the continuous variable, water volume V, evolves over time. The continuous behaviour of the water tank model is represented by a Simulink block that uses a user-defined function in MATLAB. Within this block, we implement the behaviour outlined in the Event-B model to simulate the dynamics of water flows. The output from this Simulink block is then fed into the Stateflow model as an input and is also linked to a Scope block to visualise the simulation results. Two constant blocks, D_in and D_out, are connected to the Stateflow model to specify the initial values for the inflow and outflow of water, respectively.

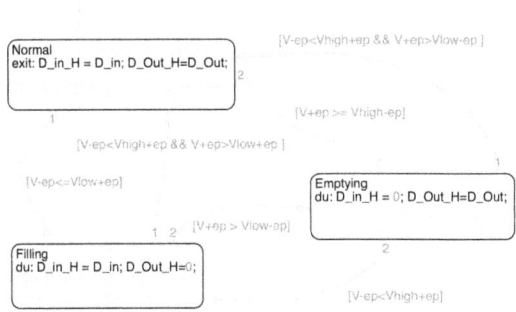

Fig. 2. Water tank Stateflow model

Figure 3 illustrates the changes in water volume during both the emptying and filling modes. In this simulation, the minimum volume V_{low} is set to 5, while the maximum volume V_{high} is set to 40. The initial flow rates for both inflow and outflow are set to 3 and 2, respectively. These parameters can be modified to explore different simulation outcomes.

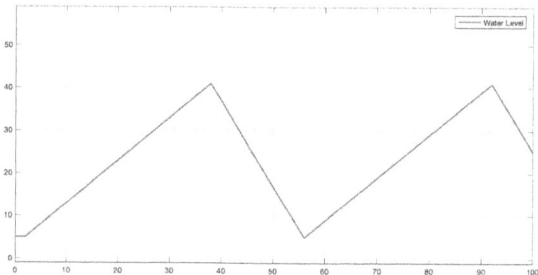

Fig. 3. Water tank simulation ($D\_in = 3$, $D\_out = 2$. $V_{high} = 40$ $V_{low} = 5$.

In our water tank simulation, we employ various input values to explore the different behaviour of the model. The simulation covers scenarios of filling, emptying, and simultaneous filling and emptying. This approach not only helps us validate the specified invariants but also allows us to identify the feasible ranges of inflow and outflow that maintain a safe water volume. Our experiments with the water tank simulation confirm the discrete and dynamic evolution of the formalised Event-B hybrid models.

Our water tank experiment leads us to conclude that simulation is an important component of our proposed methodology. In essence, the simulation allows for the animation of Event-B models across a diverse set of input values. By analysing the simulation outcomes, we can validate the discrete and dynamic behaviours of the hybrid Event-B model. This simulation reflects the desired behaviours as derived from the formal models, enabling us to effectively evaluate the hybrid system under development. Additionally, the results from the simulation can help identify potential flaws within the model. If any errors are uncovered during the simulation process, we can correct the hybrid Event-B model accordingly. This iterative approach can be employed until we achieve a robust hybrid model that meets both continuous and discrete behaviour criteria. Importantly, generating Simulink models is cost-effective and facilitates the implementation of a system that can be deployed in real-world applications.

To demonstrate the scalability of our approach, we developed several complex hybrid systems, including the ETCS train system, the Signalised Left-Turn Assist (SLTA) system, the Planar Robot system, and an inverted pendulum case study. All of these models are available at https://www.irit.fr/~Guillaume.Dupont/models. This demonstrates the potential of our approach, which can be used in a variety of complex applications.

6 Assessment

The hybridised Event-B approach facilitates the progressive design of complex hybrid systems by enabling the simultaneous modelling of both discrete and continuous behaviours. This approach allows for the generation of a set of proof obligations (POs) that ensure the correctness of both discrete and continuous system properties. Through formal verification, inconsistencies within system requirements and refinement relations can be detected, enhancing system reliability. However, the current methodology lacks a simulation framework for validating the intended behaviours of the modelled system. To overcome this limitation, our approach introduces a mechanism to generate a Simulink model. This model can be utilised to simulate the system with specified parametric values, while also accommodating system constraints. The primary advantages of incorporating simulation into this workflow include the ability to identify unwanted behaviours and to verify system correctness by examining a range of possible concrete values. Note that, this simulation approach is applicable at any level of refinement, making it a versatile tool in the validation process as well as allowing users to intuitively visualise and build complex systems related to the hybrid Event-B model without requiring extensive coding skills. Furthermore, the generated Simulink model facilitates system-level design and supports real-time simulations. This approach enables rapid prototype development, and Simulink's code generation tools can be utilised to implement algorithms in embedded systems.

To ensure the accuracy of our transformation, we base our approach on the following assumptions. First, we assume that the simulation aligns perfectly with the formalised Event-B model. While it is important to acknowledge that real simulations inevitably introduce some degree of error, these errors can be minimised by utilising smaller time steps in the simulation. The second assumption involves the selection of a very small value for ϵ, which allows for precise execution of the simulation and verification of transition enabling conditions. For instance, in the water tank scenario, the condition $V \leq V_{low}$ is approximated as $V - \epsilon \leq V_{low} + \epsilon$. Finally, we assume that the Simulink model accurately reflects the transformation process and correctly encodes the hybrid Event-B semantics. To validate the correctness of our approach, we developed and validated several complex examples that not only test the assumptions outlined but also show the robustness of the transformation process. These examples demonstrate that our assumptions hold true in a variety of scenarios, increasing our confidence in the reliability and accuracy of the transformation we aim to achieve.

7 Conclusion

The hybridised Event-B framework enables the design of complex systems using a correct-by-construction methodology, allowing for the gradual integration of both discrete and continuous behaviours. A significant challenge is conducting simulations on hybrid Event-B models while ensuring synchronisation between the discrete and continuous components. This paper proposed a method for translating trajectory-equivalent hybridised Event-B models into Simulink models. To achieve this, we utilise Stateflow for the discrete components, coordinating it with MATLAB function blocks to capture the continuous aspects. Our approach enables designers to construct complex controllers using a correct by construction methodology, and facilitating the transformation of the final model into a Simulink representation. We have empirically validated our approach with several challenging hybrid systems developed in hybridised Event-B. This methodology proves beneficial for animating and validating verified hybridised Event-B models across different abstraction levels, and supports the development of complex hybrid systems. The resulting Simulink model can serve purposes of implementation, further enhancing the practical utility of our approach.

In the future, two major challenges have been identified. The first is the development of an automatic and certified translation tool as a Rodin plugin to generate a Simulink model from the verified hybridised Event-B model, and the second is the handling of non-determinism in the generated Simulink model. Furthermore, to perform advanced simulation for under- and over-approximations, determining the optimal relaxation (ϵ) can be considered.

References

1. Abrial, J.R., Butler, M., Hallerstede, S., Hoang, T.S., Mehta, F., Voisin, L.: Rodin: an open toolset for modelling and reasoning in Event-B. Int. J. Softw. Tools Technol. Transfer **12**(6), 447–466 (2010)
2. Abrial, J.R., Butler, M., Hallerstede, S., Leuschel, M., Schmalz, M., Voisin, L.: Proposals for mathematical extensions for Event-B. Tech. rep. (2009)
3. Ameur, Y.A., Bogomolov, S., Dupont, G., Singh, N.K., Stankaitis, P.: Reachability analysis and simulation for hybridised event-b models. In: ter Beek, M.H., Monahan, R. (eds.) Integrated Formal Methods - 17th International Conference, IFM 2022, Lugano, Switzerland, 7-10 June 2022, Proceedings. LNCS, vol. 13274, pp. 109–128. Springer (2022). https://doi.org/10.1007/978-3-031-07727-2_7
4. Bak, S., Beg, O.A., Bogomolov, S., Johnson, T.T., Nguyen, L.V., Schilling, C.: Hybrid automata: from verification to implementation. Int. J. Softw. Tools Technol. Transf. **21**(1), 87–104 (2019). https://doi.org/10.1007/s10009-017-0458-1
5. Bert, D., Cave, F.: Construction of finite labelled transition systems from B abstract systems. In: Grieskamp, W., Santen, T., Stoddart, B. (eds.) IFM 2000. LNCS, vol. 1945, pp. 235–254. Springer, Heidelberg (2000). https://doi.org/10.1007/3-540-40911-4_14
6. Bert, D., Potet, M.-L., Stouls, N.: GeneSyst: a tool to reason about behavioral aspects of B event specifications. application to security properties. In: Treharne, H., King, S., Henson, M., Schneider, S. (eds.) ZB 2005. LNCS, vol. 3455, pp. 299–318. Springer, Heidelberg (2005). https://doi.org/10.1007/11415787_18
7. Butler, M., et al.: The first twenty-five years of industrial use of the B-method. In: ter Beek, M.H., Ničković, D. (eds.) FMICS 2020. LNCS, vol. 12327, pp. 189–209. Springer, Cham (2020). https://doi.org/10.1007/978-3-030-58298-2_8
8. Butler, M.J., Maamria, I.: Practical theory extension in Event-B. In: Theories of Programming and Formal Methods - Essays Dedicated to Jifeng He on the Occasion of His 70th Birthday, pp. 67–81 (2013)

9. Chaudhari, D.L., Damani, O.P.: Generating hierarchical state based representation from event-b models. Electronic Notes in Theoretical Computer Science 280, 35–46 (2011), proceedings of the B 2011 Workshop, a satellite event of the 17th International Symposium on Formal Methods (FM 2011)
10. Chen, X., Ábrahám, E., Sankaranarayanan, S.: Flow*: an analyzer for non-linear hybrid systems. In: Sharygina, N., Veith, H. (eds.) CAV 2013. LNCS, vol. 8044, pp. 258–263. Springer, Heidelberg (2013). https://doi.org/10.1007/978-3-642-39799-8_18
11. Dupont, G., Ameur, Y.A., Singh, N.K., Pantel, M.: Event-b hybridation: a proof and refinement-based framework for modelling hybrid systems. ACM Trans. Embed. Comput. Syst. **20**(4), 35:1–35:37 (2021). https://doi.org/10.1145/3448270
12. Dupont, G., Ameur, Y.A., Singh, N.K., Pantel, M.: Formally verified architectural patterns of hybrid systems using proof and refinement with event-b. Sci. Comput. Program. **216**, 102765 (2022). https://doi.org/10.1016/j.scico.2021.102765
13. Frehse, G., et al.: SpaceEx: scalable verification of hybrid systems. In: Gopalakrishnan, G., Qadeer, S. (eds.) CAV 2011. LNCS, vol. 6806, pp. 379–395. Springer, Heidelberg (2011). https://doi.org/10.1007/978-3-642-22110-1_30
14. Harel, D.: Statecharts: a visual formalism for complex systems. Sci. Comput. Program. **8**(3), 231–274 (1987)
15. MathWorks, T.: Simulink user's guide (2021)
16. MathWorks, T.: Stateflow user's guide (2021)
17. Platzer, A., Quesel, J.-D.: KeYmaera: a hybrid theorem prover for hybrid systems (system description). In: Armando, A., Baumgartner, P., Dowek, G. (eds.) IJCAR 2008. LNCS (LNAI), vol. 5195, pp. 171–178. Springer, Heidelberg (2008). https://doi.org/10.1007/978-3-540-71070-7_15
18. Satpathy, M., Ramesh, S., Snook, C.F., Singh, N.K., Butler, M.J.: A mixed approach to rigorous development of control designs. In: 2013 IEEE International Symposium on Computer-Aided Control System Design, CACSD 2013, Hyderabad, India, 28-30 August 2013, pp. 7–12. IEEE (2013)
19. Singh, N.K., Lawford, M., Maibaum, T.S.E., Wassyng, A.: Stateflow to tabular expressions. In: Proceedings of the Sixth International Symposium on Information and Communication Technology, pp. 312–319. SoICT 2015, Association for Computing Machinery, New York (2015)
20. Su, W., Abrial, J., Zhu, H.: Formalizing hybrid systems with event-b and the rodin platform. Sci. Comput. Program. **94**, 164–202 (2014)
21. Taylor, J.H., Kebede, D.: Modeling and simulation of hybrid systems in matlab. IFAC Proceedings Volumes 29(1), 4700–4705 (1996), 13th World Congress of IFAC, 1996, San Francisco USA, 30 June - 5 July

Formal Specification and Model Checking of a Synchronous Leader Election Protocol in Maude

Tomoyoshi Ogura, Canh Minh Do, and Kazuhiro Ogata(✉)

JAIST, Nomi, Ishikawa 923-1292, Japan
{canhdo,ogata}@jaist.ac.jp

Abstract. We have formally specified Bully Protocol, a distributed leader election protocol, in Maude, a specification/programming language based on rewriting logic, and conducted model checking experiments with the Maude system that Bully Protocol enjoys a safety property (Non-multiple leader election) and a liveness property (Eventual leader election). Our first version supposes that once a node becomes failed, it will never become active. It is also necessary to use an anti-fairness assumption for Non-multiple leader election model checking for the first version. We have revised the first version such that it is unnecessary to use any assumptions for Non-multiple leader election model checking and failed nodes may become active, and conducted model checking experiments that the revised version also enjoys the two properties. We mainly demonstrate that Bully Protocol does not need to be fully synchronously modeled/implemented and the protocol can be revised such that the node that has the greatest ID among active ones is not necessarily always a leader, which avoids from changing the current leader as a failed node whose ID is greater than the current leader's ID becomes active.

Keywords: leader election · Bully Protocol · Maude · model checking

1 Introduction

Although distributed leader election is a classical problem in Computer Science, it is still an important one because it is essential for the blockchain technology that emerged for bitcoin and now has many applications, such as smart contracts [4] and supply chain traceability [1]. Besides, leader election protocols are non-trivial like many other distributed protocols and there are some desired properties such protocols should satisfy. Therefore, it is worth formally specifying such a protocol and verifying that such a protocol enjoys its desired properties based on its formal specification.

Bully Protocol is a famous asynchronous distributed leader election protocol proposed by Hector Garcia-Molina [6]. We have formally specified Bully

---

This work was supported by JSPS KAKENHI Grant Number JP23K28060.

Protocol in Maude [5] as a rewrite theory specification. Maude is a specification/programming language based on rewriting logic and suitable to formally specify asynchronous distributed protocols/systems. So, Bully Protocol has not been specified as a fully synchronous system but as an asynchronous system while keeping some synchronous aspects. The protocol uses three kinds of messages: Election, OK and Coordinate messages. Election and OK messages are asynchronously treated, while Coordinate messages are synchronously treated. When a node becomes a new leader, we suppose that there is no message left in the network, which is one synchronous aspect. This is because messages sent by nodes are instantaneously received by some other nodes, and then there is no message left in the network in synchronous protocols/systems, while there may be messages left in the network in asynchronous protocols/systems. In the first part of the paper, we suppose that once a node becomes failed, it will never become active.

Based on the formal specification of Bully Protocol, we model check that the protocol enjoys one safety property and one liveness property. The safety property is called Non-multiple leader election in this paper, meaning that at most one leader is elected for any period of time, while the liveness one is called Eventual leader election, meaning that a leader will be eventually elected when the current leader became failed. In the first part of the paper, we need to use an anti-fairness assumption for Non-multiple leader election model checking. The status of each node is normal, initiator, leader or failed. When the current leader becomes failed, some normal nodes become initiators, initiating leader elections, and most initiators become back normal. Such nodes may become initiators again and again. The anti-fairness assumption is as follows: normal nodes do not become initiators infinitely many times for each election period.

In the latter part of the paper, we revise the specification such that we do not need to use the anti-fairness assumption for Non-multiple leader election model checking. We also relax the assumption that once a node becomes failed, it will never become active. In the original version of Bully Protocol, the node that has the greatest ID among active ones is always a leader. This is not needed, however, and then we revise Bully Protocol such that even if a failed node whose ID is greater than the current leader's ID becomes active, the current leader will keep the leader, implying that it is not a case that the node that has the greatest ID among active ones is always a leader. The revision avoids from changing the current leader as a failed node whose ID is greater than the current leader's ID becomes active.

Our contributions are summarized as follows:

- It is demonstrated that Bully Protocol does not need to be fully synchronously modeled/implemented. Election and OK messages are asynchronously treated, while Coordinate messages are synchronously treated. Model checking has been conducted to formally verify that Bully Protocol enjoys Non-multiple leader election and Eventual leader election based on the formal specification. We suppose that once a node becomes failed, it will never become active, and need to use the anti-fairness assumption for Eventual leader election mode checking.

- In the original version of Bully Protocol, when a node i sends a message to another node j in a round, if no response is delivered to node i from node j in the next round, then node i decides that node j is failed. When such a message is treated asynchronously, we could use timeout to let node i judge if node j is failed. If so, it is necessary to deal with some realtime concepts, introducing an extra complexity. If node j is failed, instead, a Timeout message is delivered to node i from node j in order to avoid the extra complexity in our formal specification.
- We have revised the formal specification so that we do not need to use the anti-fairness assumption for Eventual leader election model checking, and relaxed the assumption that once a node becomes failed, it will never become active. We have also revised Bully Protocol such that the node that has the greatest ID among active ones is not necessarily always a leader, which avoids from changing the current leader as a failed node whose ID is greater than the current leader's ID becomes active.

The rest of the paper is organized as follows. Section 2 mentions some preliminaries. Section 3 introduces Bully Protocol. Section 4 describes how to formally specify Bully Protocol in Maude as a rewrite-theory specification. Section 5 reports on the model checking experiments that Bully Protocol enjoys Non-multiple leader election and Eventual leader election based on the formal specification. Section 6 revises the formal specification as above-mentioned. Section 7 reports on the model checking experiments based on the revised version. Section 8 mentions some related work and the paper is concluded in Sect. 9. All pieces of the source code used in the present paper are available at https://github.com/tarugo07/leader-election.

2 Preliminaries

A state machine $M \triangleq \langle S, I, T \rangle$ consists of a set S of states, the set $I \subseteq S$ of initial states, and a set $T \subseteq S \times S$ of state-pairs, where an element $(s, s') \in T$ is called a state transition that may be written $s \to s'$, and s' is a successor state of s. A Kripke structure $K \triangleq \langle S, I, A, L \rangle$ is an extension of M such that T is left-total, A is a set of atomic propositions, and $L : S \to 2^A$ is a labeling function that assigns each state a set of atomic propositions.

The syntax and semantics of Linear Temporal Logic (LTL) can be defined with Kripke structures. LTL is an extension of Propositional Logic (PL), and then all logical connectives of PL, such as $\wedge$ (infix binary, $p \wedge q$) and $\neg$ (prefix unary, $\neg p$), can be used for LTL. The present paper mainly uses two temporal connectives: $\square$ (prefix unary, $\square \varphi$) and $\rightsquigarrow$ (infix binary, $\varphi \rightsquigarrow \psi$). Given a Kripke structure K, the informal semantics descriptions of $\square \varphi$ and $\varphi \rightsquigarrow \psi$, where neither φ nor ψ have any temporal connectives, are as follows:

- $\square \varphi$ holds for K if and only if φ holds in each reachable state of K, and
- $\varphi \rightsquigarrow \psi$ holds for K if and only if whenever φ holds in a reachable state s_1 of K, there exists a state s_2 that is reachable from s_1 such that ψ holds in s_2; this can be interpreted as follows: when φ becomes true (in a reachable state s_1 of K), ψ will always be true in future (in a future state s_2 of s_1).

Maude is a specification/programming language based on rewriting logic. Maude makes it possible to treat data, such as states, atomic propositions and LTL formulas, as terms and define functions, such as L, and semantics of logics, such as LTL. For example, a state can be expressed as a braced associative-commutative collection (called soup) of name-value pairs (called observable components). Let (pc: 14), (x: 24) and (y: 5) be observable components, where pc, x and y are names, and 14, 24 and 5 are values. Then, {(pc: 14) (x: 24) (y: 5)} expresses a state. L can be described as rewrite rules in Maude. For example, let us suppose we have the following rewrite rules:

rl [upd-x]: {(pc: 14) (x: X) (y: Y)} => {(pc: 15) (x: (X * Y)) (y: Y)} .
rl [inc-y]: {(pc: 15) (x: X) (y: Y)} => {(pc: 13) (x: X) (y: (Y + 1))} .

where rl stands for rewrite rule, upd-x (update the variable named x) and inc-y (increment the variable named y) are the names given to the two rewrite rules, X and Y are Maude variables of natural numbers, and each rewrite rule says that if a state that can match the left-hand side can be transited (rewritten) to the corresponding right-hand side. For example, {(pc: 14) (x: 24) (y: 5)} can be transited to {(pc: 15) (x: 120) (y: 5)} with upd-x, and the latter state can be be transited to {(pc: 13) (x: 120) (y: 6)} with inc-y. Rewrite rule inc-y can also be described as follows:

rl [inc-y]: {(pc: 15) (y: Y) S} => {(pc: 13) (y: (Y + 1)) S} .

where S is a Maude variable of soups. This is because the observable component whose name is x is never involved in rewrite rule inc-y and soups are associative-commutative collections.

Let us consider the pseudo-code shown in Fig. 1, where l1, ..., l6 are labels given to each atomic fragment of the pseudo-code, and we suppose we have a program counter that refers to such a label. Let the pseudo-code be called Fact5. Fact5 can be formalized as a Kripke structure K_{Fact5}. {(pc: 14) (x: 24) (y: 5)}, {(pc: 15) (x: 120) (y: 5)} and {(pc: 13) (x: 120) (y: 6)} are states of K_{Fact5}. Initially, the value of the pc observable component is l1, and although the value of the x and y observable components can be arbitrary natural numbers, they are 0 in this paper. Therefore, {(pc: l1) (x: 0) (y: 0)} is the only initial state of K_{Fact5}. Let us consider four atomic propositions: init, halt, inLoop and lte5Gte1. init is given to the initial state, halt is given to the states in which the value of the pc observable component is l6, inLoop is given to the states in which the value of the pc observable component is l4 or l5, and lte5Gte1 is given to the state in which the value of the y observable component is less than or equal to 5 and greater than or equal to 1. Then, we can consider the following LTL formulas: □(inLoop → lte5Gte1) and init ⤳ halt, where → is the ordinary logical implication. Let us note that the two rewrite rules upd-x and inc-y describe part of T_{Fact5}.

l1: $x = 1$
l2: $y = 1$
l3: **while** $y \leq 5$:
l4: $x = x * y$
l5: $y = y + 1$
l6: **exit**:

Fig. 1. Fact5

The Maude system is equipped with an LTL model checker. Let `FACT5-CHECK` be the formal specification of $\mathcal{K}_{\text{Fact5}}$ in Maude. We can conduct the model checking experiments that $\mathcal{K}_{\text{Fact5}}$ satisfies $\Box$ (inLoop $\rightarrow$ lte5Gte1) and init $\rightsquigarrow$ halt as follows:

```
red in FACT5-CHECK : modelCheck(s0, [] (inLoop -> lte5Gte1)) .
red in FACT5-CHECK : modelCheck(s0, init |-> halt) .
```

where s0 is {(pc: l1) (x: 0) (y: 0)}, [] is $\Box$, -> is $\rightarrow$, and |-> is $\rightsquigarrow$. The Maude LTL model checker concludes that the two LTL formulas hold for $\mathcal{K}_{\text{Fact5}}$.

The Maude system is also equipped with a reachability analysis tool called the `search` command. The `search` command can be used as an invariant model checker. Thus, it is possible to model check $\Box$ (inLoop $\rightarrow$ lte5Gte1) for $\mathcal{K}_{\text{Fact5}}$ as follows:

```
search [1] in FACT5 : s0 =>* {(pc: L) (y: Y) S}
such that not ((L == 14 or L == 15) implies (y <= 5 and Y >= 1)).
```

where `FACT5` is the state machine part of `FACT5-CHECK`, and L, Y and S are Maude variables of labels, natural numbers and soups. If the `search` command never finds a state in which the condition just after "such that not" is broken, then $\Box$ (inLoop $\rightarrow$ lte5Gte1) holds for $\mathcal{K}_{\text{Fact5}}$. The `search` command never finds such a state in this case.

3 Bully Protocol

Bully Protocol is a distributed synchronous leader election protocol proposed by Hector Garcia-Molina [6]. Bully Protocol consists of multiple nodes that have unique IDs, such as natural numbers, that are total order. Nodes do not share memory and can only communicate by exchanging messages. Bully Protocol uses three kinds of messages: Election, OK and Coordinate messages. Each node is either active or inactive (or failed). Once a node becomes failed, we suppose that it never gets back active again in the first part of this paper. When a node is active, its status is normal, initiator or leader. The status of a node is normal in an ordinary operation situation, where there is highly likely to be a leader that is different from the node. When the status of a node is initiator, it has initiated an election process and self-nominated as a leader. When the status of a node is leader, it is a leader. When a node is failed, its status is failed.

Bully Protocol is synchronous. Each execution (or trace) of Bully Protocol is a sequence of rounds. In each round, messages are sent by some nodes to some other nodes, the latter nodes receive the messages, and the messages are handled by the nodes, all of which can be regarded as being done instantaneously, although it takes time to make them happen in a real setting.

Let us suppose that nodes know all nodes' IDs, do not know whether non-leader nodes are active or failed, and can know whether leaders are active or failed somehow. Bully Protocol is expected to satisfy the following safety property and liveness property:

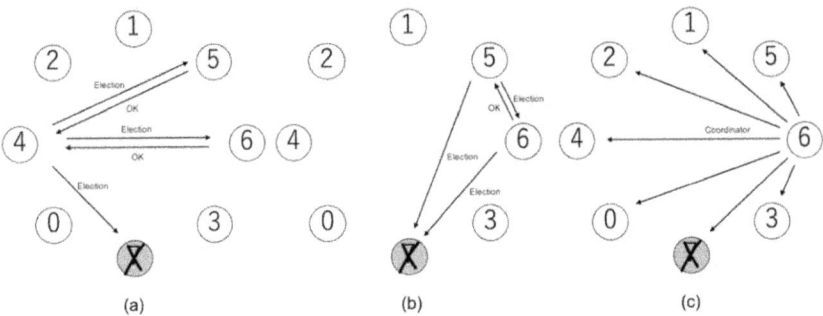

Fig. 2. A way to elect a leader with Bully Protocol

Non-multiple leader election (NonMulLElect) At most one leader is elected for any period of time;

Eventual leader election (EventLElect) A leader will be eventually elected when the current leader became failed.

When a node whose ID is i happens to know that the current leader became failed, it initiates an election process and its status becomes initiator. The following occurs in the election process:

1. Node i sends an Election message to all nodes whose IDs are greater than i;
2. If node i does not receive an OK message from any of the nodes to which the Election message has been sent, node i's status becomes leader;
3. If node i receives an OK message from at least one of the nodes to which the Election message has been sent, node i's status becomes back normal and all nodes that have sent OK messages to node i take over the election process, where each node that takes over the election process does the above-mentioned.

Each of the nodes to which node i sends an Election message in the election process is either active or failed. If it is active, it sends back an OK message to node i. Otherwise, it does nothing for the Election message because it is failed. As written, each active one of the nodes to which node i sends an Election message in the election process takes over the election process, and then there may be multiple election processes being carried out by multiple nodes. Multiple nodes may initiate multiple election processes (almost) simultaneously when they happen to know that the current leader became failed. Finally, there will be one node whose status is initiator and that does not receive an OK messages from any other nodes. The status of the node becomes leader and the node sends Coordinate messages to all the other nodes to let them know that the node is a new leader.

Let us consider a system in which there are eight nodes whose IDs are 0, 1, 2, ..., 7, respectively, node 7 was a leader, and it became failed (see Fig. 2 (a)). We suppose that node 4 happens to know it. As shown in Fig. 2 (a), node 4 sends

Election messages to nodes 5, 6 and 7, nodes 5 and 6 send back OK messages to node 4, and node 7 does nothing. As shown in Fig. 2 (b), node 5 sends Election messages to nodes 6 and 7, and node 6 sends an Election message to node 7; node 6 sends back an OK message to node 5 and node 7 does nothing. As shown in Fig. 2 (c), node 6 becomes a leader and sends Coordinate messages to all the other nodes.

4 Formal Specification

Bully Protocol is formalized as a Kripke structure, which is described as a rewrite theory specification in Maude. We suppose that only leaders can be failed, and failedLeader is used as a node status instead of failed and natural numbers are used as node IDs. As written, when node i's status becomes initiator and node i sends an Election message to a failed node, the failed node does nothing because it is failed. Timeout is often used to detect that a node is failed in a real setting. Although realtime can be formally specified, we suppose that a failed node replies to an Election message by sending a Timeout message to the node that sent the Election message to the failed node, which makes it possible not to use realtime concepts in our formal specification.

Maude makes it possible to naturally specify asynchronous systems but not necessarily to naturally specify synchronous systems. Thus, we do not handle rounds that are essence to synchronous systems. We have specified Bully Protocol as an asynchronous system but come up with specification techniques so that Bully Protocol specified as asynchronous system keeps the core part of a synchronous system.

4.1 Observable Components

We use the following observable components:

- (proc[i]: st) means the status st of node i, where st is normal, initiator, leader or failedLeader;
- (curLeader[i]: j) means that node i recognizes that node j is the leader;
- (sndElectionMsgCnt[i]: $\#ems$) means that $\#ems$ is the number of Election messages sent by node i to other nodes when node i's status is initiator;
- (rcvOkMsgCnt[i]: $\#oms$) means that $\#oms$ is the number of OK messages received by node i when node i's status is initiator;
- (rcvTimeoutMsgCnt[i]: $\#tms$) means that $\#tms$ is the number of Timeout messages received by node i when node i's status is initiator;
- (procIds[i]: ns) means that node i recognizes that ns is the set of the IDs of all nodes that participate in Bully Protocol;
- (network: ms) means that ms is a soup of messages that have been sent and not yet received;
- (tran: e) means that e is the event (or state transition) most recently taken.

(network: ms) formalizes the network with which nodes exchange messages. We need to use a condition to model check that Bully Protocol enjoys EventLElect, and then use (tran: e) to express the condition, which will be described later.

The function node is defined as follows to define initial states of Bully Protocol:

```
eq node(N,PS,LN) = (proc[N]: PS) (curLeader[N]: LN)
   (sndElectionMsgCnt[N]: 0) (rcvOkMsgCnt[N]: 0) (rcvTimeoutMsgCnt[N]: 0).
```

When there are two nodes, the initial state denoted init2 is defined as follows:

```
eq init2 = {node(0,normal,1) node(1,leader,1)
   (procIds: (0, 1)) (network: empty) (tran: notran)} .
```

When there are three nodes, the initial state denoted init3 is defined as follows:

```
eq init3 = {node(0,normal,2) node(1,normal,2) node(2,leader,2)
   (procIds: (0, 1, 2)) (network: empty) (tran: notran)} .
```

When there are four, five and six nodes, the initial states denoted init4, init5 and init6 are defined likewise.

4.2 Rewriting (or Transition) Rules

We suppose that a leader may become failedLeader anytime. This can be specified as the following rules:

```
rl [become-failed-leader] :
 {(proc[ID]: leader) (tran: E) S} =>
 {(proc[ID]: failedLeader) (tran: bfl(ID)) S} .
```

where ID and E are Maude variables of natural numbers and events, and (tran: bfl(ID)) means that the rule become-failed-leader has been most recently taken by node ID just after applying the rule to a state. Words only consisting of capital letters are used as Maude variables and their sorts can be understood from the context.

A node ID becomes initiator whenever it detects that the current leader LID became failedLeader. This can be specified as the following rules:

```
rl [become-initiator] :
 {(proc[ID]: normal) (proc[LID]: failedLeader) (curLeader[ID ]: LID)
  (sndElectionMsgCnt[ID]: SEC) (rcvOkMsgCnt[ID]: ROC)
  (rcvTimeoutMsgCnt[ID]: RTC) (tran: E) S} =>
 {(proc[ID]: initiator) (proc[LID]: failedLeader) (curLeader[ID]: LID)
  (sndElectionMsgCnt[ID]: 0) (rcvOkMsgCnt[ID]: 0) (rcvTimeoutMsgCnt[ID]: 0)
  (tran: bi(ID)) S} .
```

The values of the three observable components related to the numbers of Election, OK and Timeout messages are set to 0.

When node ID became initiator and has not yet sent Election messages to all nodes whose IDs are greater than ID, it does so. This can be specified as the following rules:

```
crl [start-election] :
 {(proc[ID]: initiator) (sndElectionMsgCnt[ID]: SEC)
  (procIds: IDS) (network: NW) (tran: E) S} =>
 {(proc[ID]: initiator) (sndElectionMsgCnt[ID]: | biggerThanIds(ID,IDS) |)
  (procIds: IDS) (network: (sndElectionMsgs(ID,biggerThanIds(ID,IDS)) NW))
  (tran: se(ID)) S}
 if SEC == 0 .
```

Node ID checks if SEC equals 0 and if so, it decides that it has not yet sent Election messages to some other nodes. biggerThanIds(ID,IDS) calculates the set of all nodes whose IDs are greater than ID. Given a set s, $|s|$ calculates the number of elements in s. sndElectionMsgs(ID,biggerThanIds(ID,IDS)) makes the Election messages addressed to all nodes whose IDs are greater than ID. Node ID puts all such Election messages in the network, meaning that it broadcasts the Election messages to all the nodes concerned, while the latter nodes do not immediately receive the Election messages because Bully Protocol is formally specified as an asynchronous system.

Whenever node ID0 whose status is normal receives an Election message from node ID1 such that ID0 > ID1 and the current leader LID is failedLeader, node ID0 becomes initiator and sends an OK message to node ID1. This can be specified as the following rules:

```
crl [normal-execution-election] :
 {(proc[ID0]: normal) (proc[LID]: failedLeader)
  (curLeader[ID0]: LID) (sndElectionMsgCnt[ID0]: SEC)
  (rcvOkMsgCnt[ID0]: ROC) (rcvTimeoutMsgCnt[ID0]: RTC)
  (network: (message(ID1,ID0,election) NW)) (tran: E) S} =>
 {(proc[ID0]: initiator) (proc[LID]: failedLeader)
  (curLeader[ID0]: LID) (sndElectionMsgCnt[ID0]: 0)
  (rcvOkMsgCnt[ID0]: 0) (rcvTimeoutMsgCnt[ID0]: 0)
  (network: (sndOkMsg(ID0,ID1) NW)) (tran: nee(ID0)) S}
 if ID0 > ID1 .
```

message(ID1,ID0,election) is an Election message addressed to node ID0 from node ID1, and sndOkMsg(ID0,ID1) is an OK message addressed to node ID1 from node ID0.

As written, instead of use of timeout, if a node whose status is failedLeader receives an Election message from a node, the failed node sends a Timeout message to the latter node. This can be specified as the following rules:

```
crl [election-timeout] :
 {(proc[ID0]: failedLeader) (network: (message(ID1,ID0,election) NW))
  (tran: E) S} =>
 {(proc[ID0]: failedLeader) (network: (sndTimeoutMsg(ID0,ID1) NW))
  (tran: et(ID0)) S}
 if ID0 > ID1 .
```

sndTimeoutMsg(ID0,ID1) is a Timeout message addressed to node ID1 from node ID0.

If node ID0 whose status is `initiator` receives an Election message from node ID1 such that ID0 > ID1, the former sends an OK message to the latter. This can be specified as the following rules:

```
crl [initiator-execution-election] :
 {(proc[ID0]: initiator) (network: (message(ID1,ID0,election) NW))
  (tran: E) S} =>
 {(proc[ID0]: initiator) (network: (sndOkMsg(ID0,ID1) NW))
  (tran: iee(ID0)) S}
 if ID0 > ID1 .
```

If the current leader becomes `failedLeader`, any nodes whose statuses are normal may become `initiator`. This is what we need to take this case into account. Because node ID0 may have already initiated an election process, the values stored in the observable components related to the numbers of Election, OK and Timeout messages are not initialized.

When node ID0 receives an OK message from node ID1 such that ID0 < ID1, it increments the number ROC of OK messages received that is stored in the rcvOkMsgCnt[ID0] observable component. This can be specified as the following rules:

```
crl [initiator-execution-ok] :
 {(proc[ID0]: initiator) (rcvOkMsgCnt[ID0]: ROC)
  (network: (message(ID1,ID0,ok) NW)) (tran: E) S} =>
 {(proc[ID0]: initiator) (rcvOkMsgCnt[ID0]: ROC + 1)
  (network: NW) (tran: ieo(ID0)) S}
 if ID0 < ID1 .
```

When node ID0 receives a Timeout message from node ID1 such that ID0 < ID1, it increments the number RTC of Timeout messages received that is stored in the rcvTimeoutMsgCnt[ID0] observable component. This can be specified as the following rules:

```
crl [initiator-execution-timeout] :
 {(proc[ID0]: initiator) (rcvTimeoutMsgCnt[ID0]: RTC)
  (network: (message(ID1,ID0,timeout) NW)) (tran: E) S} =>
 {(proc[ID0]: initiator) (rcvTimeoutMsgCnt[ID0]: RTC + 1)
  (network: NW) (tran: iet(ID0)) S}
 if ID0 < ID1 .
```

If node ID0 whose status is `initiator` receives OK and Timeout messages from all nodes to which node ID0 has sent Election messages and at least one OK message has been received, the status of node ID0 becomes back `normal`. This can be specified as the following rules:

```
crl [initiator-become-normal] :
 {(proc[ID0]: initiator) (sndElectionMsgCnt[ID0]: SEC)
  (rcvOkMsgCnt[ID0]: ROC) (rcvTimeoutMsgCnt[ID0]: RTC) (tran: E) S} =>
 {(proc[ID0]: normal) (sndElectionMsgCnt[ID0]: 0)
  (rcvOkMsgCnt[ID0]: 0) (rcvTimeoutMsgCnt[ID0]: 0) (tran: ibn(ID0)) S}
 if SEC > 0 and SEC == (ROC + RTC) and ROC > 0 .
```

If node ID0 whose status is initiator receives OK and Timeout messages from all nodes to which node ID0 has sent Election messages and no OK message has been received, the status of node ID0 becomes back leader, provided that the network is empty. This can be specified as the following rules:

```
crl [initiator-become-leader] :
 {(proc[ID0]: initiator) (curLeader[ID0]: ID1)
  (sndElectionMsgCnt[ID0]: SEC) (rcvTimeoutMsgCnt[ID0]: RTC)
  (rcvOkMsgCnt[ID0]: ROC) (procIds: IDS) (network: empty) (tran: E) S} =>
 {(proc[ID0]: leader) (curLeader[ID0]: ID0)
  (sndElectionMsgCnt[ID0]: 0) (rcvTimeoutMsgCnt[ID0]: 0)
  (rcvOkMsgCnt[ID0]: 0) (procIds: IDS) (network: empty) (tran: ibl(ID0))
  syncCurLeader(S,ID0,smallerThanIds(ID0,IDS))}
 if SEC > 0 and SEC == RTC and ROC == 0 .
```

Bully Protocol has node ID0 broadcast Coordinate messages to all the other nodes, letting them know that node ID0 has just become the new leader. In our formal specification, however, the function syncCurLeader lets all nodes whose IDs are less than ID0 know that ID0 has just become the new leader and make the initiator status of each node normal. Because all nodes whose IDs are greater than ID0 are failed because of our assumption, it is not necessary to let such nodes know it.

Both sides of initiator-become-leader have (network: empty). This is reasonable because when an initiator becomes a leader, the network is empty because Bully Protocol is synchronous. Use of (network: empty) in both sides (especially the left-hand side) of initiator-become-leader can be considered to simulate a synchronous aspect of Bully Protocol in an asynchronous systems specification.

In summary, we have formally specified Bully Protocol as an asynchronous system in Maude but keep the core part of a synchronous system because of the following two ideas:

1. A node whose status is initiator decides whether its status becomes leader or normal if and only if the node has received OK and Timeout messages from all nodes to which the node has sent Election messages, which is implemented in the two rules initiator-become-normal and initiator-become-leader;
2. Instead of broadcasting Coordinate messages to all the other nodes when a node whose ID is i has just become a new leader, the function syncCurLeader is used to let all nodes whose IDs are less than i know that node i has become a new leader.
3. When a node whose status is initiator becomes a leader, the network is empty, meaning that all messages in the network have been processed (or received) by nodes. Otherwise, messages may be accumulated and affect EventLElect, which will be described later. The assumption that the network is empty can be considered to simulate a synchronous aspect of Bully Protocol in an asynchronous systems specification.

4.3 Atomic Propositions and LTL Formulas

Three kinds of atomic propositions are used: leader(i), initiator(i) and applied(e). leader(i) holds for a state s if and only if s has (proc[i]: leader) as its observable component. initiator(i) holds for a state s if and only if s has (proc[i]: initiator) as its observable component. applied(e) holds for a state s if and only if s has (tran: e) as its observable component.

We consider a system in which there are a finite number of nodes, and suppose that once a node becomes failed, it will never become active. Thus, there may be a case such that all nodes are finally failed. For example, when there are three nodes, the LTL formula for EventLElect

$$(\neg\text{leader}(0) \land \neg\text{leader}(1) \land \neg\text{leader}(2)) \rightsquigarrow (\text{leader}(0) \lor \text{leader}(1) \lor \text{leader}(2))$$

is not adequate for our assumption. An informal description of the formula is as follows: whenever no node is a leader, a node will be eventually a leader. As written, because all nodes may be finally failed, the formula does not hold for our formal specification of Bully Protocol. However, the formula will be used later and then it is referred to as leaderLiveness3-2. When there are two, four, five and six nodes, the LTL formulas can be defined likewise, which are referred to as leaderLiveness2-2, leaderLiveness4-2, leaderLiveness5-2 and leaderLiveness6-2, respectively.

Instead, we use the following LTL formula:

$$(\text{initiator}(0) \lor \text{initiator}(1) \lor \text{initiator}(2))$$
$$\rightsquigarrow (\text{leader}(0) \lor \text{leader}(1) \lor \text{leader}(2))$$

The LTL formula is referred to as leaderLiveness3. An informal description of leaderLiveness3 is as follows: whenever a node is an initiator, a node will be eventually a leader. When there is an initiator node, the node is not failed, which means that all nodes are not failed. Moreover, a node becomes an initiator only when the current leader is failed. This is why leaderLiveness3 is adequate for EventLElect under our assumption. Model checking leaderLiveness3 for our formal specification of Bully Protocol without using any assumptions, however, a counterexample is generated, which will be described in the next section. When there are two, four, five and six nodes, the LTL formulas can be defined likewise, which are denoted leaderLiveness2, leaderLiveness4, leaderLiveness5 and leaderLiveness6, respectively.

5 Model Checking

The search command is used to model check NonMulLElect for our formal specification of Bully Protocol when there are 2, 3, 4, 5 and 6 nodes, respectively. The LTL model checker is used to model check EventLElect for our formal specification of Bully Protocol when there are 2, 3, 4, 5 and 6 nodes, respectively. We need to use an assumption for model checking EventLElect. The model checking experiments used an Apple Mac Pro computer that carries a 2.5 GHz microprocessor with 28 cores and 1.5 TB memory of RAM.

Table 1. Times taken for model checking (a) NonMulLElect and (b) EventLElect (1)

#nodes	2	3	4	5	6
(a)	0 ms	3 ms	26	18 m 3 s	NT
(b)	1 ms	5 ms	324	18 m 15 s	NT

5.1 Non-multiple Leader Election

When there are three nodes, the search command can be used to model check NonMulLElect as follows:

```
search [1] in BULLY :
  init3 =>* {(proc[ID0]: leader) (proc[ID1]: leader) S} .
```

BULLY is the module in which our formal specification of Bully Protocol is written. No counterexample is found, meaning that Bully Protocol enjoys NonMulLElect when there are three nodes. When there are 2, 4, 5 and 6 nodes, the search command can be used to model check NonMulLElect likewise, although it was not terminated to conduct the model checking experiment when there were 6 nodes within three months (denouted as NT). Table 1 (a) shows times taken for model checking NonMulLElect when there are 2, 3, 4, 5 and 6 nodes, where NT stands for non-termination within 46 d in this paper.

5.2 Eventual Leader Election

When there are three nodes, the LTL mode checker can be used to model check EventLElect as follows:

```
red in BULLY-CHECK : modelCheck(init3,leaderLiveness3) .
```

BULLY-CHECK is the module in which the atomic propositions, the labeling function and the LTL formulas as well as our formal specification of Bully Protocol are written. A counterexample is found. Node 0 repeatedly becomes an initiator and becomes back to a normal node, preventing node 2 from becoming a leader when node 3 becomes failed. To prevent a node from repeatedly becoming an initiator and back to a normal node, it suffices for the transition rule `become-initiator` not to be taken infinitely many times for each node. When there are three nodes, this can be expressed as the following LTL formula:

$$\neg\Box\Diamond\text{applied}(\text{bi}(0)) \wedge \neg\Box\Diamond\text{applied}(\text{bi}(1)) \wedge \neg\Box\Diamond\text{applied}(\text{bi}(2))$$

where $\text{bi}(i)$ for $i = 0, 1, 2$ is the event name of the rule `become-initiator` in the formal specification and $\Diamond \varphi$ is defined as $\neg\Box\neg\varphi$. The LTL formula is referred to as `afair3`. When there are 2, 4, 5, and 6 node, the counterparts of the LTL formula are referred to as `afair2`. `afair4`. `afair5` and `afair6`, respectively.

We then model check EventLElect under the assumption `afair3` as follows:

```
red in BULLY-CHECK : modelCheck(init3,afair3 -> leaderLiveness3) .
```

No counterexample is found. When there are 2, 4, 5 and 6 nodes, EventLElect can be model checked likewise under `afair2`. `afair4`. `afair5` and `afair6`, respectively, although it was not terminated to conduct the model checking experiment when there were 6 nodes over three months. Table 1 (b) shows times taken for model checking EventLElect when there are 2, 3, 4, 5 and 6 nodes.

Let us note that if `(network: empty)` is deleted from `initiator-become-leader`, EventLElect does not hold even under the assumption `afair`i when there are three nodes or more. Let us suppose that there are three nodes: node 0, node 1 and node 2. Initially, node 2 is a leader and node 0 and node 1 are normal. Let us suppose that node 2 becomes failed, and both node 0 and node 1 become initiators. Node 0 sends Election messages to node 1 and node 2, node 1 replies to the message by sending node 0 an OK message, and node 2 replies to the message by sending node 0 a Timeout message. We also suppose that the OK message is received by node 0, while the Timeout message is not by node 0. Node 1 also sends an Election message to node 2, which replies to the message by sending node 1 a Timeout message that is received by node 1. Node 1 then becomes a leader. Note that there is one Timeout message left in the network that was sent by node 2 and was not yet received by node 0. Let us suppose that node 1 becomes failed, and node 0 becomes an initiator. Node 0 sends Election messages to node 1 and node 2. We suppose that both node 1 and node 2 reply to the messages by sending node 0 Timeout messages. Note that there are now three Timeout messages addressed to node 0. If node 0 receives three Timeout messages, node 0 does not become a leader with the rule `initiator-become-leader` because the condition `SEC == RTC` does not hold, where SEC is 2 and RTC is 3. This is why it is necessary to have `(network: empty)` in both sides of `initiator-become-leader`.

6 Some Revisions of Formal Specification

One possible way to make the assumption `afair`i unnecessary for model checking EventLElect is as follows: when the current leader became failed, each node can at most once become an initiator. To this end, we add one observable component as follows:

- $(flag[i]:b)$ means the if b is true, node i can become an initiator and makes b false, and otherwise node i cannot.

The definition of `node(N,PS,LN)` is revised as follows:

```
eq node(N,PS,LN) = (proc[N]: PS) (flag[N}: true) (curLeader[N]: LN)
   (sndElectionMsgCnt[N]: 0) (rcvOkMsgCnt[N]: 0) (rcvTimeoutMsgCnt[N]: 0) .
```

Transition rule `become-initiator` is revised as follows:

```
rl [become-initiator] :
 {(proc[ID]: normal) (flag[ID]: true) (proc[LID]: failedLeader)
  (curLeader[ID ]: LID) (sndElectionMsgCnt[ID]: SEC)
  (rcvOkMsgCnt[ID]: ROC) (rcvTimeoutMsgCnt[ID]: RTC) (tran: E) S} =>
 {(proc[ID]: initiator) (flag[ID]: false) (proc[LID]: failedLeader)
  (curLeader[ID]: LID) (sndElectionMsgCnt[ID]: 0) (rcvOkMsgCnt[ID]: 0)
  (rcvTimeoutMsgCnt[ID]: 0) (tran: bi(ID)) S} .
```

The function `syncCurLeader` is revised as follows: it also makes b of $(\text{flag}[i]:b)$ true as the status of node i is made `normal` if the status of node i is `initiator`.

Then, we do not need to use any assumptions for model checking EventL-Elect. When there are three nodes, it suffices to use the following command:

```
red in BULLY-CHECK : modelCheck(init3,leaderLiveness3) .
```

No counterexample is found. The revision shows one possible way to implement the assumption used for model checking EventLElect.

One more revision is made. We assumed that once a leader becomes failed, it never becomes active. We relax this assumption. In the original version of Bully Protocol [6], when a failed node i becomes back active, it starts an election and may become a leader even though there is a leader j if $j < i$. The goal of a leader election protocol is to eventually elect a leader if there is no leader and not to elect two leaders or more. Thus, it is not necessary to elect a new leader if there is a leader, and we take a different option in this paper as follows: a failed leader can become a normal node provided that a new leader has been elected. So, we add one transition rule as follows:

```
rl [become-active] :
  {(proc[ID]: failedLeader) (flag[ID]: B) (curLeader[ID]: ID0)
   (proc[LID]: leader) (tran: E) S} =>
  {(proc[ID]: normal) (flag[ID]: true) (curLeader[ID]: LID)
   (proc[LID]: leader) (tran: ba(ID)) S} .
```

Only with this revision, however, there is a possibility left such that all nodes are failed and no failed node can become a normal one. To address this issue, there are at least two options we can take:

1. when all nodes are failed, one node randomly chosen can become alive as a leader;
2. the current leader can become failed if there exists at most one normal node.

When all nodes are failed, human operators are likely to be involved. So, we adopt the second option in this paper. To this end, we revise the rule `become-failed-leader` as follows:

```
rl [become-failed-leader] :
  {(proc[ID]: leader) (proc[ID0]: normal) (tran: E) S} =>
  {(proc[ID]: failedLeader) (proc[ID0]: normal) (tran: bfl(ID)) S} .
```

Under the assumption that failed leader never become active, the node whose ID is the largest never becomes an initiator. To relax the assumption, however, such a node may do so. The rule `start-election` does not work well for such a node. This is because there is no node whose ID is greater than the node and the node never sends Election messages to any other nodes. The rule `start-election` should be revised as two rules. One rule deals with nodes whose IDs are not the greatest, while the other deals with the node whose ID is the greatest. The two rules are as follows:

```
crl [start-election] :
 {(proc[ID]: initiator) (sndElectionMsgCnt[ID]: SEC) (procIds: IDS)
    (network: NW) (tran: E) S} =>
 {(proc[ID]: initiator) (sndElectionMsgCnt[ID]: | biggerThanIds(ID, IDS) |)
    (procIds: IDS) (network: (sndElectionMsgs(ID, biggerThanIds(ID, IDS)) NW))
    (tran: se(ID)) S}
 if SEC == 0 /\ | biggerThanIds(ID, IDS) | > 0 .

crl [start-election2] :
 {(proc[ID0]: initiator) (curLeader[ID0]: ID1) (sndElectionMsgCnt[ID0]: SEC)
    (rcvTimeoutMsgCnt[ID0]: RTC) (rcvOkMsgCnt[ID0]: ROC) (procIds: IDS)
    (network: empty) (tran: E) S} =>
 {(proc[ID0]: leader) (curLeader[ID0]: ID0) (sndElectionMsgCnt[ID0]: 0)
    (rcvTimeoutMsgCnt[ID0]: 0) (rcvOkMsgCnt[ID0]: 0) (procIds: IDS)
    (network: empty) (tran: se2(ID0)) syncCurLeader(S, ID0)}
 if SEC == 0 /\ | biggerThanIds(ID0, IDS) | == 0 .
```

The initiator node whose ID is the greatest can become a leader immediately because it does not send Election messages to any other nodes and then does not need to wait for any replies from any other nodes, which is handled by the rule `start-election2`. Any other nodes are handled by the rule `start-election`.

In summary, we have revised the formal specification of Bully Protocol as follows:

1. We make the assumption afair$i$ unnecessary for model checking EventL-Elect by adding the observable component (flag$[i]$: b) and revising the rule `become-initiator` and the function `syncCurLeader`.
2. We relax the assumption that once a leader becomes failed, it never becomes active by revising the rules `become-active`, `become-failed-leader` and `initiator-become-leader`.

7 Model Checking for the Revised Version

The same search command is used for NonMulLElect. The LTL formula leader-Liveness$i$ for $i = 2, 3, 4, 5, 6$ is used for EventLElect, where afair$i$ is not used. Table 2 (a) shows times taken for model checking NonMulLElect when there are 2, 3, 4, 5 and 6 nodes. Table 2 (b) shows times taken for model checking EventLElect. The experimental data show that the revised version of the formal specification has larger reachable states than the first version of the formal specification. This is because when there are 5 nodes, it took much more time (over

Table 2. Times taken for model checking (a) NonMulLElect and (b) EventLElect (2)

#nodes	2	3	4	5	6
(a)	0 ms	17 ms	4700 ms	46 d 17 h 30 m 19 s	NT
(b)	0 ms	18 ms	4714 ms	46 d 20 h 5 m 9 s	NT

46 d) to complete the model checking experment of both (a) and (b) than the time (about 18 min) taken for the first version. It is one piece of our future work to make it possible to conduct the model checking experiments of both properties for the revised version by coming up with a better formal specification and/or using a technique to mitigate the state space explosion problem, such as a divide & conquer approach to model checking.

8 Related Work

Bitcoin still gets attention. Blockchain is the core of the technology behind Bitcoin and needs to use a distributed consensus protocol, such as Paxos and Raft. Although Paxos is one good candidate as a distributed consensus protocol, it is not straightforward to implement Paxos. Raft is likely to be implemented more often than Paxos because one main goal of Raft is to make Raft easier-to-comprehend than Paxos. Raft divides the consensus problem into two subproblems: leader election and log replication. Bao, Li, Hu and Cao [3] formally specified the Raft leader election in Promela and conducted model checking experiments with Spin that the Raft leader election satisfies three desired properties (stability, liveness and uniqueness) expressed in LTL. They found that the Raft leader election does not satisfy liveness and uniqueness and suggested for making the properties hold by analyzing the counterexamples. Our research group has formally verified that Raft Log Replication as well as Raft Leader Election enjoy some desired properties with Maude [7,8]. Because both Raft Log Replication and Raft Leader Election are asynchronous, it is rather straightforward to formalize them as state machines and formally specify the state machines in Maude. Our research group has conducted some model checking experiments that Raft enjoys some safety properties.

André, Fribourg, Mota and Soulat [2] formally verify that a variant of an industrial asynchronous leader election protocol enjoys some desired properties with counter abstraction, bounded model checking and parametric timed model checking. The techniques used by them can deal with a large number p of processes (up to $p = 5000$). The industrial asynchronous leader election protocol was developed in Thales, a French company, and is an asynchronous version of Bully Protocol. We have formalized Bully Protocol as an asynchronous state machine and formally specified the state machine in Maude, but keep the essential synchronous aspects of Bully Protocol in our formal specification. The formal verification technique used by them is more scalable than ours. Our research group uses an interactive theorem proving technique called the proof score approach to formal verification as well as model checking. One piece of our future work is to use the proof score approach to formal verification to formally verify that the asynchronous version of Bully Protocol enjoys desired properties. Because the proof score approach to formal verification is a theorem proving technique, it can deal with an arbitrary number of processes.

9 Conclusion

We have formally specified Bully Protocol in Maude and conducted the model checking experiments that the protocol enjoys the two properties. We have revised the formal specification and conducted the model checking experiments that the revised version also enjoys the two properties. Our contributions are described in Introduction.

References

1. Agrawal, T.K., Kumar, V., Pal, R., Wang, L., Chen, Y.: Blockchain-based framework for supply chain traceability: a case example of textile and clothing industry. Comput. Ind. Eng. **154**, 107130 (2021). https://doi.org/10.1016/J.CIE.2021.107130
2. André, É., Fribourg, L., Mota, J.-M., Soulat, R.: Verification of an industrial asynchronous leader election algorithm using abstractions and parametric model checking. In: Enea, C., Piskac, R. (eds.) VMCAI 2019. LNCS, vol. 11388, pp. 409–424. Springer, Cham (2019). https://doi.org/10.1007/978-3-030-11245-5_19
3. Bao, Q., Li, B., Hu, T., Cao, D.: Model checking the safety of raft leader election algorithm. In: 22nd IEEE International Conference on Software Quality, Reliability and Security, QRS 2022, pp. 400–409. IEEE (2022). https://doi.org/10.1109/QRS57517.2022.00048
4. Buterin, V.: Ethereum white paper: A next generation smart contract & decentralized application platform (2013). https://ethereum.org/en/whitepaper/
5. Clavel, M., et al.: All About Maude - A High-Performance Logical Framework. LNCS, vol. 4350. Springer, Heidelberg (2007). https://doi.org/10.1007/978-3-540-71999-1
6. Garcia-Molina, H.: Elections in a distributed computing system. IEEE Trans. Comput. **31**(1), 48–59 (1982). https://doi.org/10.1109/TC.1982.1675885
7. Ishibashi, T., Ogata, K.: Formal specification and model checking of raft leader election in maude. In: 12th International Conference on Software and Computer Applications (ICSCA 2023), pp. 41–45. ACM (2023). https://doi.org/10.1145/3587828.3587835
8. Ishibashi, T., Ogata, K.: Formal specification and model checking of raft log replication in maude. In: 29th International DMS Conference on Visualization and Visual Languages (DMSVIVA 2023), pp. 1–6. KSI Research Inc. (2023). https://doi.org/10.18293/DMSVIVA2023-010

Relational Denotational and Algebraic Semantics Based on UTP

Zhiru Hou and Huibiao Zhu(✉)

Shanghai Key Laboratory of Trustworthy Computing, East China Normal University, Shanghai, China
hbzhu@sei.ecnu.edu.cn

Abstract. Relational Hoare logic [18] extends the applicability of modular deductive verification to encompass the verification of crucial 2-run properties, such as confidentiality. Most of the current research on relational Hoare logic primarily focuses on its practical applications. However, incorporating parallel programs into the logic may further complicate the system design, which is an aspect that most research has overlooked. Therefore, this paper updates the previous system, referred to as the relational system, by incorporating parallel composition. Based on the Unifying Theories of Programming (UTP), we further explore the denotational semantics and algebraic semantics of the system with 2-runs, employing relational denotational and algebraic semantics for representation. And the study of the conditional construct and parallel composition are the crucial points. To facilitate the algebraic exploration of parallel expansion laws, we extend the system with a new concept called guarded choice, enabling the transformation of any program into a guarded choice form.

Keywords: Relational Hoare Logic · Unifying Theories of Programming (UTP) · Denotational Semantics · Algebraic Semantics

1 Introduction

Program verification typically focuses on demonstrating that all executions of a program lie within a specified set of executions, where properties are represented as sets of traces. However, this approach is not general enough to capture various fundamental properties, such as non-interference [1] and robustness [2]. These notions are naturally modeled as relational properties, which are properties over sets of pairs of traces. Relational properties are special instances of hyperproperties [3], which are formally defined as sets of sets of traces.

Verification of relational properties can be achieved through different approaches. One method is to reduce the verification of the program, such as through self-composition [4,5] and product programs [6,7]. Another approach to verify relational properties is to use relational Hoare logic [8] or specialized logics for specific properties [9]. While both of these methods have been successfully applied in some use cases, they may have certain limitations, such as the inability to handle the parallel program in relational Hoare logic.

Formal verification techniques are essential for ensuring the correctness and reliability of both software and hardware systems. These techniques leverage mathematical foundations to rigorously specify and verify system properties. In this context, Barthe et al. [13] have successfully reduced the verification of relational properties in imperative programs to a validity problem in trace logic. Dardinier et al. [14] proposed Hyper Hoare Logic, a generalized version of Hoare logic capable of expressing arbitrary hyperproperties over the terminating executions of a program. Clarkson and Schneider [3] formally defined hyperproperties as sets of sets of traces, providing a broader framework for reasoning about security and correctness properties across multiple executions. This framework encompasses relational properties as special cases, thus establishing a direct connection between relational Hoare logic and hyperproperties. Additionally, Finkbeiner et al. [20] defined concurrent hyperproperties by generalizing traces to concurrent traces, which are partially ordered multisets. And they take Petri nets as the basic semantic model. Moreover, the approach is grounded in the perspective of model checking methods. Naumann [18] provided a comprehensive overview of the development of relational Hoare logic over the past thirty-seven years, providing a structured organization of its rules. This provides us with significant inspiration. And these contributions have provided valuable insights. However, due to the current limitations of relational Hoare logic in effectively handling parallel programs, this paper aim to update the previous system by incorporating parallel composition, and we call the new system is relational system.

The Unifying Theory of Programming (UTP) [10] was proposed by Hoare and He in 1998. It aims to provide a convincing unified framework for combining and linking operational semantics, denotational semantics [11], algebraic semantics [12] and Hoare logic. Denotational semantics provides a mathematical interpretation of programming languages, explaining *what a program does*. The algebraic semantics involves a set of algebraic laws that are well-suited for symbolic computation of parameter optimization and structural design. In this paper, following the methodology of relational Hoare logic, we investigate the denotational and algebraic semantics of programs with 2-runs, named as relational denotational semantics and relational algebraic semantics. In contrast to relational Hoare logic, which considers a pair of programs, the program discusses in this paper primarily focuses on a single program with 2-runs. Firstly, as the programs in relational Hoare logic are sequential, we extend the language by incorporating the parallel components. Consequently, we investigate our relational denotational semantics using two traces to represent 2-runs. This includes the semantics of conditional statement and parallel composition. Additionally, we delve into the relational algebraic semantics, particularly examining the rules for conditional statement. By establishing algebraic laws for the parallel composition of guarded choice components, we can describe any program in the form of guarded choice.

The rest of the paper is structured as follows. Section 2 proposes the modeling language and introduces three types of guarded choices. In Sect. 3, we study the relational denotational semantics of our language. We first give the semantic model and healthiness conditions. Then, we explore the denotational semantics of the system using two traces, referring 2-runs. In Sect. 4, we investigate the relational algebraic semantics, including the algebraic laws for the conditional statement and the parallel composition. Section 5 summarizes the paper and outlines future research directions.

2 Syntax

In this section, we give the syntax of our language for modeling the system. Subsequently, we introduce three types of guarded choices defined to facilitate the application of our algebraic expansion laws.

Table 1. Syntax

Process	$P, Q ::= x := e$	(Assignment Operation)
	$\mid @gd$	(Event Guard)
	$\mid P; Q$	(Sequential Composition)
	$\mid$ **if** b **then** P **else** Q	(Conditional Construct)
	$\mid$ **while** b **do** P	(Iteration Construct)
	$\mid P \| Q$	(Parallel Composition)
Event Guard $gd ::= true \mid x = e \mid x < e \mid x > e \mid gd \vee gd \mid gd \wedge gd \mid \neg gd$		

2.1 Syntax of the Relational System

Here we expand the syntax foundation of relational Hoare logic by incorporating parallel components and guarded choice. And we designate this system as the relational system. As shown in Table 1, we give the syntax of the system. Here, x is a variable, e represents an expression, b is a Boolean condition.

- $x := e$ is a variable assignment. In this assignment, the expression e is evaluated to obtain a value, which is then assigned to the variable x. This assignment is considered atomic.
- $@gd$ is an event guard. This action is triggered when the guard condition gd is satisfied. If the condition is not met, the action enters a waiting state.

Then, a process can consist of the commands mentioned above. Additionally, this language offers diverse compositions and constructs to enhance its functionality and flexibility.

- $P; Q$ is a sequential composition. The process P is executed initially, and if it terminates successfully, the process Q is subsequently executed.

- **if** b **then** P **else** Q is a conditional construct. The process P is executed if the condition b is $true$. If b is $false$, the process Q is executed instead.
- **while** b **do** P is an iteration construct. The process P is executed repeatedly until the Boolean condition b becomes $false$.
- $P||Q$ is a parallel composition. It indicates P executes in parallel with Q. The parallel mechanism is based on shared variables.

2.2 Guarded Choice

To accommodate the expansion laws of the parallel construct, the system introduces the concept of guarded choice. In other words, the purpose of introducing guarded choice is to sequentialize parallel programs. And in this paper, we present two types of guarded components and three types of guarded choices in order to support the algebraic parallel expansion laws in Sect. 4.

$h \to P$ is a guarded component if h is $\langle\!\langle b_1 \langle\!\langle \bullet \rangle\!\rangle b_2 \rangle\!\rangle \& @(\overleftarrow{x:=e} \bullet \overrightarrow{x:=e})$ or $@(gd)$, where b_1 and b_2 represent the Boolean conditions. In $\langle\!\langle b_1 \langle\!\langle \bullet \rangle\!\rangle b_2 \rangle\!\rangle \& @(\overleftarrow{x:=e} \bullet \overrightarrow{x:=e})$, we use $\bullet$ to differentiate between the 1st and 2nd runs of the program, where the left side of $\bullet$ represents the Boolean condition and program involved in the 1st run, and the right side represents those involved in the 2nd run. Furthermore, we use $\langle\!\langle \ \langle\!\langle$ and $\rangle\!\rangle \rangle\!\rangle$ to represent the evaluation of b_1 and b_2 in the 1st and 2nd runs, respectively. And $\overleftarrow{x:=e}$ and $\overrightarrow{x:=e}$ represent the programs that can be executed in the 1st and 2nd runs, respectively. In addition, $@(gd) \to P$ is an event guarded component.

$[]\{h_1 \to P_1, ..., h_n \to P_n\}$ is a guarded choice if every element in $\{h_1 \to P_1, ..., h_n \to P_n\}$ is a guarded component. In our language, we present three types of guarded choices. The first two are composed of a set one type of guarded components and the last one is hybrid guarded choice.

- **Assignment Guarded Choice:**
  $[]_{i \in I} \{\langle\!\langle b_{1i} \langle\!\langle \bullet \rangle\!\rangle b_{2i} \rangle\!\rangle \& @(\overleftarrow{x_i:=e_i} \bullet \overrightarrow{x_i:=e_i}) \to (\overleftarrow{P_i} \bullet \overrightarrow{S_i})\}$: It is composed of several assignment guarded components, and we have the constraint "$\bigvee_{i \in I}(b_{1i} \vee b_{2i}) = true$". When the condition b_{1i} and b_{2i} is fulfilled, $@(\overleftarrow{x_i:=e_i} \bullet \overrightarrow{x_i:=e_i})$ is executed followed by the corresponding program $(\overleftarrow{P_i} \bullet \overrightarrow{S_i})$. In some certain cases, S_i can be equal to P_i. It is important to note that if b_{1i} and b_{2i} are not simultaneously satisfied, the program will choose either the case where b_{1i} is true and the following program $\overleftarrow{P_i}$ will be executed in 1st run, or the case where b_{2i} is true and the following program $\overrightarrow{S_i}$ will be executed in 2nd run. And the formal definition of assignment guarded choice can be found in Sect. 3.
- **Event Guarded Choice:**
  $[]_{i \in I}\{@(gd_i) \to P_i\}$: It is composed of several event guarded components. And it waits for any one of the guards to be triggered. If $@(gd_i)$ is triggered, P_i will be executed.
- **Assignment & Event Hybrid Guarded Choice:**
  $[]_{i \in I}\{\langle\!\langle b_{1i} \langle\!\langle \bullet \rangle\!\rangle b_{2i} \rangle\!\rangle \& @(\overleftarrow{x_i:=e_i} \bullet \overrightarrow{x_i:=e_i}) \to (\overleftarrow{P_i} \bullet \overrightarrow{S_i})\}[]\,[]_{j \in J}\{@(gd_j) \to Q_j\}$: It contains assignment guarded components and event guarded components. If

the conditions b_{1i} and b_{2i} are satisfied, $@(\overleftarrow{x_i:=e_i} \bullet \overrightarrow{x_i:=e_i})$ can be selected for execution, followed by the execution of program $(\overleftarrow{P_i} \bullet \overrightarrow{S_i})$. Simultaneously, the system waits for the event guard $@(gd_j)$ to be triggered. If $@(gd_j)$ can currently be triggered, the subsequent program Q_j will be executed. Like assignment guarded choice, if b_{1i} and b_{2i} are not simultaneously satisfied, the program will choose either the case where b_{1i} is true or the case where b_{2i} is true.

3 Relational Denotational Semantics

In this section, we explore the relational denotational semantics of our language using the UTP (Unifying Theories of Programming) approach. We begin our formalization by presenting the semantic model and healthiness conditions. Building upon this foundation, we further study the denotational semantics of the relational system (i.e., relational denotational semantics).

3.1 Semantic Model

As the parallel mechanism of our language is based on shared variables, a trace variable is introduced to record the states contributed by the program itself or its environment. Therefore, two traces, denoted as tr_1 and tr_2, are introduced in our relational denotational semantics, representing for the 2-runs.

For the execution of a program, it can be in one of three execution states (i.e., terminating state, waiting state, divergent state). Therefore, a state variable is introduced to record the current execution state of a program. Similarly, due to the 2-runs, two state variables, denoted as st_1 and st_2, are introduced in our semantics model. Thus, we take a tuple $(st_1, st_1', tr_1, tr_1', st_2, st_2', tr_2, tr_2')$ to represent the observation of a program.

Here, variables without $'$ and with $'$ stand for the variables at the initial state and final state, respectively. And we use Fig. 1 to illustrate the variables in the 2-runs.

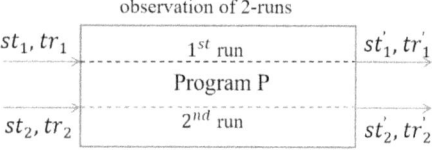

Fig. 1. Observation Diagram of 2-runs

- For the execution state of a program, st_1 and st_1' indicate the 1st run of the program at the start point and the end point respectively, st_2 and st_2' correspond to the 2nd run. Due to the consistent interpretation of st_1 and st_2, as well as st_1' and st_2', we now focus on explaining the specific meaning of st_1 and st_1'. In our system, we consider that the program may have three types of execution state: $term$, $wait$ and div.
  - $term$: If $st_1 = term$, it signifies that the predecessor program has finished executing, allowing the current program to start its execution. If $st_1' = term$, it signifies the completion of the current program, indicating that the subsequent program can be executed.

- *wait*: If $st_1 = wait$, it indicates that the current program cannot be activated because the predecessor program has not terminated (i.e., in the waiting state). If $st'_1 = wait$, it signifies that the current program is waiting, preventing the activation of the next program.
- *div*: If $st_1 = div$, it indicates that the previous program has entered a divergent state, meaning it never terminates, and as a result, the current program cannot be executed. If $st'_1 = div$, it signifies that the current program enters a divergent state, preventing the execution of the subsequent program.

• tr_1 and tr'_1 are the traces of the 1st run at the start point and the end point respectively, and tr_2 and tr'_2 correspond to the 2nd run. To describe the behavior of a program, a trace is expressed as a series of snapshots that capture a sequence of actions. In our semantic model, a snapshot can be represented as a pair (σ, μ).
  - σ: We use σ to record the data contributed by the program itself or its environment during the program runtime.
  - μ: We introduce it to distinguish whether the action is performed by the program itself or by the environment. In the case where the program executes the action, we set μ to 1. However, if the action is a result of the environment's behavior, μ is set to 0.

To extract the i-th component of a snapshot, we utilize the projection function π_i ($i = 1, 2$). Then, we can have $\pi_1((\sigma, \mu)) = \sigma$, $\pi_2((\sigma, \mu)) = \mu$. Additionally, we designate the last snapshot in trace s with the symbol $last(s)$. If trace t is a prefix of trace s (denoted as $t \leqslant s$), the notation $s - t$ represents the remaining portion of s after removing the snapshots from t. The notation $s \frown t$ denotes the concatenation of the traces s and t.

Furthermore, our model incorporates some healthiness conditions that programs must meet. And the healthiness conditions have nine scenarios shown in Table 2.

Table 2. Healthiness condition with 9 scenarios

st_1 \ st_2	term	div	wait
term	①	②	③
div	④	⑤	⑥
wait	⑦	⑧	⑨

① When $st_1 = term \wedge st_2 = term$, the traces cannot be shortened, therefore we use $tr_1 \leq tr'_1 \wedge tr_2 \leq tr'_2$ to represent this situation.

② When $st_1 = term \wedge st_2 = div$, it indicates the first trace cannot be shortened, therefore we can have $tr_1 \leq tr'_1$. For the second trace, the behavior of program is totally unpredictable, it still needs to satisfy $st'_2 = div \wedge tr_2 \leq tr'_2$.
③ When $st_1 = term \wedge st_2 = wait$, it means the first trace cannot be shortened. For the second trace, the current program is waiting for the termination of the previous program so that all variables remain unchanged, and as a result, the second state and trace should remain unchanged. Therefore we can have $tr_1 \leq tr'_1 \wedge st_2 = st'_2 \wedge tr_2 = tr'_2$.
④ When $st_1 = div \wedge st_2 = term$, it is similar to ②. Therefore, the program still needs to satisfy $st'_1 = div \wedge tr_1 \leq tr'_1 \wedge tr_2 \leq tr'_2$.
⑤ When $st_1 = div \wedge st_2 = div$, it represents that the behaviors of P in 2-runs are totally unpredictable. Therefore program P needs to satisfy $st'_1 = div \wedge tr_1 \leq tr'_1 \wedge st'_2 = div \wedge tr_2 \leq tr'_2$.
⑥ When $st_1 = div \wedge st_2 = wait$, it means the second state and trace are unchanged, therefore $st_2 = st'_2 \wedge tr_2 = tr'_2$. For the first trace, it still needs to satisfy $st'_1 = div \wedge tr_1 \leq tr'_1$.
⑦ When $st_1 = wait \wedge st_2 = term$, it represents the first state and trace are unchanged, and the second trace cannot be shortened, therefore the program needs to satisfy $st_1 = st'_1 \wedge tr_1 = tr'_1 \wedge tr_2 \leq tr'_2$.
⑧ When $st_1 = wait \wedge st_2 = div$, it indicates the first state and trace are unchanged, therefore $st_1 = st'_1 \wedge tr_1 = tr'_1$. For the second trace, it still needs to satisfy $st'_2 = div \wedge tr_2 \leq tr'_2$.
⑨ When $st_1 = wait \wedge st_2 = wait$, the current program is waiting for the termination of the previous program. Therefore, all variables remain unchanged in 2-runs. Then $st_1 = st'_1 \wedge tr_1 = tr'_1 \wedge st_2 = st'_2 \wedge tr_2 = tr'_2$ should be satisfied.

Based on the nine scenarios mentioned above, we have identified two specific healthiness conditions as follows. $H1$ states that two traces must only increase and cannot be shortened. The healthiness condition $H2$ describes the nine cases in Table 2. And we use the formula "$H(true, true)$" to reflect $H2$.

$H1: P = P \wedge Inv(tr_1, tr_2)$,
where, $Inv(tr_1, tr_2) =_{df} (tr_1 \leq tr'_1 \wedge tr_2 \leq tr'_2)$
$H2: H(true, true)$,
where, $H(X_1, X_2) =_{df}$
$(st_1 = div \wedge st_2 = div) \rightarrow (st'_1 = div \wedge tr_1 \leq tr'_1 \wedge st'_2 = div \wedge tr_2 \leq tr'_2)$
$\vee (st_1 = div \wedge st_2 = wait) \rightarrow (st'_1 = div \wedge tr_1 \leq tr'_1 \wedge st_2 = st'_2 \wedge tr_2 = tr'_2)$
$\vee (st_1 = div \wedge st_2 = term) \rightarrow (st'_1 = div \wedge tr_1 \leq tr'_1 \wedge X_2)$
$\vee (st_1 = wait \wedge st_2 = div) \rightarrow (st_1 = st'_1 \wedge tr_1 = tr'_1 \wedge st'_2 = div \wedge tr_2 \leq tr'_2)$
$\vee (st_1 = wait \wedge st_2 = wait) \rightarrow (st_1 = st'_1 \wedge tr_1 = tr'_1 \wedge st_2 = st'_2 \wedge tr_2 = tr'_2)$
$\vee (st_1 = wait \wedge st_2 = term) \rightarrow (st_1 = st'_1 \wedge tr_1 = tr'_1 \wedge X_2)$
$\vee (st_1 = term \wedge st_2 = div) \rightarrow (X_1 \wedge st'_2 = div \wedge tr_2 \leq tr'_2)$
$\vee (st_1 = term \wedge st_2 = wait) \rightarrow (X_1 \wedge st_2 = st'_2 \wedge tr_2 = tr'_2)$
$\vee (st_1 = term \wedge st_2 = term) \rightarrow (X_1 \wedge X_2)$

The parameters X_1 and X_2 in the H function, represent the behavior of the program when its predecessor program has terminated through 1st run and 2nd run respectively. Function $H(X_1, X_2)$ can be used to establish the denotational semantics for our language, and it caters for the healthiness conditions $H1$ and $H2$ if X_1 and X_2 both satisfy $Inv(tr_1, tr_2)$.

3.2 Semantics of Basic Statements

In this subsection, we provide the denotational semantics for basic statements. To distinguish between the syntax and semantics of program P, we represent the denotational semantics of P using the notation $beh(P)$ in this paper.

(1) **x := e**

The assignment operation is an instantaneous action that immediately terminates without any delay. This operation assigns the value of e to the variable x. In this context, $\sigma_1[e/x]$ stands for the state that is the same as σ_1, except that the value of variable x is now associated with the value e. We update the trace tr' by appending the assignment result to the end. There is a requirement that $\pi_2(envtr) \in 0^*$ for trace $envtr$, indicating that the environment contributes to trace $envtr$. In addition, $\sigma_1 =_{df} \pi_1(last(tr_1 \wedge envtr))$ and $\sigma_2 =_{df} \pi_1(last(tr_2 \wedge envtr))$.

$$beh(x := e) =_{df} H \left(\begin{array}{l} st'_1 = term \wedge tr'_1 = tr_1 \wedge envtr \wedge (\sigma_1[e/x], 1), \\ st'_2 = term \wedge tr'_2 = tr_2 \wedge envtr \wedge (\sigma_2[e/x], 1) \end{array} \right)$$

(2) **@(gd)**

$@(gd)$ is an event guard that can be triggered when the guard condition gd is satisfied. We consider the following two scenarios.

- Scenario 1: Consider the program P as below. Since the assignment statement $x := 1$ in program P changes the value of x, causing $x > 0$ to hold $true$, and $@(x > 0)$ is triggered.
$$P = x := 0; x := 1; @(x > 0)$$
- Scenario 2: Consider the parallel program $P \| Q$ as below. After the execution of program P, the value of x is 1. Therefore, $@(x > 1)$ cannot be triggered by the program itself, and it needs to wait for the environment to trigger it. In this example, $@(x > 1)$ can be triggered by the assignment statement $x := 2$ in program Q, as it changes the value of x to 2 after running Q.
$$P = x := 1; @(x > 1), \qquad Q = x := 2$$

Based on the analysis above, we can draw the conclusion that the trigger $@gd$ can be activated by either the program itself or the environment. Here, we provide the denotational semantics as below. And since this paper involves 2-runs of the denotational semantics, four different cases are presented.

$beh(@gd) =_{df} selftrig(gd) \vee selfenvtrig(gd) \vee envselftrig(gd) \vee doublenvtrig(gd)$

– Case 1: In two runs, the trigger $@gd$ can be activated by the program itself. In this case, $selftrig(gd)$ implies that the event guard $@gd$ is triggered by the own action of the program.

$$selftrig(gd) =_{df} H \begin{pmatrix} st'_1 = term \wedge tr'_1 = tr_1 \wedge gd(\pi_1(last(tr_1))), \\ \hline st'_2 = term \wedge tr'_2 = tr_2 \wedge gd(\pi_1(last(tr_2))) \end{pmatrix}$$

For this $selftrig(gd)$ case, the event guard can terminate immediately, resulting in $st'_1 = term$ and $st'_2 = term$. Additionally, as the trigger @gd does not alter the data state of the program, the trace remains unchanged, i.e., $tr'_1 = tr_1$ and $tr'_2 = tr_2$. Here, $gd(\sigma)$ represents the event guard condition gd holding $true$ in the data state σ, while $\pi_1(last(tr_1))$ and $\pi_1(last(tr_2))$ can respectively project to the current two data states. Thus, $gd(\pi_1(last(tr_1)))$ and $gd(\pi_1(last(tr_2)))$ signify that due to the program's own behavior, the event guard condition gd can be triggered at the starting point of the program through 2-runs.

- Case 2: For the 1st run, the trigger @gd can be activated by the program itself, and in the 2nd run, the trigger @gd cannot be triggered by the program itself. And it needs to wait for the environment to trigger it.

$$selfenvtrig(gd) =_{df} H \begin{pmatrix} \boxed{(st'_1 = term \wedge tr'_1 = tr_1 \wedge gd(\pi_1(last(tr_1))))}, \\ \begin{pmatrix} st'_2 \neq div \wedge \neg gd(\pi_1(last(tr_2))) \wedge \\ \forall s \in (tr'_2 - tr_2) \cdot \neg gd(\pi_1(s)) \wedge \pi_2(tr'_2 - tr_2) \in 0^* \end{pmatrix} ; \\ \begin{pmatrix} st'_2 = term \wedge gd(\pi_1(last(tr'_2))) \wedge \\ \pi_2(tr'_2 - tr_2) = 0 \wedge len(tr'_2 - tr_2) = 1 \end{pmatrix} \end{pmatrix}$$

Since in the 1st run, the guard @gd can be triggered by the program itself, it is similar to Case 1. For the 2nd run, the event guard cannot be triggered by the program itself, that is, $\neg gd(\pi_1(last(tr_2)))$, it needs to wait for the environment to trigger it. "$\forall s \in (tr'_2 - tr_2) \cdot \neg gd(\pi_1(s)) \wedge \pi_2(tr'_2 - tr_2) \in 0^*$" describes the waiting behavior of the program, indicating that during the waiting period for a trigger, the environment can perform its actions, and none of these actions will trigger the event guard.

After the waiting behavior, there will be the behavior of the environment program ultimately triggering the event guard. Similar to the definition of $selftrig(gd)$, this behavior terminates immediately, so we have $st'_2 = term$. And "$\pi_2(tr'_2 - tr_2) = 0$" represents this triggering behavior initiated by the environment program. In addition, $len(tr'_2 - tr_2) = 1$ emphasizes that this triggering behavior is the last action in the trace.

- Case 3: In 2nd run, the trigger @gd can be activated by the program itself, and in the 1st run, the trigger @gd can be activated by the environment. Similar to Case 2, we present the denotational semantics of the event guard gd in this case as below.

$$envselftrig(gd) =_{df} H \begin{pmatrix} \boxed{\begin{pmatrix} \begin{pmatrix} st'_1 \neq div \wedge \neg gd(\pi_1(last(tr_1))) \wedge \\ \forall s \in (tr'_1 - tr_1) \cdot \neg gd(\pi_1(s)) \wedge \pi_2(tr'_1 - tr_1) \in 0^* \end{pmatrix} ; \\ \begin{pmatrix} st'_1 = term \wedge gd(\pi_1(last(tr'_1))) \wedge \\ \pi_2(tr'_1 - tr_1) = 0 \wedge len(tr'_1 - tr_1) = 1 \end{pmatrix} \end{pmatrix}}, \\ (st'_2 = term \wedge tr'_2 = tr_2 \wedge gd(\pi_1(last(tr_2)))) \end{pmatrix}$$

– Case 4: In 2-runs, the trigger @gd cannot be activated by the program itself, and it needs to wait for the environment's trigger. This behavior is precisely defined by $doublenvtrig(gd)$.

$$doublenvtrig(gd) =_{df} H \left(\begin{pmatrix} \begin{pmatrix} st'_1 \neq div \land \neg gd(\pi_1(last(tr_1))) \land \\ \forall s \in (tr'_1 - tr_1) \cdot \neg gd(\pi_1(s)) \land \pi_2(tr'_1 - tr_1) \in 0^* \\ st'_1 = term \land gd(\pi_1(last(tr'_1))) \land \\ \pi_2(tr'_1 - tr_1) = 0 \land len(tr'_1 - tr_1) = 1 \end{pmatrix} ; \\ \begin{pmatrix} st'_2 \neq div \land \neg gd(\pi_1(last(tr_2))) \land \\ \forall s \in (tr'_2 - tr_2) \cdot \neg gd(\pi_1(s)) \land \pi_2(tr'_2 - tr_2) \in 0^* \\ st'_2 = term \land gd(\pi_1(last(tr'_2))) \land \\ \pi_2(tr'_2 - tr_2) = 0 \land len(tr'_2 - tr_2) = 1 \end{pmatrix} ; \end{pmatrix} \right)$$

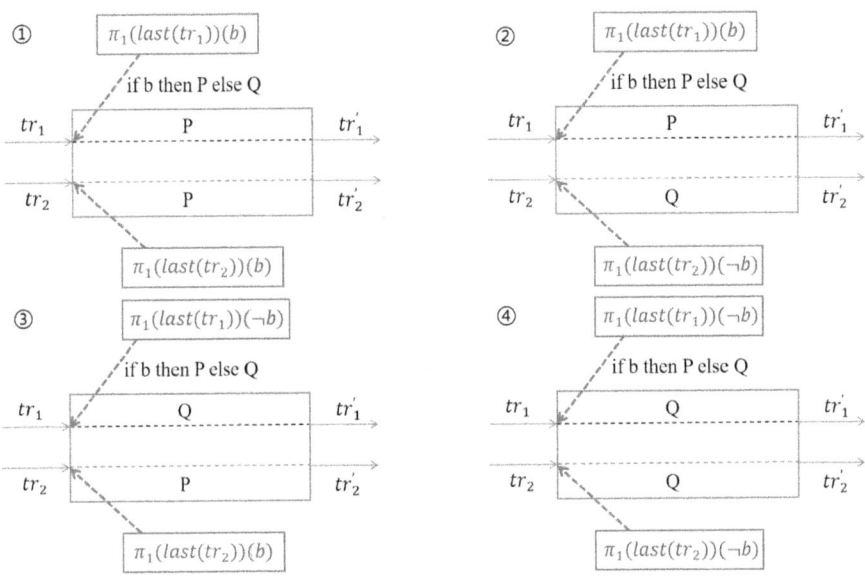

Fig. 2. Four Cases of Conditional Construct.

(3) Conditional Construct

Since this paper primarily focuses on describing the relational system, there are four cases for the denotational semantics of conditional construct. And here, $\sigma_1 =_{df} \pi_1(last(tr_1))$ and $\sigma_2 =_{df} \pi_1(last(tr_2))$. In addition, we utilize Fig. 2 to illustrate the four execution scenarios of the conditional construct.

$beh(\textbf{if } b \textbf{ then } P \textbf{ else } Q) =_{df}$

$$\left(\left(\begin{array}{l} beh(P) \triangleleft \sigma_2(b) \triangleright \\ \left(st'_1 = term \wedge st'_2 = term \wedge \; 1strun(beh(P)) \wedge 2ndrun(beh(Q)) \right) \end{array}\right) \triangleleft \sigma_1(b) \triangleright \left(\begin{array}{l} \left(st'_1 = term \wedge st'_2 = term \wedge \; 1strun(beh(Q)) \wedge 2ndrun(beh(P)) \right) \\ \triangleleft \sigma_2(b) \triangleright beh(Q) \end{array}\right)\right)$$

Firstly, we check if the condition b holds $true$ in the 1st run, which is represented by $\sigma_1(b)$. If it does, we further examine if condition b holds $true$ in the 2nd run, and it is represented by $\sigma_2(b)$. If $\sigma_2(b)$ is $true$, then program P is selected to execute, and case ① of Fig. 2 illustrates this scenario; otherwise, the 1st run executes program P, indicated as $1strun(beh(P))$, while the 2nd run executes program Q, indicated as $2ndrun(beh(Q))$, and case ② of Fig. 2 illustrates this scenario. In addition, $1strun(beh(P))$ utilizes a renaming operation to shield other variables, thus focusing on the changes caused by P on tr_1. Similarly, $2ndrun(beh(Q))$ captures the effects of Q on tr_2.

If $\sigma_1(b)$ is $false$, we also need to check if the condition b holds $true$ in the 2nd run. If $\sigma_2(b)$ is $true$, the 1st run executes program Q, and the 2nd run executes program P, case ③ of Fig. 2 illustrates this scenario. Otherwise, if $\sigma_2(b)$ is $false$, program Q is executed, and case ④ of Fig. 2 illustrates this scenario.

$1strun(beh(P)) =_{df} \exists m_1, m'_1, m_2, m'_2, t_2, t'_2 \cdot$
$$\left(\begin{array}{l} beh(P)[m_1/st_1, m'_1/st'_1, m_2/st_2, m'_2/st'_2, t_2/tr_2, t'_2/tr'_2] \wedge \\ m_1 = st_1 \wedge m_2 = st_2 \wedge t_2 = tr_2 \end{array}\right)$$

$2ndrun(beh(P)) =_{df} \exists m_1, m'_1, m_2, m'_2, t_1, t'_1 \cdot$
$$\left(\begin{array}{l} beh(P)[m_1/st_1, m'_1/st'_1, m_2/st_2, m'_2/st'_2, t_1/tr_1, t'_1/tr'_1] \wedge \\ m_1 = st_1 \wedge m_2 = st_2 \wedge t_1 = tr_1 \end{array}\right)$$

(4) **Sequential Composition**

$P;Q$ represents the sequential execution of program P followed by program Q. Here, the definition of the sequential operation ";" in the semantics model is given.

$P;Q =_{df} \exists m, s, n, k \cdot P[m/st'_1, s/st'_2, n/tr'_1, k/tr'_2] \wedge$
$\qquad\qquad Q[m/st_1, s/st_2, n/tr_1, k/tr_2]$

Further, we give the semantics of sequential composition.
$beh(P;Q) = beh(P); beh(Q)$

(5) **Iteration Construct**

The iteration construct "**while** b **do** P" can be understood as the conditional construct "**if** b **then** $(P; \textbf{while } b \textbf{ do } P)$ **else** $skip$" for interpretation. In this way, the denotational semantics of the iteration construct can be obtained through the denotational semantics of conditional statements and fixed point theory. $\mu \, F(X)$ represents the weakest fixed point of the monotonic function F.

$beh(\textbf{while } b \textbf{ do } P) =_{df} \mu \, X \bullet beh(\textbf{if } b \textbf{ then } (P; X) \textbf{ else } skip)$

3.3 Semantics of Guarded Choice

As mentioned previously, there are three types of guarded choices. Now we provide the denotational semantics for them.

- **Assignment Guarded Choice:**
  The program $[]_{i \in I}\{(b_{1i}(\bullet) b_{2i}) \& @(\overleftarrow{x_i := e_i} \bullet \overrightarrow{x_i := e_i}) \to (\overleftarrow{P_i} \bullet \overrightarrow{S_i})\}$ nondeterministically selects one of the assignment guards to execute, and then proceeds with the subsequent program. It is important to note that if b_{1i} and b_{2i} are not simultaneously satisfied, the program will choose either the case where b_{1i} is true or the case where b_{2i} is true. And in order to ensure the proper execution of the program even when only one run is valid, we define the other program whose Boolean condition is currently not satisfied as $skip$.

$$beh([]_{i \in I}\{(b_{1i}(\bullet) b_{2i}) \& @(\overleftarrow{x_i := e_i} \bullet \overrightarrow{x_i := e_i}) \to (\overleftarrow{P_i} \bullet \overrightarrow{S_i})\})$$

$$=_{df} \bigvee_{i \in I} \begin{pmatrix} beh(\{(b_{1i}(\bullet) b_{2i}) \& @(\overleftarrow{x_i := e_i} \bullet \overrightarrow{x_i := e_i}); (\overleftarrow{P_i} \bullet \overrightarrow{S_i})\}) \\ \vee\, beh(\{(b_{1i}(\bullet) \neg b_{2i}) \& @(\overleftarrow{x_i := e_i} \bullet \overrightarrow{skip}); (\overleftarrow{P_i} \bullet \overrightarrow{skip})\}) \\ \vee\, beh(\{(\neg b_{1i}(\bullet) b_{2i}) \& @(\overleftarrow{skip} \bullet \overrightarrow{x_i := e_i}); (\overleftarrow{skip} \bullet \overrightarrow{S_i})\}) \end{pmatrix}$$

where,

$beh((b_{1i}(\bullet) b_{2i}) \& @(\overleftarrow{x_i := e_i} \bullet \overrightarrow{x_i := e_i})) =_{df} \sigma_1(b_{1i}) \wedge \sigma_2(b_{2i}) \wedge beh(x_i := e_i),$

$beh((b_{1i}(\bullet) \neg b_{2i}) \& @(\overleftarrow{x_i := e_i} \bullet \overrightarrow{skip})) =_{df} \sigma_1(b_{1i}) \wedge \sigma_2(\neg b_{2i}) \wedge beh(\overleftarrow{x_i := e_i}),$

$beh((\neg b_{1i}(\bullet) b_{2i}) \& @(\overleftarrow{skip} \bullet \overrightarrow{x_i := e_i})) =_{df} \sigma_1(\neg b_{1i}) \wedge \sigma_2(b_{2i}) \wedge beh(\overrightarrow{x_i := e_i}).$

And here, $\sigma_1 =_{df} \pi_1(last(tr_1))$ and $\sigma_2 =_{df} \pi_1(last(tr_2))$. The definition of $beh(\overleftarrow{P} \bullet \overrightarrow{S})$ is as below. In addition, $beh(\overleftarrow{P})$ utilizes a renaming operation to shield other variables, thus focusing on the changes caused by program P on st_1 and tr_1. Similarly, $beh(\overrightarrow{S})$ captures the effects of S on st_2 and tr_2.

$$beh(\overleftarrow{P} \bullet \overrightarrow{S}) =_{df} beh(\overleftarrow{P}) \wedge beh(\overrightarrow{S}),$$

where,

$beh(\overleftarrow{P}) =_{df} \exists m_2, m_2', t_2, t_2' \cdot$
$beh(P)[m_2/st_2, m_2'/st_2', t_2/tr_2, t_2'/tr_2'] \wedge m_2 = st_2 \wedge t_2 = tr_2,$

$beh(\overrightarrow{S}) =_{df} \exists m_1, m_1', t_1, t_1' \cdot$
$beh(S)[m_1/st_1, m_1'/st_1', t_1/tr_1, t_1'/tr_1'] \wedge m_1 = st_1 \wedge t_1 = tr_1$

- **Event Guarded Choice:**
  The program $[]_{i \in I}\{@(gd_i) \to P_i\}$ is composed of several event guarded components. And it waits for one of the guards to be triggered. If $@(gd_i)$ is triggered, P_i is executed which is the subsequent program.
  $beh([]_{i \in I}\{@(gd_i) \to P_i\}) =_{df}$
  $\bigvee_{i \in I}\{(selftrig(gd_i) \vee selfenvtrig(gd_i) \vee envselftrig(gd_i) \vee doublenvtrig(gd_i)); beh(P_i)\}$

- **Assignment & Event Hybrid Guarded Choice:**
$HAE =_{df} \quad []_{i \in I}\{(\!|b_{1i}(\!|\bullet|\!)b_{2i}|\!) \& @(\overleftarrow{x_i := e_i} \bullet \overrightarrow{x_i := e_i}) \to (\overleftarrow{P_i} \bullet \overrightarrow{S_i})\}$
$\quad []\!|_{j \in J}\{@(gd_j) \to Q_j\}$

The program HAE first executes the selected assignment guard $@(\overleftarrow{x_i := e_i} \bullet \overrightarrow{x_i := e_i})$, followed by the execution of its subsequent program. Furthermore, if there exist event guard $@(gd_j)$ in 2-runs that can be triggered, the program also allows for the selection of an event guard to be executed first, followed by the execution of the subsequent program Q_j. And in this case, due to the presence of assignment guard, environmental triggering is not considered.

$beh(HAE) =_{df}$

$$\left(\begin{array}{l} \bigvee_{i \in I} \left(\begin{array}{l} beh(\{(\!|b_{1i}(\!|\bullet|\!)b_{2i}|\!) \& @(\overleftarrow{x_i := e_i} \bullet \overrightarrow{x_i := e_i}); (\overleftarrow{P_i} \bullet \overrightarrow{S_i})\}) \\ \bigvee beh(\{(\!|b_{1i}(\!|\bullet|\!) \neg b_{2i}|\!) \& @(\overleftarrow{x_i := e_i} \bullet \overrightarrow{skip}); (\overleftarrow{P_i} \bullet \overrightarrow{skip})\}) \\ \bigvee beh(\{(\!|\neg b_{1i}(\!|\bullet|\!)b_{2i}|\!) \& @(\overleftarrow{skip} \bullet \overrightarrow{x_i := e_i}); (\overleftarrow{skip} \bullet \overrightarrow{S_i})\}) \end{array} \right) \bigvee \\ \bigvee_{j \in J}\{(selftrig(gd_j)); beh(Q_j)\} \end{array} \right)$$

3.4 Parallel Composition

We present the denotational semantics of the parallel composition below.
$beh(P||Q) =_{df} beh(P)||beh(Q)$
where, $beh(P)||beh(Q) =_{df}$

$$\left(\begin{array}{l} \exists st_1, st'_1, tr_1, tr'_1, st_2, st'_2, tr_2, tr'_2 \bullet \\ \quad st_{11} = st_{21} = st_1 \wedge tr_{11} = tr_{21} = tr_1 \wedge \\ \quad st_{12} = st_{22} = st_2 \wedge tr_{12} = tr_{22} = tr_2 \wedge \\ \quad beh(P)[st_{11}/st_1, st'_{11}/st'_1, st_{12}/st_2, st'_{12}/st'_2, \\ \qquad tr_{11}/tr_1, tr'_{11}/tr'_1, tr_{12}/tr_2, tr'_{12}/tr'_2] \wedge \\ \quad beh(Q)[st_{21}/st_1, st'_{21}/st'_1, st_{22}/st_2, st'_{22}/st'_2, \\ \qquad tr_{21}/tr_1, tr'_{21}/tr'_1, tr_{22}/tr_2, tr'_{22}/tr'_2] \\ \wedge mergeState(st'_{11}, st'_{21}, st'_1) \\ \wedge mergeState(st'_{12}, st'_{22}, st'_2) \\ \wedge mergeTrace(tr'_{11}, tr'_{21}, tr'_1) \\ \wedge mergeTrace(tr'_{12}, tr'_{22}, tr'_2) \end{array} \right)$$

In the above definition, $beh(P)$ and $beh(Q)$ represent the denotational semantics of programs P and Q, respectively. For the 1st run, it requires that P and Q have the same initial values on st_1 and tr_1. Similarly, for the 2nd run, it requires that P and Q have the same initial values on st_2 and tr_2. Additionally, $mergeState$ and $mergeTrace$ define the final state and final trace when performing parallel composition. Specifically, if the final state of both parallel components P and Q are $term$, then the final execution state for their parallel composition $P||Q$ is $term$. If any component program is in a $wait$ state, then $P||Q$ stays $wait$ as well. $P||Q$ is divergent when either component behaves chaotically. Due to the similarity between $mergeState(st'_{11}, st'_{21}, st'_1)$ and $mergeState(st'_{12}, st'_{22}, st'_2)$, we only provide the definition of $mergeState(st'_{11}, st'_{21}, st'_1)$ as shown below.

$$mergeState(st'_{11}, st'_{21}, st'_1) =$$

$$\begin{pmatrix} ((st'_{11} = term \land st'_{21} = term) \to (st'_1 = term)) \land \\ \begin{pmatrix} ((st'_{11} = wait \land st'_{21} \neq div) \lor \\ (st'_{11} \neq div \land st'_{21} = wait)) \to (st'_1 = wait) \end{pmatrix} \land \\ ((st'_{11} = div \land st'_{21} = div) \to (st'_1 = div)) \end{pmatrix}$$

The trace (i.e., snapshot sequence) of a parallel composition program is formed by the interleaving of actions from its component programs. As defined in Sect. 2, each snapshot in the trace is in the form of a triple (σ, μ). In the definition of $mergeTrace$, the definition of π^* migrates from the symbol definition of a single snapshot to the snapshot sequence. In this function, the first line ensures that the data states in the trace of $P||Q$ remain the same as P and Q individually. The second line indicates that the action in the parallel composition is formed by the interleaving of the component programs. The third line restricts every state in the trace sequence to be contributed by only one component program.

$$mergeTrace(tr'_{11}, tr'_{21}, tr'_1) =$$

$$\begin{pmatrix} (\pi_1^*(tr'_1) = \pi_1^*(tr'_{11}) = \pi_1^*(tr'_{21})) \land \\ (\pi_2^*(tr'_1) = \pi_2^*(tr'_{11}) + \pi_2^*(tr'_{21})) \land \\ 2 \notin \pi_2^*(tr'_1) \end{pmatrix}$$

Example 1. Consider the process $P =_{df} x := y + 1$, and the process $Q =_{df} y := y + 2$. Assume that $P||Q$ is activated with two states $\{x \mapsto 0, y \mapsto 1\}$ and $\{x \mapsto 1, y \mapsto 0\}$, which are contributed by the 2-runs of the predecessor programs. If P is scheduled to execute first, it can produce the snapshot as below.

$$seq_{11} = \langle (\{x \mapsto 1, y \mapsto 1\}, 1), (\{x \mapsto 1, y \mapsto 3\}, 0) \rangle$$

$$seq_{12} = \langle (\{x \mapsto 1, y \mapsto 0\}, 1), (\{x \mapsto 1, y \mapsto 2\}, 0) \rangle$$

The first line is the trace of the 1st run, and the second line is the trace of the 2nd run. And in both lines, the first snapshot is made by the action $x := y + 1$ of P, and the second one represents an action engaged by the environment of P, which is Q. Corresponding to seq_{11} and seq_{12}, the following two traces can be yielded from the viewpoint of Q,

$$seq_{21} = \langle (\{x \mapsto 1, y \mapsto 1\}, 0), (\{x \mapsto 1, y \mapsto 3\}, 1) \rangle$$

$$seq_{22} = \langle (\{x \mapsto 1, y \mapsto 0\}, 0), (\{x \mapsto 1, y \mapsto 2\}, 1) \rangle$$

where second snapshot for both the two traces is given by the assignment $y := y + 2$ of Q. Based on the definition of $mergeTrace$, their merge gives rise to the traces of $P||Q$:

$$seq_1 = \langle (\{x \mapsto 1, y \mapsto 1\}, 1), (\{x \mapsto 1, y \mapsto 3\}, 1) \rangle$$

$$seq_2 = \langle (\{x \mapsto 1, y \mapsto 0\}, 1), (\{x \mapsto 1, y \mapsto 2\}, 1) \rangle$$

3.5 Application of Denotational Semantics

After describing the denotational semantics of the relational system, we can use it to verify some properties from the perspective of traces. It is necessary to note that security levels in information flow control are viewed as a lattice, allowing information to flow only upwards [19]. And the researchers always use *high* and *low* to represent the security labels. The following are the properties we list.

Determinism. For the program P, it has two traces: the initial trace tr_1 changes to tr_1' after the execution of program P, and the other initial trace tr_2 becomes tr_2'. If $\pi_1(last(tr_1)) = \pi_1(last(tr_2))$ and $\pi_1(last(tr_1')) = \pi_1(last(tr_2'))$, then program P is called satisfying determinism.

Non-interference. For a deterministic program P, let Low stand for all low level variables. P is called satisfying the non-interference property if: $\forall x \in Low$, the two conditions $\pi_1(last(tr_1))(x) = \pi_1(last(tr_2))(x)$ and $\pi_1(last(tr_1'))(x) = \pi_1(last(tr_2'))(x)$ are met.

Example 2. Consider the process $P =_{df} x := x+1; y := y+2$, and it is activated with two states σ_1 (i.e., $\{x \mapsto 0, y \mapsto 0\}$) and σ_2 (i.e., $\{x \mapsto 0, y \mapsto 1\}$). Then we can get the following traces.

$$seq_1 = \langle(\{x \mapsto 1, y \mapsto 0\}, 1), (\{\boxed{x \mapsto 1}, y \mapsto 2\}, 1)\rangle$$

$$seq_2 = \langle(\{x \mapsto 1, y \mapsto 1\}, 1), (\{\boxed{x \mapsto 1}, y \mapsto 3\}, 1)\rangle$$

If we assume that $x \in Low$, then we need to compare $\pi_1(last(tr_1'))(x) = \pi_1(last(tr_2'))(x)$, and here $tr_1' = tr_1 \wedge seq_1$, $tr_2' = tr_2 \wedge seq_2$. Based on the results provided above, we can conclude that program P satisfies non-interference.

4 Algebraic Semantics

Program properties can be represented and verified using algebraic laws within a formalized semantics framework. In this section, we delve into the concept of algebraic semantics.

4.1 Algebraic Laws for Basic Statements

First, we study the algebraic laws of basic statements outlined below. These laws indicate that a program written in our language can be transformed into the form of guarded choice. In this context, the symbol ε represents an empty program.

- (assign-1) $x := e = []\{\langle true\{\bullet\}true\rangle \& @(\overrightarrow{x := e} \bullet \overrightarrow{x := e}) \to (\overleftarrow{\varepsilon} \bullet \overrightarrow{\varepsilon})\}$
- (guard-1) $@gd = []\{@(gd) \to \varepsilon\}$

- (cond-1) if b then P else Q
  $= []\{\langle b\{\bullet\}b\rangle \& @(\overleftarrow{skip} \bullet \overrightarrow{skip}) \to (\overleftarrow{P} \bullet \overrightarrow{P}),$
  $\langle b\{\bullet\}\neg b\rangle \& @(\overleftarrow{skip} \bullet \overrightarrow{skip}) \to (\overleftarrow{P} \bullet \overrightarrow{Q}),$
  $\langle \neg b\{\bullet\}b\rangle \& @(\overleftarrow{skip} \bullet \overrightarrow{skip}) \to (\overleftarrow{Q} \bullet \overrightarrow{P}),$
  $\langle \neg b\{\bullet\}\neg b\rangle \& @(\overleftarrow{skip} \bullet \overrightarrow{skip}) \to (\overleftarrow{Q} \bullet \overrightarrow{Q})\}$
- (iter-1) while b do P
  $= []\{\langle b\{\bullet\}b\rangle \& @(\overleftarrow{skip} \bullet \overrightarrow{skip}) \to (\overleftarrow{(P; while\ b\ do\ P)} \bullet \overrightarrow{(P; while\ b\ do\ P)}),$
  $\langle b\{\bullet\}\neg b\rangle \& @(\overleftarrow{skip} \bullet \overrightarrow{skip}) \to (\overleftarrow{(P; while\ b\ do\ P)} \bullet \overrightarrow{\varepsilon}),$
  $\langle \neg b\{\bullet\}b\rangle \& @(\overleftarrow{skip} \bullet \overrightarrow{skip}) \to (\overleftarrow{\varepsilon} \bullet \overrightarrow{(P; while\ b\ do\ P)}),$
  $\langle \neg b\{\bullet\}\neg b\rangle \& @(\overleftarrow{skip} \bullet \overrightarrow{skip}) \to (\overleftarrow{\varepsilon} \bullet \overrightarrow{\varepsilon})\}$
- (seq-1) $(P;Q);R = P;(Q;R)$
- (seq-2) If $P = []\{g_1 \to P_1, ..., g_n \to P_n\}$, then $P;Q = []\{g_1 \to (P_1;Q), ..., g_n \to (P_n;Q)\}$

For (cond-1), the conditional construct is transformed into the form of an assignment guarded choice. In the 2-runs representation, the conditional construct has four cases: (1) If both runs satisfy condition b, then the conditional statement selects program P; (2) If the 1st run satisfies condition b but the 2nd run does not, the 1st run executes P and the 2nd run executes program Q, denoted as $\overleftarrow{P} \bullet \overrightarrow{Q}$; (3) Case (3) is the opposite of case (2), denoted as $\overleftarrow{Q} \bullet \overrightarrow{P}$; (4) If neither run satisfies condition b, the conditional statement selects program Q. These four cases correspond to the scenarios shown in Fig. 2 (Page 10). The denotational semantics presented in this paper provides a foundation for verifying these algebraic laws. Due to space limitations, we do not provide the detailed proofs here.

4.2 Algebraic Laws for Parallel Composition

Parallel composition is symmetric and associative.

- (par-1) $P||Q = Q||P$
- (par-2) $(P||Q)||R = P||(Q||R)$

In our investigation, we focus on the algebraic laws governing the parallel composition of guarded choices. As mentioned previously, there are three types of guarded choices, resulting in a total of 9 expansion laws. However, due to the symmetry of the parallel composition (par-1), we only need to present 6 laws, as illustrated in Table 3.

Table 3. Compositions of guarded choices

	Assignment	Event	Assign&Event
Assignment	(par-1-1)	(par-1-2)	(par-1-3)
Event		(par-2-2)	(par-2-3)
Assign&Event			(par-3-3)

Due to the page limit, we only present the algebraic laws **(par-1-1)** and **(par-3-3)**.

(par-1-1) Let $P = []_{i \in I}\{(b_{1i}\{\bullet\}b_{2i})\&@(\overleftarrow{x_i := e_i} \bullet \overrightarrow{x_i := e_i}) \to (\overleftarrow{P_i} \bullet \overrightarrow{S_i})\}$
$Q = []_{j \in J}\{(b_{1j}\{\bullet\}b_{2j})\&@(\overleftarrow{x_j := e_j} \bullet \overrightarrow{x_j := e_j}) \to (\overleftarrow{Q_j} \bullet \overrightarrow{R_j})\}$
then,
$P||Q = []_{i \in I}\{(b_{1i}\{\bullet\}b_{2i})\&@(\overleftarrow{x_i := e_i} \bullet \overrightarrow{x_i := e_i}) \to (\overleftarrow{P_i||Q} \bullet \overrightarrow{S_i||Q})\}$
$[][]_{i \in I}\{(b_{1i}\{\bullet\}\neg b_{2i})\&@(\overleftarrow{x_i := e_i} \bullet \overrightarrow{skip}) \to (\overleftarrow{P_i||Q} \bullet \overrightarrow{skip||Q})\}$
$[][]_{i \in I}\{(\neg b_{1i}\{\bullet\}b_{2i})\&@(\overleftarrow{skip} \bullet \overrightarrow{x_i := e_i}) \to (\overleftarrow{skip||Q} \bullet \overrightarrow{S_i||Q})\}$
$[][]_{j \in J}\{(b_{1j}\{\bullet\}b_{2j})\&@(\overleftarrow{x_j := e_j} \bullet \overrightarrow{x_j := e_j}) \to (\overleftarrow{P||Q_j} \bullet \overrightarrow{P||R_j})\}$
$[][]_{j \in J}\{(b_{1j}\{\bullet\}\neg b_{2j})\&@(\overleftarrow{x_j := e_j} \bullet \overrightarrow{skip}) \to (\overleftarrow{P||Q_j} \bullet \overrightarrow{P||skip})\}$
$[][]_{j \in J}\{(\neg b_{1j}\{\bullet\}b_{2j})\&@(\overleftarrow{skip} \bullet \overrightarrow{x_j := e_j}) \to (\overleftarrow{P||skip} \bullet \overrightarrow{P||R_j})\}$

(par-1-1) is the parallel composition for the two assignment guarded choices. There are six cases in total, where each line represents a possible execution case for $P||Q$. The first line indicates that the Boolean conditions b_{1i} and b_{2i} in the 2-runs of program P can be both satisfied, allowing the scheduling of two assignment guards (i.e., $\overleftarrow{x_i := e_i}$ and $\overrightarrow{x_i := e_i}$). Therefore, the subsequent behavior of the 2-runs consists of the respective subsequent programs combined with the other parallel component. Similarly, the fourth line represents that both Boolean conditions in the 2-runs of program Q can be satisfied, respectively.

Subsequently, if none of the above two cases can apply, we can consider the scenario where the Boolean condition is satisfied in one run. We take the second line as an example. It indicates that the Boolean condition b_{1i} is satisfied in the 1st run of program P, allowing the scheduling of the corresponding assignment guard (i.e., $\overleftarrow{x_i := e_i}$). The subsequent program can also be combined with the other parallel component, regarded as the subsequent program of $P||Q$. However, in the 2nd run of program P, the Boolean condition b_{2i} is not satisfied. In this case, we use $skip$ to represent no action is taken, and the subsequent program becomes $skip$ combined with the other parallel component.

(par-3-3) Let $P = []_{i \in I}\{(b_{1i}\{\bullet\}b_{2i})\&@(\overleftarrow{x_i := e_i} \bullet \overrightarrow{x_i := e_i}) \to (\overleftarrow{P_i} \bullet \overrightarrow{S_i})\}$
$[][]_{j \in J}\{@(\xi_j) \to T_j\}$
$Q = []_{k \in K}\{(b_{1k}\{\bullet\}b_{2k})\&@(\overleftarrow{x_k := e_k} \bullet \overrightarrow{x_k := e_k}) \to (\overleftarrow{Q_k} \bullet \overrightarrow{R_k})\}$
$[][]_{n \in N}\{@(\eta_n) \to M_n\}$
then,
$P||Q = []_{i \in I}\{(b_{1i}\{\bullet\}b_{2i})\&@(\overleftarrow{x_i := e_i} \bullet \overrightarrow{x_i := e_i}) \to (\overleftarrow{P_i||Q} \bullet \overrightarrow{S_i||Q})\}$
$[][]_{i \in I}\{(b_{1i}\{\bullet\}\neg b_{2i})\&@(\overleftarrow{x_i := e_i} \bullet \overrightarrow{skip}) \to (\overleftarrow{P_i||Q} \bullet \overrightarrow{skip||Q})\}$
$[][]_{i \in I}\{(\neg b_{1i}\{\bullet\}b_{2i})\&@(\overleftarrow{skip} \bullet \overrightarrow{x_i := e_i}) \to (\overleftarrow{skip||Q} \bullet \overrightarrow{S_i||Q})\}$
$[][]_{k \in K}\{(b_{1k}\{\bullet\}b_{2k})\&@(\overleftarrow{x_k := e_k} \bullet \overrightarrow{x_k := e_k}) \to (\overleftarrow{P||Q_k} \bullet \overrightarrow{P||R_k})\}$
$[][]_{k \in K}\{(b_{1k}\{\bullet\}\neg b_{2k})\&@(\overleftarrow{x_k := e_k} \bullet \overrightarrow{skip}) \to (\overleftarrow{P||Q_k} \bullet \overrightarrow{P||skip})\}$
$[][]_{k \in K}\{(\neg b_{1k}\{\bullet\}b_{2k})\&@(\overleftarrow{skip} \bullet \overrightarrow{x_k := e_k}) \to (\overleftarrow{P||skip} \bullet \overrightarrow{P||R_k})\}$
$[][]_{j \in J}\{@(\xi_j \wedge \neg \eta) \to (T_j||Q)\}$
$[][]_{n \in N}\{@(\eta_n \wedge \neg \xi) \to (P||M_n)\}$
$[][]_{j \in J \wedge n \in N}\{@(\xi_j \wedge \eta_n) \to (T_j||M_n)\}$

where, $\xi = or_{j \in J}\{@(\xi_j)\}$ and $\eta = or_{n \in N}\{@(\eta_n)\}$, which mean ξ and η are the or-compounds of all $@\xi_j (j \in J)$ and all $@\eta_n (n \in N)$, respectively.

(par-3-3) reflects the parallel composition where the two parallel components are all assign&event guarded choices. According to the scheduling rules, assignment guards can have the choice to be executed first, the analysis is similar to **(par-1-1)**. Meanwhile, the event guard can also be triggered first, there are three other cases where the event guard is scheduled. If one event guard from one parallel part is triggered and all the guards from another parallel part cannot be triggered currently, the behavior after this triggered case is the parallel composition of the subsequent process of one parallel part after the triggered guard and another parallel part. If two guards from different parallel parts are triggered simultaneously, the behavior after this type of triggered case is the parallel composition of the subsequent processes after two triggered guards from each parallel part.

5 Conclusion

In this paper, we have introduced a relational system for analyzing 2-runs of a program, grounded in relational Hoare logic. Additionally, we also presented two types of guarded components and three types of guarded choices to support the algebraic parallel expansion laws. By leveraging the UTP approach [10], we have further explored the denotational and algebraic semantics of our language, which are the relational denotational and relational algebraic semantics. Our main contributions lie in providing the denotational semantics for the conditional statement and parallel program, and summarizing the algebraic laws for the parallel composition. Building upon these foundations, we have achieved the transformation of every program in our language into a unified form known as the guarded choice form, supporting the realization of the sequentialization of parallel programs.

In the future, we plan to study the relational Hoare logic with parallel composition. We also plan to dive into the semantics linking theory [10] of our language. Additionally, we plan to use the theorem proof assistant Coq [15–17] to formalize the UTP-based semantics.

Acknowledgements. The authors would like to acknowledge Dr. Qiwen Xu of University of Macau for his help in discussion of this study. This work was partially supported by the National Natural Science Foundation of China (Grant No. 62032024), the "Digital Silk Road" Shanghai International Joint Lab of Trustworthy Intelligent Software (No. 22510750100), and Shanghai Trusted Industry Internet Software Collaborative Innovation Center.

References

1. Goguen, J.A., Meseguer, J.: Security policies and security models. In: IEEE Symposium on Security and Privacy, pp. 11–20 (1982)
2. Chaudhuri, S., Gulwani, S., Lublinerman, R.: Continuity analysis of programs. In: Proceedings of the 37th Annual ACM SIGPLAN-SIGACT Symposium on Principles of Programming Languages, pp. 57–70 (2010)
3. Clarkson, M.R., Schneider, F.B.: Hyperproperties. J. Comput. Secur. **18**(6), 1157–1210 (2010)
4. Barthe, G., D'argenio, P.R., Rezk, T.: Secure information flow by self-composition. Math. Struct. Comput. Sci. **21**(6), 1207–1252 (2011)
5. Darvas, Á., Hähnle, R., Sands, D.: A theorem proving approach to analysis of secure information flow. In: Security in Pervasive Computing: Second International Conference, pp. 193–209 (2005)
6. Barthe, G., Crespo, J.M., Kunz, C.: Relational verification using product programs. In: International Symposium on Formal Methods, pp. 200–214 (2011)
7. Churchill, B., Padon, O., Sharma, R., Aiken, A.: Semantic program alignment for equivalence checking. In: Proceedings of the 40th ACM SIGPLAN Conference on Programming Language Design and Implementation, pp. 1027–1040 (2019)
8. Benton, N.: Simple relational correctness proofs for static analyses and program transformations. ACM SIGPLAN Not. **39**(1), 14–25 (2004)
9. Amtoft, T., Bandhakavi, S., Banerjee, A.: A logic for information flow in object-oriented programs. ACM SIGPLAN Not. **41**(1), 91–102 (2006)
10. Hoare, C.A.R., He, J.: Unifying Theories of Programming. Prentice Hall, Englewood Cliffs (1998)
11. Stoy, J.E.: Denotational Semantics: The Scott-Strachey Approach to Programming Language Theory. MIT Press, Cambridge (1981)
12. Hoare, C.A.R., et al.: Laws of programming. Commun. ACM **30**(8), 672–686 (1987)
13. Barthe, G., Eilers, R., Georgiou, P., Gleiss, B., Kovács, L., Maffei, M.: Verifying relational properties using trace logic. In: 2019 Formal Methods in Computer Aided Design (FMCAD), pp. 170–178 (2019)
14. Dardinier, T., Müller, P.: Hyper Hoare Logic: (dis-) proving program hyperproperties (extended version). arXiv:2301.10037 (2023)
15. Sheng, F., Zhu, H., He, J., Yang, Z., Bowen, J.P.: Theoretical and practical aspects of linking operational and algebraic semantics for MDESL. ACM Trans. Softw. Eng. Methodol. (TOSEM) **28**(3), 1–46 (2019)
16. Huet, G., Kahn, G., Paulin-Mohring, C.: The Coq Proof Assistant a Tutorial (2005)
17. Bertot, Y., Casteran, P.: Interactive Theorem Proving and Program Development: Coq'Art: The Calculus of Inductive Constructions. Springer, Heidelberg (2013)
18. Naumann, D.A.: Thirty-seven years of relational Hoare logic: remarks on its principles and history. In: Leveraging Applications of Formal Methods, Verification and Validation: Engineering Principles: 9th International Symposium on Leveraging Applications of Formal Methods, pp. 93–116 (2020)
19. Denning, D.E.: A lattice model of secure information flow. Commun. ACM **19**(5), 236–243 (1976)
20. Finkbeiner, B., Olderog, E.R.: Concurrent hyperproperties. In: Theories of Programming and Formal Methods: Essays Dedicated to Jifeng He on the Occasion of His 80th Birthday, pp. 211–231 (2023)

ASTD Patterns for Integrated Continuous Anomaly Detection in Data Logs

Chaymae El Jabri, Marc Frappier, and Pierre-Martin Tardif

Université de Sherbrooke, Sherbrooke, Canada
eljc3201@usherbrooke.ca

Abstract. This paper investigates the use of the ASTD language for ensemble anomaly detection in data logs. It uses a sliding window technique for continuous learning in data streams, coupled with updating learning models upon the completion of each window to maintain accurate detection and align with current data trends. It proposes ASTD patterns for combining learning models, especially in the context of unsupervised learning, which is commonly used for data streams. To facilitate this, a new ASTD operator is proposed, the Quantified Flow, which enables the seamless combination of learning models while ensuring that the specification remains concise. Our contribution is a specification pattern, highlighting the capacity of ASTDs to abstract and modularize anomaly detection systems. The ASTD language provides a unique approach to develop data flow anomaly detection systems, grounded in the combination of processes through the graphical representation of the language operators. This simplifies the design task for developers, who can focus primarily on defining the functional operations that constitute the system.

Keywords: ASTD · Anomaly detection · Continuous learning

1 Introduction

In today's digital age, protecting IT infrastructure from cyberattacks and security breaches is critical for organizations to ensure daily operations, store sensitive data and manage customer information. Anomaly detection techniques can help organizations identify unusual patterns and behaviors in their systems so they can respond quickly and prevent potential security incidents. Anomaly detection techniques are instrumental in diverse areas, including fraud detection, network security, and intrusion detection within business applications [1].

Recognizing the pivotal role of anomaly detection systems in ensuring the security and reliability of various applications, from cybersecurity to industrial monitoring, it is crucial to acknowledge the challenges associated with their development [2]. Effectively addressing these challenges becomes imperative for successfully deploying robust and adaptive detection systems.

In the realm of anomaly detection systems, a formidable challenge arises from the dynamic nature of data patterns. To maintain the system's accuracy over time, periodic model re-training becomes imperative. Nils Baumann et al. [3] underscore the critical importance of automating the re-training process to adapt to evolving data patterns seamlessly. This challenge necessitates implementing robust mechanisms that detect anomalies and autonomously refine their understanding of normal and abnormal behaviors in the ever-changing data landscape.

The intricacy of learning systems poses yet another significant challenge, encompassing multifaceted phases such as data pre-processing and model training. Benjamin Benni et al. [4] delve into a comprehensive analysis of this complexity, shedding light on the intricate processes that form the backbone of effective anomaly detection. Addressing this challenge requires the development of streamlined strategies to simplify the various phases, ensuring that the learning system can efficiently navigate the intricacies of data preprocessing and model training. Overcoming this hurdle is crucial for enhancing anomaly detection systems' overall effectiveness and efficiency.

As detection systems scale up to handle vast amounts of data, a distinct challenge emerges in maintaining modularity to ensure scalability and ease of maintenance. The development of large-scale detection systems demands a careful balance to prevent unwieldy complexity. Baldwin and Clark [5] stress the significance of modularity in such systems, emphasizing its pivotal role in facilitating scalability and simplifying maintenance efforts. Successfully addressing this challenge involves designing detection systems with modular architectures that can seamlessly adapt to the increasing demands of data volume and computational resources, ensuring both scalability and ease of long-term maintenance.

This article introduces a method for developing anomaly detection systems using a specification language called Algebraic State Transition Diagram (ASTD) [6]. It investigates the extent to which this language reduces the complexity of the detection system by adding an abstraction layer. Additionally, it examines how the graphical representation of the language's operators contributes to easing development efforts by managing the scheduling of various processes within the detection system. ASTD is a graphical and executable notation for composing state machines, offering modularity and flexibility in system development [7]. The paper's contributions include (1) The extension of the ASTD language by the Quantified Flow operator to allow the combination of an arbitrary number of models while keeping the specification compact, and (2) The definition of an ASTD specification that represents a pattern on which to base the development of more complex systems; this specification has the following features: - Automated re-training of learning models, - Composition of a set of learning models to detect anomalies in data logs, - Combination of the decisions of each model for each event. The intent is to provide an illustrative example of specifications of anomaly detection systems that can be easily adapted for other contexts or learning methods.

The paper is divided into six sections. In Sect. 2, we emphasize the importance of automating the renewal of the learning model in the context of dynamic data, the role of abstraction in reducing system complexity, and modularity, which facilitates maintenance and extension without introducing errors. Section 3 introduces the Quantified Flow operator as an extension of the ASTD language to easily combine an arbitrary number of learning models. In Sect. 4, we present a case study on the detection of unexpected events, implementing the following essential features for unsupervised anomaly detection: - Automation of retraining of learning models using the Sliding Window technique. - Model composition using the Quantified Flow operator. - Decision combination of models through Majority Voting. In Sect. 5, we assess the performance of the specification in detecting unexpected events during a day of activity, while highlighting the effect of training data renewal and the combination of unsupervised models. Finally, in Sects. 6 and 7, we summarize our findings and conclude.

2 Related Work

The MLOps [8] approach presents a set of principles aimed at standardizing the deployment, management, and monitoring processes of machine learning models in production environments. This approach integrates best practices and tools to optimize the model lifecycle, ensuring their effectiveness and robustness throughout their usage. In this work, we propose a development framework for an unsupervised anomaly detection pipeline, based on statistical learning models. This framework aims to incorporate features that align with certain technical aspects of MLOps, such as:

1. **Periodic Learning**: Regular updating of data using a sliding window approach [9,10]. Gamma [9] suggests that in most cases, we are primarily concerned with computing statistics for the recent past rather than the entire history. The sliding window method is useful in this regard as it allows us to focus on the relevant data. There are various window models, including the sequence-based model where the window size is determined by the number of observations, and the timestamp-based model where the window size is determined by duration.
2. **Metadata Storage**: Storage of intermediate results associated with the learning model.
3. **Entity-Based Data Processing**: Separation and processing of data based on specific entities, such as users or machines, to customize analyses and anomaly detection.

By implementing these features, we aim to create a flexible pipeline that optimizes the development lifecycle of anomaly detection models.

The development of the Anomaly Detection System using ASTD language follows the Model-Driven Engineering (MDE) paradigm, which provides a potential solution to reduce complexities through abstraction [11]. MDE advocates for using software models at different levels of abstraction to (semi-) automatically construct software systems. Models serve as abstractions of complex entities; they conceal unwanted details so that modelers can easily focus on their areas of interest. The ASTD language ensures, through the graphical representation of its operators, the combination and scheduling of processes, enabling a focus on the core operations of the detection system.

Modularity in software design is crucial for enhancing maintainability and extensibility by breaking down complex systems into smaller, independent modules. This approach simplifies debugging and maintenance, as changes can be made to individual modules without affecting the entire system. It also promotes code reuse, saving time and effort. Studies such as [11] and [12] emphasize modularity's importance for building scalable and maintainable software systems. The ASTD language embodies this principle, with its specifications organized in a tree structure where each branch represents a specific functionality of the system.

3 Extended ASTD Formalism

The Algebraic State Transition Diagram (ASTD) [6] is a specification language for modeling and integrating complex systems by extending traditional state machines with process algebra operators. To enable anomaly detection models to work concurrently and independently within an ensemble system, we propose the Quantified Flow operator as an extension of the standard ASTD Flow operator.

The Flow operator is an operator similar to the AND state in statecharts. In [13], the flow operator is used for combining the processes of data preprocessing, training, and detection during the development of anomaly detection systems by ASTDs. This is possible thanks to the fact that a single input event can be processed differently in each of the sub-ASTDs of the flow operator according to two distinct actions. This is represented in Fig. 1: When event e() is received, act_1 is executed, followed by act_2.

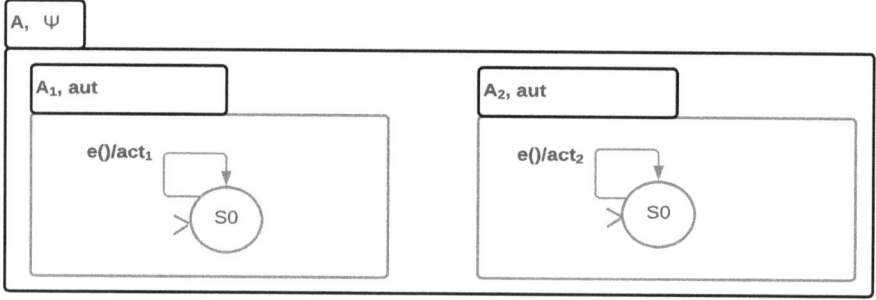

Fig. 1. Flow operator

The Quantified Flow was introduced to enable support for combining learning models, which involve two phases: training and detection. This operator allows the independent invocation of methods for each phase within the models.

In anomaly detection systems, managing both the training and detection phases across multiple models is important. These models typically perform two main tasks: **training** and **evaluation**. During training, the model is updated with new data to improve its performance, while in the evaluation phase, it processes new input to identify anomalies.

Each task can be executed independently and in parallel across models. To achieve this, we define an abstract structure that captures the general functions of anomaly detection models. In object-oriented programming, this is done by specifying the skeleton of detection models in an abstract class, with methods for training and scoring implemented in subclasses tailored to each model (see Fig. 2).

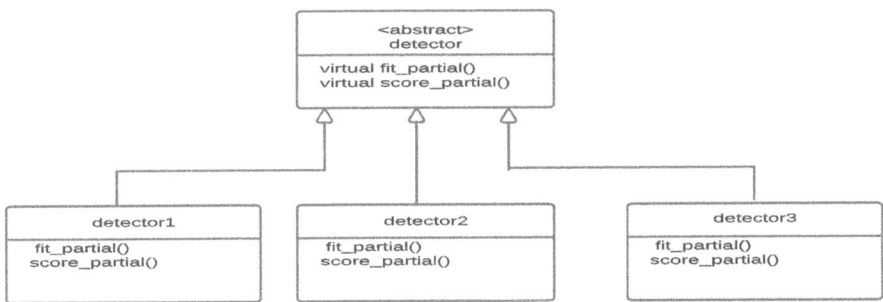

Fig. 2. Class hierarchy for anomaly detection using multiple techniques

In order to effectively combine a set of heterogeneous anomaly detection models while maintaining the abstraction of their functioning in an ASTD, we use the abstract class *detector* (shown in Fig. 2), which encapsulates the general functions of the detection models. This class defines two primary methods: fit_partial(): Trains the model incrementally by incorporating each new instance of data, score_partial(): Returns the score of the input data based on the reference model, indicating whether it represents an anomaly.

In Fig. 3, we present the specification for combining multiple detectors using the Quantified Flow operator. In this example, the attribute **detectors** is associated with the quantified flow ASTD A, and it is of type map<string, detector*>. This map holds references to instances of the detection models, associating each model's name with its class: {'detector1': new detector1(), 'detector2': new detector2(), 'detector3': new detector3()}. Upon receiving an event e(), the Quantified Flow operator uses the quantification variable d to traverse the set of detectors {detector1, detector2, detector3}. For each detector, two key actions are sequentially executed, each with its corresponding guard condition: $g_1(d)$ checks if training for model d can begin, and $g_2(d)$ verifies if model d is fully computed and ready to perform detection. The actions involves:

- fit_partial(): The model is trained with the new instance of data.
- score_partial(): The model evaluates the data and returns an anomaly score.

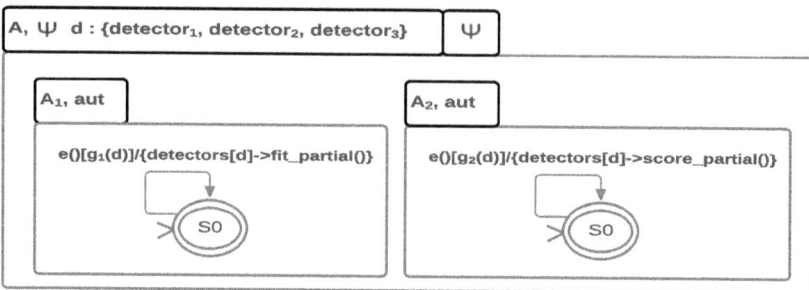

Fig. 3. An ASTD pattern for combining three anomaly detection models using the quantified flow

This allows each detector to perform its operations independently, without waiting for the others. The Quantified Flow operator facilitates this parallelism while maintaining the abstraction of each model's function. The use of the detector class ensures that each model behaves according to its unique characteristics, yet all are managed through a unified interface. This structure allows the Quantified Flow operator to handle any learning model—such as k-means, KDE, and LOF—in an integrated and scalable way.

The example in Fig. 3 illustrates how the hierarchical nature of ASTDs integrates seamlessly with object-oriented class hierarchies. The detector abstract class is utilized to declare the detectors map in the quantified ASTD A, where each instance of A can be associated with its specific type of detector. This design promotes reusability and modularity, ensuring that the system can easily incorporate additional detectors or modify existing ones by simply altering the map and the class instantiations. To generalize to any set of detectors, we must first define classes that inherit from the detector interface, implementing the fit_partial() and score_partial() methods. Next, pass a JSON configuration file as a parameter to the specification, containing the list of detector names and the constructors initializing each detector. This will enable dynamic loading of the set of detectors.

Syntax The quantified flow ASTD subtype has the following structure:

$$\text{Qflow} \triangleq \langle \Psi :, x, T, b \rangle$$

where $x \in \mathsf{Var}$ denotes a quantified variable that can be accessed in read-only mode. The type of this variable is represented by T. $b \in \mathsf{ASTD}$ refers to the body of the flow, which represents the ASTD that will be executed for each instance of the quantified variable. ASTD is the abstract type that identifies all the shared characteristics of all ASTD types, $\mathsf{ASTD} \triangleq \langle n, P, V, A_{astd} \rangle$ where $n \in \mathsf{Name}$ is the name of the ASTD, P is a list of parameters, V is a list of attributes, A_{astd} is an action.

Each ASTD has a set of states, with State representing all states. Final states are determined by the function $\mathit{final} : \mathsf{State} \to \mathsf{Boolean}$, and $\mathit{init} : \mathsf{ASTD} \to \mathsf{State}$ returns the initial state. For a quantified flow, the state is of type $\langle \Psi :_\circ, E, f \rangle$, where $\Psi :_\circ$ is the constructor, E is the attribute set, and $f : T \to \mathsf{State}$ maps elements x of T to states of b, with each state corresponding to an instance of the quantified flow.

Initial and final states are defined as follows. Let a be a quantified flow ASTD:

$$\mathit{init}(a) \triangleq (\Psi :_\circ, a.E_{init}, T \times \{\mathit{init}(a.b)\})$$

$$\mathit{final}(a, (\Psi :_\circ, E, f)) \triangleq \forall c : T \cdot \mathit{final}(a.b, f(c))$$

Semantics. The semantics of an ASTD consists of a labeled transition system (LTS), computed based on the inference rules of ASTD operators [14], which is a subset of $\mathsf{State} \times \mathsf{Event} \times \mathsf{State}$ representing a set of transitions of the form $s \xrightarrow{\sigma}_a s'$. It means that ASTD a can execute event σ from state s and move to state s'. The semantics of a nested ASTD depends on the variables declared in its enclosing ASTDs; we use *environments* to represent the values of these variables and the values of ASTD parameters. An environment is a function of $\mathsf{Env} \triangleq \mathsf{Var} \nrightarrow \mathsf{Term}$ which assigns values to variables. We need to introduce an auxiliary transition relation that handles environments: $s \xrightarrow{\sigma, E_e, E'_e}_a s'$, where environments E_e, E'_e denote the before and after values of variables in the ASTDs enclosing ASTD a.

Rule $\Psi :_1$ describes the execution of an event in the quantified flow ASTD. The rule applies when a transition occurs in the body of the ASTD.

$$\Theta \triangleq \left(E_g = E_e \triangleleft E \quad a.A_{astd}(E''_g, E'_g) \quad E'_e = E_e \triangleleft (V \triangleleft E'_g) \quad E' = V \triangleleft E'_g \right)$$

where environments E_e, E'_e denote the before and after values of variables in the ASTDs enclosing ASTD a. The ASTD action A_{astd} defines the computation of E'_g from E''_g. E'_e and E' are extracted by partitioning E'_g using V, the set of attributes. Θ defines the transformation of environments during a sub-ASTD transition execution.

$$\Psi :_1 \frac{\Omega_{qflow} \quad \Theta}{(\Psi :_\circ, E, f) \xrightarrow{\sigma, E_e, E'_e}_a (\Psi :_\circ, E', f')}$$

In this context, $(\Psi :_\circ, E, f)$ represents the current state of the quantified flow, where E denotes the environment and f is the function that maps elements of T to the state of the body ASTD b. The event σ triggers the transition, which changes the enclosing environment from E_e to E'_e. After this transition, the function is updated to f', reflecting the changes in the state of the body ASTD. The action A_{astd} governs the changes in the global environment E'_g.

We use the following abbreviation to indicate that an ASTD cannot execute a transition from a state s and global attributes E_g:

$$s \xrightarrow{\sigma, E_g}_a \triangleq \neg \exists E'_g, s' \cdot s \xrightarrow{\sigma, E_g, E'_g}_a s'$$

This notation expresses that no transition exists from state s under the event σ with global attributes E_g.

Premiss Ω_{qflow} non-deterministically selects a permutation p of T (noted $p \in \pi(T)$) and a sequence of environments Es, which store the intermediate results of the computation of E''_g from E_g by iterating over the elements $p(i)$ of p and executing the instances of the quantified flow. The execution order of the instances is chosen non-deterministically.

If the specifier wants deterministic results for the values of attributes, they must ensure that the actions of the instances are commutative. Let $k = |T|$ (the size of T):

$$\Omega_{qflow} \triangleq \begin{pmatrix} p \in \pi(T) \land Es \in 0..k \to \mathsf{Env} \land Es(0) = E_g \land Es(k) = E''_g \land \\ \forall i \in 1..k \cdot \begin{pmatrix} f(p(i)) \xrightarrow{\sigma, Es(i-1) \triangleleft \{x \mapsto p(i)\}, Es(i)}_{a.b} f'(p(i)) \\ \lor \\ Es(i) = Es(i-1) \land f(p(i)) \xrightarrow{g, Es(i)}_{a.b} \end{pmatrix} \end{pmatrix}$$

This expression defines the non-deterministic execution of the quantified flow instances, where p is a permutation of T, and Es is a sequence of environments that capture intermediate states of the system as each element $p(i)$ is processed.

The existing synchronization operators are not suitable for this application. Quantified synchronization, for instance, allows the parallel execution of its sub-instances and synchronizes their actions based on a set of events called Δ. The events in Δ are executed only when all sub-instances are able to perform them. If learning models are synchronized during the training and detection phases, all models must train simultaneously. This prevents adapting the training of each model to specific conditions, unless these conditions are implemented at the action level rather than the model level. However, this approach limits the extensibility and modularity of the specification: any modification to the quantification set would also require changes to the action code. With Quantified Flow, modifications are localized: only the quantification set needs to be adjusted. Quantified interleave, on the other hand, is a special case of quantified synchronization where the Δ set is empty ($\Delta = \varnothing$), allowing only one of the sub-instances to execute an event at a time. In this case, there is more independence than necessary to trigger the training or detection of each model, as it requires calling the event $e(x)$, where x is the name of the model one wishes to use, for each model individually. In contrast, with Quantified Flow, the independence is optimized: by simply calling the event e, it is executed automatically for all models capable of processing it at the given moment.

ASTDs are supported by the tools eASTD and cASTD [15]. eASTD is a graphical editor of ASTD specifications. cASTD is a compiler that translates

ASTD specifications into executable code. It first generates an implementation in an abstract, intermediate, imperative language that can be translated into an equivalent executable imperative language like C++, Java, Python. Currently, C++ is the sole translation implemented. The generated code can read the data continuously from a data source, and apply the operations contained in the specification in the order that has been defined thanks to the process algebra operators.

4 ASTD Specification for Combining Anomaly Detection Models

In this section, we present a generic ASTD specification for combining a set of heterogeneous detectors. For this purpose, we introduce a real application case, in which we will determine all the components and elements of the specification. The complete specification is found in [16]. The main goal of this application is to identify unusual or unexpected events within user activities. These "unexpected events" typically manifest as activities occurring at times when a user is not usually active. Our example is based on the time of occurrence of an event, for illustrative purposes and the sake of simplicity. Other criteria, or more general techniques for identifying anomalies, could easily be used with our ASTD pattern. For our example, we select three attributes from those available in the log files which are:

- Id: uniquely identifies each event, designated in the specification by eventId.
- CreationTime: determines the date and time in Coordinated Universal Time (UTC) when the user performed the activity, designated in the specification by eventDate.
- UserId: the user who performed the action

Anomaly Detection Models. We utilize three heterogeneous learning models, which are:

- K-means: a clustering algorithm for batch learning adapted to circular data. The number of clusters used is optimized using the silhouette coefficient. The distance used for clustering refers to the time interval between two events occurring at different hours, denoted as a and b. The formula to compute this distance is as follows:

$$\text{distance}(a, b) = \begin{cases} \min(b - a, a - b + 24), & \text{if } a < b \\ \min(a - b, b - a + 24), & \text{otherwise} \end{cases} \quad (1)$$

- KDE: is a non-parametric statistical technique for estimating the probability density of a random variable.
- LOF: is an unsupervised anomaly detection method that calculates the local density deviation of a given data point from its neighbors. It considers as outliers the samples whose density is significantly lower than that of their neighbors.

The data used during the training of the different models consists of the hours of events performed by a user within a day, which means the data is circular in an interval of [0,24[.

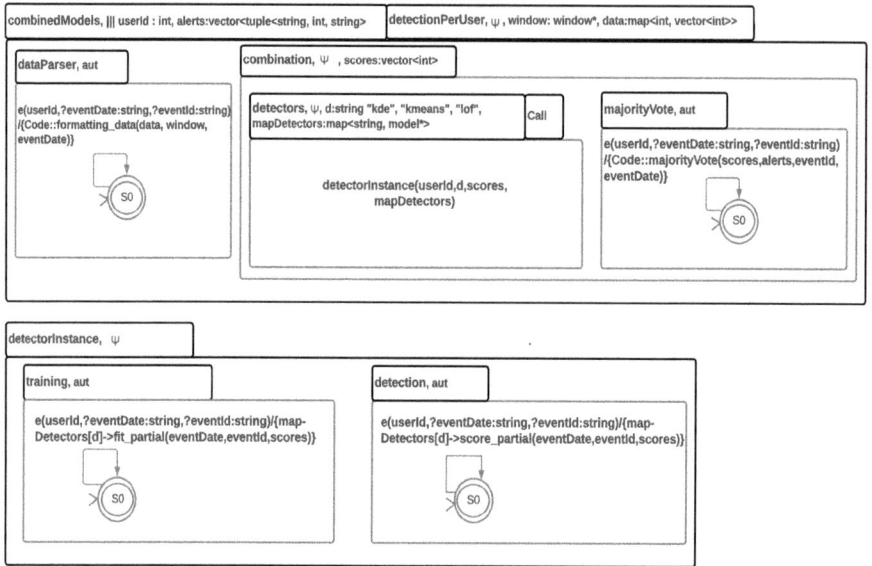

Fig. 4. Specification pattern

ASTD Specification. In Fig. 4, we present the top-level ASTD named combinedModels of type quantified interleave, denoted by ||| in the upper left tab. It declares a quantification variable userId of type int with an $UnboundedDomain$, which allows the processing of all the users received without the need to identify them a priori. The quantified interleave allows each user to be treated independently by associating an instance of the flow sub-ASTD for each user. The flow combines two sub-ASTDs dataParser, and combination

It has the following attributes:

- window of type window* initialized by new window(window_parameters).
- data of type $map\langle int, vector\langle int\rangle\rangle$. In cases where the period type is either 'week' or 'day', the keys of the map represent the period number. However, if the type of window is 'instance', the map contains a single key with a value of '0'. The values in the map are the minutes of the occurrence of the events, stored in a vector.
- alerts, which is of type $vector\langle tuple\langle string, int, string\rangle\rangle$. The alerts attribute stores information about abnormal events, including the event identifier, the number of models that flagged the event, and the date of its occurrence.

Additionally, the following parameters are defined:

- **window_parameters** of type json that respects the following structure $\{window\_size: int, sliding\_size: int, type \in \{'day', 'week', 'instance'\}\}$
- **kde_parameter**: double; the value of the k-percentile that will determine the threshold of probability densities below which an event is considered abnormal. It takes values in [0.5, 5].
- **kmeans_parameter**: double; the threshold to which the absolute value of the events cluster's z-score is compared. It takes values in [1.5, 2.5].
- **lof_parameter**: double; the value of the k-percentile that will determine the threshold of LOF scores for the training data, above which any score from the test data is considered abnormal. It takes values in [75, 95].

The sub-ASTD named **detectionPerUser** is of type flow denoted by $\Psi:$, which is a binary operator. It allows the same event to be treated by its two sub-ASTDs, and the combination of the latter two by sharing inherited variables. The right sub-ASTD is **DataParser** of automaton type, consisting of a single initial and final state (S0) having a loop transition labeled with the event pattern e(userId, ?eventDate: string, ?eventId: string) and the action formatting_data(data, window, eventDate), which adds each received event to the training set and defines the data belonging to the current window according to the type of period chosen as shown in the Algorithm 1, The methods $add\_instance$ and add_period of the window class can be found in the window.cpp file at [17].

Algorithm 1. formatting_data

1: **Input:** $data, window, eventDate$
2: **Output:** $data, window$ updated
3: int $hour$ = get_hour(CreationDate)
4: string $type$ = window → getType()
5: **if** $type$ == "day" or $type$ == "week" **then**
6:     $period$ = Compute_period(CreationDate, $type$)
7:     add $minute$ to $data[period]$
8:     std::vector⟨int⟩periodsToDelete = window → add_period($period$)
9:     delete the periods in $periodsToDelete$ from the map $data$
10: **if** $type$ == "instance" **then**
11:     add $minute$ to $data[0]$
12:     bool $sliding\_on$ = window → add_instance($minute$)
13:     int $sliding\_size$ = window → getSliding_size()
14:     **if** $sliding\_on$ **then**
15:         $data[0] \leftarrow$ delete elements from $data[0]$ from start to $sliding\_size$

The left sub-ASTD is named **Combination** it is a flow with the parameter: **scores** of type $vector\langle int\rangle$. It stores the scores of value 0 or 1 of an input data for each detection model. At the level of the left ASTD referred to as **detectors**, we establish an attribute called $mapDetectors$, which is of type $map\langle string, model*\rangle$. Here, the term "model" represents an abstract class from which three distinct learning models inherit: namely, k-means, kernel density estimation (KDE), and the local outlier factor (LOF). mapDetectors is initialized using the function $init\_map(kmeans\_parameters, kde\_parameters, lof\_parameters)$ (Algorithm 2).

Algorithm 2. Initialize Map of Models

1: **function** INIT_MAP($kmeans\_parameters, kde\_parameters, lo$ $f\_parameters$)
2:     Map⟨String, Model*⟩ map_classes
3:     map_classes["kde"] ← new kde($kde\_parameters$)
4:     map_classes["kmeans"] ← new kmeans($kmeans\_parameters$)
5:     map_classes["lof"] ← new lof($lof\_parameters$)
6:     **return** map_classes

ASTD detectors respects the structure presented in Sect. 3, except that in order to modularise the specification we use the operator Call, which calls the ASTD DetectorInstance containing the actions allowing the training and the detection by each model. It has two sub-ASTDs training and detection which are of type automaton having both a single state which is initial and final with a loop transition labeled by the same event e(userId, ?eventDate: string, ?eventId: string) and with the following actions:

- $mapDetectors[d] \rightarrow fit\_partial(data)$ at the training ASTD which launches the computation of the three learning models each time there is enough data in the current window.
- $mapDetectors[d] \rightarrow score\_partial(eventDate, event_Id, scores)$ in the detection ASTD, which populates the scores vector with predictions from each model, while adhering to the discrimination criteria set for each of the models.

After having obtained the score of each model, we perform a Majority Voting in the majorityVote ASTD by the action Code::majorityVote(scores, alerts, eventId,eventDate), which scans scores and in the case that more than 50% are positive (of value 1), it adds the event data in alerts, as shown in the Algorithm 3.

The Method for Renewing Training Data. To apply these models to data streams they are integrated in a sliding window. We have defined three distinct types of windows, to capture relevant information for anomaly detection in various applications, each with varying window sizes. Specifically, we have timestamp-based windows that are categorized based on the number of days or weeks, where each event is associated with a unique day or week number defined by YYYYDDD or YYYYWW, respectively; where YYYY denotes the year, DDD denotes the day's number, and WW denotes the week's number. We refer to these values as *periods*. Additionally, we have a sequence-based window type whose size is determined by the number of events. In all cases, the window's initialization involves the following three parameters:

Algorithm 3. majorityVote: Majority Vote Algorithm

```
1: procedure MAJORITYVOTE(scores, alerts, eventId, eventDate)
2:     if scores.size() ≠ 0 then
3:         count ← 0
4:         for i ← 0 to scores.size() − 1 do
5:             if scores[i] = 1 then
6:                 count ← count + 1
7:         if count > ⌊labels.size()/2⌋ then
8:             alerts.push_back(⟨eventId, count, eventDate⟩)
9:             print eventId is malicious
10:        scores.clear()
```

- *window_size*: the number of days, weeks, or events the window covers.
- *sliding_size*: the number of days, weeks, or events the window moves.
- *type*: 'day', 'week', or 'instance'.

Window sliding is shown in Fig. 5, and depends on two parameters: *window_size* (ws) and *sliding_size* (ss). *Window_size* consists of three units, representing the window size, and *sliding_size* consists of one unit, which determines the number of units by which the window moves; data associated with old units is deleted. The window moves when we obtain the necessary data to complete the *sliding_size*, at which point we update the window and delete the data from the previous window's old units

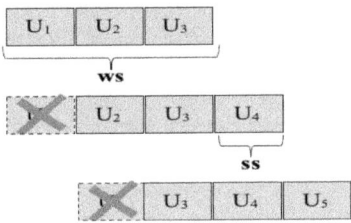

Fig. 5. Sliding window

The training and detection by each model occurs as follows:

- **K-means:** Throughout the training process, our objective is to identify the clusters within the data of the current time window. We optimize the number of clusters, denoted as 'k', by evaluating the silhouette coefficient, a measure of cluster quality. In addition to identifying the clusters, we also compute and store the standard deviation and mean values for each cluster. During the detection phase, our system identifies anomalies by a two-step process. First, we determine the cluster that is closest to the input minute, and then

we calculate the z-score. If the computed z-score exceeds a threshold defined by 'kmeans_parameter', we classify it as an anomaly.
- KDE: The training involves modeling the probability density of a user's activity over the 24 h of the day based on the data contained in the current window. The percentile of the probability densities of the training data is calculated according to kde_parameter, which represents the detection threshold. Then, when a new event is received, the time of its occurrence is calculated. If the probability density associated with this time is below the threshold, the event is assigned a value of 1, indicating that the event is considered an anomaly.
- LOF: We use the algorithm from the sklearn library, choosing cosine as the metric. Before providing the data to the training model, we convert it into Cartesian space to ensure compatibility with the chosen metric. The percentile of the LOF scores of the training data is calculated according to lof_parameter, which represents the detection threshold. When a new event is received, we compare its score with the threshold. If the score exceeds the threshold, the data is considered abnormal and is assigned a value of 1.

5 Experiment

The initial goal of this case study was to detect user activities occurring at unusual times within the activity logs of various Microsoft Office 365 services [13]. However, since there is no ground truth available for this type of application, we will apply the case study to a dataset from CERT Insider Threat version 4.2 [18], which simulates the activity of 1,000 employees, 70 of whom are malicious according to three malicious scenarios. The dataset that will be used is logon.csv, which contains user IDs, logon and logoff dates, and the PC on which the activity was performed. We will focus on the anomalies associated with the first scenario, which identifies users who logged in after working hours to upload data to wikileaks.org.

Although we will concentrate on a subset of the available information, our main interest in this application lies in the detection rate. We will also examine the effect of combining models through majority voting and the impact of the data renewal method. We are not concerned with false positives since we are not using the complete dataset, and an event occurring outside regular working hours may be normal, considering the role of the employee who performed it, as well as the nature of the PC (shared or private).

First, we convert each line of the logon.csv file into an event in the form of e(userId, date, eventId), and then we provide these as input to the executable C++ code that translates the ASTD specification.

The evaluation is performed using the detection rate (DR) for different models. The detection rate (DR) is defined as follows:

$$DR = \frac{\text{True Positive}}{\text{True Positive} + \text{False Negative}}$$

The Table 1, highlights the performance metrics of different anomaly detection configurations, revealing notable improvements when combining KDE, LOF,

Table 1. Performance metrics for an anomaly detection configuration using KDE, LOF, and KMeans models with different window settings.

Thresholds (kde, lof, kmeans)		(1.5, 0.5, 95)			
window (window_size, sliding_size, type)		kde	lof	kmeans	combined models
(10,5,week)	DR	0.89	0.89	0.94	0.92
	Number of alerts	109060			
(10,0,week)	DR	0.73	0.19	0.54	0.48
	Number of alerts	175995			
(100,50,instance)	DR	0.60	0.56	0.84	0.76
	Number of alerts	100948			

and KMeans models using a majority voting method. Cross all scenarios, the combined models show enhanced detection rates (DR), indicating that leveraging the strengths of multiple models results in more robust and accurate anomaly detection. This ensemble approach reduces the likelihood of missing true anomalies while maintaining a high overall performance.

Comparing the different window configurations, we observe that the first case (10,5, weeks), with a window size of 10 weeks, a sliding size of 5 weeks, performs the best. This setup achieves the highest DR value across all models, The large number of alerts generated in this configuration indicates the model's high sensitivity. In contrast, the second case (10,0, week), which lacks a sliding window, shows significantly lower performance metrics. The absence of overlapping windows reduces the model's ability to renew data, leading to decreased detection rates, although it generates more alerts, potentially increasing false positives. The third case (100,50, instance) uses an instance-based sliding window, resulting in moderate performance. While the combined models still outperform individual ones, The overall DR values are lower than in the first case, and the number of alerts is the lowest, suggesting fewer false positives but an increased risk of missing true anomalies.

The use of a sliding window improves anomaly detection by enabling continuous data renewal, which helps maintain high accuracy values. The ASTD specification ensures consistent performance across users by standardizing data size.

Choosing optimal parameters such as window size and sliding size is crucial for effective anomaly detection and minimizing false alerts. Optimal parameter selection enhances model accuracy and reliability across various scenarios.

6 Discussion

The ASTD specification in Sect. 4 uses the quantified interleave operator, which provides processing independence for each user and allows separation of the variables common to all users from those associated with each user. The common variables are defined at the level of the quantified interleave, while the user-specific variables are declared below the quantified interleave in the specification hierarchy. These variables can be accessed by their names in the specification, and the cASTD compiler forwards them to the associated userId instance. Data renewal is performed using a sliding window approach, which requires three specified parameters: *window_size*, *sliding_size*, and *type*. The management of data and launching of recomputation of learning models for each user are dependent on these parameters.

The ASTD specification in Sect. 4 illustrates the utility of the Quantified Flow operator, which preserves the modularity and extensibility of the specification, while effectively leveraging object-oriented principles. It also enables the execution of the three learning models while maintaining the functioning of each abstract. The combination of learning models is achieved through Majority Voting, but other combination techniques can be employed by modifying the action at the left sub-ASTD of the ASTD combination.

The ASTD language provides a framework for better structuring the code by its operators. It enables us to determine the different components of the system, in our case: user, learning models, and window, as well as their interrelationships. This promotes the adoption of a robust development approach. However, the C++ language, which is employed at the level of actions in an ASTD specification, does not currently provide a comprehensive set of machine-learning libraries. This limitation could be addressed by integrating Python code that handles these tasks.

It's worth noting that the ASTD specification presented here is not limited to the specific anomaly detection methods described. Instead, it can be easily adapted to accommodate various other anomaly detection techniques by simply modifying the ASTD components specific to the chosen method. This flexibility underscores the generative power of the ASTD language.

Additionally, the object-oriented architecture of the classes representing the learning models plays a pivotal role in abstracting the specific behavior of each model. This architectural choice harmonizes seamlessly with the ASTD framework within a Quantified Flow. As such, our contribution extends beyond a practical implementation and serves as a specification pattern, emphasizing the language's capacity to abstract and modularize complex systems.

The ASTD language, through its visual approach, provides a detailed view of the various stages of the pipeline, thus allowing for a better understanding and maintenance of the system. This becomes more apparent when using the eASTD editor of the language, where for each component of the specification, one can see its various properties and also assign comments describing its function in the overall system.

One of the major properties of the ASTD language lies in the modularity it brings to the development of detection systems. This modular approach not only facilitates the initial development of the system but also its subsequent evolution. A designer can make targeted modifications without compromising the overall integrity of the system.

Another important aspect of the ASTD language lies in the scheduling of the features of the detection system. The language's operators play a central role in this task, enabling smooth and efficient process management. By entrusting scheduling to these operators, the ASTD language significantly reduces development effort. Designers can focus on business logic, leaving operators to handle the coordination of different stages of the system.

The drawback of this method lies in the fact that it requires an understanding of the functioning of each of the ASTD language operators. Indeed, although the clear visualization and modularity offered by the language facilitate system design and maintenance, dependence on operators can pose a challenge for developers less familiar with them. Note that the purpose of this experiment is not to evaluate the accuracy of the produced detection model. This is a separate issue that is orthogonal to the objective of this paper, which is to streamline the construction of models.

7 Conclusion

In this study, we use the ASTD language for anomaly detection in data logs. Our focus centered on the sliding window technique for continuous learning in data streams, coupled with updating learning models upon the completion of each window to maintain accurate detection and align with current data trends. Additionally, we emphasized the significance of employing methods for combining learning models, especially in the context of unsupervised learning, which is commonly used for data streams. To facilitate this, we extended the ASTD language with a new operator, the Quantified Flow, which enables the seamless combination of learning models while preserving the functioning of each of them in an abstract manner. Therefore, our contribution extends beyond a mere implementation and serves as a specification pattern, highlighting the language's capacity to abstract and modularize anomaly detection systems. In conclusion, the ASTD language provides a unique approach to developing data flow anomaly detection systems, grounded in the combination of processes through the graphical representation of the language operators. This simplifies the design task for developers, who can focus primarily on defining the functional operations that constitute the system.

References

1. Ahmed, M., Mahmood, A.N., Islam, M.R.: A survey of anomaly detection techniques in financial domain. Futur. Gener. Comput. Syst. **1**(55), 278–88 (2016)
2. Yao, D., Shu, X., Cheng, L., Stolfo, S.J., Bertino, E., Sandhu, R.: Anomaly Detection as a Service: Challenges, Advances, and Opportunities. Morgan & Claypool, New York (2018)
3. Baumann, N., Kusmenko, E., Ritz, J., Rumpe, B., Weber, M.B.: Dynamic data management for continuous retraining. In: Proceedings of the 25th International Conference on Model Driven Engineering Languages and Systems: Companion Proceedings, 23 October 2022, pp. 359–366 (2022)
4. Benni, B., Blay-Fornarino, M., Mosser, S., Precisio, F., Jungbluth, G.: When DevOps meets meta-learning: a portfolio to rule them all. In: 2019 ACM/IEEE 22nd International Conference on Model Driven Engineering Languages and Systems Companion (MODELS-C), 15 September 2019, pp. 605–612. IEEE (2019)
5. Baldwin, C.Y., Clark, K.B.: Design Rules: The Power of Modularity. MIT Press, Cambridge (2000)
6. Frappier, M., Gervais, F., Laleau, R., Fraikin, B., St-Denis, R.: Extending statecharts with process algebra operators. Innov. Syst. Softw. Eng. **4**, 285–92 (2008)
7. Tidjon, L.N., Frappier, M., Mammar, A.: Intrusion detection using ASTDs. In: Barolli, L., Amato, F., Moscato, F., Enokido, T., Takizawa, M. (eds.) AINA 2020. AISC, vol. 1151, pp. 1397–1411. Springer, Cham (2020). https://doi.org/10.1007/978-3-030-44041-1_118
8. Kreuzberger, D., Kühl, N., Hirschl, S.: Machine learning operations (MLOps): overview, definition, and architecture. IEEE Access **11**, 31866–31879 (2023)
9. Gama, J.: Knowledge Discovery from Data Streams. CRC Press, Boca Raton (2010)
10. Jankov, D., et al.: Real-time high performance anomaly detection over data streams: grand challenge. In: Proceedings of the 11th ACM International Conference on Distributed and Event-Based Systems (2017)
11. Moin, A., Challenger, M., Badii, A., Günnemann, S.: A model-driven approach to machine learning and software modeling for the IoT: generating full source code for smart Internet of Things (IoT) services and cyber-physical systems (CPS). Softw. Syst. Model. **21**(3), 987–1014 (2022)
12. Van Vliet, H., Van Vliet, H., Van Vliet, J.C.: Software Engineering: Principles and Practice. Wiley, Hoboken (2008)
13. Chaymae, E.J., et al.: Development of monitoring systems for anomaly detection using ASTD specifications. In: Ait-Ameur, Y., Craciun, F. (eds.) Theoretical Aspects of Software Engineering, TASE 2022. LNCS, vol. 13299, pp. 274–289. Springer, Cham (2022). https://doi.org/10.1007/978-3-031-10363-6_19
14. Tidjon, L.N., et al.: Extended algebraic state-transition diagrams. In: 2018 23rd International Conference on Engineering of Complex Computer Systems (ICECCS). IEEE (2018)
15. GRIF. ASTD Tools (2023). https://github.com/eljabrichaymae/ASTD-tools.git
16. El Jabri, C.: Case_Study-ASTD_Patterns- (2023). https://github.com/eljabrichaymae/Case_Study-ASTD_Patterns-.git
17. El Jabri, C.: window.cpp file (2023). https://github.com/eljabrichaymae/Case_Study-ASTD_Patterns-/blob/main/generatedCode/window/window.cpp
18. CERT and ExactData, LLC. Insider Threat Test Dataset. https://kilthub.cmu.edu/articles/dataset/Insider_Threat_Test_Dataset/12841247. Accessed 8 July 2024

Towards a Novel Approach to Railway Safety Using STPA and Promise Theory

Felix Schaber[1](✉), Atif Mashkoor[2], and Michael Leuschel[3]

[1] Hitachi Rail GTS, Vienna, Austria
felix.schaber@urbanandmainlines.com
[2] Johannes Kepler University Linz, Linz, Austria
[3] Heinrich Heine University Düsseldorf, Düsseldorf, Germany

Abstract. The safety of railway systems requires cooperation between many interdependent subsystems. As safety responsibilities are split between these subsystems, modeling cooperation, and conditional dependencies between subsystems become a central issue. This paper proposes the safety promise assessment method (SafePAM), an iterative approach to modeling these dependencies formally. SafePAM enriches the STPA - a structured hazard analysis technique based on systems theory - resulting in a formal description of dependencies provided by the promise theory. Together, this yields a flexible method of iterative refinement, which allows the embedding of novel system designs within their environment while upholding the overall system safety properties. In contrast to previous approaches, SafePAM permits integrating conditional dependencies within the model description without assuming pairwise independence between conditions. We evaluate the proposed method in a case study from the railway domain. We describe the system behavior based on promises that allow a seamless link between domain-specific properties and the system's physical properties, enabling domain experts to validate the resulting model.

Keywords: STPA · Promise Theory · Railway Safety · Safety Analysis · Formal Methods

1 Introduction

Safety is a system property. In mission-critical software systems, this is often associated with complex interactions of multiple controllers and processes. System theoretic process analysis (STPA) [1] is an emerging method to model these

---

The research presented in this paper has been partly conducted within the IVOIRE project, which is funded by "Deutsche Forschungsgemeinschaft" (DFG) and the Austrian Science Fund (FWF) grant # I 4744-N. The work of Atif Mashkoor has been partly funded by the LIT Secure and Correct Systems Lab, which is sponsored by the province of Upper Austria. The work of Felix Schaber has been partly funded by the European Union ▓ Grant Agreement # 101102001.

© The Author(s), under exclusive license to Springer Nature Singapore Pte Ltd. 2025
S. Liu (Ed.): SFPVV 2024, LNCS 15393, pp. 263–279, 2025.
https://doi.org/10.1007/978-981-96-1621-3_17

interactions and judge their impact on safety. A safety-guided design process can be built upon these foundations, systematically considering safety from the onset of system design. However, building executable software controllers based on these results calls for a systematic extension of the STPA method. The classical STPA method describes a methodology for analyzing a system for safety properties but does not prescribe a method for building a system that fulfills these properties. Building an executable system description requires formalizing the safety controller's process model (controller view of its environment) and control algorithm (behavioral patterns when the controller provides actions to its environment).

Deriving a correct controller process model depends on environmental assumptions. These assumptions are critical for the safety of the overall system. The promise theory [2] provides a systematic treatment of these assumptions. It allows for tracking and assessing dependencies, the dependability and stability of individual assumptions, and their impact on safety. A promise is a statement of behavior between agents. If the promise depends on a condition, it is called a conditional promise.

This paper uses conditional promises to model conditional dependencies between multiple assumptions, making the causal chains explicit. These causal chains link the behavior of multiple controllers, providing a basis for assessing if the overall system can uphold its safety promises in the real world. Therefore, we propose the safety promise assessment method (SafePAM) to model these conditional dependencies formally. Its key contribution is extending STPA to describe the details necessary to describe cooperation formally and systematically. We combine a top-down hazard analysis to generate a safety model (STPA) with a bottom-up approach to ensure the implementation of this safety model (formalized promises from the promise theory).

The SafePAM method exploits STPA to abstractly describe automated controllers by their process model and control algorithm. Multiple controllers' process models and control algorithms are viewed independently by default. The promise theory then adds explicit dependencies between the control algorithms of multiple controllers and their environment. This is especially beneficial for large cyber-physical systems, whose dependencies can span many controllers due to functional and physical interactions. Since SafePAM describes a method for systematically deriving the conditions of the analysis to be valid and provides an approach to assessing the stability of cooperation, this differs from existing STPA-based approaches, where the assumptions are taken as given, and the validity of the approach fades once assumptions are violated.

We evaluate the efficacy of the SafePAM method in a case study from the railway domain. In the next-generation train control system case study, we use the SafePAM method to systematically model the interaction of as many as five controllers (driver, onboard unit, braking system, trackside control, and tracks) to constrain the train movement successfully. The conditions under which these dependencies are valid can become quite complex to model otherwise.

The rest of the paper is structured as follows: In Sect. 2, we provide an overview of STPA and the promise theory. Section 3 presents the proposed safety promise assessment method (SafePAM). Section 4 applies the SafePAM method to the railway case study. Section 5 discusses the important lessons learned. Section 6 discusses the related work. The paper is concluded in Sect. 7, while hinting at the future direction.

2 Background

The SafePAM method builds upon STPA and promise theory results. The concepts used from these methods are described below for the context.

2.1 STPA

STPA is a top-down safety analysis method based on systems theory. It describes safety as emergent system behavior, including controller interactions and individual controller failures. The concept of controllers is very general and includes both automated systems and human controllers or organizations. Controllers enforce controller constraints by providing control actions and receiving feedback from their environment. The constraints are designed to prevent unsafe control actions. Loss scenarios build upon these unsafe control actions and describe concrete scenarios (traces) of how the unsafe control action could occur. The control structure can be decomposed hierarchically, allowing the controller model to be refined to the required level of detail. SafePAM uses controller constraints and loss scenarios as inputs.

2.2 Promise Theory

The promise theory describes agent interactions as promises of intended behavior. It is based on a bottom-up approach and is used to model the stability of cooperative behavior. In SafePAM, agents are modeled after the STPA controllers and can be refined to fine-grained sub-controllers if needed. Formally, a promise is described as a tuple $\langle S, R, b(\tau, \chi_\tau), \pi_n \rangle$ where S is the sender, R the receiver, b the body of the promise and π_n the name of the promise. The body is parameterized by a type $\tau \in \{+, -\}$, representing either a promise to give($+$) or to receive($-$) and a constraint χ_τ, which expresses the constraint of the promise. The promise can be made conditional on keeping another promise c by another agent. This can also be expressed in infix notation, where the arrow symbolizes a promise, and the content of the promise body is written above the arrow. The body consists of the actual promise p, the symbol | indicating conditional dependence, and the actual condition c. A conjunction of multiple conditions is denoted by separating the conditions with a semicolon.

$$\pi_n : S \xrightarrow{\pm p | c} R \qquad (1)$$

Stable cooperation requires a binding between a promise to give and a promise to receive. For the sake of brevity, we will focus solely on the promises to give (+) in the case study.

Together, the promises form a graph, which tracks the influence of the individual promises on the overall system behavior. An example of such a graph is shown in Fig. 1. Whether a promise is kept is judged by each agent individually.

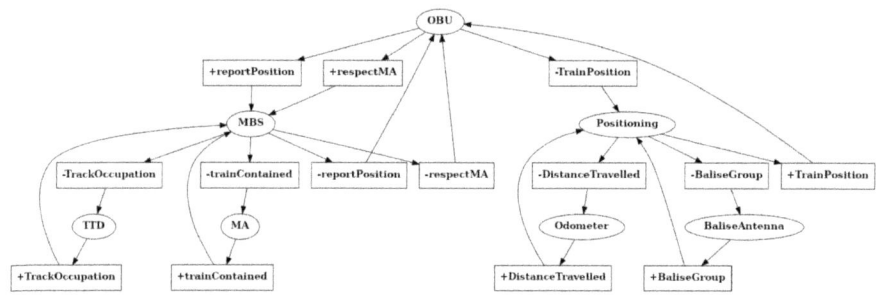

Fig. 1. Simplified example of a promise graph from the railway domain. Ellipsoids represent actors, while rectangles represent promise bodies between the actors connected by the arrow.

Formally, the assessment is a mapping from promises to the interval $[0, 1]$, where 1 represents complete confidence in keeping the promise. For SafePAM, this value depends on the judgment of domain experts and documented agent behavior and dependencies.

3 Safety Promise Assessment Method

The SafePAM uses the STPA system analysis. This consists of defining the system boundary and purpose and performing the STPA analysis. Figure 2 gives a graphical overview of the SafePAM approach, which is based on these central ideas:

– Interpret STPA unsafe controller actions (which include the context of unsafe system behavior) as loss patterns, defining behavioral patterns that the control algorithms are designed to prevent. These unsafe controller actions are translated into formal controller constraints, which describe invariants on the controller behavior. STPA loss scenarios are concrete examples of how an unsafe controller action could occur. These scenarios can be used for acceptance tests to validate that the solution concept meets the controller's safety requirements.
– Build an abstract process model for the safety controller as the controller's view of the world, guided by the STPA hierarchical controller structure of the overall system.

- Sub-states and all their possible dependencies are added, driven by the need to describe and fulfill the formalized controller constraints.
- The analyst's assumptions are modeled using promise theory. Conditional promises systematically link the interaction of multiple controllers, allowing us to assess their stability and dependability. The concrete process model is derived from this, limiting all possible dependencies in the abstract world to those relevant to a concrete situation.
- Derive a dynamic concrete safety model for hazard assessment in real-time from the generic abstract safety model by combining it with observed data about the current real-time environment.

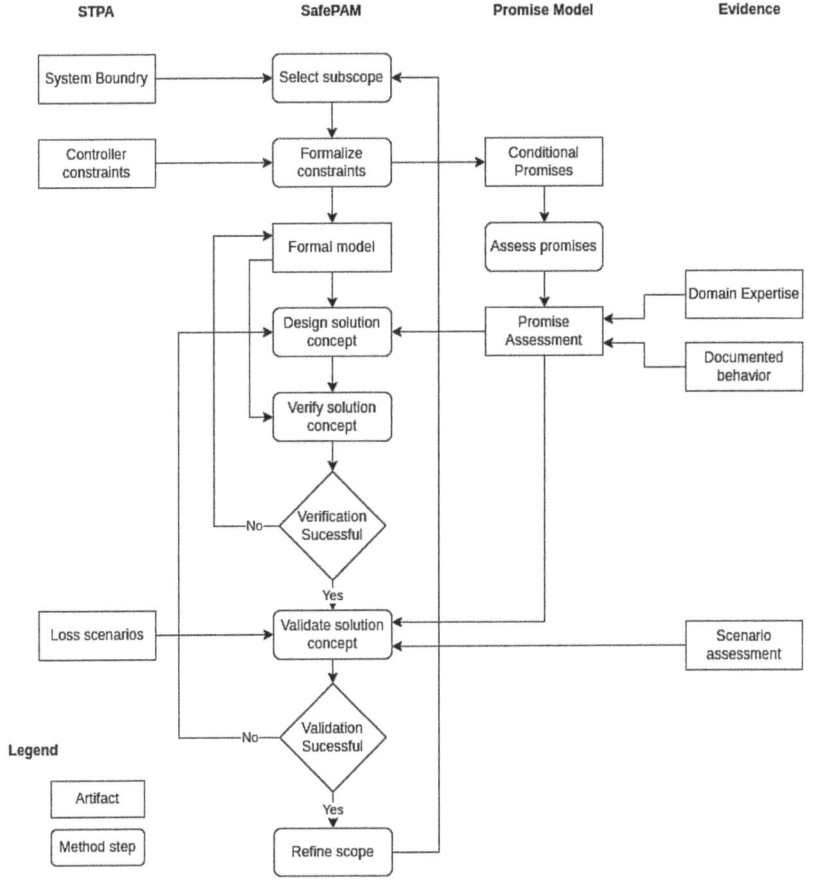

Fig. 2. Graphical overview of SafePAM as simplified flowchart

1. Formalize Controller Constraints. This step extends STPA by formalizing process model variables and controller constraints. It starts by selecting a system to model in detail (usually a single controller) and a scope for the iteration. Promise Theory enables the systematic modeling of assumptions and conditional dependencies. The scope can be extended in later iterations. However, all promises made at the previous iterations shall be kept, possibly by a different combination of promises.

1a. Formalize Process Model Variables. The individual controller constraints are derived from the unsafe control actions. The context under which the control action is unsafe shall be formalized. All process model variables shall have delimited, non-overlapping states. The variables used in the context often depend on other process model variables. The conditional dependence of the context on these variables is modeled as well.

1b. Model Conditional Dependencies Using Promises. The conditional dependencies found in step 1a are described using promise theory. In addition, the influence of other controllers on the internal process model variables (transmitted through commands or feedback) is formulated as promises. If these, in turn, depend on the behavior of other controllers, this is modeled in the condition of the promise body.

2. Assess Promises. All promises found in the previous step should be assessed for their dependability. This may depend on knowledge about the operating environment, system specifications, domain expert judgment, etc. The assessment results should be documented for each promise, along with supporting evidence. In addition, the dependability assessment may change when additional information about the dependencies becomes available later (e.g., information supplied at runtime). For conditional promises, the dependability of the conditions provides an upper limit for the dependability of the whole promise.

This also provides an early opportunity for system validation. Domain experts may identify promises likely to be broken, and the search for evidence during the assessment may highlight unpromised but necessary behavior or common environmental dependencies. When expanding the scope in a new iteration, the conditions of the promises shall also be checked to ensure they remain satisfied. If they are unsatisfied, this may indicate that the scope change affects assumptions within the solution concept.

3. Develop Solution Concepts. This step takes the found promises as inputs and provides a structured methodology for developing solution concepts based on these promises.

3a. Design Solution Concept. In this step, the desired properties of the solution concepts are modeled. This also reflects the environmental constraints under which the system will operate, as informed by the assessment promised in the previous step. Sometimes, choosing between different strategies may be necessary to handle inconsistencies and promises that are known to be unreliable. The choice of strategy should be documented and explained here. This is similar to documenting the architectural assumptions of the solution concepts. These assumptions should be relatively stable and change only infrequently.

3b. Model the Solution Concept and Add It to the System Model. Here, the concrete solution concept is built. The solution concept is described as an agent within the controller, promising the properties in step 3a. The dependencies on the environmental promises are documented, linking the solution model and the environmental conditions and assumptions under which the system was designed.

4. Verify Solution Concepts Against the System Model. Verification can be performed by model checking the controllers against the desired behavior. The promises from the solution concepts and the environmental promises shall be checked. The verification conditions can be expressed, e.g., as invariants or temporal properties.

5. Validate Solution Concept. Validate that the environment fulfills the promises of the solution concepts. Domain experts (e.g., end users and system suppliers) can be asked to assess the promises used during the development of the solution concepts if they have not already been performed in Step 2. Visualization of the solution concepts (e.g., animation) and their current reported state and actual state may greatly aid domain expert assessment. Loss scenarios found in the STPA can be used as example scenarios. As loss scenarios are known to lead to hazards, their unfolding should be prevented by the developed solution concepts.

6. Iterate Model. Returning to step 1, the model can be enhanced iteratively by adding environmental assumptions or modeling additional hazardous control actions. Care must be taken at each iteration to verify that the promises used when developing the solution concepts of previous situations still hold. Otherwise, the promises shall be updated, and the solution concepts will be adapted to continue to hold under the changed scope.

4 Case Study

We use a simplified model of the European train control system (ETCS) train protection system as a case study. The fundamental purpose of such a system is to avoid trains colliding. This requires the system to detect the presence of trains and other obstacles within its control area. Detection may be performed by sensors with fixed positions along the track or by moving sensors. For example, the presence of trains may be determined by fixed sensors along the track-sensing train wheelsets (i.e., track-side train detection systems). Alternatively, the train itself may report where it believes to be within regular intervals (i.e., train position report). This section describes how the method was applied to the case study.

4.1 Controllers

Moving Block System. The moving block system (MBS) is the trackside control system that assesses the risk of Movement Permission commands and object state change requests (i.e., changing the position of a railway point). It only grants a request if it does not result in a hazardous situation (now or in the future) and translates it into movement authorities (MA). MBS intervenes if the risk of a hazardous situation becomes intolerable after a movement is granted. In addition, it sends configuration values for the controlled region to the OBU.

Train. The train is the physical configuration of train cars moving on the track, with at least one traction unit. It can accelerate or brake but not determine its running path. The driver and the OBU (see below) can command the brakes. To simplify the analysis for this case study, we assume that the train consists of a single car only.

On-Board Unit. The on-board unit (OBU) continuously supervises the braking curve until the end of the movement authority (MA) and commands the brakes if the driver brakes too late. It also continuously supervises the permitted speed and commands the brakes if the speed is significantly exceeded. It shows the driver the current braking curve, permitted speed, and ETCS mode. These ETCS modes influence the split of responsibility between OBU, the train driver, and the trackside control. For example, under full supervision mode, the MBS is responsible for ensuring the train route is passable (i.e., railway points are in the correct position for the route) and that no obstacles are present within the MA. This contrasts with on-sight (OS) mode, where the driver monitors the track for potential obstacles. Finally, when in staff-responsible mode, the driver is responsible for monitoring the route and the track to ensure it is passable and free of obstacles.

The OBU also requests movement authorities from the MBS. When a new movement authority is received from the MBS, supervision is updated to the end of the new movement authority. It also sends train position reports to the MBS to inform them of the current train positions.

Trackside Train Detection. Trackside train detection (TTD) continuously supervises a fixed track section for the presence of vehicles. It provides feedback on whether the track section is free or occupied by the trackside control. TTDs are commonly implemented either by using track circuits or by axle counters. Track circuits detect the presence of train axles by utilizing the electrical conductance of the axles. In contrast, axle counters count the number of axes entering and leaving the track section and declare the section free if the difference between these numbers is zero. The trackside system can provide a command to reset the axle counter to zero to address miscounts.

Braking. The braking system reduces train speed when commanded by the driver or OBU. The system differentiates between service brakes for graceful deceleration and emergency brakes for maximum brake performance. It also selects the suitable physical brake type(s) for the commanded brake deceleration (e.g., recuperation brake, block brake, eddy brake, etc.). Actual braking performance also depends on the adhesion conditions on the track/wheel interface. It shall reduce skidding and sliding as much as possible for situations with reduced adhesion conditions.

Positioning. The positioning system measures the position of the train front relative to fixed location balises based on the track. It detects the passing of location balises and measures the distance traveled since reading the last valid location reference. It also calculates the confidence interval and train speed and determines the train running direction. This information is summarized in the train position report and regularly sent to the trackside system via a radio link.

Track. The track provides physical guidance and steering for the train. Track conditions (e.g., curve radius, cant deficiency, etc.) strongly influence the train's maximum running speed. Adhesion conditions between the track and the train wheel are essential to limit braking performance.

4.2 Formalized Controller Constraints

The STPA analysis starts with defining the losses. For this case study, the focus is on the first loss:

L-1. Loss of life or injury to people on the train

This, in turn, leads to the following hazards, where the identifier in the square brackets refers to the linked loss.

H-1. Trains don't maintain a safe distance from other trains. [L-1]

H-2. Train doesn't maintain a safe distance from other obstacles. [L-1]

For the train control system, we select the following unsafe control action found using the STPA approach as an example for further analysis:

UCA-MBS-1. MBS provides MA to the OBU when the risk of the MA intersecting with other trains or obstacles is intolerable. [H-1,H-2]

This unsafe control action corresponds to the following controller constraints:

C-MBS-1. MBS shall not provide a full supervision MA to the OBU when the MA may intersect with other trains or obstacles known at the time of the MA request. [UCA-MBS-1]

C-MBS-2. MBS shall not provide an on-sight MA to the OBU when the MA may potentially include infrastructure elements that are not passable. [UCA-MBS-1]

C-MBS-3. MBS shall not provide a staff-responsible MA to the OBU when the MA may potentially intersect with the movement authorizations of other trains. [UCA-MBS-1]

These, in turn, depend on process model inputs:

- Granted movement authorities
- Reported train positions
- Region between retarded train rear (min safe rear end) and advanced train front (max safe front end)

- Time of position report
- Reported track occupation
- Fixed region on track

Based on these inputs, the internal process model of the MBS consists of the following:

- Regions where train presence is known
- Regions where train presence is likely (now or in the future)
- Regions where train presence is possible (now or in the future)
- Regions where obstacle presence is likely (now or in the future)
- Movement authorities
- Regions where trains may move without authorization (uncontrolled regions)

For stable cooperative behavior, promise theory requires matching a promise to give (+) with a promise to receive (−) between agents. For the sake of brevity, this case study only lists the promises to give.

Using the process model inputs listed above to determine obstacle presence requires modeling additional domain assumptions. The remainder of this section describes how to model such promises.

One such assumption is that all trains within the control area report their position at regular time intervals *tReport* and known accuracy. The following promise expresses this assumption:

$$OBU \xrightarrow{+reportPosition|Connection,TrainPosition,Config(tReport)} MBS \quad (2)$$

However, this assumption is conditional on multiple other assumptions. For example, the train must have the equipment for position reporting (i.e., an OBU) with an established communication session. This, in turn, requires the train to have radio signal reception and, therefore, electrical power. The following promises express this.

$$Odometer \xrightarrow{+DistanceTravelled|ElectricalPower} Positioning \quad (3)$$

$$BaliseAntenna \xrightarrow{+BaliseGroup|ElectricalPower} Positioning \quad (4)$$

$$Positioning \xrightarrow{+TrainPosition|DistanceTravelled,BaliseGroup} OBU \quad (5)$$

In addition, information about the train position can also be obtained from trackside train detectors (TTD). These systems are installed at a fixed location along the tracks and detect whether a monitored section is occupied by a train or empty. For the MBS to notice the change, this requires an established connection between the TTD and MBS as well as enough time to detect the change (*tDetection*):

$$TTD \xrightarrow{+TrackOccupation|Connection,StateChange(tDetection)} MBS \quad (6)$$

The purpose of the movement authority (MA) is to constrain the train dynamics within a region permitted by MBS. An additional promise is therefore necessary to describe this behavior. We introduce MA as a separate agent to embody this behavior:

$$MA \xrightarrow{+trainContained|respectMA} MBS \qquad (7)$$

This has the advantage of tightly linking the information contained within the MA to the desired behavior. However, the OBU needs environmental conditions to be fulfilled to respect the constraints of the MA. One significant promise is that the braking performance is sufficient to stop the train within the MA region. This, again, can be modeled as a promise of the braking system on the train to the OBU.

$$OBU \xrightarrow{+respectMA|MA,sufficientBrakes} MBS \qquad (8)$$

$$Braking \xrightarrow{+sufficientBrakes|sufficientAdhesion} OBU \qquad (9)$$

As promise (9) shows, sufficient adhesion between the train wheels and the track is another requirement for sufficient braking. This depends on the physical track conditions and is therefore modeled as a promise of the physical TrackState.

$$TrackState \xrightarrow{+sufficientAdhesion} OBU \qquad (10)$$

4.3 Assess Promises

Assessing whether these dependencies hold for the given system depends on domain knowledge.

Train Position Reporting. Starting with promise (2), we see the ability to determine the train position (*TrainPosition*) is itself conditional. The *TrainPosition* promise (5) indirectly depends through promises (3) and (4) on the availability of *ElectricalPower* to the *Odometer* and *BaliseAntenna*, which are located onboard the train. Therefore, we must assume that train position reports could be missing if a radio hole or *ElectricalPower* is unavailable to *Odometer* or *BaliseAntenna*. The promise (2) to report positions regularly is violated, necessitating the design of solution concepts with this restriction in mind. We treat this as a possible condition that can occur at any time, as the numerical conditional probabilities between multiple dependencies depend on the concrete operational situation and may be unknown for the general case.

Enforcing the Movement Authority. Limiting the area where the train is allowed to run must be enforced by other means. Promise (8) shows the mechanism within ETCS for that purpose: the train OBU promises to the trackside MBS that the end of the movement authority will be respected. This is achieved by calculating the train braking curve on-board and preventively applying the brakes if the train driver does trigger the brakes before the relevant supervision limit of the braking curve. To calculate the braking curve, promise (9) relating to the assumed braking performance is required. However, sufficient adhesion between the physical tracks and train wheels expressed by promise (10) is required to achieve the specified braking performance.

The OBU depends on additional input to adjust for reduced adhesion conditions. These inputs can either come from the MBS or the train driver. But even then, the reduced adhesion factor does sometimes not enter the braking curve calculation. Therefore, even a reliable promise to provide the reduced adhesion factor is insufficient to fulfill the promise (8). The MBS will require additional solution concepts to ensure the train remains within its allowed region in case of reduced conditions.

Combining TTDs with Train Position Reports. The train position reports may be combined with reports from the track-side train detection systems to detect non-communicating trains and reduce the time to position updates. Promise (6) describes the information about track occupation transmitted to MBS. However, this combination is non-trivial.

The two types of reports describe fundamentally different information at different times. Train position is reported as distance to a known location, while train detection monitors a fixed section along the track and transmits the state change after *tDetection*. The reports have different transmission times and transmission triggers. Therefore, they can also interleave and remain inconsistent for short enough periods. A systematic way to model and discuss these domain assumptions with domain experts in an easily accessible way for all parties is beneficial in such cases.

4.4 Develop Solution Concept

With the promise model, the controller constraint can be restated as follows:

C-MBS-1. The MBS shall not provide a full supervision MA to the OBU when the MA may contain regionWithObstacles.

regionWithObstacles is defined as the region where a train presence (i.e., by train position reports) is either known or is expected (i.e., due to a granted movement authority).

To compute this concept, we must know when a train has reliably vacated an area within an MA. Only then can this region be declared free of obstacles, allowing the MBS system to reduce the size of the granted MA. This requires that the vacated region always increase, as future observations may indicate obstacles after the region has already been declared vacant. Nevertheless, complete removal of the vacated region is allowed to reduce an MA region.

We introduce a new agent *vacatedMARegion* instead of overloading the existing MBS with this solution concept. This allows a clear separation between the dependencies of this concept and the rest of MBS.

In addition, a promise is also dependent on the concepts always (**A**) and until (**U**) from linear temporal logic. Where there is a need to separate previous from current states, states with a tick($'$) represent the new state, while states without represent the previous state.

$$vacatedMARegion \xrightarrow{+\chi_{noTrainPresence}|monoIncreasing(vacatedMARegion)} MBS$$

$$\chi_{noTrainPresence} \equiv \mathbf{A}(trainPresenceImplausible\,\mathbf{U}\,MARegionReduced)$$

A train is known to only move forward, with the running direction being enforced by the OBU.

$$OBU \xrightarrow{+runningDirectionEnforced|MA(runningDirection)} MBS \quad (11)$$

$$physicalTrain \xrightarrow{+\chi_{movingForward}|runningDirectionEnforced} MBS \quad (12)$$

$$\chi_{movingForward} \equiv trainPos(rear)' \geq trainPos(rear) \quad (13)$$

The reported track occupation and train position always describe a past situation. Under the condition that the running direction is enforced (*runningDirectionEnforced*), the last known rear position is always in the rear of the physical train position.

$$knownTrainPos \xrightarrow{+\chi_{confirmedRear}|Connection(tDelivery>0)} MBS \quad (14)$$

$$\chi_{confirmedRear} \equiv \mathbf{A}\,knownTrainPos(rear) <= physicalTrainPos(rear)$$

knownTrainPos shall then delimit the region where the train was at some time in the past based on the information received by MBS. To keep the promise to *vacatedMARegion*, it is vital that *runningDirectionEnforced* holds, so the rear of the known train position moves only forward. $\chi_{confirmedRear}$ expresses that this shall hold even if reports (of train position or track occupation) are missing or arrive in the wrong sequence.

$$knownTrainPos \xrightarrow{+increasing(vacatedMARegion)|\chi_{rearMoved}} vacatedMARegion$$

$$\chi_{rearMoved} \equiv knownTrainPos(rear)' \geq knownTrainPos(rear)$$

This constrains the update behavior of *knownTrainPos*. The rear shall only be moved forward once it is inevitable that new reports do not invalidate previous updates. This assumption shall guarantee that the rear may only move forward or remain in the same position.

We know that the information we received about the train position will only eventually be consistent. An update should, therefore, be delayed until enough time has passed for the information to be consistent, or additional domain promises allow an update beforehand. Such domain promises are defined below.

$$TTD \xrightarrow{+\chi_{forwardMovingOcc}|MA,!(trainPresenceKnown \vee trainPresenceExpected)} MBS$$

$$\chi_{forwardMovingOcc} \equiv state = occupied \quad \& \quad state' = free$$
$$\Rightarrow \mathbf{A} state = free$$
$$OBU \xrightarrow{+\chi_{forwardMovingRear}|MA,Odometer} MBS$$
$$\chi_{forwardMovingRear} \equiv \mathbf{A} time(PosReport2) > time(PosReport1)$$
$$\Rightarrow minSafeRear(PosReport2) > minSafeRear(PosReport1)$$

Implementing this promise amounts to implementing the solution concepts. We use a formal description in the promise bodies to allow a formal verification and validation of the solution concepts.

As the formal verification of the case study is ongoing, the following sections give an overview of these steps.

4.5 Verification

Verification (i.e., is the model sound and do all invariants hold) can be performed, i.e., model checking of the controllers against the desired behavior. The promises from the solution concepts and the environmental promises shall be checked. The verification conditions can be directly derived from the promises and expressed as invariants or temporal properties.

4.6 Validation

Validate (i.e., does the model match the end-user's perception) that the environment fulfills the promises of the solution concepts. Domain experts can be asked to assess the promises used to develop the solution concepts. Visualization of the solution concepts, together with its current reported state and actual state, may greatly aid expert assessment.

4.7 Iterative Model Enhancement

The model can be iteratively enhanced by adding environmental assumptions or modeling additional hazardous control actions. Care must be taken at each iteration to verify that the promises used when developing the solution concepts of previous situations still hold. If this is not the case, then the promises shall be updated, and the solution concepts will be adapted to continue to hold under the new promises.

5 Lessons Learned

By applying SafePAM, we have successfully established solution concepts for the MBS train protection system case study.

- We learned that to limit train movement to known regions, the concept of MA needs to be extended with additional solution concepts to contain the train. As shown by the assessment of the conditional promises, this depends on other promises beyond the MBS control (*sufficientAdhesion*).

- Even if the MBS provides the OBU with information about the current adhesion conditions, this information is not always used to calculate the braking characteristics.
- We also learned under which conditions an MA can be released behind the train and showed how this is connected to sequential promises of train position reports.

6 Related Work

Formalization of STPA. Formal descriptions of the STPA artifacts have been proposed early on. Thomas described an extension of STPA for requirements generation and analysis [3]. This work formalizes the process model and addresses the issue of completeness through a systematic and exhaustive state space search. Another approach proposed by Colley and Butler is to iteratively formalize the system requirements using the Event-B language, which supports a refinement workflow [4]. Howard et al. also proposed to combine the analysis of safety and security of critical infrastructure [5] and formalized the requirements using Event-B [6]. To detect when changes in assumption may impact the STPA analysis results, Leveson and Thomas also proposed introducing assumption-based leading indicators [7] within the context of STPA. These indicators are designed to detect the violation of assumptions early, which indicates a migration to a state of higher risk and increases the likelihood of an accident.

Formal Description of Conditional Dependencies. A well-known approach to formalize conditional dependencies is the Rely-Guarantee Method [8], also known as the Assume-Guarantee method [9]. This method describes the assumptions of each agent regarding its environment, relying on invariants. Only if the rely conditions are fulfilled will the agent provide its guarantees to its environment. In contrast to the Promise Theory, each rely-guarantee binding assessment is considered unanimous and globally valid. In addition, partial fulfillment of bindings is not considered in the Rely-Guarantee Method. Specific frameworks indented for risk modeling and supporting conditional dependencies have also been proposed [10,11]. Within model-based system engineering, an approach to safety analysis by probabilistically modeling faulty dependencies has also been proposed [12]. In contrast to promise theory, faults are assumed to occur independently and the assessment if a fault occurred is global rather than local for each agent.

Formalization of Moving Block. The verification of ETCS has been studied for some time in the formal methods community. For example, [13] discusses the formal verification of ETCS as a case study. There are few recent surveys about the use of formal methods for railways, in general, [14,15] and for using the B-method, in particular, [16]. There are several industrial Event-B models for the safety analysis of railway systems [17–19]. Of particular relevance for our case study is the Event-B model in [20] (inspired by [19]), which focuses on the core safety aspect of an ETCS moving block system. This could, in principle, be integrated into SafePAM.

7 Conclusion

This paper proposes SafePAM, a method to iteratively model and design a critical safety system based on promises. We validated the approach for a selected subset of the safety analysis of a train protection system based on the moving block concepts. Results show that the required domain details can be formalized, and the resulting promises can describe the system sufficiently for a domain expert to assess. The method includes a systematic validation of domain assumptions based on promise assessment. Finally, the solution concepts are validated based on loss scenarios.

The use case in this paper represents a simplified subset of the complete train protection system. All relevant parts of the safety analysis must be included to study the overall system's real-life complexity. Therefore, in the future, we would like to iteratively expand the model to include all relevant constraints of the safety analysis and study the method's behavior as it scales to a system of real-life complexity.

References

1. Leveson, N.: Engineering a Safer World: Systems Thinking Applied to Safety. The MIT Press, Cambridge (2016). ISBN: 9780262533690
2. Bergstra, J.A., Burgess, M.: Promise Theory: Principles and Applications. XtAxis, Oslo (2014). ISBN: 978-1-4954-3777-9
3. Thomas, J.: Extending and automating a systems-theoretic hazard analysis for requirements generation and analysis. SAND2012-4080, 1044959 (2012). https://doi.org/10.2172/1044959
4. Colley, J., Butler, M.: A Formal, Systematic Approach to STPA Using Event-B Refinement and Proof (2013). https://eprints.soton.ac.uk/352155/1/STPAandEventB.pdf
5. Howard, G., et al.: Formal analysis of safety and security requirements of critical systems supported by an extended STPA methodology. In: 2017 IEEE European Symposium on Security and Privacy Workshops (EuroS&PW), Paris, pp. 174–180. IEEE, April 2017. ISBN: 978-1-5386-2244-5. https://doi.org/10.1109/EuroSPW.2017.68
6. Howard, G., et al.: A methodology for assuring the safety and security of critical infrastructure based on STPA and Event-B. Int. J. Crit. Comput.-Based Syst. **9**, 56–74 (2019)
7. Leveson, N., Thomas, J.: STPA Handbook (2018). https://psas.scripts.mit.edu/home/get_file.php?name=STPA_handbook.pdf
8. Nieto, L.P.: The rely-guarantee method in Isabelle/HOL. In: Degano, P., Goos, G., Hartmanis, J., Van Leeuwen, J. (eds.) Programming Languages and Systems, vol. 2618, pp. 348–362. Springer, Heidelberg (2003). https://doi.org/10.1007/3-540-36575-3_24
9. Feng, X., Ferreira, R., Shao, Z.: On the relationship between concurrent separation logic and assume-guarantee reasoning. In: De Nicola, R., Hutchison, D., et al. (eds.) Programming Languages and Systems, vol. 4421, pp. 173–188. Springer, Heidelberg (2007). https://doi.org/10.1007/978-3-540-71316-6_13

10. Gleirscher, M., Calinescu, R.: Safety controller synthesis for collaborative robots. In: 2020 25th International Conference on Engineering of Complex Computer Systems (ICECCS), pp. 83–92, October 2020. https://doi.org/10.1109/ICECCS51672.2020.00017, arXiv: 2007.03340 [cs, eess]
11. Gleirscher, M., Calinescu, R., Woodcock, J.: RiskStructures: a design algebra for risk-aware machines. Formal Aspects Comput. **33**(4–5), 763–802 (2021). https://doi.org/10.1007/s00165-021-00545-4
12. Stewart, D., et al.: AADL-based safety analysis using formal methods applied to aircraft digital systems. Reliab. Eng. Syst. Saf. **213**, 107649 (2021)
13. Platzer, A., Quesel, J.-D.: European train control system: a case study in formal verification. In: Breitman, K., Cavalcanti, A., Hutchison, D., et al. (eds.) Formal Methods and Software Engineering, vol. 5885, pp. 246–265. Springer, Heidelberg (2009). https://doi.org/10.1007/978-3-642-10373-5_13
14. ter Beek, M.H., et al.: Adopting formal methods in an industrial setting: the railways case. In: ter Beek, M.H., McIver, A., Oliveira, J.N., et al. (eds.) Formal Methods – The Next 30 Years, pp. 762–772. Springer, Cham (2019). ISBN: 978-3-030-30942-8. https://doi.org/10.1007/978-3-030-30942-8_46
15. Ferrari, A., et al.: Survey on formal methods and tools in railways: the ASTRail approach. In: Collart-Dutilleul, S., Lecomte, T., Romanovsky, A. (eds.) RSSRail 2019. LNCS, vol. 11495, pp. 226–241. Springer, Cham (2019). ISBN: 978-3-030-18744-6. https://doi.org/10.1007/978-3-030-18744-6_15
16. Butler, M., et al.: The first twenty-five years of industrial use of the B-method. In: ter Beek, M.H., Ničković, D. (eds.) FMICS 2020. LNCS, vol. 12327, pp. 189–209. Springer, Cham (2020). https://doi.org/10.1007/978-3-030-58298-2_8
17. Comptier, M., Leuschel, M., Mejia, L.F., Perez, J.M., Mutz, M.: Property-based modelling and validation of a CBTC zone controller in Event-B. In: Collart-Dutilleul, S., Lecomte, T., Romanovsky, A. (eds.) Reliability, Safety, and Security of Railway Systems. Modelling, Analysis, Verification, and Certification. RSSRail 2019. LNCS, vol. 11495, pp. 202–212. Springer, Cham (2019). ISBN: 978-3-030-18743-9. https://doi.org/10.1007/978-3-030-18744-6_13
18. Comptier, M., et al.: Safety analysis of a CBTC system: a rigorous approach with Event-B. In: Fantechi, A., Lecomte, T., Romanovsky, A. (eds.) Proceedings RSSRail 2017. LNCS, vol. 10598, pp. 148–159. Springer, Cham (2017). ISBN: 978-3-319-68498-7. https://doi.org/10.1007/978-3-319-68499-4_10
19. Sabatier, D.: Using formal proof and B method at system level for industrial projects. In: Lecomte, T., Pinger, R., Romanovsky, A. (eds.) RSSRail 2016. LNCS, vol. 9707, pp. 20–31. Springer, Cham (2016). ISBN: 978-3-319-33950-4. https://doi.org/10.1007/978-3-319-33951-1_2
20. Leuschel, M., Nayeri, N.: Modelling, visualisation and proof of an ETCS level 3 moving block system. In: Proceedings RSSRail 2023, pp. 193–210 (2023). https://doi.org/10.1007/978-3-031-43366-5_12

Functional Modelling of the Matroid and Application to the Knapsack Problem

Zikang Wan[1,2], Zhen You[1,2(✉)], Chen Zhang[1,2], Zhengkang Zuo[2], Changjing Wang[2], and Qimin Hu[1,2]

[1] State International S&T Cooperation Base of Networked Supporting Software, Jiangxi Normal University, Nanchang 330022, China
youzhen@jxnu.edu.cn
[2] Computer Information Engineering School, Jiangxi Normal University, Nanchang 330022, China

Abstract. The matroids have a wide range of applications in discrete mathematics, combinatorial mathematics, computer science and other fields. However, most of the researches about matroids focus on the mathematical level, and there is a lack of exploration on functional modelling and formal verification. In this paper, we propose a general functional modeling framework for matroids, which consists of the basic elements of matroids, the verification functions of basic properties, and the verification functions of matroids. Finally, the functional modeling framework of this paper is used to verify whether the 0-1 knapsack problem and the fractional knapsack problem conform to the matroid structure, thus exemplifying the correctness of the matroid functional modeling and the matroid verification function, and reflecting the validity and extensibility of this framework.

Keywords: matroid · knapsack problem · functional modelling · formal verification

1 Introduction

Matroids were introduced by Whitney in 1935 to capture the nature of dependence in the abstract, and their definition encompasses the rich diversity of combinatorial structures [1]. Nowadays, the matroid is used in many fields including discrete mathematics, combinatorial mathematics, and computer science, and plays an important role in solving applications such as the maximum flow problem and the knapsack problem. In the process of solving optimization problems, the proposed array can be used to determine whether the greedy algorithm can

---

This work was funded by Projects of Jiangxi Provincial Nature Science Foundation (Grant No. 20212BAB202018), Provincial Virtual Simulation Experiment Education Project of Jiangxi Education Department (Grant No. 2020-2-0048) and the Science and Technology Research Project of Jiangxi Province Educational Department (Grant No. GJJ210333).

lead to the optimal solution of the problem, and it is necessary to use formal methods to model the proposed array functionally, which is convenient to check whether the optimization problem conforms to the structure of the proposed array or not. The Isabelle/HOL theorem prover, as a formal modeling and validation tool, has the advantage of not being restricted to state space, and can guarantee correctness and high confidence.

At present, many scholars have studied the matroid, but most of them study the application of the matroid in mathematics, while there is a lack of exploration on functional modelling and formal verification. Literature [2] proposed the matroid mean and knapsack mean problems, i.e., replacing the base constraints in the mean with the matroid constraints and knapsack constraints, respectively, in order to solve many types of problems. Literature [3] focuses on the relationship between knowledge spaces and simple proposed matrices and concludes that they are one-to-one correspondence. Literature [4] defines the combinatorial structure of independent systems and matroids and provides the basic concepts and theorems related to them, but it is incomplete about the basic properties of matroids, and lacks effective algorithms for verifying matroids.

In this paper, we propose a functional modelling framework for matroids. Firstly, the basic elements of the matroid are modelled according to the definition of the matroid. Then, the verification functions corresponding to the three basic properties of the matroid definition are modelled, and a generic matroid verification algorithm is given. Finally, the general functional modeling framework implemented in this paper is applied to the 0-1 knapsack problem and fractional knapsack problem, which ensures the correctness of the matroid verification algorithm and lays a good foundation for future mechanized theorem proving of matroids.

2 Background Knowledge

This section introduces the basic definition of a matroid and gives a simple example of a matroid based on the definition, and then introduces the Isabelle/HOL theorem prover, a tool used in the work of this paper, and the notion of Locale in it.

2.1 Definition of the Matroid

Based on the literature [1,5,9], the matroid is defined as a binary set $M = (S, L)$, where S is a finite set and L is a family of sets (i.e. $L \subseteq 2^{|S|}$) consisting of some subsets of S called independent sets, and the subsets in an independent set can be called independent.

The matroid can be defined in terms of an independent set L. Then L needs to satisfy the properties.

1. Non-empty: there is $\emptyset \in L, L \neq \emptyset$, i.e. L is non-empty.
2. Heritability: if $A \subseteq B$, for any $B \in L$, then $A \in L$, i.e. if the subset of any set of elements in L is also an element in L.

3. Exchangeability: if for any $A, B \in L, |A| > |B|$, then $\exists i \in (A-B), (B \cup \{i\}) \in L$, i.e. take any two sets of elements in L with different bases, and there exists at least one element in the set of differences between the two, and after merging it into the set of elements with smaller bases, the new set obtained is also a set of elements in L.

For example, the sets $S1 = \{2, 3, 4\}, L1 = \{\emptyset, \{2\}, \{3\}, \{4\}, \{2,3\}\}$ satisfy the non-emptiness and heredity of the matroid, but do not satisfy the exchange property of the matroid (there is no element i in the set of the difference between the two when $A = \{2,3\}, B = \{4\}$, such that $(B \cup \{i\}) \in L$), and thus L1 is not a matroid. On the other hand, $L2 = \{\emptyset, \{2\}, \{3\}, \{2,3\}\}$ satisfies all the properties of the matroid, and hence L2 is a matroid.

2.2 Isabelle/HOL Theorem Prover

Isabelle/HOL [6] is a general-purpose interactive theorem prover based on higher-order logic (HOL). It is an LCF (Logic for Computable Functions) style proof aid implemented in the Standard ML language under the BSD license. It has a minimalist logic core, which means that proofs and formal verifications using it have strong confidence.

Locale is the basic method of program parameterization in Isabelle/HOL language, which provides a modular and parameterised mechanism for programs that can effectively express complex dependencies between functional program structures [7]. Locale is similar to interface in object-oriented languages, which provide more flexible parameterization and logical statutes than interfaces [8]. The following is an example of the declaration structure of Locale in Isabelle/HOL.

```
1    locale additive_group
2        fixes add (infixl "+" 65)
3        assumes assoc: "∀x y z. (x + y) + z = x + (y + z)"
```

The declaration of a Locale consists of three parts: the name of the region (e.g. additive_group), the local parameters of the locale (using the fixes keyword), and the logical statute of the Locale (using the assumes keyword). The local parameter fixes of a Locale defines a addition operation, where add (infixl "+" 65) defines a binary operation add, represented by the symbol '+'. The logical statute of locale assumes defines that this binary operation add needs to satisfy associative law of addition.

3 Functional Modelling Framework for Matroids

The functional modelling framework for matroids provides more than ten basic operations. These operations include modelling the basic elements of an array, set operations implemented as lists, matroid property validation operations, and matroid verification functions. Compared to set types, Isabelle/HOL provers provide more functions for list types, and list types have ordering, more convenient to achieve recursion, so as to achieve more diversified methods of filtering subsets Indep. In this section, these basic operations are depicted using the locale in Isabelle/HOL. This is shown in Fig. 1.

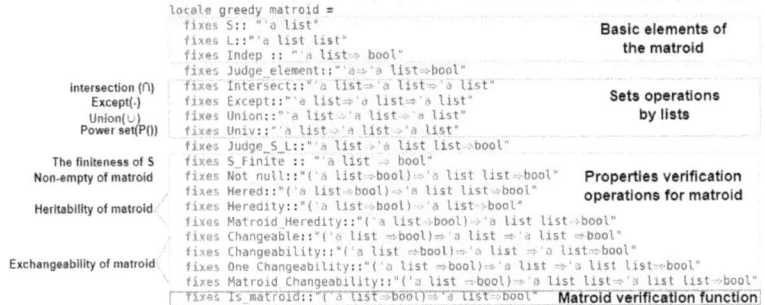

Fig. 1. Functional Modelling Framework Diagram for the Matroid

3.1 Functional Modelling of Basic Elements

The matroid M = (S, L), consists of three basic elements: S, L and Indep. S is a finite set, L is a family of sets consisting of some subsets of S, which can be regarded as a kind of special set whose elements are sets. Indep is a method to judge which subsets of S can be used as elements in L. The data types in Isabelle/HOL contain the definitions of a set, and a list, where the definition of list structure fits the idea of recursion, and the correctness verification of the corresponding function is relatively simple. The data types in Isabelle/HOL include the definition of 'a set, 'a list, where the definition of a list structure fits the idea of recursion, and the correctness of the corresponding function is simpler to verify. The functions that can be realized are more extensive. Therefore, S, L and Indep can be defined as follows.

```
1  type_synonym S    = " 'a list "
2  type_synonym L    = " 'a list list "
3  type_synonym Indep = " 'a list ⇒ bool "
```

In the definition of the above three basic elements, 'a is abstract and can be instantiated into different concrete types according to the need, in different application scenarios, it can be instantiated into different types according to the need to obtain more complex structures. For example, it can be instantiated into complex structures such as sequential pairs or tuples to cope with more complex requirements.

3.2 Functional Modelling of Property Verifications

This part is the core work of this paper, which proposes a functional modelling of the matroid verification based on the verification of three basic properties of the matroid (non-empty verification, heritability verification, and exchangeability verification).

Non-empty Verification. The non-empty of the matroid requires that L is a non-empty set. We can define the function Not_null, its function is the subset screening method indep with the full set of S as a parameter, the use of the list of recursive, in turn, the elements of the full set of S to do the judgement, if all are False, then the function output False, otherwise output True.

```
1  fun Not_null::"(S⇒ bool)⇒ L ⇒bool"
2    where"Not_null indep    [[]]  =False"|
3  "Not_null indep (s#ts)=(if (indep s) then
4  True else Not_null indep ts) "
```

Heritability Verification. The heritability of the matroid requires that the subsets of any set of elements in L are also elements in L. We can first define the function Hered, its function is to subset screening method indep and a certain set family as a parameter, the use of the recursive nature of the list, in turn, on the set family of elements in the set of sets to do the judgement, if all are True, then the function output True, otherwise output False. Function Add, its function is to insert a single element into a set of family of each element in the collection, to get a new set of family. The function of univ is to complete the power set operation of the collection in the form of a list.

Then, define the function Heredity, its function is to subset screening method indep and a subset of S as parameters, the use of the function Hered, judge if the subset of the use of the method indep, the result is True, whether all the subsets of the subset of the use of the same method, the result is True, if so, then return True, otherwise return False.

Finally, define the function Matroid_Heredity, its function is to subset screening method indep and the full set of S as a parameter, the use of the function Heredity, to determine if the subset of any S using the method indep, the result is True, whether the subset of all subsets of the use of the same method, the result is True, if so, return True, otherwise Returns False.

```
1  fun Hered::"(S⇒bool)⇒L⇒bool"
2    where"Hered indep    [[]]  =True"|
3  "Hered indep (s#ts)
4  =(if (indep s) =False then False else Hered indep ts)"
5
6  fun Add::"(real×real)⇒L⇒L"
7    where"Add a [] =[]"|
```

```
8   "Add a (s#ts) = ([a]@s) # Add a ts"
9
10  fun univ::"S⇒L"
11    where" univ [] = [[]]"|
12  " univ (s#ts)= ( Add s ( univ ts))@ univ ts "
13
14  definition Heredity::"(S⇒bool)⇒S⇒bool"
15    where" Heredity indep  r ≡( indep r⟶
16    Hered indep (univ r))"
17
18  fun Matroid_Heredity::"(S⇒bool)⇒L⇒bool"
19    where" Matroid_Heredity indep  [[]] =True"|
20  "Matroid_Heredity indep (s#ts) =
21   (if (Heredity (indep) (s)) =False then False
22   else Matroid_Heredity indep ts)"
```

Exchangeability Verification. The exchangeability of the matroid requires to take any two sets of elements in L with different bases, and there exists at least one element in the set of differences between the two, which is merged into the set of elements with smaller bases, and then the new set obtained is also the set of elements in L. We can first define the function Changeable, its function is to subset screening method indep and a certain two sets as a parameter, in turn, the former set of all the elements of a single set into the latter set, each time the new set of methods indep, if all False, then the function output False, otherwise output True. The function intersect is to complete the set of intersection operations in the form of a list and the function except is to complete the set of exception operations.

Then, define the function Changeability, its function is to subset screening method indep and S of a two subsets as a parameter, the use of the function Changeable, determine if the two subsets of the use of method indep, the results are True, and the two sets of different bases, whether the difference between the two subsets of the set of the existence of an element, will be merged into the base of the smaller subset, the new set obtained using the method indep, if all are False, then the function output False, otherwise output True. set, the new set obtained using the same method, the result is True, if so, then return True, otherwise return False.

Finally, define the function One_Changeability and Matroid_Changeability, its function is to determine whether any two subsets of S, using the function Changeability, the result is True, if so, then return True, otherwise return False.

```
1   fun Changeable::"(S⇒bool)⇒S⇒S⇒bool"
2     where" Changeable indep [] s2 =False"|
3   "Changeable indep (s#ts) s2=(if indep ([s]@s2)
4    then True else Changeable indep ts s2)"
5
6   fun intersect::"S⇒S⇒S"
```

```
7      where"intersect s1 s2=filter (λx. judge_ele x s1) s2"
8
9   fun except::"S⇒S⇒S"
10     where"except s1 s2 =filter(λx.
11     judge_ele x (intersect s1 s2) =False) s1"
12
13  definition Changeability::"(S⇒bool)⇒S⇒S⇒bool"
14     where" Changeability indep   r r1 ≡
15  ((indep r ∧indep r1 ∧ length r =
16  Suc (length r1)) ⟶(Changeable indep (except r r1) r1) )"
17
18  fun One_Changeability::"(S⇒bool)⇒S⇒L⇒bool"
19     where" One_Changeability indep s1 [[]]= True"|
20  "One_Changeability indep s1 (t1#ts) =
21  (if (Changeability indep s1 t1) =False then False
22  else One_Changeability indep s1 ts)"
23
24  fun Matroid_Changeability::"(S⇒bool)⇒L⇒L⇒bool"
25     where"Matroid_Changeability indep [[]] l= True"|
26  "Matroid_Changeability indep   (l1#ls) l =
27  (if ( One_Changeability indep l1 l) =False then False
28  else Matroid_Changeability indep ls l)"
```

3.3 Functional Modelling of the Matroid Verification

In addition to the three basic properties of the matroid, to perform the matroid verification operation, the finiteness of S needs to be verified. Here, the length of S is directly verified and if the length is less than a natural number, it means that S is finite.

```
1   definition finite_list::"S⇒bool"
2      where"finite_list r≡(length r<=9999)"
```

This function verifications the set S and the set screening function indep (the result of indep's screening of S is denoted as L), and if the finiteness of S and the non-emptiness of L, the heritability of L, and the exchange of L are satisfied at the same time, then the subset system can be judged to be a matroid.

```
1   definition is_matroid_list::"(S⇒bool)⇒S⇒bool"
2    where" is_matroid_list indep r≡
3    (finite_list r ∧not_null indep (univ r) ∧
4      Matroid_Heredity indep (univ r) ∧
5      Matroid_Changeability indep (univ r) (univ r))"
```

3.4 Comparison of Mathematical Definitions and Functional Model

This section describes in table form the difference between the mathematically defined form of the matroid and functional modelling, where the advantage of functional modelling lies in its formal nature, which is easier and quicker compared to the manual form and facilitates subsequent validation work (Table 1).

Table 1. Mathematical Definitions and Functional Modelling

	Mathematical Definitions	Functional Modelling
Basic elements	Semi-formal definitions	Formal definition
Basic properties	Semi-formal description using mathematical and natural language	Formal description using a functional language
Judge a problem satisfies the matroid structure or not	Manual mathematical derivation and judgment	Mechanized verification using our defined matroid functions
Verification framework	None	Using Locale to design the Verification Framework of Matroid

4 Application of the Modelling Framework

The matroid can be used to study the greedy algorithm, it is the mathematical basis of the greedy algorithm. A problem can be solved by a simple greedy strategy if it can be shown to fit the model of the matroid[10]. This modelling framework can be used to solve a range of real-world greedy algorithmic problems. In order to verify the validity of the property verifications and the matroid verification function, we apply the function to two classic cases of the greedy algorithm: the 0-1 knapsack problem and the fractional knapsack problem, exemplifying the correctness of the matroid functional modeling and the matroid verification function.

4.1 0-1 Knapsack Problem

Description of the problem: There are n items, which have their own weights as well as values, and there is a backpack with a given capacity w. How to maximize the sum of the values of the items loaded into the backpack, where the items are indivisible.

Specific example: There are 4 items with weights of 1, 2, 3, and 4; values corresponding to 8, 6, 4, and 10; and a backpack capacity of 6.

Mathematical derivation: $M = (S, L), S = \{(1,8), (2,6), (4,4), (5,10)\}$, fst (Si) is the weight, and snd(Si) is the value. $L = \{x | x \subseteq S, \text{ and } \sum fst(x) \leq 6\} = \{\emptyset, \{S1\}, \{S2\}, \{S3\}, \{S4\}, \{S1, S2\}, \{S1, S3\}, \{S1, S4\}.\{S2, S3\}\}$. $Let A =$

$\{S4\}, B = \{S2, S3\}, |A| < |B|, B - A = \{S2, S3\}, \{S2, S4\}, \{S3, S4\}$, by the commutativity of the matroid. There exists at least one $\in L$, but they are all $\notin$ L, and therefore do not satisfy the exchangeability of the matroid (and obviously satisfy the other properties of the matroid, which will not be repeated), and this subset system is not a matroid.

The definitions involving S, L, and Indep in Isabelle/HOL are as follows. S' is an instance of S, and S' is an ordinal pair of real numbers, before the weight, after the value, L' is an instance of L. Function Add_fst, its function is to find the sum of the weight of the elements in the set. function Backpack_judge_01 for the Indep method instance, the function is to filter the subset of S, so that the subset of elements within the weight of the sum is less than or equal to the backpack capacity.

```
1   type_synonym  S' ="(real×real) list"
2   type_synonym  L'="S list"
3
4   fun Add_fst::"S'⇒real"
5       where " Add_fst [] = 0"|
6   " Add_fst ((x,y)#ts)=x+(Add_fst ts)"
7
8   definition Backpack_judge_01::"S'⇒bool"
9       where"Backpack_judge_01 s=(if (Add_fst s)≤6
10          then True else False)"
```

As can be seen in Fig. 2, the 0-1 knapsack instance successfully passes the non-empty verification, the heritability verification, and the exchange verification using the non-empty verification, the heritability verification, and the exchange verification in the framework of this paper, but fails the exchange verification, and thus fails the matroid verification, and the results are as expected.

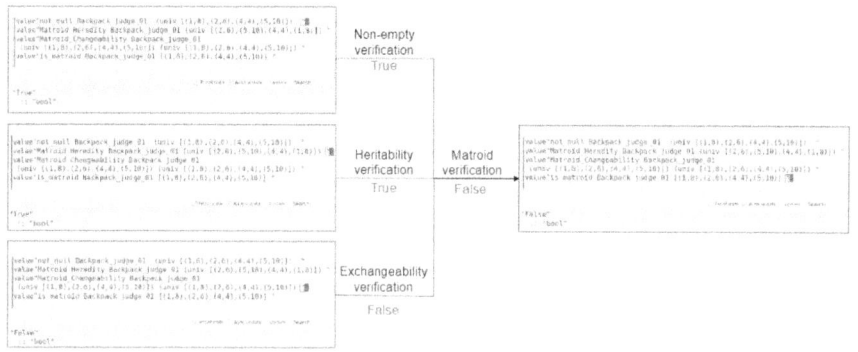

Fig. 2. Properties Verifications and Matroid Verification for 0-1Knapsack Instances

4.2 Fractional Knapsack Problem

Problem Description: There are n items, which have their own weight as well as value, and there exists a backpack with a given capacity w. How to make the items filled in the backpack have the maximum sum of values, where the items are divisible.

Specific example: same as previous section.

Mathematical derivation: M = (S, L), S as in the previous section, L = $\{x|x \subseteq S,$ and $\sum fst(x) < 6$(which does not contain Si, which can be any of the items in x)$\}$ = $\{\emptyset, \{S1\}, \{S2\}, \{S3\}, \{S4\}, \{S1, S2\}, \{S1, S3\}, \{S1, S4\},$ $\{S2, S3\}, \{S2, S4\}, \{S3, S4\}, \{S1, S2, S3\}, \{S1, S2, S4\}, \{S1, S3, S4\}\}$ it is clear that for any A, B $\in$ L and $|A| < |B|$, there exists x $\in$ (B-A) such that $(A \cup \{x\}) \in$ L, and hence the proposed matrix exchangeability is satisfied (and obviously the other properties of proposed matrices are satisfied and will not be repeated), and the subset system is a matroid.

The definitions involving S, L, and Indep in Isabelle/HOL are as follows. Where S' is an instance of S, S' is an ordinal pair of real numbers preceded by a weight and followed by a value, and L' is an instance of L. Function subtract_1, its function is to remove a set of a set of elements, to get a set of families, set of families containing all the removal of the situation. Function Cond, its function is to determine in a set of families, whether there is a collection of elements, the sum of their weight is less than the backpack capacity. Function Backpack_judge for the Indep method instance, the function is to screen all subsets of S, so that the subset to remove any one element after the weight of the sum is less than the backpack capacity (the last one can be cut).

```
type_synonym S ="(real×real) list"
type_synonym L ="S list"

fun subtract_1::"S⇒L"
  where"subtract_1 [] =[]"|
  "subtract_1 (s#ts) =(Add s (subtract_1 ts))@[ts]"

fun Cond::"L⇒bool"
  where "Cond [] = False"|
  "Cond (s#ts)=(if Add_fst s<6  then True else Cond ts)"

definition Backpack_judge::"S⇒bool"
  where"Backpack_judge s=(if Cond (subtract_1 s)
     then True else False)"
```

As can be seen from Fig. 3, the fractional knapsack example successfully passes the verification using the non-emptiness verification, the heritability verification, and the exchange verification in the framework of this paper, and the example in this section clearly satisfies the finiteness of S and thus passes the matroid verification with the expected results.

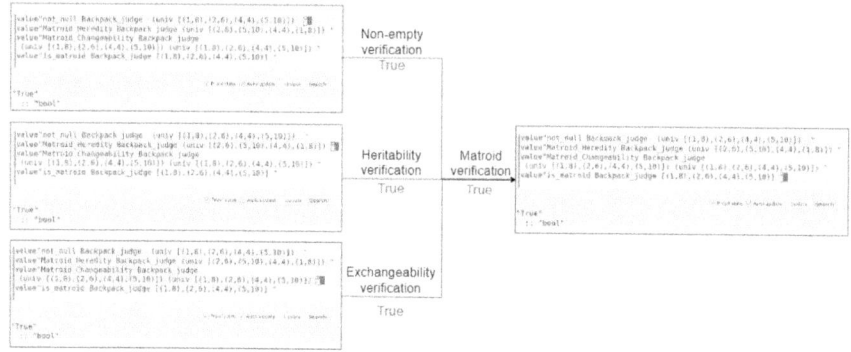

Fig. 3. Properties Verification and Matroid Verification for Fractional Knapsack Instances

5 Conclusion and Future Work

The work of this paper is divided into two parts. (1) A functional modelling framework for the matroid is proposed, and the basic elements of the matroid are functionally modelled. Then, the basic properties of the matroid are functionally modelled and the verification function of the matroid is proposed. (2) The functional modeling framework of the matroid is applied to the 0-1 knapsack problem and the fractional knapsack problem to ensure the correctness of the matroid checking algorithm, and then the effectiveness and scalability of the method are exemplified.

In this paper, a functional modeling framework for the matroid is implemented in Isabelle/HOL, which can be instantiated into various algorithms including the greedy algorithm according to different application scenarios. The next step can be to further optimise and extend the modelling framework proposed in this paper and perform mechanical validation, which can model and validate more applications of the matroid checking algorithm in different scenarios.

References

1. Oxley, J.: What is a matroid? Cubo **5**, 179–218 (2003)
2. Ao, Z.: Approximation algorithms for the matroid and knapsack mean problems. Shandong Normal University (2023). (in Chinese). https://doi.org/10.27280/d.cnki.gsdsu.2023.000736
3. Taoli, Y., Yinfeng, Z.: Relationship between knowledge spaces and simple matroids. J. Minnan Normal Univ. (Nat. Sci. Ed.) **34**(03), 30–38 (2021). (in Chinese). https://doi.org/10.16007/j.cnki.issn2095-7122.2021.03.005
4. Keinholz, J.: Matroids (2024)
5. Guizhen, L., Qinghua, C.: Matroids. National University of Defense Technology Press (1994)

6. Nipkow, T., Klein, G.: Concrete Semantics. Springer, Cham (2014). https://doi.org/10.1007/978-3-319-10542-0
7. Yongwang, Z.: Functional Programming and Proofs (2023). (in Chinese). https://www.yuque.com/zhaoyongwang/fpp
8. Zhengkang, Z., Yuhan, K.: Trie+ structural functional modelling, mechanistic verification and its applications. J. Softw. **35**(09), 4242–4264 (2024). (in Chinese). https://doi.org/10.13328/j.cnki.jos.007135
9. Oxley, J.: Matroid Theory. Oxford University Press, Oxford (2006)
10. Qianlan, Y.: An introduction to some extensions of the matroid and their applications (2018). (in Chinese). https://chxulong.oss-cn-shenzhen.aliyuncs.com

Author Index

A
Aït Ameur, Yamine 189

C
Cai, Yong 141
Constantinides, Constantinos 158

D
Deng, Xiong 177
Do, Canh Minh 208
Dohi, Tadashi 32
Du, Yu 1
Dupont, Guillaume 189

E
El Jabri, Chaymae 245

F
Feng, Jincao 115
Frappier, Marc 245

G
Guo, Xiujing 32

H
Hieu, Doan Minh 49, 64
Hou, Zhiru 226
Hu, Qimin 280

J
Jacobsen, Jonas Brager 79
Jannatpour, Ali 158
Jin, Zhi 97

K
Khoa, Tran Dang 49, 64

L
Leuschel, Michael 263
Li, Jiandong 97
Li, Jingyue 79

Liang, Jinhao 115
Liu, Shaoying 1, 97, 177
Liu, Yanli 177
Loc, Van Cao Phu 49, 64

M
Mashkoor, Atif 263
Miao, Weikai 115, 141
Minh Do, Canh 15
Mohus, Mathias Lundteigen 79

N
Nagoya, Fumiko 131
Nam, Tran Ba 49, 64
Ngan, Nguyen Thi Kim 49, 64
Nghiem, Thanh Pham 49, 64

O
Ogata, Kazuhiro 15, 208
Ogura, Tomoyoshi 208
Okamura, Hiroyuki 32

P
Pantel, Marc 189
Pu, Geguang 115

S
Schaber, Felix 263
Singh, Neeraj Kumar 189

T
Tardif, Pierre-Martin 245
Trung, Phan Hoang Tuan 49, 64

W
Wan, Zikang 280
Wang, Changjing 280
Wang, Jiangtao 115
Wang, Zhewei 115
Wang, Zhouyang 141

X
Xu, Yilongfei   115

Y
You, Zhen   280

Z
Zhang, Chen   280
Zhang, Jilu   141
Zhang, Yueling   115
Zhu, Huibiao   226
Zhu, Yujin   32
Zuo, Zhengkang   280

GPSR Compliance

The European Union's (EU) General Product Safety Regulation (GPSR) is a set of rules that requires consumer products to be safe and our obligations to ensure this.

If you have any concerns about our products, you can contact us on

ProductSafety@springernature.com

In case Publisher is established outside the EU, the EU authorized representative is:

Springer Nature Customer Service Center GmbH
Europaplatz 3
69115 Heidelberg, Germany

www.ingramcontent.com/pod-product-compliance
Ingram Content Group UK Ltd.
Pitfield, Milton Keynes, MK11 3LW, UK
UKHW021844060925
462651UK00010B/114